Early praise for *Apple Game Frameworks and Technologies*

I wish I had something like this when I first started learning game development. I can't think of a better way to get started than by building a game from start to finish (or three in this case), not to mention all of the other modern, essential concepts like Game Center, GameplayKit, and In-App Purchases.

➤ **Ryan McLeod**
Creator of Blackbox, Winner of the 2017 Apple Design Award

This is a smart, modern, and fun guide to getting into building games on Apple's platforms, and it manages to make even complex topics seem achievable. If you're keen to get into SpriteKit, Tammy is here to help!

➤ **Paul Hudson**
Creator of Hacking with Swift

If you're looking to learn how to make your first iOS game in Swift, this is the book for you. Tammy will guide you step by step, and she'll make your journey feel so simple—and so fun!

➤ **Ray Wenderlich**
Founder of Razeware, raywenderlich.com

Want to build a great iOS game? Start here! This is the ideal, easy-to-follow guide to understanding and using Apple's own game frameworks. But it's so much more than dry syntax. Tammy covers it all: game design, art, physics, social and multi-player aspects, monetization—everything you need to make your iOS game a success.

➤ **Simon Allardice**
Author, Pluralsight

Tammy has put together a super informative and fun set of tutorials here, shining a light on what I've always thought was one of Apple's more underrated APIs. I've never built a game of my own with SpriteKit and shipped it to the App Store, but now I kinda want to.

➤ **Joe Cieplinski**
   Independent Developer and Designer

If only I had a copy of *Apple Game Frameworks and Technologies* when I created my first game. Oh, right—that was before Apple released iOS and the Mac. Regardless, I predict you'll have a lot of fun reading this book—and who knows, maybe you'll even create an award-winning game or two!

➤ **Al Lowe**
   Game Designer and Programmer, Formerly with Sierra On-Line, Creator of the Leisure Suit Larry series

Apple Game Frameworks and Technologies

Build 2D Games with SpriteKit & Swift

Tammy Coron

The Pragmatic Bookshelf

Raleigh, North Carolina

Many of the designations used by manufacturers and sellers to distinguish their products are claimed as trademarks. Where those designations appear in this book, and The Pragmatic Programmers, LLC was aware of a trademark claim, the designations have been printed in initial capital letters or in all capitals. The Pragmatic Starter Kit, The Pragmatic Programmer, Pragmatic Programming, Pragmatic Bookshelf, PragProg and the linking *g* device are trademarks of The Pragmatic Programmers, LLC.

Every precaution was taken in the preparation of this book. However, the publisher assumes no responsibility for errors or omissions, or for damages that may result from the use of information (including program listings) contained herein.

For our complete catalog of hands-on, practical, and Pragmatic content for software developers, please visit *https://pragprog.com*.

The team that produced this book includes:

CEO: Dave Rankin
COO: Janet Furlow
Managing Editor: Tammy Coron
Development Editor: Margaret Eldridge
Copy Editor: Katharine Dvorak
Indexing: Potomac Indexing, LLC
Layout: Gilson Graphics
Founders: Andy Hunt and Dave Thomas

For sales, volume licensing, and support, please contact *support@pragprog.com*.

For international rights, please contact *rights@pragprog.com*.

ISBN-13: 978-1-68050-784-3
Book version: P1.0—April 2021

To my children, Travis and Jake, and to my husband, Bill: I love you guys so very, very much. Life wouldn't be the same without you.

Contents

Part II — Use the Scene Editor to Build Games

Part III — Scale Your Games with GameplayKit

Part IV — Enhance the Player's Experience

Foreword

I first met Tammy Coron through the raywenderlich.com developer website. If you're familiar with the Apple developer community, you probably already know about Ray Wenderlich and his online tutorial site, raywenderlich.com. If not, you may want to spend a few minutes checking it out.

Anyway, Tammy and I were—and still are—part of the raywenderlich.com team, which means we get to work with some of the best developers and technical educators around the world. In addition to being an author and editor on the site, Tammy was also one of the founding co-hosts of The raywenderlich.com podcast as well as the Apple Game Frameworks Team Lead.

I remember one of the first conversations we had: I was interested in writing a book and had just started the More Than Just Code (MTJC) podcast along with my co-hosts, Jaime Lopez Jr. and Mark Rubin. And Tammy—well, she was just hanging around the raywenderlich.com Slack channel waiting to connect with other team members.

MTJC was on a small break in its recording schedule, so I reached out to Tammy on Slack to ask her about the book-writing process. About five minutes into our discussion, we decided to fire up the microphones and record our conversation. Oddly enough, that conversation turned into a crossover episode between Roundabout: Creative Chaos (Tammy's podcast) and the More Than Just Code podcast. In that "episode," we talked about writing books, learning code, and whatever else came to mind; if you go back into the MTJC archives, you can still find that episode today.

Shortly after our recorded conversation, Tammy became a "sometimes" co-host of the More Than Just Code podcast. Despite her "sometimes" appearances on the show, Tammy always presents a fresh perspective, especially when we do our recap shows—like our year-end shows and WWDC recaps. Her focus is usually on the gaming side of things, while I focus more on the arts—although Tammy is also an artist. Jaime is our resident game player, which plays nicely against Tammy's game-development career. And Mark is the intellectual who tends to dive deep into the nuts and bolts of code.

But Tammy isn't just a game developer or "sometimes" co-host. She's what you call a multipotentialite—a term coined by TED speaker Emilie Wapnick. A multipotentialite is someone who is equally good at multiple things—a sort of modern renaissance person, which Tammy certainly is.

On the More Than Just Code podcast, Tammy is our go-to person for gaming tech—and not just because she's the one who's made the most games. Tammy has a lot of experience with game development. She's a champion of Apple's SpriteKit and GameplayKit frameworks, and she also works with other gaming technologies like Unity and Unreal Engine.

But Tammy's experience goes beyond simply using this tech; she also teaches others how to use it. With the backing of some of the most well-known technical publishers in the industry, Tammy has delivered video courses on LinkedIn Learning (formally known as Lynda.com) and raywenderlich.com. She's also written countless tutorials and articles for print and online publication. She's even co-authored a few books.

In addition to her teaching accomplishments, Tammy is also a skilled development editor (sometimes called a final pass editor), technical editor, and copy editor. One of her more recent edits is the new *Apple Augmented Reality by Tutorials* book, written by her friend and fellow raywenderlich.com team member, Chris Language. It's funny—when you work with Tammy, you not only write a book; you also make a friend.

When it comes to Tammy's book—*Apple Game Frameworks and Technologies*—she's effectively combined all of her skills, distilling what she knows about 2D Apple game design and development, and then placing that information into a thoughtfully organized and substantial resource. Like a true renaissance person, Tammy has a way of taking complicated ideas and presenting those ideas so that they are easy to understand and fun to learn about and pull apart.

Tammy delivers the complete package. As an artist, she's always drawing, so she creates all of the artwork for her games. As a writer, she's always cooking up story ideas—and, yes, every game tells a story. As a developer, she's always looking for the best way to write readable code. As an editor, she does her best to be clear and concise in her writing (although she does have a wonderful editor on this book, Margaret Eldridge, to help her stay on track). But her biggest asset—the thing she brings most to this book—is her commitment to guiding you on your hero's journey to Apple game development.

We hope you enjoy the book as much as we do!

Respectfully yours,

Tim Mitra, with input from Jaime Lopez Jr. and Mark Rubin (hosts of the More Than Just Code podcast)

Acknowledgments

First, I want to thank all of the technical reviewers for their time in making sure the information in this book is accurate and complete: Jimmy Ti, Dominik Hauser, Jeremy Sydik, Jeff Kelley, Mads Ohm Larson, Ryan Huber, Joshua Smith, Hung Fioramonti, and Trevor Burnham. You all did an amazing job. Thank you.

Equally important is my editor, Margaret Eldridge. Her guidance, encouragement, and attention to detail is greatly appreciated. Thank you.

I also want to thank my family and friends for their continued love and support in everything I do. Thank you.

Finally, a special thanks to all of the animals in my life, both past and present. Thank you for always being there and never judging me.

Preface

Why SpriteKit? Well, that's a good question—and one that I get asked quite often. For those who ask, my response is always the same: "Why *not* SpriteKit? It has everything you need to build great games."

With SpriteKit and the rest of the Apple game frameworks and technologies—like GameplayKit, Game Center, Xcode, and Swift—you have access to the tools you need to create high-performance, power-efficient games that work across the entire Apple ecosystem.

What's especially neat about SpriteKit is that it's built on top of Metal,[1] a robust Apple framework that provides near-direct access to the *graphics processing unit (GPU)*. Because SpriteKit leverages Metal, it's possible to tap into your game's full graphics and compute potential (using Metal) while also providing a simpler programming interface (using SpriteKit).

Another benefit of using SpriteKit, especially if you're already familiar with Xcode and Swift—even more so if you're new to game development—is that the learning curve isn't as steep as something like Unity or Unreal Engine. Don't get me wrong, Unity and Unreal Engine are phenomenal tools and well worth learning—I've used them both and will continue to do so—but there's something so beautifully simple, yet strangely powerful about SpriteKit.

So, is SpriteKit the best tool for making games? Well, maybe. It all depends on what you're trying to do and why you're doing it.

Suppose you have a fantastic idea for an exciting new game you want to make, but you're not sure what tools are best for making it, so you ask me for some advice. My first question for you would be, "Why do you want to make a game?" But I wouldn't stop there. I'd also ask you questions like:

- What kind of game are you making?

- What genre? Action, adventure, simulation, role-playing?

---

1.   https://developer.apple.com/documentation/metal

- Is it a 2D game or a 3D game?

- What about making an augmented reality (AR) or virtual reality (VR) version? Do you have plans to do that?

- Are you looking to make a prototype, a full game, or both?

- Where do you want to publish your game?

- How much time do you want to spend developing your game?

- What about money and other resources? Are you funding the project yourself?

- Are you working with other developers or is this a solo project?

- Do you have any prior experience with programming or game development?

Without knowing *what* you want to do, it's a little difficult to suggest *how* to do it. For me, deciding what to use to build a game is rarely a difficult decision—for 2D games, I almost always start with SpriteKit. If SpriteKit isn't powerful enough or doesn't have a way to include a specific feature I want in my game, then I move on to something else. Most often, that's Unity.

So far, the only thing I can't do with the Apple game frameworks and technologies is create games for other platforms—so, if you want to build games for Android, Windows, or any other device outside of the Apple platform, this book may not be right for you. Then again, it's a great place to start if you're new to game development.

Who Should Read This Book

You should read this book, that's who! Yes, I realize I just made a very bold statement—heck, I even went against my own rule about using exclamation points (sorry about that).

So, how can I make such a bold statement? How do I know *you* should read this book? Simple. You're reading *this* page *right now*, so evidently you're curious what this book is all about. There's a reason for that—maybe even more than one.

Perhaps you think game development will be fun. Maybe you've tried it before but got so lost in the learning that you gave up, and now you're ready to try again. Or perhaps you're already familiar with Apple game frameworks and technologies and you're ready to see what you can *really do* with it.

Whatever your reasons were (and are) for picking up this book and reading this page (and hopefully all the ones that come next), thank you. Thank you for taking that first step, scary as it may be, to trying something new.

What Are Apple Game Frameworks and Technologies

Apple game frameworks and technologies[2] refers to a suite of related tools and application programming interfaces (APIs) that you can use to build games for the Apple platforms. This suite includes:

- ARKit
- Metal
- SceneKit
- SpriteKit
- ReplayKit
- GameplayKit
- Model I/O
- Game Center
- Game Controller
- On-Demand Resources
- Apple Arcade

Some of these frameworks and technologies listed are covered in this book.

What's in This Book

In this book, you'll build three exciting games: Gloop Drop—a new twist on a classic arcade game; Val's Revenge—a roguelike dungeon crawler; and Hog Dice—a social player versus player dice game.

Although the primary focus of this book is on building games in Xcode using SpriteKit and Swift, you'll also discover how to use other Apple game frameworks and technologies like GameplayKit and Game Center. You'll learn how to add pathfinding, artificial intelligence (AI), complex rule systems, and social player versus player features to your games.

But the learning (and fun) doesn't stop there. With the bonus chapters, you'll get to dip a proverbial toe or two into the waters of monetization. You'll find out what it takes to include in-app purchases and third-party ads with your games. (Seriously, who doesn't want to earn some extra money doing something they love, right?)

---

2. https://developer.apple.com/games

What's Not in This Book

Not many people want to read an 800+ page book while trying to learn something new—and even if they did, how many of those 800 pages would stick in their brains afterward?

There's a lot to Apple game frameworks and technologies, and although I eventually want to cover all of it, doing so in a single book is a terrible idea. The goal of learning (and teaching) shouldn't be about who makes it to the finish line first. Instead, it should be about the journey. With that thought in mind, I took a considerable amount of time deciding what to include in this book and what to save for another day.

So there is no confusion, misunderstanding, or disappointment for a lack of coverage, please understand that the following Apple game frameworks and technologies are *not covered* in this book:

- ARKit
- Metal
- SceneKit
- ReplayKit
- Game Controller
- On-Demand Resources
- Apple Arcade

How to Read This Book

If you're new to game development or Apple game frameworks and technologies, your best bet is to read this book cover-to-cover. The chapters and sample projects were carefully crafted and their order well planned. In a sense, these chapters tell a story and take you on a journey—some would say a hero's journey. (I don't want to spoil the surprise, but you, my friend, are the hero in this book. I'm just your guide.)

If reading something cover-to-cover isn't your style, don't worry; reading this book linearly is not mandatory. If there's a specific topic that interests you—let's say you want to know how to create and use tile maps or add physics to your games—no problem; every chapter in this book includes a starter project, so you can jump right in at any point without having to worry. I also include an ending project for every chapter, so if you get stuck, you can use those projects as a reference.

Conventions Used in This book

For the most part, this book uses standard conventions when it comes to programming in Swift. However, if you ask a group of 10 programmers how to create a method that returns some value, you're bound to get back 12 or so different solutions.

Is this difference in technique a bad thing? No, not at all. Having different choices is a good thing. If there was only one way for you to apply physics within your games, it might limit the types of games you can build—and making games shouldn't limit your imagination—it should help it flourish.

Don't misunderstand my words. There are rules you must (or at least should) follow and certain best practices and design guidelines[3] developers need to use—I encourage you to read them—but don't lose sight of your goal.

Game development should be fun, and how you code is an art unto itself. As developers, we all code differently. We have certain patterns we favor and stylistic choices we make. For instance, I use the prefix setup rather than setUp when naming methods that "set up" stuff. Is this wrong? Well, technically, it breaks the camel case of naming conventions. Set up (the verb) is two words, not one (as in setup, the noun or adjective).

The point is, as you work through the examples in this book, you'll more than likely come across some code or solution that you either 1) may have done differently yourself, or 2) had been taught to do another way. Try not to get distracted by these nuances—the diversity in code makes us all grow and discover new ways of doing things.

Your suggestions on how to improve the book's projects are welcome. Better yet, I encourage you to play around and find new ways of doing things. Remember, this is your journey; I'm simply your guide.

Online Resources

Several resources are available on the interwebs about game development, fewer about SpriteKit. For Apple-related resources and help, your first stop should always be the official Apple documentation.[4]

---

3.   https://swift.org/documentation/api-design-guidelines
4.   https://developer.apple.com/documentation/technologies

If you're new to Xcode[5] and Swift[6] development, you may want to read through the documentation for each.

Finally, if you find any errors in this book, need access to its source code, or want to discuss what you've read within its pages, you can find out more by visiting the book's website.[7]

Next Steps

I'm incredibly excited that you're taking this journey into the world of game development using the Apple game frameworks and technologies. I'm even more excited that you're bringing this book along with you.

Sure, you may not be fighting fire-breathing dragons or protecting some far off land from a band of evil forest dwellers, but it's still going to be a lot of fun. So, strap yourself in, because the adventure is about to begin.

---

5. https://developer.apple.com/documentation/xcode
6. https://swift.org/documentation
7. https://pragprog.com/titles/tcswift

Get Ready for Game Development

In this short introduction, you'll get what I call a 30,000-foot game development flyover. This flyover isn't really about the tools you need to develop your game. To be honest, this flyover isn't really about game development at all. Instead, it covers game design and the steps you need to take *before* you write your first line of code—and it all starts with an idea.

Discover Your Idea

So, how do you come up with a good game idea? Well, that is the million-dollar question now, isn't it?

The best advice I can give is to use your imagination and recall your past gaming experiences. While I'm not encouraging you to copy or steal other games—please, don't do that—I am encouraging you to look at the games you enjoy playing, whether it be in the past or present, and think about how you can add your own spin to make it uniquely yours.

You can also look at movies, books, and other non-video game–related material. For example, if you're a horror fan, like me, maybe you want to make a game that includes zombies or demons. Or, perhaps you like science fiction. In that case, you may want to make a space-related game where the player gets to explore strange new worlds.

Whatever your idea is, run with it...play with it...enjoy it. And, when you're ready to turn that idea into a playable game, you're ready to make a plan.

Make a Plan

Before you fire up Xcode and write that first line of code, make a plan. Without a plan, you could find yourself in the frustrating position of trying to design your game while also trying to develop it. Sure, it's possible to throw everything you have at the code—whatever it may be—but it's almost always better to start with a plan.

To help plan out your games, you can use what's known as a *game design document (GDD)*. With a GDD, you'll have a much better idea of the game you're trying to make.

In addition to the technical specifications of your game, the design document should include:

- A short description of the game, including the genre.

- Character bios and/or descriptions of the main characters, enemies, and other key players in the game.

- Location and/or scene information—especially if your game is story-driven.

- Any design considerations, concept art, and mock-ups. The GDD is a good place to decide the game's art style and camera angle.

- Level design ideas. Are the levels randomly generated or made purposefully? Is your game an endless runner, or are there distinct levels the player must clear before moving on to the next?

- Music and sound ideas or examples that will help set the tone of your game.

- The gameplay mechanics, such as items and power-ups, goals and challenges, and movement and control systems.

The level of detail you include in a GDD depends not only on the size of your game, but also on the size of your team. Even if you're working alone, make a plan and document it.

Also, it's important to understand that the GDD is a *living document*. A living document is a document that is always evolving and changing. As your game develops, so too should your design document. Because no two GDDs are alike, your best bet is to start with a blank page and add the information that is relevant to your game and its design. Alternatively, you can do a web search to find a free template or an open example.

Now that you have an idea and a plan, the next step is to gather your resources.

Gather Your Resources

When I talk about resources, I mostly mean the graphics and sound included in the game, but I also mean the people involved in making it (as well as the software and hardware required to do so), so let's start there.

Choosing Your Game Development Environment

When it comes to Apple game development, you have a few options from which to choose. One of those options is to use the native Apple development tools and its supported languages. For Apple, that means using Xcode and Swift. Another popular option is to use Unity and C#.

Deciding which tools to use is mostly a matter of preference. Still, it can also depend on your game's design and technical specifications.

This book focuses on native Apple development, and more specifically, the Apple game frameworks and technologies. It's not that Xcode and Swift are any *better* or *worse* than other development tools; it just that, in this book, the focus is on native development tools, and the games you'll be making here fall well within the range of what's possible with those tools.

To follow along with the examples in this book, you'll need:

- macOS Mojave 10.14.6 or newer
- Xcode 11.3 or newer
- Basic knowledge of Swift 5.1.4 or newer

With the tech out of the way, the next thing you need to consider is your game's assets and whether you're going to make them yourself, hire a professional, or use royalty-free resources.

Creating Assets for Your Game

Creating a good game isn't only about writing good, clean code; it's also about making sure the game looks and sounds good. Now, of course, audio and visual appeal are subjective, and you know what they say: you can't please all of the people all of the time. To that end, if you're creating the assets for your game, the design is entirely up to you.

For most games I create, I make all of the visual assets myself using a handful of applications. My go-to design tools include Adobe Photoshop, Affinity Designer, and Clip Studio Paint. This book doesn't focus on asset creation, but there are a lot of great resources you can use to learn how to use each of these programs. I recommend starting with the resources provided by the individual software publishers:

- Adobe Photoshop Tutorials[1]
- Affinity Designer Tutorials[2]
- Clip Studio Paint Tutorials[3]

When it comes to making visual assets for your games, the rule of thumb to follow is known as the *power of two*. Simply put, the power of two rule states that either one or both of the following conditions must be met:

- The width and/or height of the image should be divisible by 8.
- The width and/or height of the image can be doubled-up or divided-down by 2.

In other words, any image that is 8, 16, 32, 64, 128, 256, 512, 1024, or 2048 pixels (or higher) in width and/or height is considered valid and properly optimized. When an image is properly optimized, it tends to load faster, and the graphics pipeline can take advantage of other optimizations. However, nowadays, that rule tends to be more relaxed, but if you can follow it without too much trouble, why not, right?

You'll learn more about visual assets and how to add them to your own projects in Add Image Assets, on page 17.

When it comes to creating sound assets, my go-to tool is usually Adobe Audition, although I don't typically make the sound assets for my games. There are a few audio formats that work well, especially with mobile games, including .wav and .mp3. The .wav format has slightly better quality compared to the .mp3 format, but it tends to have a larger footprint.

If you're not too keen on making your own assets, that's okay, too. You can always hire a professional (or ask a friend).

Hiring a Professional

The first step to hiring a professional to make your assets is finding an individual or a group of individuals who can produce resources that match the design specs of your game. The best advice I can give here is to do a web search and make inquiries. Once you find a match, be clear about the resources you need. No one likes surprises, so make sure you have a clear contract drawn up and that all parties agree to its terms.

---

1. https://helpx.adobe.com/photoshop/tutorials.html
2. https://affinity.serif.com/en-gb/tutorials/designer/desktop
3. https://tips.clip-studio.com/en-us/official

For this book, and specifically for the Val's Revenge game, I hired my longtime friend, Chris Language.[4] Well, I didn't really hire him; I sort of just asked him if he wanted to help create the music for the game, and thankfully, he said yes.

If you're not sure what assets you need, you may want to consider using programmer art and/or temporary resources. Programmer art doesn't have to look good, but it can help you figure out what you need—and more important, it can help you get the programming-end of things done while you wait for the final assets to arrive.

Alternatively, you could skip using custom assets altogether and, instead, use royalty-free assets.

Using Royalty-Free Assets

Another popular option for audio and visual resources is to use *royalty-free* assets. With royalty-free assets, developers can either obtain the assets for free or pay a small licensing fee for the rights to use them. When exercising the royalty-free option, be sure to read the license agreements carefully.

Some of my favorite resources are from:

- gamedeveloperstudio.com[5]
- zapsplat[6]
- Epic Stock Media[7]

My recommendation is to do a web search, and when you find something you like, go from there.

Next Steps

As you work through the chapters in this book, think about the games you want to make. Consider their design. Take the information and examples in this book, and use it to build your own games. As you do, remember this: game development may not always be easy—but, then again, things that are worth doing rarely ever are.

---

4. https://twitter.com/ChrisLanguage
5. https://www.gamedeveloperstudio.com
6. https://www.zapsplat.com
7. https://epicstockmedia.com

Part I

Build Your First Game with SpriteKit

Get started with SpriteKit by building Gloop Drop, a game that shares similar gameplay to Kaboom!, a classic Atari 2600 game designed by Larry Kaplan and published by Activision in 1981.

In Kaboom!, the goal of the game is to catch all of the bombs dropped by the Mad Bomber—miss three, and you lose the game. In Gloop Drop, however, you won't be catching bombs—you'll be catching sticky globs of gloop.

CHAPTER 1

Creating Scenes with Sprites and Nodes

Now that you've decided to use SpriteKit, it's time to create your first game, Gloop Drop. In this chapter, you'll start with the basics:

- Setting up the project
- Working with the asset catalog
- Adding the background and foreground sprite nodes

If you're new to SpriteKit, this is the place to start. You'll meet the basic building blocks of SpriteKit—like sprites and nodes—and you'll work with assets and the asset catalog, setting the stage for what's to come.

If, however, this isn't your first time using SpriteKit, stick around—this chapter moves quickly, and you might find some new and useful information.

Gloop Drop is a 2D game based on the classic 1980s video game, Kaboom!. In Gloop Drop, the player's goal is to catch sticky globs of gloop—the more drops you catch, the faster they go. As you work through re-creating this game, you'll gain a deeper understanding of what it takes to make a 2D game with SpriteKit.

Although it's optional, you may want to download the full version of Gloop Drop[1] from the App Store so that you can get a feel for what you're building in this part of the book.

Create the Project

The first step is to create the Xcode project using a default template. From Xcode's App menu, select File ▶ New ▶ Project... or press ⇧⌘N on your keyboard to create a new project as shown in the image on page 4.

---

1. https://apps.apple.com/us/app/gloop-drop/id1441553754

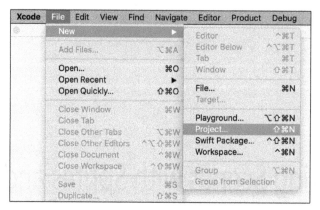

When prompted to choose a new template for your project, select the iOS Game template as shown in the following image, and click Next:

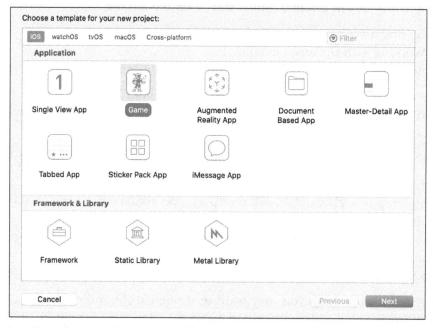

You're then prompted with the following options as shown in the image on page 5.

For the Product Name, enter gloopdrop. The text you enter here becomes part of the *Bundle Identifier (ID)*, a unique name that identifies your app on the App Store. Your project needs a Bundle ID so that you can assign app capabilities[2] and create provisioning profiles.[3]

---

2.   https://developer.apple.com/support/app-capabilities
3.   https://developer.apple.com/documentation/appstoreconnectapi/profiles

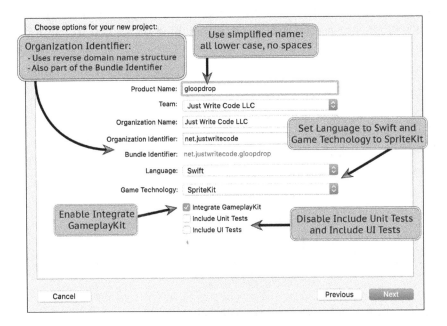

___

Entering a Product Name

Although you may be tempted to enter the full name of your game
—for example, Gloop Drop—it's better to use a simplified name
that contains no spaces or special characters, and uses only low-
ercase letters as it tends to look nicer and is more flexible.

___

For the Team, Organization Name, and Organization Identifier, use your Apple developer
information. Note that the Organization Identifier uses a reverse domain name
structure and is also part of the Bundle ID. For example, net.justwritecode is the
reverse domain name for my domain, justwritecode.net. When the Organization
Identifier of net.justwritecode is combined with the Product Name of gloopdrop, the
Bundle ID becomes net.justwritecode.gloopdrop.

You'll be using Swift and SpriteKit for this project, so set the Language to Swift
and the Game Technology to SpriteKit.

Although you won't be using the GameplayKit framework too much with this
project, you'll still need access to some of its APIs, so enable the option to
Integrate GameplayKit.

Finally, disable both the Include Unit Tests and Include UI Tests options since you
won't be using either one with this project.

When you're done entering all of the information, click Next.

When prompted, select a location to save your project, and verify that the Create Git repository on my Mac option is not enabled as shown in the following image:

Once you confirm all of the information, click Create.

At this point, your new SpriteKit project is set up and ready for you to explore as shown in the image that follows.

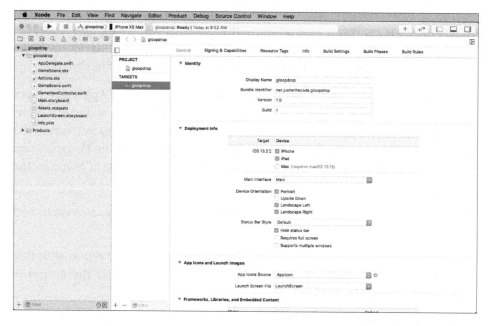

Explore the Default Template

The default iOS Game template includes some default files like AppDelegate.swift and Main.storyboard. If you've built other iOS apps before, you may recognize both of these files. The AppDelegate.swift file handles application lifecycle events,[4] and the Main.storyboard file contains the main view controller.

The default template also includes files specific to SpriteKit, like Actions.sks and GameScene.sks. Most of the time, you'll replace or modify these two files; however, using a template is preferred as it saves time in the long run.

Before you get too far into developing your first game with SpriteKit, build and run the default project to ensure everything is working. Start by setting the destination for the active scheme to the iPhone 11 Pro Max. To select the destination, click the currently selected destination on the Scheme menu located to the right of the active scheme, and choose the iPhone 11 Pro Max from the list of available destinations, like so:

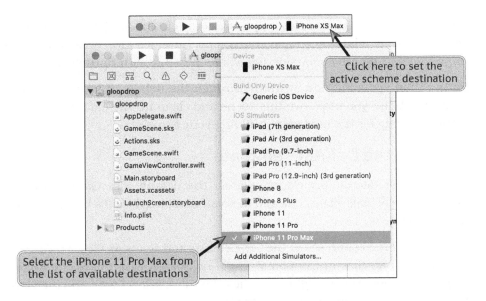

Once you've set the active scheme destination, build and run the project by selecting Product ▶ Run from Xcode's App menu. Alternatively, you can use the Run button in the top-left corner of the Xcode toolbar (it looks like a play button).

---

4.   https://developer.apple.com/documentation/uikit/uiapplicationdelegate

When the Simulator app launches, you'll see a screen with a dark-colored background and some light-colored text that reads, "Hello, World!". When you click the screen, the text shrinks and expands, and some animated colored shapes appear.

What you're seeing is the default SpriteKit project. This project uses a single scene and some relatively simple animations. Sure, it's kind of neat, but this project doesn't do much considering what's possible with SpriteKit.

Rather than spending time working through the details of how the default scene was built, you'll remove this scene and clean up the default template, getting it ready for the next step: building your game.

Clean Up the Default Template

As with most default project templates, the default iOS Game template includes a lot of boilerplate code and files you won't need, so it's best to remove these things.

In the Project Navigator, select the GameScene.sks and Actions.sks files. You'll learn more about SKS files in Chapter 7, Building Scenes with the Scene Editor, on page 143, but for now, right-click these two files, select Delete, and then Move to Trash, as shown in the image on page 9.

Still inside the Project Navigator, select the GameScene.swift file, which opens the file in the Source Editor on the right. This file controls the main game scene, and it comes packed with all sorts of properties and methods. As you work

through this book, you'll learn more about this file, but for now, delete everything in that file and replace it with this:

```swift
import SpriteKit
import GameplayKit

class GameScene: SKScene {

  override func didMove(to view: SKView) {

  }
}
```

This code imports the SpriteKit and GameplayKit frameworks and declares a GameScene class with a single, empty method named didMove(to:). This method gets called automatically when the view is about to present the scene.

Next, open the GameViewController.swift file. This is the file that controls the main view controller of your game. The view controller is responsible for loading the view.

Find and remove all of the code inside the viewDidLoad() method, leaving only the line that reads super.viewDidLoad(). Leaving this line intact ensures that the superclass loads everything it needs to function before you start overriding its method.

When you're done, the GameViewController.swift file will look like this:

```
import UIKit
import SpriteKit
import GameplayKit

class GameViewController: UIViewController {

    override func viewDidLoad() {
        super.viewDidLoad()
    }

    override var shouldAutorotate: Bool {
        return true
    }

    override var supportedInterfaceOrientations: UIInterfaceOrientationMask {
        if UIDevice.current.userInterfaceIdiom == .phone {
            return .allButUpsideDown
        } else {
            return .all
        }
    }

    override var prefersStatusBarHidden: Bool {
        return true
    }
}
```

You now have a nice clean view controller, ready and waiting. It's time to start building your game.

Set the Supported Device Orientation

The default iOS Game template is set to work in both portrait and landscape orientation. However, Gloop Drop is designed for landscape only, so you need to restrict the device orientation.

In the Project Navigator, select the gloopdrop project and look at the Deployment Info section in the Project Editor. You need to set a few options in this section.

First, verify that the iPhone and iPad devices are both enabled. Gloop Drop is also designed to work universally, so you need to let the compiler know to target both.

Next, disable the Portrait option and enable Requires full screen as shown in the following image:

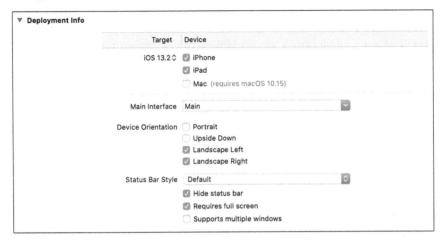

You might think that disabling the Portrait option in this section is enough to force landscape orientation on all devices, but it's not. To fix this problem, you need to temporarily disable the iPhone option while you set up the iPad options separately, like so:

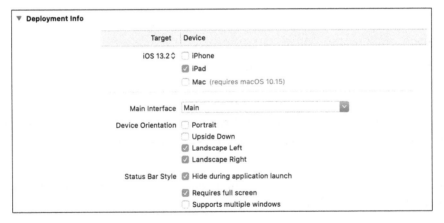

 Once you have everything set up, don't forget to re-enable iPhone support.

When you make the changes here, you're asking Xcode to reach into the Info.plist file and automatically update this file on your behalf. The information property list[5] file stores information about your project. To verify that the supported orientations are set up correctly, select the Info.plist file from the Project Navigator, and you'll see the following options near the bottom:

UIRequiresFullScreen	⌃	Boolean	YES
Status bar is initially hidden	⌃	Boolean	YES
▼ Supported interface orientations	⌃	Array	(2 items)
Item 0		String	Landscape (left home button)
Item 1		String	Landscape (right home button)
▼ Supported interface orientations (iPad)	⌃	Array	(2 items)
Item 0		String	Landscape (left home button)
Item 1		String	Landscape (right home button)

If your settings match what you see here, then your setup is correct—but hang on, you're not done yet. There's still one more thing you need to do.

In the GameViewController.swift file, modify the supportedInterfaceOrientations property from this:

```
override var supportedInterfaceOrientations: UIInterfaceOrientationMask {
  if UIDevice.current.userInterfaceIdiom == .phone {
    return .allButUpsideDown
  } else {
    return .all
  }
}
```

to this:

```
override var supportedInterfaceOrientations: UIInterfaceOrientationMask {
  return .landscape
}
```

The supportedInterfaceOrientations is an instance property that returns all of the interface orientations this view controller supports. Since this game supports only landscape, it makes sense to return only .landscape.

Build and run the project. If everything works as expected, you'll see a gray screen like the image on page 13.

(To rotate the device, select Hardware ▶ Rotate Right from the Simulator app menu until its orientation is set to landscape.)

At this point, you're ready to build your first scene.

---

5.   https://developer.apple.com/documentation/bundleresources/information_property_list

Xcode 12 and Universal Screen-Size Support

 At the time of this writing, it looks as if some key settings that enable universal support are not set when using Xcode 12. If you're using Xcode 12, you'll need to add a plist entry for Launch screen interface file base name. You can either add this entry and set its value to Main or create a custom LaunchScreen.storyboard file and set its value to LaunchScreen instead.

Alternatively, you can set this option using the drop-down list in the App Icons and Launch Images section of the General tab of the target settings. Either way, you must use an Xcode storyboard to provide a launch screen if you intend to accommodate different screen sizes. Xcode 11 automatically sets this option for you.

Create Your First SpriteKit Scene

Before building your first scene, let's go over the key components that make up a SpriteKit scene:

- SKView: This is the primary view for a SpriteKit scene. The SKView class inherits from the UIView class (or NSView on macOS).

- SKScene: This is the root node of the scene. The SKScene class includes properties and methods that define how to render content and process animation.

Typically, the view is responsible for presenting the scene.

You can create a scene in two ways: visually using the Scene Editor or pro-grammatically in code using the Source Editor. For this first game, you'll use code and the Source Editor to get better acquainted with what's going on under the hood of SpriteKit.

Open the GameViewController.swift file and in the viewDidLoad() method, add the following code below the line that reads super.viewDidLoad():

```swift
// Create the view
if let view = self.view as! SKView? {

  // Create the scene
  let scene = GameScene(size: view.bounds.size)

  // Set the scale mode to scale to fill the view window
  scene.scaleMode = .aspectFill

  // Set the background color
  scene.backgroundColor = UIColor(red: 105/255,
                                  green: 157/255,
                                  blue: 181/255,
                                  alpha: 1.0)

  // Present the scene
  view.presentScene(scene)

  // Set the view options
  view.ignoresSiblingOrder = false
  view.showsPhysics = false
  view.showsFPS = true
  view.showsNodeCount = true
}
```

First, you downcast the view as an SKView using the forced form of the type cast operator (as!). Xcode uses this type of casting in its default iOS Game template, so it makes sense to use it here, too.

After that, you create the scene and set its size and scaleMode properties. The size of your scene depends largely on the game's design and the devices it supports. With this code, you set the scene size to match the view size (view.bounds.size), and you scale the content to fill the view while also keeping the aspect ratio intact (.aspectFill). You also set the background color using the UIColor class, giving it a nice shade of blue.

You then call the presentScene(_:) method on the view, which presents the scene.

Finally, you set a few standard view properties. The SKView class has a lot of properties, so let's keep the focus on the ones you're setting up here:

- ignoresSiblingOrder: A true or false value used in part to control the rendering order of the nodes. You'll learn more about this property in Chapter 2, Adding Animation and Movement with Actions, on page 27.

- showsPhysics: A true or false value used to show or hide the physics bodies attached to your nodes.

- showsFPS: A true or false value used to show or hide the frames per second (FPS) indicator.

- showsNodeCount: A true or false value used to show or hide the number of nodes.

The last three properties are known as *performance stats* and are generally used for testing and debugging your SpriteKit scenes. There are other performance stats—like showsDrawCount, showsQuadCount, and showsFields—but you won't be using them, so there's no need to add them.

Build and run the project, and you'll see the background is now a lovely shade of blue. You'll also see the performance stats in the lower-right corner as shown in the following image:

With the view controller set up and the view presenting the scene, you're ready to start adding content.

Create Your First Sprite Node

A scene without content is like a game without a player. But before you can add content to your SpriteKit scene, you first need to learn about the SKNode class.

The SKNode class, although it doesn't render (draw) any visual content, is considered the building block of SpriteKit because every node in a SpriteKit scene is a subclass of SKNode. Each subclass has a specific function or purpose.

To draw content, you need to use a visual node, such as:

- SKSpriteNode: Perhaps the most widely used type, this node draws a rectangle texture, image, or color.

- SKShapeNode: This type of node is used along with a Core Graphics path to draw custom shapes.

- SKLabelNode: When you need text, this type of node is used to draw a text label.

- SKVideoNode: With this type of node, you can display video content.

- SKReferenceNode: Although technically not considered a visual node, this is a special node in which you can create reusable content.

Other node types modify draw behavior:

- SKEffectNode: This type of node is used for caching or for applying Core Image filters for special effects.

- SKCropNode: When you need to mask pixels, you can use this type of node.

These are just a few of the node types available in SpriteKit, some of which you'll learn more about in this book. For a full list, visit Apple's Nodes for Scene Building[6] documentation.

Although the SKNode class does not allow for visual content, it does provide some standard properties that its subclasses inherit. These properties include:

Position—

- frame: The rectangle within the parent's coordinate system.
- position: The position within the parent's coordinate system.
- zPosition: The depth within the scene relative to its parent. Using this setting, you can have content overlap in a specific order.

Scale and Rotation—

- xScale: The scaling factor of the x-axis (width).
- yScale: The scaling factor of the y-axis (height).
- zRotation: The Euler rotation around the z-axis, specified in radians[7] (a standard unit for measuring angles).

---

6. https://developer.apple.com/documentation/spritekit/nodes_for_scene_building
7. https://en.wikipedia.org/wiki/Radian

The SKNode class provides more properties (and methods), and you'll learn more about them as you go, but for now, this is a good start. Besides, you have some image assets that you need to load into your project.

Add Image Assets

In the Project Navigator, select the Assets.xcassets asset catalog. An *asset catalog* is a great way to manage and organize your assets.

With the asset catalog selected, launch a Finder window and navigate to the resources folder included with the code resources for this chapter. Once there, select the three background images:

- background_1@1x.png
- background_1@2x.png
- background_1@3x.png

Drag the background images into the Outline View (that's the view to the right of the Project Navigator) of the Assets.xcassets asset catalog, like so:

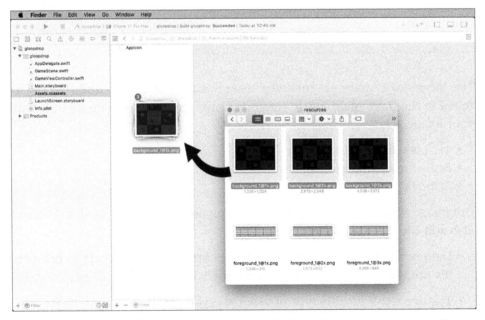

When you drag the three images into the Outline View, you create an *image set*. With an image set, you can have different image variations depending on their resolution.

In the Outline View, select the background_1 image set and look at the Detail Area to the right of the Outline View as shown in the image on page 18.

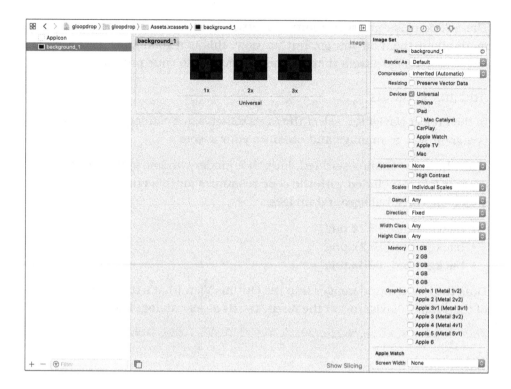

The background_1 image set includes three variations: 1x, 2x, and 3x. The #x refers to the three main image versions Apple recommends you include with your image sets:

- 1:1 pixel density (@1x)
- Scale factor of 2.0 (@2x)
- Scale factor of 3.0 (@3x)

But image sets aren't the only thing you can add to an asset catalog. You can also add the following asset types:

- Data set: You can use this type of asset set to hold binary data, provided it's not an executable. For example, a JSON file.

- Texture set: With this type of asset set, you can store an image for a 2D texture.

- Sprite atlas: Especially useful with SpriteKit projects, you can use this type of asset set to store a group of image sets. A sprite atlas is often used with frame animation or to increase runtime performance while minimizing bundle size.

These are just a few of the asset types you can add to an asset catalog, some of which you'll use in this book. For a full list, visit Xcode's Work with Assets[8] Help documentation.

Add the Background

With the background image asset added to the project, you're ready to add the background to the scene by adding a new sprite node, which will become part of the *node tree*.

A node tree is an ordered list of related parent-child nodes. You create this tree by adding nodes to other nodes. In other words, you're nesting nodes. Depending on a few properties, such as the zPosition, which indicates the node's depth within the scene, the order of the nodes in the node tree can affect their visibility—so, it's a good idea to keep things organized. You'll learn more about the node tree as you add more objects to the scene.

You can add content to a scene in many ways. Although you can use the Scene Editor to add the background, you'll continue to use the Source Editor and code in this chapter to help familiarize yourself with how things work.

Open the GameScene.swift file and locate the didMove(to:) method. This method is one of two methods automatically called when the view presents the scene. In calling order, the two methods are:

- sceneDidLoad(): Called after the scene is initialized.
- didMove(to:): Called after the view presents the scene.

Another method is automatically called, too; however, this method gets called immediately before a scene is removed from a view:

- willMove(from:): Called before the scene is removed from a view.

In the didMove(to:) method, add the following code:

```
// Set up background
let background = SKSpriteNode(imageNamed: "background_1")
background.position = CGPoint(x: 0, y: 0)
addChild(background)
```

This code declares a constant named background and uses the standard initializer to initialize a textured sprite node using the background_1 image set. The position is set to (x: 0, y: 0), and the node is added to the scene using the addChild() method on the parent node. Technically, you don't need to set a (x: 0, y: 0) position

---

8.   https://help.apple.com/xcode/mac/11.0/#/dev10510b1f7

because it's the default value. However, for clarity and instruction, it's being set by the code.

Now, switch the active scheme destination to iPad Pro (12.9-inch) (4th generation) and build and run the project. Rotate the simulator to the right (⌘→), and you'll immediately notice a problem:

The background image shows up, but it's not where it needs to be. You'll fix that next.

Set Position, Coordinates, and Anchor Points

When you add nodes to a scene and set their position, knowing how the coordinate system works in SpriteKit is key to avoiding frustration.

In SpriteKit, the bottom-left corner of the unit coordinate system is located at (x: 0, y: 0) and the top-right corner is located at (x: 1, y: 1), as shown in the following illustration:

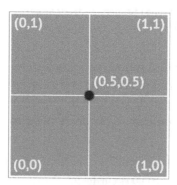

When you position a sprite node, you need to consider its anchorPoint property, which defaults to (x: 0.5, y: 0.5).

Look at the sprite node in the following image; its position property is set to (x: 0, y: 0). Notice how changing the anchorPoint can affect the node's position.

The image on the left uses the default anchorPoint value of (x: 0.5, y: 0.5), while the image on the right is using (x: 0, y: 0). Notice the left image looks a lot like the background image in the previous build and run.

When you set a node's position, it places the node at this position using the anchorPoint. In other words, the anchorPoint is what is positioned at that point specified.

Go back to the GameScene.swift file. In the didMove(to:) method, below this line:

```
let background = SKSpriteNode(imageNamed: "background_1")
```

add the following code to set the background node's anchorPoint property to location (x: 0, y: 0):

```
background.anchorPoint = CGPoint(x: 0, y: 0)
```

In the last two code blocks, you set a (x: 0, y: 0) location using CGPoint(x: 0, y: 0). If you prefer, you can instead use .zero or CGPoint.zero as these two values produce the same results. For many developers, using .zero is preferred because it's more concise and uses type inference.

Build and run the project. The background's position looks better—well, almost. Notice the blue strip down the right side. Clearly, something is wrong.

Before fixing this problem, switch the active scheme destination back to the iPhone 11 Pro Max. Then, build and run the project again.

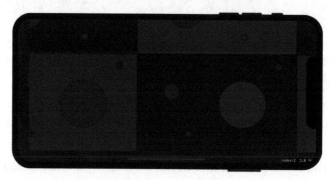

This looks even worse. Everything is scaled way up. What's happening?

The quick answer is that the assets were designed for a scene size of 1336 × 1024. However, the scene size is set using the size of the view's bounds, like so:

```
let scene = GameScene(size: view.bounds.size)
```

This is a problem because the size of the view's bounds—and therefore, the scene's size—are not a match to the original design. Here's a look at the size of the two devices:

- iPhone 11 Pro Max: (896.0, 414.0)
- iPad Pro 12.9-inch: (1366.0, 1024.0)

To get the size of the scene, you can add print("scene.size: \(scene.size)") to the viewDidLoad() method after initializing the scene.

To fix the size problem, you can manually set the size of the scene. In the GameViewController.swift file, comment out the line where you set up the scene and add a new line to set the scene size to 1336 × 1024 manually:

```
// let scene = GameScene(size: view.bounds.size)
let scene = GameScene(size: CGSize(width: 1336, height: 1024))
```

With this change, the scene size is set to match the design.

Build and run the project on both the iPad Pro and iPhone 11 Pro Max simulators and notice that everything looks as it should on both devices:

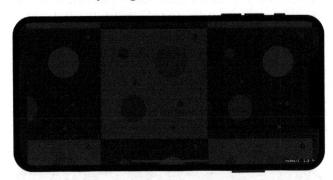

You'll learn more about designing for multiple resolutions later in Part II, Use the Scene Editor to Build Games, on page 141. This was just a quick introduction with very little explanation because you've got one more thing to do before you wrap-up this chapter: you need to add the foreground.

Add the Foreground

You've seen how to add an image set and get an SKSpriteNode object initialized, positioned, and added to the scene. You did this with the background. It's now time to apply that same knowledge and get the foreground added to your scene.

Add the Foreground Images

Before you can add a sprite node with a corresponding image file, you first need to add the images to the project as you did with the background.

In the Project Navigator, select the Assets.xcassets asset catalog.

Once again, launch a Finder window and navigate to the resources folder included with the code resources for this chapter. This time, select the three foreground images:

- foreground_1@1x.png
- foreground_1@2x.png
- foreground_1@3x.png

Drag the foreground images into the Outline View of the Assets.xcassets asset catalog.

Add the Foreground Node

Your next step is to add the code to initialize the sprite node.

Open the GameScene.swift file. In the didMove(to:) method, below the code block that sets up the background node, add the following code:

```
// Set up foreground
let foreground = SKSpriteNode(imageNamed: "foreground_1")
foreground.anchorPoint = CGPoint(x: 0, y: 0)
foreground.position = CGPoint(x: 0, y: 0)
addChild(foreground)
```

Build and run the project. You now have a foreground on which your player can stand.

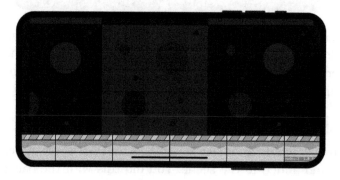

Next Steps

In this chapter, you learned how to create a new SpriteKit project using the default iOS Game template and how to clean up the boilerplate code and default files. You also learned about the SKNode class and one of its subclasses, SKSpriteNode, by adding the background and foreground nodes. While adding these two sprite nodes, you also learned about the asset catalog and how to position and anchor nodes.

In the next chapter, you'll add the player and learn the basics of movement, animation, and sound using the SKAction class.

CHAPTER 2

Adding Animation and Movement
with Actions

In the previous chapter, you created a new project using the default iOS Game template. You cleared out the boilerplate code and started to set up your first scene by adding the background and foreground sprite nodes using the SKSpriteNode class.

In this chapter, you'll add the player sprite node to the scene and focus on adding movement and animation using another SpriteKit class: SKAction.

Animation in SpriteKit

Have you ever made one of those little flip-books that when you thumb through the pages, your drawings come to life? With a flip-book, you can string together a series of static images that appear to move as you flip through them, sort of like a filmstrip animation, like so:

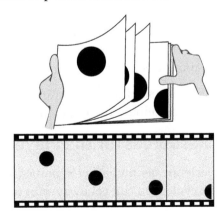

Working with animation in SpriteKit isn't much different than making a flip-book: you grab a handful of images known as *textures*, and you cycle through them one by one. The more textures you use, the smoother the animation; however, too many textures can quickly overload device resources, making the animation choppy and slow. The trick is to strike a balance between being resource-efficient and having enough images for a smooth animation.

To find the right balance, you must first understand the concept of *frame rate* and how it relates to motion. The frame rate, also known as *frames per second* (*FPS*), is the rate at which individual images show up on the screen. For SpriteKit, the default frame rate is 60 FPS.

Let's get scientific for a moment. The human eye can process 10 to 12 images per second. When animating characters and other elements, it's common practice to use the principle of *on twos*. With on twos, there's one drawing for every two frames. If you need faster animation, such as a character running or a heavy ball dropping, you can use the *on ones* principle, which uses one image per frame.

For film, the average frame rate is 24 FPS, and the general rule of thumb for a typical walk cycle is about 12 images on average using the on twos principle.

Cycle animations let you create repeating actions, like walking and running, by looping through a series of animations. A walk cycle has four main poses:

- Contact
- Recoil
- Passing
- High point

The remaining images make up the frames in between, also known as *inbetweening* or *tweening*.

You don't always need 12 images for a walk cycle; sometimes you need more, sometimes you need less—it all depends on what you're trying to do and the length of time the animation needs to run.

Now that you have a better sense of how frame animation works, it's time to load the images you'll use to animate the main character in Gloop Drop.

Add the Images Resources for the Player

In this game, the player controls a character named Blob. Because there's not much to Blob's walk cycle, you can get away with using only three images for this animation. The following image shows the individual frames you'll use for Blob's walk cycle:

blob-walk_0   blob-walk_1   blob-walk_2

Before you can animate Blob, you need to create a new sprite atlas and get these three images added to the project.

First, open the gloopdrop project in Xcode.

Using the Starter Project

You may continue using your project from the previous chapter, or you can use the starter project located in the projects/begin folder included with the code resources for this chapter. Either option is fine; the only benefit to using the starter project is that you won't get stuck going forward if you missed an earlier step.

There's also an ending project for this chapter that includes all of the code and resources you'll be adding here. The end project is located in the projects/end folder included with the code resources for this chapter.

In the Project Navigator, select the Assets.xcassets asset catalog. Click the + button at the bottom of the Outline View and select New Sprite Atlas, like so:

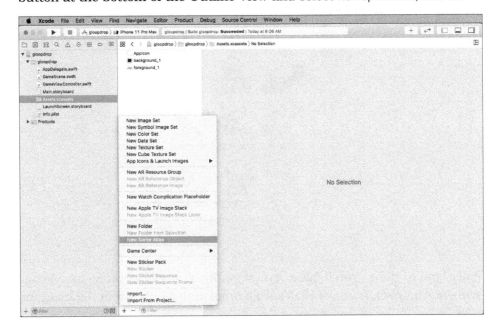

Xcode automatically creates a new sprite atlas with the name Sprites.

Xcode 12 and Sprite Atlas Creation

In Xcode 12, the New Sprite Atlas option does not exist. To create a new sprite atlas, click the + button at the bottom of the Outline View and select AR and SceneKit ▶ Sprite Atlas.

Inside the new sprite atlas folder, you'll see a single image set named Sprite, like this:

Select the Sprite image set and press the Delete key or use the - button at the bottom of the Outline View to delete the default image set.

Next, select the Sprites sprite atlas and with it highlighted, single-click the folder name and rename the sprite atlas to blob.

Finally, open Finder and drag all of the images from the resources/blob_walk folder into the blob sprite atlas, like so:

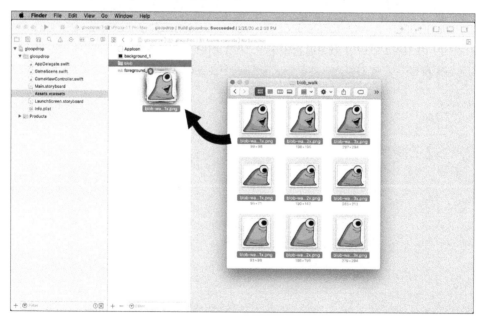

When you're done, you'll have a new sprite atlas with three new image sets—one for each frame of Blob's walk animation as shown in the image on page 31.

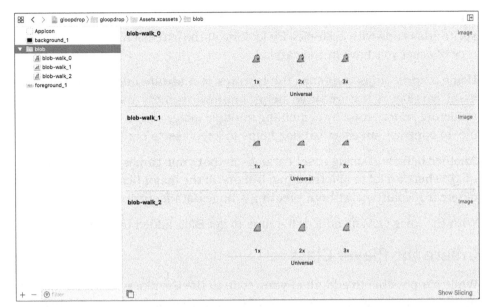

To verify that you're using a sprite atlas, right-click the folder name in the Project Navigator and select Show in Finder.

When Finder opens, you'll see something similar to this:

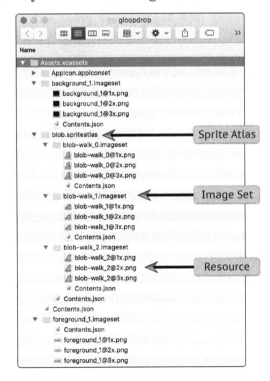

Notice the different folder extensions: an image set ends with .imageset, and a sprite atlas ends with .spriteatlas. By looking at the extension, you can tell what type of asset you have in the catalog.

Using a sprite atlas combines the features of a *texture atlas* with that of an asset catalog. A texture atlas helps improve memory usage and increase rendering performance by combining multiple image assets into a larger image file. In contrast, an asset catalog helps to keep assets organized.

Another benefit of using asset catalogs is that your games can use *app thinning*.[1] There's a lot to app thinning, but one of the major benefits is to support different resolutions without creating a huge data footprint on the device.

With the image assets added, it's time to get Blob added to the scene.

Create the Player Class

While it's possible to add all of your code to the GameScene class, it's usually not the best plan and can create problems further down the road when you want to extend your game's features. Instead, you'll create a separate Player class to keep your codebase free of the muck that causes spaghetti code.

To further organize your code, you'll put your new class in its own file. From Xcode's App menu, select File ▶ New ▶ File... or press ⌘N on your keyboard to create a new file:

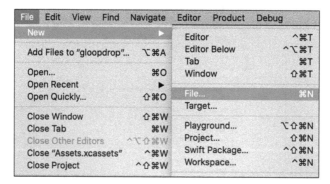

When prompted, select the iOS Swift File template as shown in the image on page 33, then click Next.

In the Save As field, enter the name, Player.swift and then click Create. This action opens the Source Editor on the right, with the newly created file loaded.

---

1. https://help.apple.com/xcode/mac/current/#/devbbdc5ce4f

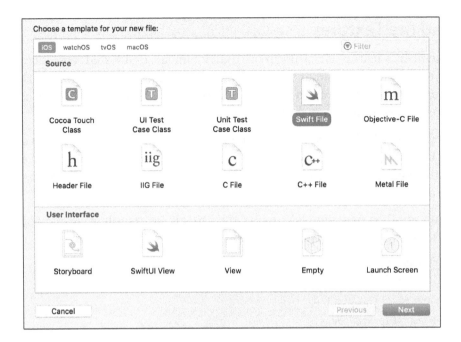

Now, replace the contents of Player.swift with the following:

```swift
import Foundation
import SpriteKit

class Player: SKSpriteNode {
  // MARK: - PROPERTIES

  // MARK: - INIT
}
```

This code sets up the foundation for the Player class by importing the SpriteKit framework and providing the class definition. By adding the MARK: prefix to the comment (//), you're able to add a heading in your jump bar and minimap. When you also add a hyphen (-), you're able to add a separator line. Adding the hyphen before the heading content places the separator bar above the heading; adding it after the heading content places the separator bar below the heading. The following image shows the headings and separator lines as they appear in the jump bar:

The next step is to get the textures loaded.

Load the Textures

Remember, a texture is nothing more than an image, or a visual representation for your sprite. To animate a sprite in SpriteKit, you can load an array of textures and cycle through them. Given this is something you'll do a lot, it makes sense to use an *extension*[2] to load the textures.

Extensions, which are common to many programming languages, are a great way to reuse code, keep things organized, and extend the functionality of an existing class. To keep your code further organized, you'll put the extensions into a separate file.

Create another new file (⌘N) using the iOS Swift File template. Name the file SpriteKitHelper.swift and replace its contents with the following:

```
import Foundation
import SpriteKit

// MARK: - SPRITEKIT EXTENSIONS

extension SKSpriteNode {

}
```

You're now ready to add your first SKSpriteNode extension method. Within the brackets ({}) of the SKSpriteNode extension, add the following code:

```
// Used to load texture arrays for animations
func loadTextures(atlas: String, prefix: String,
                  startsAt: Int, stopsAt: Int) -> [SKTexture] {
  var textureArray = [SKTexture]()
  let textureAtlas = SKTextureAtlas(named: atlas)
  for i in startsAt...stopsAt {
    let textureName = "\(prefix)\(i)"
    let temp = textureAtlas.textureNamed(textureName)
    textureArray.append(temp)
  }

  return textureArray
}
```

This method takes four parameters: an atlas name, a prefix, and the start and stop frame numbers for the animation. It then uses a for-in loop to build and return the array of textures.

Now that you have a convenient way to load textures for your sprite nodes, you can use it to load the textures for Blob's walk cycle.

---

2.   https://docs.swift.org/swift-book/LanguageGuide/Extensions.html

Use the Load Textures Extension

Open the Player.swift file. At the top of the file, below the import statements and above the class definition, add the following block of code:

```
// This enum lets you easily switch between animations
enum PlayerAnimationType: String {
  case walk
}
```

Because you'll add more animation types later, it makes sense to use an *enumeration*[3] using the keyword, enum. An enumeration is a data type you can use to store a set of named values. With the PlayerAnimationType enum, you can easily refer to specific animation types elsewhere in your code using memorable names like walk or run.

First, you need a private property to hold the walk textures. Inside the Player class below the line that reads // MARK: - PROPERTIES, add the following code:

```
// Textures (Animation)
private var walkTextures: [SKTexture]?
```

Next, you need to add the init() and init(coder:) methods. You may get some errors while adding these methods, but you can ignore them because they'll disappear once you've added all of the code.

Below the line that reads // MARK: - INIT, add the following block of code:

```
init() {
  // Set default texture
  let texture = SKTexture(imageNamed: "blob-walk_0")

  // Call to super.init
  super.init(texture: texture, color: .clear, size: texture.size())

  // Set up animation textures
  self.walkTextures = self.loadTextures(atlas: "blob", prefix: "blob-walk_",
                                        startsAt: 0, stopsAt: 2)

  // Set up other properties after init
  self.name = "player"
  self.setScale(1.0)
  self.anchorPoint = CGPoint(x: 0.5, y: 0.0) // center-bottom
}

required init?(coder aDecoder: NSCoder) {
  fatalError("init(coder:) has not been implemented")
}
```

---

3.   https://docs.swift.org/swift-book/LanguageGuide/Enumerations.html

The init() method creates an SKTexture object using the first blob-walk image. It then makes a call to super.init.

After calling super.init, the init() method calls your new extension method and passes in the name of the atlas, the prefix for the images, and the start and end numbers of the image names for this animation. To better understand how this extension method works, consider the following code (but don't add it to your project):

```
// Create the array of textures
self.walkTextures = [SKTexture(imageNamed: "blob-walk_0"),
                     SKTexture(imageNamed: "blob-walk_1"),
                     SKTexture(imageNamed: "blob-walk_2")]
```

This code creates the walkTextures array in-line rather than by calling the extension method like the following code does:

```
self.walkTextures = self.loadTextures(atlas: "blob", prefix: "blob-walk_",
                                      startsAt: 0, stopsAt: 2)
```

Either way is acceptable, but with the extension method, you're able to simplify and reuse your code with other sprite nodes, making use of the *DRY (Don't Repeat Yourself) principle.*

The init() method also sets some additional properties like the name, scale, and anchorPoint for the player sprite node.

The second method you added is init(coder:). The init(coder:) method is a required method; it's used when initializing a sprite from a scene file. You're not using scene files yet, so there's not much you need to do with this method besides include it.

With these two methods in place, you're ready to add the player to the scene.

Add the Player to the Scene

Adding the player to the scene is a lot like adding the background and foreground.

Start by opening the GameScene.swift file. At the end of the didMove(to:) method and below the code block that sets up the foreground, add the following code:

```
// Set up player
let player = Player()
player.position = CGPoint(x: size.width/2, y: foreground.frame.maxY)
addChild(player)
```

This block of code initializes an instance of the Player class and sticks that instance into a local variable. It then sets the position of the sprite node to the center of the scene and directly on top of the foreground node using the maxY property on foreground.frame. The maxY property returns the maximum y-value of a node, which in this case is the top of the foreground node.

Build and run the project.

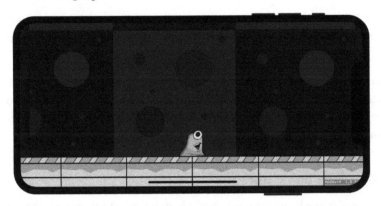

So far, everything looks as expected, but there's a potential problem. Can you guess what it is?

No spoilers, but I'll give you a hint: it has to do with the render order. To see what I mean, move the background set-up code to the end of the didMove(to:) method after adding the player. Now, build and run the project again.

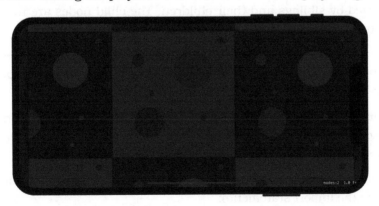

Notice how the foreground and player are missing. Well, technically, they're not missing—you just can't see them anymore because they're behind the background node. To fix this problem, you first need to learn how to control the render order using a node's z-position.

Control Render Order with Z-Position

When you add nodes to the scene, you're building a node tree, which you briefly read about in Chapter 1, Creating Scenes with Sprites and Nodes, on page 3. The order in which you add a node to the scene determines how it's rendered. In this case, you added the background node last, which places it on top of the other nodes.

Here's how it works:

- The scene renders itself, clearing its contents to its background color.
- The scene renders the foreground node, the player node, and finally, the background node.

You could build your scenes with this process in mind, but that can get complicated as you add and remove nodes. Luckily, you're able to change how things render by using a node's z-position. You can think of the z-position as the node's depth setting within the scene.

When you use z-positions to set up your nodes, the node tree gets rendered differently. Here's how it works:

- The global z-position for each node is calculated by recursively adding its z-position to its parent's z-position.

- The drawing order is determined by the node's z-position and is ordered from lowest to highest.

- If two nodes share the same z-position, parent nodes are rendered first, followed by siblings and their children. The child nodes are rendered in the order in which they appear in the parent's children array.

The default z-position for a node is 0. Setting this to a higher number brings it closer to the top. So, a z-position of 10, for example, is on top of a node whose z-position is set to 5.

Although you can set the z-position for each node using hard-coded numbers throughout your code, it's best to use an enum. Using an enum makes it easier to maintain your code as you build more advanced scenes.

Open the SpriteKitHelper.swift file and add the following code to the top of this file, below the import statements:

```
// MARK: - SPRITEKIT HELPERS

// Set up shared z-positions
enum Layer: CGFloat {
  case background
  case foreground
  case player
}
```

This code creates a new Layer enum that you can use for ordering the different nodes. Because player is last in the list, it has the highest number, which means any nodes that use this value will appear on the top-most layer.

Now that you have an enum available for setting a z-position value, you can use it to set the node's zPosition property.

Open the Player.swift file, and inside the init() method, add the following line after setting the anchorPoint:

```
self.zPosition = Layer.player.rawValue
```

Here, you're using one of the enum values you set up earlier to set the node's zPosition property. Because this is the player node, you want it to appear on top of everything else.

Next, open the GameScene.swift file, and inside the didMove(to:) method, update the code for both the background and foreground nodes.

For the background node, below the line of code that sets its anchorPoint, add the following:

```
background.zPosition = Layer.background.rawValue
```

For the foreground node, below the line of code that sets its anchorPoint, add the following:

```
foreground.zPosition = Layer.foreground.rawValue
```

Build and run the project to confirm everything is working as expected.

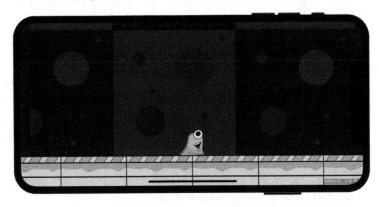

Although you can keep the code as it is now—remember, in Add the Player to the Scene, on page 36, you swapped the order in which you're adding nodes to the scene—it's better to put everything back the way it was. For reference, the didMove(to:) method should look like this:

```
override func didMove(to view: SKView) {
    // Set up background
    let background = SKSpriteNode(imageNamed: "background_1")
    background.anchorPoint = CGPoint(x: 0, y: 0)
    background.zPosition = Layer.background.rawValue
    background.position = CGPoint(x: 0, y: 0)
    addChild(background)

    // Set up foreground
    let foreground = SKSpriteNode(imageNamed: "foreground_1")
    foreground.anchorPoint = CGPoint(x: 0, y: 0)
    foreground.zPosition = Layer.foreground.rawValue
    foreground.position = CGPoint(x: 0, y: 0)
    addChild(foreground)

    // Set up player
    let player = Player()
    player.position = CGPoint(x: size.width/2, y: foreground.frame.maxY)
    addChild(player)
}
```

Build and run the project again to make sure things continue to look as expected.

A Word about Render Order

In Chapter 1, Creating Scenes with Sprites and Nodes, on page 3, you may recall a property named ignoresSiblingOrder. When ignoresSiblingOrder is set to its default value of false, nodes within a scene are sorted and rendered in a deterministic order: parents before children, and then siblings in the order in which they appear in the node tree.

 In contrast, when the ignoresSiblingOrder property is set to true, the render order is based entirely on a node's z-position. The default zPosition property value of a node is 0. While setting ignoresSiblingOrder = true offers an increase in performance, you must ensure that each node has its zPosition property set. In cases where two nodes share the same z-position, their render order is arbitrary and can change.

For most SpriteKit games, leaving ignoresSiblingOrder = false is recommended unless performance is an issue.

With your player image resources added and your base methods set up, you have everything in place to animate Blob's walk cycle.

Animate the Player with Actions

One of the more powerful features in SpriteKit is *actions*. Actions in SpriteKit are handled using the SKAction class, and they allow you to perform many types of operations on your nodes. For example, you can:

- Change a node's position and orientation.
- Change a node's size or scale properties.
- Change a node's visibility or make it translucent.
- Change a sprite node's contents so it animates through a series of textures.
- Colorize a sprite node.
- Play simple sounds.
- Remove a node from the node tree.
- Run a code block.
- Invoke a selector on an object.

You'll use most—if not all—of these types of actions in your games. However, to animate the sprite and move the player, you'll use only a handful of these actions to change the node's position, scale, and texture.

Open the SpriteKitHelper.swift file and add another method to your SKSpriteNode extension:

```
// Start the animation using a name and a count (0 = repeat forever)
func startAnimation(textures: [SKTexture], speed: Double, name: String,
                    count: Int, resize: Bool, restore: Bool) {

  // Run animation only if animation key doesn't already exist
  if (action(forKey: name) == nil) {
    let animation = SKAction.animate(with: textures, timePerFrame: speed,
                                     resize: resize, restore: restore)

    if count == 0 {
      // Run animation until stopped
      let repeatAction = SKAction.repeatForever(animation)
      run(repeatAction, withKey: name)
    } else if count == 1 {
      run(animation, withKey: name)
    } else {
      let repeatAction = SKAction.repeat(animation, count: count)
      run(repeatAction, withKey: name)
    }
  }
}
```

With this code, you're creating an extension method to start an animation. The function parameters include an array of textures, the speed at which to cycle through the textures, a key name for the animation (so you can identify it later), a count, and two parameters that control how to handle the images.

Looking closer at this extension method, you'll notice that three SKAction methods are used:

- SKAction.animate(with:timePerFrame:resize:restore:)
- SKAction.repeatForever(_:)
- SKAction.repeat(_:count:)

The first action sets up the frame-by-frame animation using the supplied textures. The code then cycles through these textures based on the value of timePerFrame. The timePerFrame is the amount of time, in seconds, each texture is displayed. The other parameters, resize and restore, indicate how the action should handle the size and final texture for the node. When resize = true, the sprite's size matches the image size. When restore = true, the original texture is restored when the action completes.

The other two actions, repeatForever(_:) and repeat(_:count:), determine how many times to repeat the action. You can either repeat forever or repeat the number of times specified in the count parameter.

With this extension method, you're using the count parameter to determine how often to repeat the action: when a value of 0 is passed into the method, the action repeats forever, whereas if any other number is passed in, the action repeats the specified number of times.

Once you have the action set up, you use the run(_:withKey:) method on the node to execute that action. Excellent, you're ready to animate Blob using your new animation extension.

Use the Animation Extension

Open the Player.swift file. Below the initialization methods, add a new method to handle the walk action:

```
// MARK: - METHODS

func walk() {
  // Check for textures
  guard let walkTextures = walkTextures else {
    preconditionFailure("Could not find textures!")
  }
  // Run animation (forever)
  startAnimation(textures: walkTextures, speed: 0.25,
                 name: PlayerAnimationType.walk.rawValue,
                 count: 0, resize: true, restore: true)
}
```

This new method calls the animation extension method you just created and passes in the values for textures, speed, name, count, resize, and restore. The speed parameter is set to 0.25. Setting this number higher or lower will result in a slower or faster animation. The higher the number, the longer each frame is on screen, which creates a slower animation cycle. For Blob's walk cycle, 0.25 gives him a good swagger.

With your new walk() method in place, you're ready to get Blob's animation running from within the scene.

Open the GameScene.swift file and add the following line to the end of the did-Move(to:) method:

```
player.walk()
```

Build and run the project, and watch as Blob bounces up and down in place as the animation cycles repeatedly through the three textures.

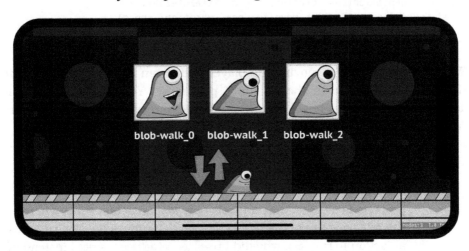

That's great, but now Blob needs to get moving across the platform.

Move the Player with Actions

Currently, the player object is defined in the scene using a local variable within a single method. This approach won't work because you need access to the player object from outside of that single method. To fix this problem, you'll add a new player property to the GameScene and remove the local player variable from the didMove(to:) method.

Still inside the GameScene.swift file, add the following property to the GameScene class, just above the didMove(to:) method:

```
let player = Player()
```

Then, change the player set-up code in the didMove(to:) method to match this:

```
// Set up player
player.position = CGPoint(x: size.width/2, y: foreground.frame.maxY)
addChild(player)
player.walk()
```

This code gives you access to the player object from other methods within the game scene. The next step is to move the player node left and right when the user, your human player, touches the screen.

Add the Move Action

First, you need a new method that moves the player node. For this new method, you'll use another action.

Open the Player.swift file and add your new method below the walk() method:

```
func moveToPosition(pos: CGPoint, speed: TimeInterval) {
  let moveAction = SKAction.move(to: pos, duration: speed)
  run(moveAction)
}
```

With this action, you're moving the player node from its current position to the position indicated in the pos input parameter. You're also setting the duration, which specifies how long it should take to move the node from point A to point B.

Speed versus Duration

When you're working with actions, a handful of properties control the timing. Two of those properties are speed and duration. The speed property is a CGFloat that controls how *fast* an action runs, whereas the 'duration property is a TimeInterval that determines *how long* it takes an action to run. So, why did I use moveToPosition(pos:speed:) instead of moveToPosition(pos:duration:), which is closer to the SKAction.move(to:duration:) method?

When I name custom methods, I tend to think in terms of gameplay rather than what the method is technically doing. You could argue that I'm using the Swift API guideline that states you should "name variables, parameters, and associated types according to their roles, rather than their type constraints," but in this case, it's a fine line. The length it takes Blob to move across the scene, in my mind, is his speed—how fast he's moving.

Respond to Touch

When you create a new project, the iOS Game template creates some useful methods, including its touch handlers. In Clean Up the Default Template, on page 8, you removed those handlers for clarity—it's time to add them back into the code.

In the GameScene.swift file, add the following code below the didMove(to:) method:

```
// MARK: - TOUCH HANDLING

/* ################################################################## */
/*                    TOUCH HANDLERS STARTS HERE                      */
/* ################################################################## */
func touchDown(atPoint pos : CGPoint) {

}

override func touchesBegan(_ touches: Set<UITouch>, with event: UIEvent?) {
  for t in touches { self.touchDown(atPoint: t.location(in: self)) }
}
```

This boilerplate code handles one of the standard touch events.

A Word about Comment Blocks

You might be wondering why so many comments are included with the code examples you're adding. For example, the large comment block, TOUCH HANDLERS STARTS HERE, that immediately proceeds the // MARK: - TOUCH HANDLING comment.

While it's generally a good idea to include some comments with your code, adding larger blocks helps to visually break up your code without having to rely on the jump bar or separator lines.

If you're typing this code into your editor, and you'd rather skip the comments, that's fine.

For the code you just added, your focus is on the touchDown(atPoint:) method. This method is indirectly called whenever the user touches the screen. It works that way because the touchesBegan(_:with:) method is automatically called by the system when the user touches the screen, and this method now passes the touch location to your custom method.

In the touchDown(atPoint:) method, add the following line:

```
player.moveToPosition(pos: pos, speed: 1.0)
```

This line of code passes the desired position and speed to the moveToPosition(pos:speed:) method you created earlier.

Build and run the project, and then start tapping anywhere on the screen.

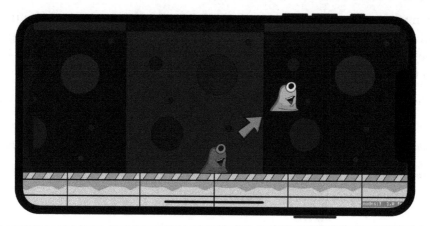

You likely already noticed a problem. Well, actually, three problems:

- Blob moves anywhere you tap, including off the platform.
- The direction Blob is facing doesn't always match the direction he's going.
- Blob's speed is inconsistent.

The good news is that all of Blob's movement issues are fixable, which you'll do next.

Testing with the Simulator

As you start to add more features to your SpriteKit games, such as animation and movement, you'll notice that running things on the simulator is very slow. To get around this problem, you can test on a physical device rather than using the simulator. As a matter of fact, you should never ship your games or apps without proper testing on a physical device first.

Use Constraints to Limit Movement

At the moment, the player node moves to the tap location instead of staying on the platform. There's a way to fix this problem using constraints and the SKConstraint class.

With constraints, you can restrict a node's movement to a specific area. In this case, you need to limit the player.position.y value to keep Blob firmly on the platform.

Open the Player.swift file and add a new method above the walk() method:

```
func setupConstraints(floor: CGFloat) {
  let range = SKRange(lowerLimit: floor, upperLimit: floor)
  let lockToPlatform = SKConstraint.positionY(range)

  constraints = [ lockToPlatform ]
}
```

This new method sets up a range with an upper and lower limit using the values you pass in for the lowerLimit and upperLimit parameters.

Go back to the GameScene.swift file, and where you set up the player node, add the following line above the line that adds that node to the scene:

```
player.setupConstraints(floor: foreground.frame.maxY)
```

This line of code calls the new method and passes in the foreground frame's maxY value, which it uses to keep the player node's position.y value constrained to the platform.

Build and run the project, and tap anywhere you'd like.

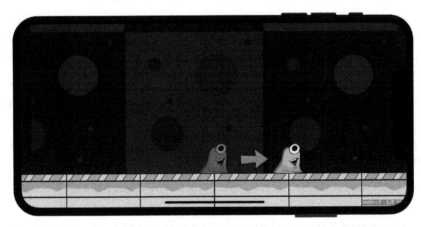

Notice that no matter where you tap, Blob stays firmly planted on top of the platform. But don't celebrate yet. You need to work out the next problem: Blob's inability to pay attention to where he's going. Silly, Blob, what are you thinking?

Set the Player's Direction Using Scales

The next problem you need to fix is Blob's inability to switch direction visually. At the moment, Blob only faces in one direction regardless of where he's headed. You can fix Blob's misguided behavior using the xScale property of the node.

First, open the Player.swift file and modify the moveToPosition(pos:direction:speed:) method to match the following:

```
func moveToPosition(pos: CGPoint, direction: String, speed: TimeInterval) {
  switch direction {
  case "L":
    xScale = -abs(xScale)
  default:
    xScale = abs(xScale)
  }

  let moveAction = SKAction.move(to: pos, duration: speed)
  run(moveAction)
}
```

The switch statement evaluates the value in the direction parameter (R=Right/L=Left) and adjusts the node's xScale property accordingly:

- direction = "R": Sets the xScale property value to a positive number.
- direction = "L": Sets the xScale property value to a negative number.

Setting the value to positive or negative is handled with the built-in abs() method,[4] which returns an absolute value. You're using an absolute value to ensure that you're always starting with a positive number. You then convert that positive value to a negative value only when necessary.

Next, open the GameScene.swift file, and in the touchDown(atPoint:) method, modify the call that moves the player:

```
if pos.x < player.position.x {
  player.moveToPosition(pos: pos, direction: "L", speed: 1.0)
} else {
  player.moveToPosition(pos: pos, direction: "R", speed: 1.0)
}
```

This code checks if the touch location (pos.x) is less than the player's current x-position (player.x). If it is, that means Blob is headed left; otherwise, Blob is headed right.

Build and run the project to test Blob's new superpower of looking where he's going as shown in the image on page 49.

Great, you're almost done. The last thing to fix is Blob's inconsistent speed problem.

---

4. https://developer.apple.com/documentation/swift/2885649-abs

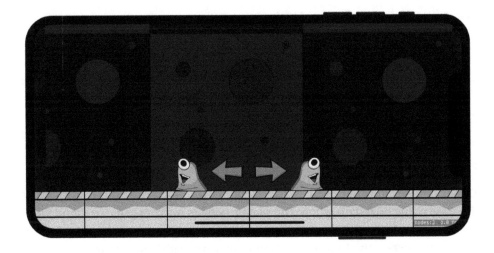

Keep the Player's Speed Consistent

When you first built the move action, you set a duration for the action using the speed parameter (yeah, I know). As a reminder, here's the original method (it looks a little different now since you just added a direction parameter, too):

```
func moveToPosition(pos: CGPoint, speed: TimeInterval) {
  let moveAction = SKAction.move(to: pos, duration: speed)
  run(moveAction)
}
```

The trouble with Blob's movement is the duration of the action: it can't be the same every time. When Blob is at the far left of the scene and travels to the far right, the duration of the action needs to be different than when he's already halfway across the scene. In other words, Blob will need to go faster when he's farther from his target location and slower when he's closer to it.

Although you're starting to get into the nitty-gritty of the *game loop* and how and when frames are updated, you don't have to worry about that too much at this point. For now, you can leverage a little math to solve this problem.

Open the GameScene.swift file and add a new property to hold the player's base speed:

```
let playerSpeed: CGFloat = 1.5
```

Then, modify the touchDown(atPoint:) method so that it matches this:

```
func touchDown(atPoint pos : CGPoint) {
  // Calculate the speed based on current position and tap location
  let distance = hypot(pos.x-player.position.x, pos.y-player.position.y)
  let calculatedSpeed = TimeInterval(distance / playerSpeed) / 255
  // print(" distance: \(distance) \n calculatedSpeed: \(calculatedSpeed)")

  if pos.x < player.position.x {
    player.moveToPosition(pos: pos, direction: "L", speed: calculatedSpeed)
  } else {
    player.moveToPosition(pos: pos, direction: "R", speed: calculatedSpeed)
  }
}
```

This code uses another built-in function, hypot(),[5] and some math to calculate the speed value based on where the player node is currently located and where it's headed. The hypot() function uses a bit of trigonometry to calculate the distance between the two points. Remember, the value stored in speed is used to determine the duration of the move action; in this case, moving the player node from point A to point B.

Build and run the project. Notice that Blob's movement speed is now consistent regardless of where he starts or where he's going.

Next Steps

In this chapter, you learned how to animate and move a sprite node using the SKAction class, and you dipped a toe in the proverbial water, learning how to use one of the more powerful and lesser-known classes of SpriteKit, SKConstraint.

As a bonus, you got to create a custom Player class and use a few built-in functions to manipulate the direction and speed of the player node. You also got to add some useful and reusable extensions to the SKSpriteNode class.

In the next chapter, you'll add the gloop drops to your game and build on what you learned about actions. You'll also discover how to use iterative design as you modify the movement of the player node.

---

5. https://developer.apple.com/documentation/simd/hypot?language=objc

CHAPTER 3

Chaining Actions and Using Iterative Design

In the previous chapter, you added the player sprite node to the scene, worked with animations, and got Blob moving around at a consistent speed by using a touch event and some built-in functions. In this chapter, you'll add the drops (collectible items) and learn how to improve and iterate your design by modifying how the player moves.

As you work through the beginning sections of this chapter, you'll notice many similarities to the previous chapter. For this reason, some of the instructions—like adding a new Swift file and creating a new sprite atlas—will be simplified and won't include screenshots or detailed explanations. Thanks to this accelerated pace, you'll have more time to dive deeper into actions and strengthen your SpriteKit skills.

Add Your First Collectible Item

Most games worth playing include some type of goal or reward system—without it, players would quickly get bored playing your game and move on to something else.

In Gloop Drop, the player's goal is to collect sticky globs of gloop (drops) as they fall from the sky without letting them hit the platform. Each time the player catches a drop, the player earns points.

Your first step to implementing Gloop Drop's goal and reward system is to add the image resources for the sticky globs of gloop.

Add the Gloop Drop Image Resources

Similar to what you did in Add the Images Resources for the Player, on page 28, you'll add a new sprite atlas to hold the three gloop drop images—one for each resolution (@1x, @2x, and @3x):

gloop@1x.png
34×54

gloop@2x.png
67×106

gloop@3x.png
101×160

To begin, open the gloopdrop project in Xcode.

Using the Starter Project

You may continue using your project from the previous chapter, or you can use the starter project located in the projects/begin folder included with the code resources for this chapter. Either option is fine; the only benefit to using the starter project is that you won't get stuck going forward if you missed an earlier step.

There's also an ending project for this chapter that includes all of the code and resources you'll be adding here. The end project is located in the projects/end folder included with the code resources for this chapter.

From the Project Navigator, select the Assets.xcassets asset catalog. Click the + button at the bottom of the Outline View and select New Sprite Atlas. Rename the Sprites sprite atlas to collectibles, and delete the empty Sprite image set.

Open Finder and drag all of the images from the resources/collectibles folder into the newly created sprite atlas, like the first image on page 53.

When you're done, your new sprite atlas will look like the second image on page 53.

With the image resources added, you're ready to create the custom class for the collectible items.

Create the Collectible Class

Similar to what you did in Create the Player Class, on page 32, you'll create a custom class for the collectible items.

From Xcode's App menu, select File ▶ New ▶ File... or press ⌘N on your keyboard to create a new file. Select the iOS Swift File template and name the file,

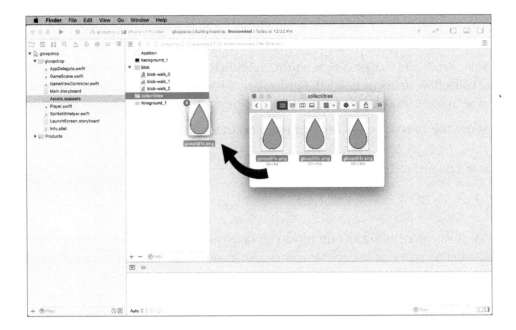

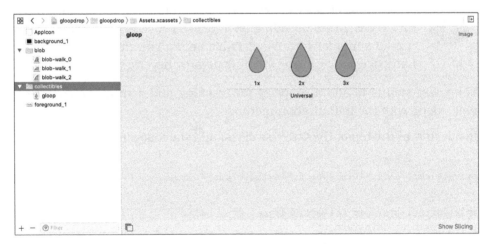

Collectible.swift. When the new file opens in the Source Editor, replace its contents with the following code:

```
import Foundation
import SpriteKit

class Collectible: SKSpriteNode {

}
```

Like the Player class, this new class imports the Foundation and SpriteKit frameworks and provides the Collectible class definition.

Next, you'll add a CollectibleType enum, making it easier to set up different types of collectible items as needed. Remember, with an enum, you can use memorable names, making it easier to refer to them in a type-safe way.

Above the Collectible class declaration, add the following code:

```
// This enum lets you add different types of collectibles
enum CollectibleType: String {
  case none
  case gloop
}
```

Because you're using an enum, you can now extend the game later to include additional types of collectible items like power-ups, extra lives, and other goodies.

Adding More Collectible Types

In this book, you'll only be adding one type of collectible item—the sticky globs of gloop—however, it's good practice to consider your future design when coding, so it doesn't hurt to plan ahead and use an enum for future collectible items. The alternative is to hardcode your values, which is usually never a good idea.

Your next step is to add a property for tracking and setting the collectible type, along with the initialization methods.

Inside and at the top of the Collectible class, add the following block of code:

```
// MARK: - PROPERTIES
private var collectibleType: CollectibleType = .none

// MARK: - INIT
init(collectibleType: CollectibleType) {
  var texture: SKTexture!
  self.collectibleType = collectibleType

  // Set the texture based on the type
  switch self.collectibleType {
  case .gloop:
    texture = SKTexture(imageNamed: "gloop")
  case .none:
    break
  }

  // Call to super.init
  super.init(texture: texture, color: SKColor.clear, size: texture.size())
```

```
  // Set up collectible
  self.name = "co_\(collectibleType)"
  self.anchorPoint = CGPoint(x: 0.5, y: 1.0)
  self.zPosition = Layer.collectible.rawValue
}
// Required init
required init?(coder aDecoder: NSCoder) {
  fatalError("init(coder:) has not been implemented")
}
```

This code initializes a Collectible object and sets its texture, name, anchorPoint, and zPosition properties.

Notice that you get the following error when setting the zPosition: Type Layer has no member collectible. To fix this error, open the SpriteKitHelper.swift file and modify the Layer enum so that it matches this:

```
enum Layer: CGFloat {
  case background
  case foreground
  case player
  case collectible
}
```

This updated code adds a new case for the z-position—essentially, another layer—above the player layer and clears the error.

Now that you have the groundwork laid for your collectible items, you're ready to get the collectible drops added to the game scene using the process of *iterative and incremental development.*

Improve Code with Iterative and Incremental Development

With iterative and incremental development, you can shake out any potential problems with your code and your game's design. Adding code in smaller chunks makes it much faster and easier to pinpoint code that's causing issues.

The phrase, "iterative and incremental development" is a combination of *iterative design* and the *incremental build model.* With iterative design, you develop your game using a set of repeated cycles. With the incremental build model, you develop your code in smaller chunks. With each iteration and chunk of code you add, you get closer to your end goal.

For the collectible items, you'll start with a single, stationary collectible—a gloop drop. Once you get that working, you'll move on to adding more functionality with every iteration.

The first method you'll add is spawnGloop(). You'll use this method to spawn a single drop and add it to the scene.

Start by opening the GameScene.swift file. Immediately below the didMove(to:) method, add the following code:

```
// MARK: - GAME FUNCTIONS
/* ################################################################# */
/*                    GAME FUNCTIONS START HERE                      */
/* ################################################################# */
func spawnGloop() {
  let collectible = Collectible(collectibleType: CollectibleType.gloop)
  collectible.position = CGPoint(x: player.position.x,
                                 y: player.position.y * 2.5)
  addChild(collectible)
}
```

With this code, you initialize a collectible object using the new Collectible class. You then set its position to be directly above the player node. You also set its y-position to be 2.5 times higher than that of the player.position.y. Finally, you add the collectible node to the scene.

Your next step is to call the new spawnGloop() method. Inside the didMove(to:) method, below the line that reads player.walk(), add the following code:

```
// Set up game
spawnGloop()
```

This code calls the spawnGloop() method you added earlier.

Build and run the project to ensure everything is working so far. If all is well, you'll see a single drop of gloop above the player, and your first iteration is complete as shown in the image on page 57.

At this point, you're ready for the next iteration (and to learn how to chain SpriteKit actions together).

Chain Actions Together to Create a Sequence

Using a single action in SpriteKit is powerful, but even more powerful are actions that you chain together. When you chain actions together, you can create a complex system of actions that you can run either as a *group* or a *sequence*. You can also set up your actions to repeat forever or for a set

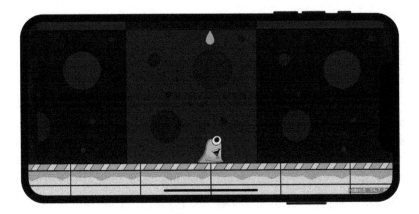

number of times, as you saw earlier in Animate the Player with Actions, on page 41.

To make the collectible drops fall from the sky, you'll use several actions chained together, creating a single sequence of actions. You'll build this sequence of actions in a new drop(dropSpeed:floorLevel) method.

Open the Collectible.swift file. Below the initialization methods, add the following code:

```swift
// MARK: - FUNCTIONS
func drop(dropSpeed: TimeInterval, floorLevel: CGFloat) {
  let pos = CGPoint(x: position.x, y: floorLevel)

  let scaleX = SKAction.scaleX(to: 1.0, duration: 1.0)
  let scaleY = SKAction.scaleY(to: 1.3, duration: 1.0)
  let scale = SKAction.group([scaleX, scaleY])

  let appear = SKAction.fadeAlpha(to: 1.0, duration: 0.25)
  let moveAction = SKAction.move(to: pos, duration: dropSpeed)
  let actionSequence = SKAction.sequence([appear, scale, moveAction])

  // Shrink first, then run fall action
  self.scale(to: CGSize(width: 0.25, height: 1.0))
  self.run(actionSequence, withKey: "drop")
}
```

Here, you're setting the end position of the drop, in other words, where you want the drop to land. You're then creating a series of actions to present that drop to the player, making it appear to fall to the floor. Here's how it works:

- First, you set the y-position using the input value stored in floorLevel.

- Then, you add two scale actions to make the drop stretch a little; this gives it a drip-like appearance.

- Next, you create actions to fade-in and move the drop down the scene.

- Finally, for some more visual appeal, you tweak the scale of the drop and then run this sequence of actions. You give it a named key so that you can access this action later using its name.

Notice that the first set of actions are grouped, meaning they run at the same time, whereas the second set of actions are individually run as part of the sequence. Also, notice how it's possible to run grouped actions within a sequence of actions. Ah, yes, the power of actions—this is where SpritKit really shines.

You're almost done: open the GameScene.swift file and at the end of the spawnGloop() method, add this line of code:

```
collectible.drop(dropSpeed: TimeInterval(1.0),
                 floorLevel: player.frame.minY)
```

With this code, the collectible node is executing the drop(dropSpeed:floorLevel) method on itself.

For clarity, the updated spawnGloop() method looks like this:

```
func spawnGloop() {
  let collectible = Collectible(collectibleType: CollectibleType.gloop)
  collectible.position = CGPoint(x: player.position.x,
                                 y: player.position.y * 2.5)
  addChild(collectible)

  collectible.drop(dropSpeed: TimeInterval(1.0),
                   floorLevel: player.frame.minY)
}
```

Build and run the project. Notice how a single drop falls straight down and then stops at the platform. As the drop is making its journey to the platform, notice how it's slightly elongated—thanks to the SKAction.scaleY(to: 1.3, duration: 1.0) action in the drop(dropSpeed:floorLevel) method as shown in the image on page 59.

At this point, your second iteration is complete: a single collectible falls from the sky and lands at the top of the platform. Your next task is to add more collectibles.

Use Actions to Run Code Blocks

The spawnGloop() method you added in the GameScene.swift file drops a single drop of gloop. Although that's a great start, what you really need now is a way to drop multiple drops at specific time intervals. For that, you'll rely on another

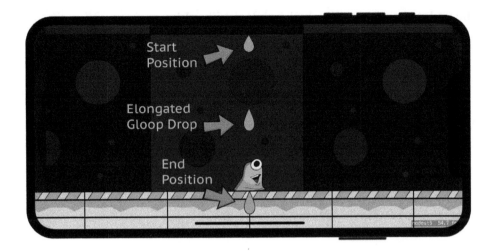

powerful feature of SpriteKit actions: running a block of code after the action completes.

Open the GameScene.swift file. Above the spawnGloop() method, add the following new method, which you'll use to spawn multiple drops:

```
func spawnMultipleGloops() {
  // Set up repeating action
  let wait = SKAction.wait(forDuration: TimeInterval(1.0))
  let spawn = SKAction.run { [unowned self] in self.spawnGloop() }
  let sequence = SKAction.sequence([wait, spawn])
  let repeatAction = SKAction.repeat(sequence, count: 10)

  // Run action
  run(repeatAction, withKey: "gloop")
}
```

This new method uses a *completion block* to call spawnGloop(). It also wraps it up in a nifty sequence of actions that are set to repeat 10 times.

Now that you have a method that repeatedly spawns collectible drops, you need to call it when the game scene launches.

In the didMove(to:) method, replace this line of code:

```
spawnGloop()
```

with this line of code:

```
spawnMultipleGloops()
```

The updated didMove(to:) method now looks like this:

```
override func didMove(to view: SKView) {
    // Set up background
    let background = SKSpriteNode(imageNamed: "background_1")
    background.anchorPoint = CGPoint(x: 0, y: 0)
    background.zPosition = Layer.background.rawValue
    background.position = CGPoint(x: 0, y: 0)
    addChild(background)

    // Set up foreground
    let foreground = SKSpriteNode(imageNamed: "foreground_1")
    foreground.anchorPoint = CGPoint(x: 0, y: 0)
    foreground.zPosition = Layer.foreground.rawValue
    foreground.position = CGPoint(x: 0, y: 0)
    addChild(foreground)

    // Set up player
    player.position = CGPoint(x: size.width/2, y: foreground.frame.maxY)
    player.setupConstraints(floor: foreground.frame.maxY)
    addChild(player)
    player.walk()

    // Set up game
    spawnMultipleGloops()
}
```

Build and run the project. Notice how all 10 drops spawn from the same location. Kind of boring, right? To fix that problem and enhance gameplay, you'll add a little randomness.

Locate the spawnGloop() method and modify it so that it matches this:

```
func spawnGloop() {
    let collectible = Collectible(collectibleType: CollectibleType.gloop)

    // set random position
    let margin = collectible.size.width * 2
    let dropRange = SKRange(lowerLimit: frame.minX + margin,
                            upperLimit: frame.maxX - margin)
    let randomX = CGFloat.random(in:
                          dropRange.lowerLimit...dropRange.upperLimit)

    collectible.position = CGPoint(x: randomX,
                                   y: player.position.y * 2.5)
    addChild(collectible)

    collectible.drop(dropSpeed: TimeInterval(1.0),
                     floorLevel: player.frame.minY)
}
```

Here, you're using the SKRange class to define the lower and upper limits for the x-position. You might remember this class from Use Constraints to Limit

Movement, on page 46. Specifically, you're using the min and max values of frame.x to keep the drops within the visible area of the view. You then use CGFloat.random to grab a random value that falls between that range.

Build and run the project, and watch in awe as 10 glorious gloop drops fall from the sky to the platform below.

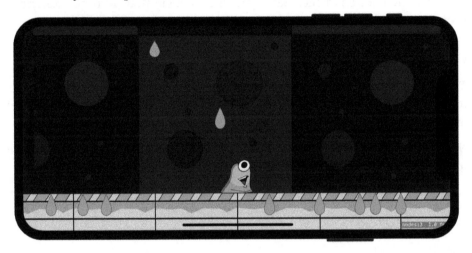

Now that you have multiple drops falling and accumulating on the platform, it's time to move on to the next iteration: using the current game level to add incremental challenge to the game.

Use Level Data to Add Challenging Gameplay

A game that doesn't challenge its players is a game that won't have many players. Likewise, a game that can't grow with its players will suffer the same fate. While those two phrases may sound zen, they're at the heart of a principle known as *dynamic difficulty adjustment (DDA)*.

With DDA, the goal is to adjust the game's difficulty over time based on the player's skill level. While you can incorporate DDA into your games in many ways, such as the rate of successful shots or how quickly a player completes a specific task, most are overkill for a game like Gloop Drop. Instead, you'll be using a more traditional approach of stepped-level progression. In other words, the difficulty of the game will increase as the player completes each level.

Your first step in getting this stepped-level progression implemented is to set up and use some level data.

Modify the Number of Collectibles Using Level Data

To increase game difficulty in Gloop Drop based on the player's current level, you'll add some properties to track both the level and the number of drops to release.

Open the GameScene.swift file. Below the line of code that adds the playerSpeed property, add the following two properties with their default values:

```
var level: Int = 1
var numberOfDrops: Int = 10
```

These two properties track the player's current level and the number of drops to release. (You'll learn how to advance levels in Advancing to the Next Level, on page 104.)

Next, locate the spawnMultipleGloops() method and add the following code at the top of the method:

```
// Set number of drops based on the level
switch level {
case 1, 2, 3, 4, 5:
  numberOfDrops = level * 10
case 6:
  numberOfDrops = 75
case 7:
  numberOfDrops = 100
case 8:
  numberOfDrops = 150
default:
  numberOfDrops = 150
}
```

(Note: You could have also used case 1...5: instead of case 1, 2, 3, 4, 5:, taking advantage of ranged operators; however, with case statements, I tend to be explicit, especially when the range is small. Either way is acceptable, so use whatever you like better.)

As the player progresses through each level, more drops will fall. The switch statement sets the numberOfDrops property based on the current value stored in level. For example, when players reach Level 6, 75 drops will fall; when they reach level 8, 150 drops will fall.

Finally, still within the spawnMultipleGloops() method, change this line of code:

```
let repeatAction = SKAction.repeat(sequence, count: 10)
```

to match this:

```
let repeatAction = SKAction.repeat(sequence, count: numberOfDrops)
```

Instead of hardcoding a number for the repeat count, you're now using a dynamically generated number based on the current level.

For reference, the updated spawnMultipleGloops() method now looks like this:

```
func spawnMultipleGloops() {
  // Set number of drops based on the level
  switch level {
  case 1, 2, 3, 4, 5:
    numberOfDrops = level * 10
  case 6:
    numberOfDrops = 75
  case 7:
    numberOfDrops = 100
  case 8:
    numberOfDrops = 150
  default:
    numberOfDrops = 150
  }

  // Set up repeating action
  let wait = SKAction.wait(forDuration: TimeInterval(1.0))
  let spawn = SKAction.run { [unowned self] in self.spawnGloop() }
  let sequence = SKAction.sequence([wait, spawn])
  let repeatAction = SKAction.repeat(sequence, count: numberOfDrops)

  // Run action
  run(repeatAction, withKey: "gloop")
}
```

It's nice that the number of drops increases as the game progresses, but if you want this game to be fun, it has to be more challenging. One way to do that is to increase the drop speed per level.

Increase Collectible Drop Speed Using Level Data

To make Gloop Drop more challenging as the game progresses, you'll increase the speed at which the drops fall to the ground. To help with this new functionality, you'll create three new properties: dropSpeed, minDropSpeed, and maxDropSpeed.

Open the GameScene.swift file and add the following three properties to the GameScene class below the existing properties:

```
var dropSpeed: CGFloat = 1.0
var minDropSpeed: CGFloat = 0.12 // (fastest drop)
var maxDropSpeed: CGFloat = 1.0 // (slowest drop)
```

You'll use the values stored in these three properties to control the wait time (in seconds) between drops. Essentially, you're controlling how fast the drops will fall to the ground, and you're capping the minimum and maximum delay between each drop for better gameplay. However, to implement this speed change, you'll need to modify the method that spawns the drops.

Inside the spawnMultipleGloops() method, below the code that sets the numberOfDrops property, add the following block of code:

```
// Set up drop speed
dropSpeed = 1 / (CGFloat(level) +
            (CGFloat(level) / CGFloat(numberOfDrops)))
if dropSpeed < minDropSpeed {
  dropSpeed = minDropSpeed
} else if dropSpeed > maxDropSpeed {
  dropSpeed = maxDropSpeed
}
```

Here, you're using some math to set the drop's traveling speed based on the current level. Essentially, this code states that the higher the level, the faster the drops will fall. You're also making sure not to drop the gloop too slowly or too quickly.

Finally, still inside the spawnMultipleGloops() method, find this line of code:

```
let wait = SKAction.wait(forDuration: TimeInterval(1.0))
```

and change it to match this:

```
let wait = SKAction.wait(forDuration: TimeInterval(dropSpeed))
```

This code adjusts the repeat method's time interval using a wait action, the value of which is based on the math you added earlier to determine the value to use for the dropSpeed property.

For reference, the updated spawnMultipleGloops() method now looks like this:

```
func spawnMultipleGloops() {
  // Set number of drops based on the level
  switch level {
  case 1, 2, 3, 4, 5:
    numberOfDrops = level * 10
  case 6:
    numberOfDrops = 75
  case 7:
    numberOfDrops = 100
  case 8:
    numberOfDrops = 150
  default:
    numberOfDrops = 150
  }
```

```
// Set up drop speed
dropSpeed = 1 / (CGFloat(level) +
            (CGFloat(level) / CGFloat(numberOfDrops)))
if dropSpeed < minDropSpeed {
  dropSpeed = minDropSpeed
} else if dropSpeed > maxDropSpeed {
  dropSpeed = maxDropSpeed
}
// Set up repeating action
let wait = SKAction.wait(forDuration: TimeInterval(dropSpeed))
let spawn = SKAction.run { [unowned self] in self.spawnGloop() }
let sequence = SKAction.sequence([wait, spawn])
let repeatAction = SKAction.repeat(sequence, count: numberOfDrops)

// Run action
run(repeatAction, withKey: "gloop")
}
```

Build and run the project. Take notice of the speed of the drops and how many are released because you're about to cheat and move up a few levels.

Scroll up to the top of the GameScene class and change the value of the level property from 1 to 8, like so:

```
var level: Int = 8
```

With this change, you set the start level to Level 8. Build and run the project again.

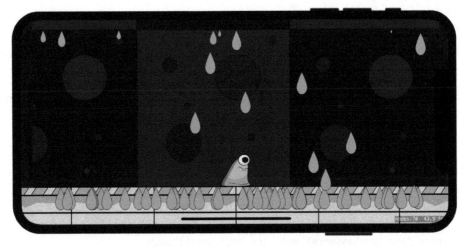

Notice that there are a lot more drops, and they're coming at a faster rate.

While you're running the game, move the player left and right by tapping on either side.

Blob is moving a little too slowly to catch these drops, don't you think? To fix this problem, you'll need to make some changes to the game's design concerning Blob's movement or players won't be able to collect the drops. This is a great time to take a little dip into the pool of iterative design.

Use Iterative Design to Adjust the Player's Movement

In Create the Collectible Class, on page 52, you were introduced to the term, iterative design. If you recall, iterative design is the process by which you prototype, test, analyze, and refine.

Currently, the player moves Blob by tapping either side of the screen. You could alter the code to move Blob faster, but that type of movement is not ideal for this type of game. Instead, you'll make it so that players can slide Blob around by moving their fingers left and right. Not only will this make for better gameplay, but also you'll get a chance to see what's involved with getting a node to follow the touch location.

First, you need two new properties to track whether or not the player is moving and the last known position of the player node. You'll name these properties movingPlayer and lastPosition, respectively.

Open the GameScene.swift file and add these new properties to the GameScene class below the playerSpeed property:

```
// Player movement
var movingPlayer = false
var lastPosition: CGPoint?
```

Using these two properties, you can now track if the player is moving and the last known position of the player node.

Next, you need to override three touch methods. Scroll down to the bottom of the GameScene class and add the following three overrides:

```
override func touchesMoved(_ touches: Set<UITouch>, with event: UIEvent?) {
  for t in touches { self.touchMoved(toPoint: t.location(in: self)) }
}

override func touchesEnded(_ touches: Set<UITouch>, with event: UIEvent?) {
  for t in touches { self.touchUp(atPoint: t.location(in: self)) }
}

override func touchesCancelled(_ touches: Set<UITouch>,
                                            with event: UIEvent?) {
  for t in touches { self.touchUp(atPoint: t.location(in: self)) }
}
```

When you create a new project, the iOS Game template creates these touch handlers. In Clean Up the Default Template, on page 8, you removed them for clarity—it's time to add them back into the code.

For now, ignore the three errors you see about the value of type GameScene not containing these members—you'll fix those in a moment—and modify the touchDown(atPoint:) method so that it matches this:

```
func touchDown(atPoint pos: CGPoint) {
  let touchedNode = atPoint(pos)
  if touchedNode.name == "player" {
    movingPlayer = true
  }
}
```

With this code, you get the touched node and check to see if its name property is equal to player. If so, you set the movingPlayer property to true.

It's time to fix those errors. Immediately below the touchDown(atPoint:) method, add the following two methods:

```
func touchMoved(toPoint pos: CGPoint) {
  if movingPlayer == true {
    // Clamp position
    let newPos = CGPoint(x: pos.x, y: player.position.y)
    player.position = newPos

    // Check last position; if empty set it
    let recordedPosition = lastPosition ?? player.position
    if recordedPosition.x > newPos.x {
      player.xScale = -abs(xScale)
    } else {
      player.xScale = abs(xScale)
    }

    // Save last known position
    lastPosition = newPos
  }
}
func touchUp(atPoint pos: CGPoint) {
  movingPlayer = false
}
```

The first method, touchMoved(pos:), verifies that the player is moving by ensuring that the movingPlayer property is true. It then clamps the player node's position along the y-axis, and using the last known touch location and the current touch location, the node's position is updated and the new location stored.

The second method, touchUp(pos:), gets called when the player stops touching the screen, which means the player is also not moving Blob anymore, so it sets movingPlayer to false.

Build and run the project. Touch Blob to get him to track with your finger, moving him as quickly or as slowly as you want.

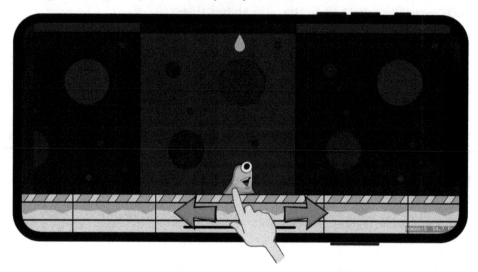

For now, leave the level property set to 8, and consider this chapter complete.

Next Steps

In this chapter, you learned how to chain actions together. You also learned how to add to your code little-by-little and tweak your design using the iterative and incremental development process. You even saw how to use level data to increase the game's difficulty as the player progresses, effectively implementing stepped-level progression.

At this point, all that's left to do for the basic gameplay mechanics is to implement a way for Blob to collect the drops of gloop.

CHAPTER 4

Working with Physics and Collision Detection

In the previous chapter, you added the drop collectible items and learned how to chain actions together so that the gloop drops appear to be dripping from the top of the scene. You also got your feet wet with the iterative and incremental development process by adding your code in smaller chunks and modifying the way the player moves.

In this chapter, you'll get your first look at using the SpriteKit *physics engine*. The SpriteKit physics engine makes it possible for your SpriteKit games to simulate physics and detect collisions.

When you attach physical properties to your game objects, they can interact with each other in the game world as they would outside of it. But don't worry; you won't need to be a rocket scientist or astrophysicist to play with the SpriteKit physics engine.

Run a Playground Physics Simulation

Before jumping back into the Gloop Drop game project, open the PhysicsSimulation.playground file in the projects/playgrounds folder. Playgrounds offer an interactive development environment where you can prototype and test your code in real time. The PhysicsSimulation playground is a small, custom playground that you can use to play around with the SpriteKit physics engine.

The image on page 70 shows the PhysicsSimulation playground in its running state.

To run the playground, click the Execute button in the bottom-left corner. This action runs the code and loads the SpriteKit scene in the Live View. You may

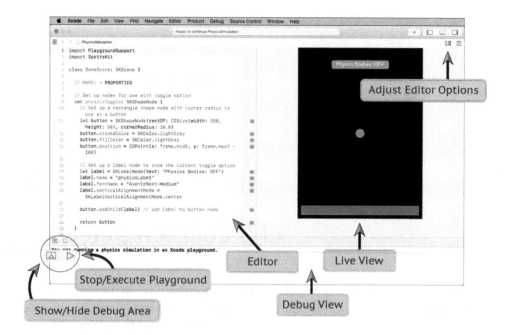

need to start and stop the playground more than once to get it to respond to clicks.

If you don't see the Live View, click the Adjust Editor Options button in the top-right corner and turn on the Live View option. The menu looks like this:

You won't need to write any code in this section, except for a handful of lines. Instead, you'll use the existing code in the PhysicsSimulation playground to learn more about the SpriteKit physics engine. Later in this chapter, you'll apply what you've learned to the gloopdrop project.

With the PhysicsSimulation playground running, click a few random places on the Live View scene, and you'll see something similar to the image on page 71.

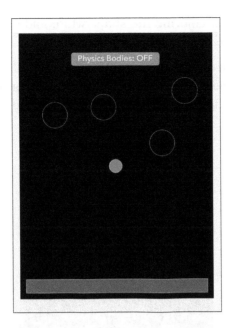

To understand what's happening, look through the code in the playground. You'll find that the touchDown(atPoint:) method contains the following code:

```
// Check if toggle button was clicked
if physicsToggle.contains(pos) {
  withBody.toggle()
  return
}
// Set up a circle shape node to use for the ball
let ball = SKShapeNode(circleOfRadius: 50)
ball.name = "ball"
ball.position = pos

// Check value of `withBody` to determine if physics is enabled
if withBody == true {
  ball.fillColor = SKColor.white
  ball.physicsBody = SKPhysicsBody(circleOfRadius: ball.frame.width/2)

  // Set up physics properties
  ball.physicsBody?.restitution = 0.2 // Bounce: 0.0-1.0 (default: 0.2)
}
// Add the ball node to the scene
addChild(ball)
```

This code, among other things, places a shape node named ball at each touch location (pos). The withBody property is currently set to its default value of false, so the code skips over coloring the shape white and adding a *physics body* to the node—more on physics bodies in a moment.

Click the "Physics Bodies: OFF" button at the top of the scene to toggle the withBody property to true. Once again, click anywhere on the Live View scene and notice that this time, the balls react to gravity and to each other.

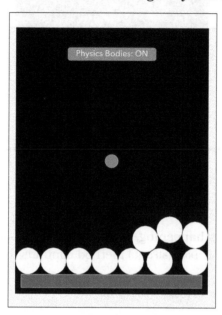

In this second example, where withBody = true, the three lines that were skipped earlier now run:

```
ball.fillColor = SKColor.white
ball.physicsBody = SKPhysicsBody(circleOfRadius: ball.frame.width/2)

// Set up physics properties
ball.physicsBody?.restitution = 0.2 // Bounce: 0.0-1.0 (default: 0.2)
```

The fillColor property—which is not part of the physics engine and is only being used as a visual cue for this example—sets the shape node's color to white. After that, the physicsBody property of that same node gets set using one of the SKPhysicsBody class initializers. The type of initializer you use depends largely on the shape of the physics body you need. In this case, your node is shaped like a circle, so it makes sense to use init(circleOfRadius:).

Finally, the restitution property of the physics body attached to the ball node is set to 0.2. (The restitution property determines the node's bounciness, in other words, how much kinetic energy the body loses or gains from collisions.) It's this physics body that makes everything come alive in the SpriteKit physics engine. In fact, change the restitution to 1.0, restart the playground, and you'll see a big difference in how the balls react when hitting the floor—the higher the number, the more bouncy things get. The restitution property is but one of many properties available for physics bodies.

To better understand the SKPhysicsBody class and how physics bodies work, you'll continue to use the PhysicsSimulation playground in the next section before returning to the gloopdrop project.

A Closer Look at Physics Bodies

There are two types of physics bodies: *volume-based* bodies and *edge-based* bodies, which are illustrated in the images that follow.

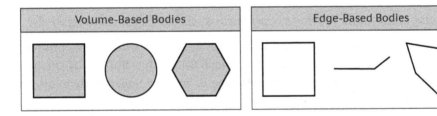

To create these physics bodies, you use the SKPhysicsBody class and one of its initializers. Typically, you'll use an initializer that matches your sprite node's shape, such as a rectangle, circle, polygon, or custom path. You then assign this physics body to the node's physicsBody property, like so:

```
ball.physicsBody = SKPhysicsBody(circleOfRadius: ball.frame.width/2)
```

When defining shapes, always consider performance. A circle is the most efficient shape, whereas a path-based polygon is the least efficient shape. As you add complexity to these custom shapes, the overall performance of your scene decreases. Also, consider that not every object (node) within a scene needs a physics body; you only need to add a physics body if you intend to apply physics to the node or track it for collision detection.

A volume-based body, such as the ball in the previous example, reacts according to its mass, density, and other properties. For example, in the touchDown(atPoint:) method after setting the restitution property, add the following line:

```
ball.physicsBody?.mass = 5.0 // in kilograms
```

This code sets the mass of the ball to 5 kilograms. The default value is based on the size of the physics body and the body's default density, which is 1.0. Because these two values are related, changing one automatically changes the other to be consistent. This number is arbitrary, so as long as you keep things consistent in your physics world, you won't have a problem. In other words, don't set one body's mass to 5 kilograms and another to 500 kilograms if they're supposed to represent a similarly sized object.

Now, look at the didMove(to:) method. There, you'll see the following three lines that set up the floor node's physics body:

```
// Set up its physics body using a rectangle
floor.physicsBody = SKPhysicsBody(rectangleOf: floor.frame.size)
floor.physicsBody?.isDynamic = false // static, not moved by physics engine
floor.physicsBody?.affectedByGravity = false // ignores world gravity
```

Like the ball node's physics body, this type of physics body is also a volume-based body. However, unlike the ball node, which uses a circle shape, the floor node's initializer uses a rectangle.

Something else to note is two new properties: isDynamic and affectedByGravity.

The isDynamic property for the floor node is set to false. By setting this property to false, you tell the physics engine not to move this body—that's why the floor doesn't move when the balls hit it. This type of volume-based body is known as a *static volume* body because it never moves.

It's time for a little science experiment. Set the isDynamic property of the floor node to true, which is the default value, and run the playground again. Notice that this time the floor falls to the edge of the scene after the first ball hits it. The floor node moves because it's now using a *dynamic volume* body like the balls, so the physics simulation can move it.

Go back to the touchDown(atPoint:) method and change the mass of the ball node from 5 to 50, like so:

```
ball.physicsBody?.mass = 50
```

Restart the playground and notice how much heavier the balls are this time around—so much so that they make the floor bounce when they hit it.

One more experiment. Currently, the floor node's affectedByGravity property is set to false, which means this physics body ignores gravity. Set this value to true, and restart the playground. Notice this time, as soon as you start the playground, the floor falls to the bottom of the scene, but it doesn't fall out of the scene. Instead, it stops precisely at the bottom or edge of the scene.

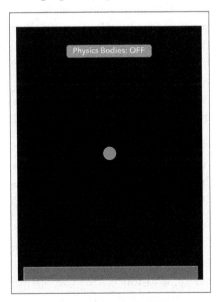

The floor node doesn't fall past the scene's edge into nothingness because the scene also has a physics body attached to it. At the end of the didMove(to:) method, notice the following code:

```
// Set up a physics body around the frame using an edge loop
physicsBody = SKPhysicsBody(edgeLoopFrom: frame)
```

This code sets the scene's physicsBody property using what's known as an *edge-based* body. Unlike volume-based bodies, edge-based bodies do not have mass and are never moved by the physics simulation, which makes them a great choice for providing invisible boundaries like a scene's edge. If you were to comment out that line and restart the playground, the floor would fall into nothingness. In fact, it would happen so fast that it's unlikely you'd even see it fall.

To finish out this final experiment, you'll adjust the gravity of the simulated physics world. At the top of the didMove(to:) method, add the following code:

```
// Adjust the physics world gravity
physicsWorld.gravity = CGVector(dx: 0, dy: -1.62)

// Earth's gravity: -9.8 meters per second
// Moon's gravity: -1.62 meters per second
```

This code changes the physicsWorld.gravity from its default of -9.8, which simulates Earth's gravity, to -1.62, which simulates the gravity on the Moon. Build and run the project, start dropping balls with physics bodies attached, and you'll notice a significant difference in how the balls react to gravity.

The Gravity of the Situation

 Gravity is measured by how fast an object falls to the ground. On planet Earth, the acceleration at which an object falls is about 9.8 meters (32 feet) per second. In SpriteKit, you can simulate Earth's gravity by setting the physicsWorld.gravity to (dx: 0, dy: -9.8). Likewise, to simulate the Moon's gravity, you can use (dx: 0, dy: -1.62). The negative numbers in both cases indicate a downward pull, like gravity.

You may have noticed that the gravity property includes both a dx and dy value. Not only can you set the world's vertical gravity (y-axis) by setting a value for dy, but you can also set the horizontal gravity (x-axis) by providing a value for dx, too.

There's no doubt that the SpriteKit physics engine is powerful; with just a few lines of code, you can implement a sophisticated physics world, complete with mass, density, gravity, and more. But the SpriteKit physics engine and physics bodies do more than simulate physics.

In the next section, you'll return to the gloopdrop project and discover how you can use physics bodies for more than simulated physics.

Use Physics Bodies for Collision Detection

Another powerful feature of the SpriteKit physics engine is its ability to handle *collision detection*. With collision detection, you're able to tell when two physics bodies come into contact with one another, and you can use that to drive some of your game logic.

For Gloop Drop, you'll implement collision detection to track when the player catches the gloop drops. To get started, open the gloopdrop project in Xcode.

Using the Starter Project

You may continue using your project from the previous chapter, or you can use the starter project located in the projects/begin folder included with the code resources for this chapter. Either option is fine; the only benefit to using the starter project is that you won't get stuck going forward if you missed an earlier step.

There's also an ending project for this chapter that includes all of the code and resources you'll be adding here. The end project is located in the projects/end folder included with the code resources for this chapter.

Your first step is to set up the physics bodies for the player, collectible, and foreground nodes. From the Project Navigator, select the Player.swift file to open it in the Source Editor. At the end of the init() method, add the following block of code:

```
// Add physics body
self.physicsBody = SKPhysicsBody(rectangleOf: self.size,
    center: CGPoint(x: 0.0, y: self.size.height/2))
self.physicsBody?.affectedByGravity = false
```

This code creates a physics body for the player node using one of the SKPhysicsBody class initializers. In this case, it's creating a body in the shape of a rectangle with the same size as the player node. It also manually sets the center point using a point within the node's coordinate space. This is necessary because the node's anchorPoint property is set to CGPoint(x: 0.5, y: 0.0), and the center point for the physics body is (0.5,0.5), so you need an offset. In other words, if you don't adjust this center point, your physics body won't align with your sprite node.

Also, because the player node should not be affected by gravity, you set its affectedByGravity property to false.

With the player node's physics body added, you're ready to add the physics bodies to the collectible items. Open the Collectible.swift file, and at the end of the init() method, add the following code:

```
// Add physics body
self.physicsBody = SKPhysicsBody(rectangleOf: self.size,
    center: CGPoint(x: 0.0, y: -self.size.height/2))
self.physicsBody?.affectedByGravity = false
```

Similar to the code in Player.swift, this code sets the collectible's physics bodies; however, in this case, rather than set the center of the physics body near the top of the node, this code sets it near the bottom of the node and does so by using a negative value. The reason for this is because the anchorPoint property of the collectible node is set to CGPoint(x: 0.5, y: 1.0), so you need the offset in the other direction.

You also set the collectible node's affectedByGravity property to false so that the node isn't affected by gravity. Remember, you're moving these drops using actions, so there's no need to add gravity.

Move Nodes with Actions or Use the Physics Engine

You might be wondering why Gloop Drop doesn't use gravity to drop the drops. While it's entirely possible to do so, you need to consider your gameplay mechanics. With Gloop Drop, the drops must fall at a consistent rate of speed and with a deliberate pattern in mind.

Furthermore, because the speed increases with every new level, you'd have to muck around with additional physics settings to achieve the desired results—and because you generally don't want to mix moving nodes manually with actions and moving those same nodes using the physics engine, it's best to pick the method that makes the most sense for your game.

The last physics body you need to add is on the foreground node. Open the GameScene.swift file, and in the didMove(to:) method, add the following code above the code that adds the foreground node to the scene—for reference, that line of code is included in the code listing:

```
// Add physics body
foreground.physicsBody = SKPhysicsBody(edgeLoopFrom: foreground.frame)
foreground.physicsBody?.affectedByGravity = false

addChild(foreground) // do not add this line again; it already exists.
```

This code sets up a physics body on the foreground node; however, instead of using a rectangle shape for the physics body, it uses an SKPhysicsBody class initializer that creates an edge-based physics body. Remember, edge-based bodies are the most appropriate choice for nodes that act as boundaries. It also sets the affectedByGravity property to false.

While you're in the GameScene.swift file, switch the level property's default value back to 1:

```
var level: Int = 1
```

Before you build and run the project, there's one more change you need to make. Open the GameViewController.swift file and locate this line of code:

```
view.showsPhysics = false
```

Once you find it, replace it with this:

```
view.showsPhysics = true
```

With the showsPhysics property set to true, you're able to see the physics bodies around each node. While testing, set this option to true so that you can see exactly where the physics body exists in relation to its node. In the following image taken from the PhysicsSimulation playground, you can see an example of this relationship.

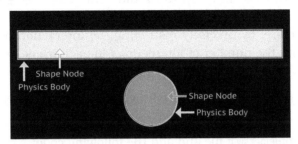

Now, build and run the project.

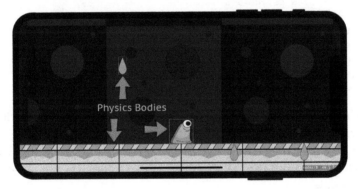

Notice the light blue lines around the nodes? These are the physics bodies—one for the player, one for the foreground, and one for each of the collectible items.

With the physics bodies set up, you're ready to move on to the next step: configuring *physics categories*.

Configure Physics Categories

Before you can set up physics categories, you first need to understand what SpriteKit does when two physics bodies attempt to occupy the same space, and what types of interactions are possible. With SpriteKit, there are two types of interactions: a *contact* and a *collision*. A contact occurs the moment body A touches body B. A collision occurs when two bodies collide. The difference between these two interactions is subtle but important. The first type of interaction is generally used to handle some type of game logic. For example, knowing when the player collects an item. The second type of interaction is used more for simulating real-world physics—for example, a ball bouncing off the side of a wall.

SpriteKit determines how to handle contacts and collisions between bodies through the use of physics categories. Physics categories are set up by you, the developer; you can have up to 32 different categories per scene. With physics categories, you're able to set up game logic based on these interactions. Furthermore, by precisely restricting the interaction between certain bodies, you limit the number of interactions in each frame, which increases your game's overall performance.

For Gloop Drop, you'll use four physics categories: none, player, collectible, and foreground.

Open the SpriteKitHelper.swift file and add the following code:

```
// SpriteKit Physics Categories
enum PhysicsCategory {
    static let none:        UInt32 = 0
    static let player:      UInt32 = 0b1    // 1
    static let collectible: UInt32 = 0b10   // 2
    static let foreground:  UInt32 = 0b100  // 4
}
```

Here, you're using an enum to set up the different physics categories to keep track of what nodes belong to what category. You could also use a struct if you prefer, but it's unnecessary because you're not going to add any members or methods. Also, note that the names you use here do not need to match the node names.

Numbers and Physics Categories

By default, integer literals are expressed in decimals using the numbers 0 through 9. However, you can modify this default behavior and use binary literals instead, which might make it easier. With binary literals, you use the prefix 0b. Unlike integer literals, binary literals use only 0 and 1. So, in this example, 0b100 equals the number 4. Essentially, this is shorthand for 000000100. When setting your categories, it's best to do so using powers of two: 1, 2, 4, 8, 16, and so on.

You can also use the OptionSet protocol[1] inside a custom struct to represent the different categories. Sometimes, it's just a matter of preference.

---

1. https://developer.apple.com/documentation/swift/optionset

Your next step is to apply these categories to the different physics bodies. Open the GameScene.swift file, and in the didMove(to:) method, after the code that sets up the foreground.physicsBody, add this block of code:

```
// Set up physics categories for contacts
foreground.physicsBody?.categoryBitMask = PhysicsCategory.foreground
foreground.physicsBody?.contactTestBitMask = PhysicsCategory.collectible
foreground.physicsBody?.collisionBitMask = PhysicsCategory.none
```

This code sets the category, contact, and collision bit masks for the foreground node's physics body. Effectively, this code tells SpriteKit that the foreground node's physics body belongs to the PhysicsCategory.foreground. It also tells SpriteKit that it should be concerned only about contacts from the PhysicsCategory.collectible category and to ignore collisions altogether. For an in-depth look at bit masks and bitwise operators, read the Advanced Operators section in *The Swift Programming Language* guide.[2]

Now it's time to set up the player node. Open the Player.swift file, and at the end of the init() method, add this code:

```
// Set up physics categories for contacts
self.physicsBody?.categoryBitMask = PhysicsCategory.player
self.physicsBody?.contactTestBitMask = PhysicsCategory.collectible
self.physicsBody?.collisionBitMask = PhysicsCategory.none
```

Like the foreground node, you're setting up the player node's physics body category and its contact and collision bit masks. In this case, SpriteKit will react only to a player/collectible contact event.

Finally, open the Collectible.swift file, and at the end of the init() method, add this code:

```
// Set up physics categories for contacts
self.physicsBody?.categoryBitMask = PhysicsCategory.collectible
self.physicsBody?.contactTestBitMask = PhysicsCategory.player
                                     | PhysicsCategory.foreground
self.physicsBody?.collisionBitMask = PhysicsCategory.none
```

Notice here that the contactTestBitMask is set to both the PhysicsCategory.player | PhysicsCategory.foreground categories, which means SpriteKit will keep tabs when a collectible makes contact with either the player or the foreground.

Now that your categories and physics bodies are set up, you're ready to handle the interactions.

---

2. https://docs.swift.org/swift-book/LanguageGuide/AdvancedOperators.html

Configure the Physics Contact Delegate

Before you can take action on these physics body interactions, the GameScene class needs to declare its intention to implement the SKPhysicsContactDelegate protocols—in other words, it needs to conform to that protocol.[3] Like other protocols in Swift, your class, structure, or enumeration needs to implement the protocol's requirements. In this case, the SKPhysicsContactDelegate protocols, didBegin(_:) and didEnd(_:), are what makes it possible for your scenes to respond to contact events.

While you could update the GameScene class definition to implement the SKPhysicsContactDelegate directly, it's better to use an extension to keep your code better organized. Open the GameScene.swift, and at the bottom of the file, add a new extension to handle the collision detection:

```
// MARK: - COLLISION DETECTION

/* ##################################################################### */
/*                 COLLISION DETECTION METHODS START HERE                */
/* ##################################################################### */

extension GameScene: SKPhysicsContactDelegate {

}
```

This extension declares that the GameScene class can act as a delegate for SKPhysicsContactDelegate. Your next step is to make it official by setting the delegate in the game scene. In the didMove(to:) method, add the following code at the top:

```
// Set up the physics world contact delegate
physicsWorld.contactDelegate = self
```

This code sets the physicsWorld.contactDelegate property to self, making the scene the contact delegate. The next step is to implement the protocol responsible for handling contacts.

Detect Contact Between Physics Bodies

Inside the SKPhysicsContactDelegate extension, add the following method:

```
func didBegin(_ contact: SKPhysicsContact) {
  // Check collision bodies
  let collision = contact.bodyA.categoryBitMask |
                  contact.bodyB.categoryBitMask
```

```
// Did the [PLAYER] collide with the [COLLECTIBLE]?
if collision == PhysicsCategory.player | PhysicsCategory.collectible {
  print("player hit collectible")
}

// Or did the [COLLECTIBLE] collide with the [FOREGROUND]?
if collision == PhysicsCategory.foreground | PhysicsCategory.collectible {
  print("collectible hit foreground")
}
}
```

With this protocol method, you are grabbing the value stored in the categoryBit-Mask of each body involved, and you are printing a statement to the console depending on those results.

Build and run the project to see the collision detection in action.

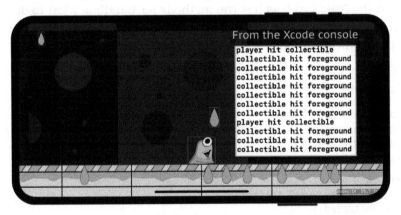

Each time the player hits a collectible or a collectible hits the foreground, you'll see the corresponding statement print to the console. This is the beginning of adding your game logic based on those contacts.

Now that you know when and what type of contact was made between physics bodies, you're ready to handle those interactions.

Handle Contact Between Physics Bodies

Your next step is to write the methods that handle what happens when the player misses and catches a drop. Rather than stuff these actions inside the didBegin(_:) method of the SKPhysicsContactDelegate extension, you'll place them inside the Collectible class.

Open the Collectible.swift file, and at the end of the class, add two functions—one to handle the collected event and one to handle the missed event:

```
// Handle Contacts
func collected() {
  let removeFromParent = SKAction.removeFromParent()
  self.run(removeFromParent)
}

func missed() {
  let removeFromParent = SKAction.removeFromParent()
  self.run(removeFromParent)
}
```

These two methods handle removing the nodes from the scene. Although you could have combined them into a single method and processed the outcome using an if statement and a parameter, it's best to keep these events separate for clarity, making it easier to modify them later.

Now that the Collectible class has the methods for handling what to do when a collectible item hits either the player (collected) or the foreground (missed), you can call these methods when contact occurs.

Open the GameScene.swift file, and inside the didBegin(_:) method, add the following code inside the first if block:

```
// Find out which body is attached to the collectible node
let body = contact.bodyA.categoryBitMask == PhysicsCategory.collectible ?
  contact.bodyA.node :
  contact.bodyB.node

// Verify the object is a collectible
if let sprite = body as? Collectible {
  sprite.collected()
}
```

With this code, when contact occurs between the player and a collectible, it will verify that the sprite object is a Collectible object and run its collected() method.

Next up: handling the missed event. Scroll down to the second if statement and add this block of code:

```
// Find out which body is attached to the collectible node
let body = contact.bodyA.categoryBitMask == PhysicsCategory.collectible ?
  contact.bodyA.node :
  contact.bodyB.node

// Verify the object is a collectible
if let sprite = body as? Collectible {
  sprite.missed()
}
```

Like the code in the first if statement, this code calls the missed() method on either bodyA or bodyB depending on which node is the collectible node.

For reference, the complete function looks like this:

```
func didBegin(_ contact: SKPhysicsContact) {
  // Check collision bodies
  let collision = contact.bodyA.categoryBitMask |
                  contact.bodyB.categoryBitMask

  // Did the [PLAYER] collide with the [COLLECTIBLE]?
  if collision == PhysicsCategory.player | PhysicsCategory.collectible {
    print("player hit collectible")

    // Find out which body is attached to the collectible node
    let body = contact.bodyA.categoryBitMask == PhysicsCategory.collectible ?
      contact.bodyA.node :
      contact.bodyB.node

    // Verify the object is a collectible
    if let sprite = body as? Collectible {
      sprite.collected()
    }
  }
  // Or did the [COLLECTIBLE] collide with the [FLOOR]?
  if collision == PhysicsCategory.floor | PhysicsCategory.collectible {
    print("collectible hit foreground")

    // Find out which body is attached to the collectible node
    let body = contact.bodyA.categoryBitMask == PhysicsCategory.collectible ?
      contact.bodyA.node :
      contact.bodyB.node

    // Verify the object is a collectible
    if let sprite = body as? Collectible {
      sprite.missed()
    }
  }
}
```

Build and run the project. This time, notice that when the collectible hits the player or the foreground, the node is removed from the scene. Not only does this action show the player that something's happened, but it always frees up your scene's resources by removing unnecessary nodes from the node tree.

Next Steps

In this chapter, you learned a lot about the SpriteKit physics engine and physics bodies. You played inside a custom playground where you got to muck around with the physics world, and you added everything you need to handle collision detection in Gloop Drop. You also discovered the difference between moving nodes with actions versus using the built-in physics engine.

In the next chapter, you'll add the ability to track the player's score and show important messages to the player using labels. You'll also add a way to start and end the game.

More on SpriteKit Physics

The SpriteKit physics engine is very powerful, and there is a lot more to it than what you learned in this chapter. If you're interested in playing with some of the more advanced features of the SpriteKit physics engine, review the AdvancedPhysicsSimulation.playground file in the projects/playgrounds folder. The code in that file is documented to help you follow along.

CHAPTER 5

Adding Labels and Working with the Game Loop

In the previous chapter, you had an opportunity to play around with the SpriteKit physics engine—not only in the gloopdrop project, but also in an interactive Xcode playground. As you make your way through these chapters, you're strengthening your SpriteKit skills and preparing yourself for the challenge of making your own games.

Some skills that you haven't yet learned in this book include how to work with the game loop, how to manage game levels, and how to add labels to your scene—all of which are important to how the game operates and what the player needs to know.

Labels provide an excellent visual cue for the player to receive important messages. For example, in Gloop Drop, players need to know what level they're on and how many points they have. They also need to know when the game is over and when a new level is about to begin. In this chapter, you'll implement all of these labels. You'll also have an opportunity to learn about and play with the game loop and how to manage level data.

Add Labels to Show Current Level and Score

If you're familiar with UIKit, you know that you can add labels to your views using the UILabel class. In SpriteKit, however, rather than using the UILabel class, you use the SKLabelNode class.

Like other nodes in SpriteKit, the SKLabelNode class is a subclass of SKNode. That means all of the properties and functionality of the SKNode class—like position, scale, and rotation—are also available within the SKLabelNode class. However, label nodes in SpriteKit are not as intuitive as some other nodes, like sprite nodes, for example. But don't worry, this chapter will help to unravel the mystery.

Your first stop in learning about labels in SpriteKit is how to add custom fonts to your project.

Adding Custom Fonts

While using custom fonts isn't always necessary, the Gloop Drop game design document specifies the Nosifer font as its primary font. You can download this free font[1] from the Google Fonts repository. Alternatively, you can use the Nosifer-Regular.ttf font file in the Fonts folder included with the code resources for this chapter.

With the Nosifer-Regular.ttf font file in hand (so to speak), open the gloopdrop project in Xcode.

Using the Starter Project

You may continue using your project from the previous chapter, or you can use the starter project located in the projects/begin folder included with the code resources for this chapter. Either option is fine; the only benefit to using the starter project is that you won't get stuck going forward if you missed an earlier step.

There's also an ending project for this chapter that includes all of the code and resources you'll be adding here. The end project is located in the projects/end folder included with the code resources for this chapter.

To use custom fonts in your game, you need to add them to your project. As you begin to add more resources to your projects, you need to consider how to organize them. In this case, you'll create a new folder in your project to hold your custom font.

From Xcode's App menu, select File ▶ New ▶ Group or press ⌥⌘N on your keyboard to create a new group within your Xcode project as shown in the first image on page 89.

Rename the group Fonts, and drag the Nosifer-Regular.ttf font file into the group, as shown in the second image on page 89.

When prompted, ensure the Copy items if needed and Add to targets options are both checked. Also, verify that the option to Create groups is selected. Once these options are set and everything matches the first image on page 90, click Finish.

---

1. https://fonts.google.com/specimen/Nosifer

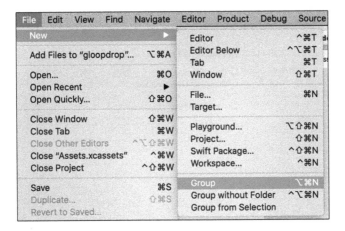

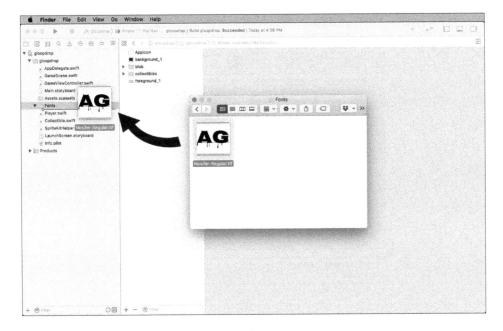

The font file now exists within the project; however, the project doesn't know about it. For the project to recognize a custom font, you need to update the Info.plist file.

In the Project Navigator, select the Info.plist file. Highlight the last item in the list and click the + button to the right of the Key's label. When the Key drop-down list appears, select Fonts provided by application. Now, click the disclosure icon to the left of the key's label to expand the list and display Item 0. For the Item 0 Value, enter Nosifer-Regular.ttf, as shown in the second image on page 90.

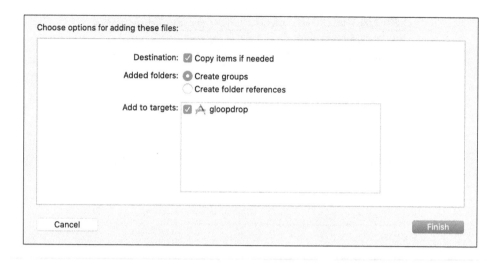

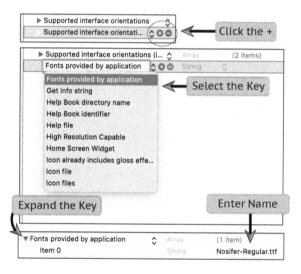

When you add the Fonts provided by application Key/Value pair to the Info.plist file, you *register the font*, which makes it available for use in your game.

Now that your custom font is registered and ready to use, you can add the score and level labels to the scene to provide players with key information.

Creating Labels in SpriteKit

Open the GameScene.swift file and add the following two properties to hold the score and level label objects:

```
// Labels
var scoreLabel: SKLabelNode = SKLabelNode()
var levelLabel: SKLabelNode = SKLabelNode()
```

This code creates the label objects using the SKLabelNode class—one for the score and one for the level.

Before you write the code to add these two labels to the scene, you need to do a few things first, staring with adding a new Layer enum to help set the z-position of the User Interface (UI) objects.

Setting Label Positions

Open the SpriteKitHelper.swift file and update the Layer enum by adding a new case:

```
enum Layer: CGFloat {
  case background
  case foreground
  case player
  case collectible
  case ui
}
```

You'll use the new ui case for the UI elements, such as the labels. If you remember from Control Render Order with Z-Position, on page 37, because ui is at the end of this list, any node that has its zPosition property set to Layer.ui will position itself at the front of the node tree—in other words, on top of the other nodes. But the z-position isn't the only position you need to consider when placing labels, especially when your game supports different screen sizes.

Working with Different Screen Sizes

Gloop Drop was designed to support multiple screen sizes, so you need to consider where your labels will appear depending on which device the player is using. Because the view size is different than the scene size and depends largely on the device in use, some clipping can occur. This happens because of the scaleMode setting.

Four modes are available: fill, aspectFit, resizeFill, and aspectFill. The default value is fill; however, when you create a new SpriteKit project using the iOS Game template, it gets set to aspectFill. That's okay, though, because Gloop Drop uses aspectFill. You can see this in the GameViewController.swift file where you set up the scene:

```
// Create the scene
// let scene = GameScene(size: view.bounds.size)
let scene = GameScene(size:CGSize(width: 1336, height: 1024))

// Set the scale mode to scale to fill the view window
scene.scaleMode = .aspectFill
```

Deciding which scale mode to use depends on the design of your game. From the Apple documentation:

- fill: Each axis of the scene is scaled independently so that each axis in the scene exactly maps to the length of that axis in the view.

- aspectFit: The scaling factor of each dimension is calculated and the smaller of the two is chosen. Each axis of the scene is scaled by the same scaling factor. This guarantees that the entire scene is visible but may require letterboxing in the view.

- resizeFill: The scene is not scaled to match the view. Instead, the scene is automatically resized so its dimensions always match those of the view.

- aspectFill: The scaling factor of each dimension is calculated and the larger of the two is chosen. Each axis of the scene is scaled by the same scaling factor. This guarantees that the entire area of the view is filled but may cause parts of the scene to be cropped.

Selecting the best scale mode—then deciding how to appropriately handle the art assets and gameplay logic based on that decision—isn't always easy as it depends largely on your game's design and the devices you intend to support.

Look at following image:

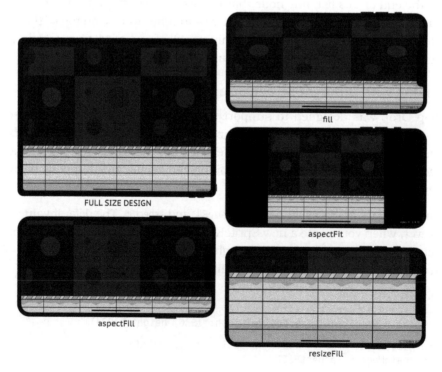

This image shows how Gloop Drop looks with each scaleMode option.

With Gloop Drop, the game design called for support on both the iPad and the iPhone. With the radically different screen sizes, and the desire to keep the art simple by only having one size in @1x, @2x, and @3x resolutions, it made sense to design the game with the iPad size in mind. With that being the case, the next decision was how to handle the size and position of sprites.

For most games, it makes sense to use aspectFill simply because it offers you a way to design with a constant-sized scene, which provides a predictable coordinate system and frame; however, if doing so, you as the designer/developer need to ensure that your gameplay logic stays visible regardless of the viewable area.

To position the level and score labels at the top right and left of the scene, and to keep them within the boundaries of the viewable area on all devices, you'll use a custom SKScene extension.

Scroll to the bottom of the SpriteKitHelper.swift file and add the following extension and two extension methods:

```swift
extension SKScene {

  // Top of view
  func viewTop() -> CGFloat {
    return convertPoint(fromView: CGPoint(x: 0.0, y: 0)).y
  }

  // Bottom of view
  func viewBottom() -> CGFloat {
    guard let view = view else { return 0.0 }
    return convertPoint(fromView: CGPoint(x: 0.0,
                                          y: view.bounds.size.height)).y

  }
}
```

This extension and its two methods convert the view's coordinates to scene coordinates. By converting the view's coordinates to scene coordinates, you're able to position the label nodes—or any node for that matter—at the top and bottom of the viewable screen.

Your next step is to add the labels to the scene.

Adding Labels to the Scene

Open the GameScene.swift file, and below the didMove(to:) method, add the following method to set up the labels:

```
func setupLabels() {
  /* SCORE LABEL */
  scoreLabel.name = "score"
  scoreLabel.fontName = "Nosifer"
  scoreLabel.fontColor = .yellow
  scoreLabel.fontSize = 35.0
  scoreLabel.horizontalAlignmentMode = .right
  scoreLabel.verticalAlignmentMode = .center
  scoreLabel.zPosition = Layer.ui.rawValue
  scoreLabel.position = CGPoint(x: frame.maxX - 50, y: viewTop() - 100)

  // Set the text and add the label node to scene
  scoreLabel.text = "Score: 0"
  addChild(scoreLabel)

  /* LEVEL LABEL */
  levelLabel.name = "level"
  levelLabel.fontName = "Nosifer"
  levelLabel.fontColor = .yellow
  levelLabel.fontSize = 35.0
  levelLabel.horizontalAlignmentMode = .left
  levelLabel.verticalAlignmentMode = .center
  levelLabel.zPosition = Layer.ui.rawValue
  levelLabel.position = CGPoint(x: frame.minX + 50, y: viewTop() - 100)

  // Set the text and add the label node to scene
  levelLabel.text = "Level: \(level)"
  addChild(levelLabel)
}
```

This code sets up the score and level labels using the available SKLabelNode properties. Here, you can see properties like fontName, fontColor, and fontSize, which set the properties for the font the label will use. Notice the fontName is the name of your custom font: Nosifer. Also, notice the two alignment-related properties: horizontalAlignmentMode and verticalAlignmentMode. These two properties control how the text is aligned within the node. In this case, the score label is right-aligned horizontally, and the level label is left-aligned horizontally; both are vertically centered. Additionally, you're setting the zPosition property to use Layer.ui.rawValue and the position property to use the extensions you created earlier, which tucks the labels into the top right and left corners of the viewable scene.

Before you build and run the project, you need to call the newly-created setupLabels() method. In the didMove(to:) method, immediately above the code that sets up the player node, add the following code that calls the new setupLabels() method:

```
// Set up User Interface
setupLabels()
```

With the call to setupLabels() added, build and run the project. If everything went according to plan, you'll see the level and score labels in place.

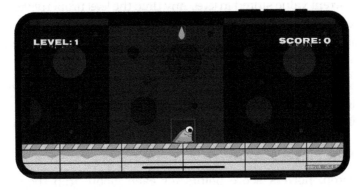

While this is a good start, the text for each label is static. In other words, when the player scores points and advances to the next level, these labels will not update. Your next step is to fix that problem.

Use Variables to Monitor Game States

In a game like Gloop Drop, you need to monitor a few values and game stats, for example, the current score and level. The GameScene class has a level property that holds the value of the current level, but it doesn't have a score property to hold the current score—at least not yet. Furthermore, you have labels in the scene that need to get updated when the level and score values change. While you could write a method to update the labels' text as the player's score and level change, a better way to keep things in sync is to use a *property observer*[2] for each property. With a property observer, you can monitor the changes in a property's value. For Gloop Drop, you'll monitor the changes for both the level and score properties.

In the GameScene.swift file, locate the line that reads var level: Int = 1, and replace it with the following code:

```
var level: Int = 1 {
  didSet {
    levelLabel.text = "Level: \(level)"
  }
}
var score: Int = 0 {
  didSet {
    scoreLabel.text = "Score: \(score)"
  }
}
```

---

2. https://docs.swift.org/swift-book/LanguageGuide/Properties.html

This code updates the level property by adding a didSet property observer. Within that property observer, the code updates the text of the levelLabel node using the current value stored in level. Any time the level property value changes or gets set, the level label text updates. This code also adds a new property named score with its own property observer—one that updates the text of the scoreLabel node when the score property value changes.

Property observers are a great way to keep your labels up to date or run a specific piece of code when a value changes. Of course, to get the most out of a property observer, you need to use it, which is what you'll do next.

Updating the Player's Score

In Gloop Drop, players score points for each gloop drop they catch. The number of points they get is based on the current level. So, for example, when players are on Level 1, they score one point for each drop they catch; when they're on Level 2, they score two points for each drop they catch, and so on.

In the GameScene.swift file, locate the didBegin(_:) method, and below the sprite.collected() line, add the following code:

```
score += level
```

This code updates the value of the score property by adding together its current value and the value stored in the level property using the shorthand notation of += (meaning, score = score + level).

Build and run the project. Do your best to catch the gloop drops as they fall; notice how each time you catch a drop, you score one point. This happens because as the score property value changes, the didSet property observer updates the text for the scoreLabel node.

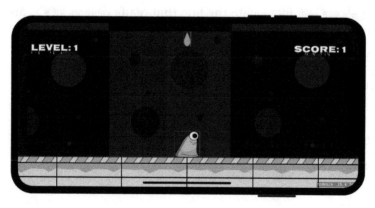

Now that the player's score is updating, it's time to code a way for players to lose the game and to reach new levels.

Losing the Game

A game without some kind of challenge isn't much fun to play. In Gloop Drop, the challenge is to catch all of the gloop drops. If you miss a drop, you fail the level and the game ends. For that to happen, you need to add some code.

The first step is to add a method that ends the game and stops the actions responsible for dropping the gloop drops. In the GameScene.swift file, below the spawnGloop() method, add the following code:

```
// Player FAILED level
func gameOver() {

  // Remove repeatable action on main scene
  removeAction(forKey: "gloop")

  // Loop through child nodes and stop actions on collectibles
  enumerateChildNodes(withName: "//co_*") {
    (node, stop) in

    // Stop and remove drops
    node.removeAction(forKey: "drop") // remove action
    node.physicsBody = nil // remove body so no collisions occur
  }
}
```

This code uses a key name to stop or remove the action of the same name; in this case, the action using the key gloop. It then uses the enumerate-ChildNodes(withName:) method to search the node tree for any node starting with the name co_. The * is a wildcard indicating any character. When a node name matches, it removes the drop action on the node and its attached physics body. You remove the physics body right away to avoid any potential collisions.

With this new gameOver() method in place, you're ready to call it when the player misses a drop. Locate the didBegin(_:) method, and below the line that reads sprite.missed(), add the following code:

```
gameOver()
```

Build and run the project. Do your best to catch a few drops and then miss one on purpose. Notice the remaining drops and corresponding actions stop immediately. Also, notice how the physics body is removed on the remaining drop as shown in the image on page 98.

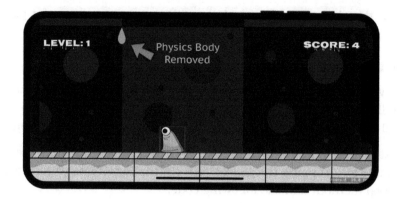

At this point, you have the basics in place for the lose condition, but something isn't quite right—Blob keeps moving after the game ends. To handle this strange-looking problem, you will swap out the walk animation with a die animation.

From the Project Navigator, select the Assets.xcassets asset catalog and expand the blob sprite atlas. Switch to Finder and drag all of the images from the resources/blob_die folder into the blob sprite atlas as shown in the following image.

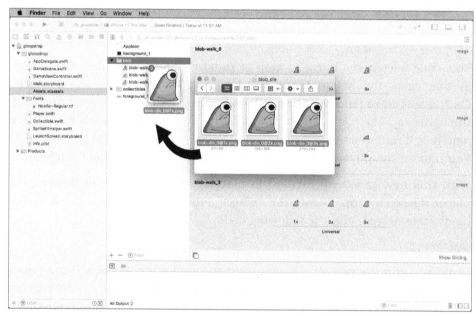

With the new image resources added to the project, you're ready to use them.

Open the Player.swift file and update the PlayerAnimationType enum to include a new die case. For reference, the updated enum looks like this:

```
enum PlayerAnimationType: String {
  case walk
  case die
}
```

In addition to having an enum case to use for Blob's die animation, you need a property to hold the textures. Below the declaration of the walkTextures property, add the following new property:

```
private var dieTextures: [SKTexture]?
```

You'll use this property to hold Blob's die textures—well, in this case, there's only one.

Scroll down to the init() method and add the following code below the line that sets the value of the self.walkTextures property:

```
self.dieTextures = self.loadTextures(atlas: "blob", prefix: "blob-die_",
                            startsAt: 0, stopsAt: 0)
```

Although there's only a single image for this animation, you're still using the loadTextures extension to keep things consistent.

The next step is to create the method that's responsible for running the die animation. Find the walk() method, and below that method, add the following code:

```
func die() {
  // Check for textures
  guard let dieTextures = dieTextures else {
    preconditionFailure("Could not find textures!")
  }

  // Stop the walk animation
  removeAction(forKey: PlayerAnimationType.walk.rawValue)

  // Run animation (forever)
  startAnimation(textures: dieTextures, speed: 0.25,
              name: PlayerAnimationType.die.rawValue,
              count: 0, resize: true, restore: true)
}
```

Before you can start the die animation, you first have to stop the walk animation action. You do this using the removeAction(forKey:) method of the SKNode class, passing in the key name. You saw this type of remove action earlier in the gameOver() method.

Just as you had to stop the walk animation before starting the die animation, you need to stop the die animation before you start the walk animation so that Blob can start moving again. Scroll up to the walk() method and add a call to remove the die animation action before starting the walk animation. For reference, the updated walk() method looks like this:

```swift
func walk() {
  // Check for textures
  guard let walkTextures = walkTextures else {
    preconditionFailure("Could not find textures!")
  }

  // Stop the die animation
  removeAction(forKey: PlayerAnimationType.die.rawValue)

  // Run animation (forever)
  startAnimation(textures: walkTextures, speed: 0.25,
                 name: PlayerAnimationType.walk.rawValue,
                 count: 0, resize: true, restore: true)
}
```

The last step is to call the die() method when the player loses the level.

Open the GameScene.swift file. Locate the gameOver() method and add the following code at the beginning of that method:

```swift
// Start player die animation
player.die()
```

For reference, the updated gameOver() method looks like this:

```swift
func gameOver() {

  // Start player die animation
  player.die()

  // Remove repeatable action on main scene
  removeAction(forKey: "gloop")

  // Loop through child nodes and stop actions on collectibles
  enumerateChildNodes(withName: "//co_*") {
    (node, stop) in

    // Stop and remove drops
    node.removeAction(forKey: "drop") // remove action
    node.physicsBody = nil // remove body so no collisions occur
  }
}
```

Build and run the project. After the game begins, miss a drop and watch Blob's reaction as shown in the image on page 101.

Despite Blob's sad face, you're well on your way to building a fun game. Your next step is to add the logic that handles restarting the game.

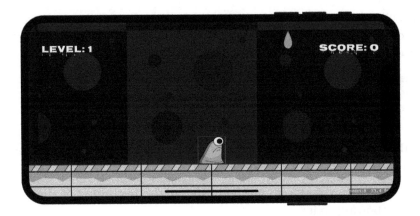

Restarting the Game

Slightly different than how the App Store version of Gloop Drop handles restarts, you'll add a simple mechanism that lets players tap the screen to start and restart the game. Because you need a way to determine when the players' touch is meant to move Blob rather than start or restart the game, you'll add a new property to the GameScene class.

In the GameScene.swift file, add the following new property, which you'll use to track when the game is in progress:

```
// Game states
var gameInProgress = false
```

This code adds a new gameInProgress property using a default value of false. A value of false means the game is *not* currently in progress.

When the player begins a new game, you need to switch the gameInProgress property value to true. Scroll down to the spawnMultipleGloops() method, and at the end of that method, add the following code:

```
// Update game states
gameInProgress = true
```

This code switches the gameInProgress property value to true after the player begins a new game.

You're almost done, but there's one problem: the game starts immediately after the scene loads. To fix this issue, you need to change the code so that it only starts—or restarts—when the player taps the screen.

In the didMove(to:) method, locate and comment out the call to spawnMultipleGloops()—it should be at the end of that method. Now, scroll down to the touchDown(atPoint:) method, and at the top of that method, add the following code:

```
if gameInProgress == false {
  spawnMultipleGloops()
  return
}
```

With this small change, you're starting the game when the player taps the screen rather than when the scene loads.

Finally, locate the gameOver() method, and at the beginning of that method, add the following code:

```
// Update game states
gameInProgress = false
```

With the addition of this code, when the player loses the game, the gameIn-Progress property value is set back to false.

Build and run the project. Tap the screen to start the game, catch a few drops, and then miss one. To restart the game, tap the screen again.

Everything seems to be working, except the game doesn't restart as you'd expect: the score doesn't get reset to zero, the drops remain on the screen, and Blob doesn't return to his starting position. To fix these *reset* problems, you'll add two new methods and update another.

Resetting the Game

Still inside the GameScene.swift file, find the gameOver() method and add calls to the yet-to-be-written resetPlayerPosition() and popRemainingDrops() methods—you can disregard the errors about unresolved identifiers since they'll disappear once you add the new methods:

```
// Reset game
resetPlayerPosition()
popRemainingDrops()
```

Now, when the gameOver() method executes, these two methods will get called.

Below the gameOver() method, add the new resetPlayerPosition() method:

```
func resetPlayerPosition() {
  let resetPoint = CGPoint(x: frame.midX, y: player.position.y)
  let distance = hypot(resetPoint.x-player.position.x, 0)
  let calculatedSpeed = TimeInterval(distance / (playerSpeed * 2)) / 255
```

```
  if player.position.x > frame.midX {
    player.moveToPosition(pos: resetPoint, direction: "L",
                          speed: calculatedSpeed)
  } else {
    player.moveToPosition(pos: resetPoint, direction: "R",
                          speed: calculatedSpeed)
  }
}
```

This new method moves Blob back to the center of the scene using a little math and the custom method you wrote in Add the Move Action, on page 44.

Below the method you just added, add the second new method that pops the remaining gloop drops:

```
func popRemainingDrops() {
  var i = 0
  enumerateChildNodes(withName: "//co_*") {
    (node, stop) in

    // Pop remaining drops in sequence
    let initialWait = SKAction.wait(forDuration: 1.0)
    let wait = SKAction.wait(forDuration: TimeInterval(0.15 * CGFloat(i)))

    let removeFromParent = SKAction.removeFromParent()
    let actionSequence = SKAction.sequence([initialWait, wait,
                                            removeFromParent])

    node.run(actionSequence)

    i += 1
  }
}
```

This second method locates the gloop drop nodes by name, and then uses a series of timed actions to remove them from the scene.

Finally, in the spawnMultipleGloops() method, *above* the switch level statement, add the following code that resets the level and score:

```
// Reset the level and score
if gameInProgress == false {
  score = 0
  level = 1
}
```

Build and run the project. Catch a few drops and then miss one. Notice that blob moves back to the center of the screen and the remaining drops disappear. Tap the screen to start a new game.

Notice how Blob's animation action is *stuck* on his sad face die animation as shown in the image on page 104.

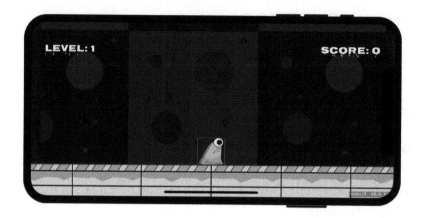

To fix that problem, and to also make the start of the game look a little better, you'll update two existing methods.

Locate the spawnMultipleGloops() method and add the following code at the beginning:

```
// Start player walk animation
player.walk()
```

Now, scroll up to the didMove(to:) method and comment out the call to player.walk().

Build and run the program. Notice this time, Blob isn't animated until you start the game, and his walk animation restarts when you start a new game.

With those changes in place, you now have a nice—yet simple—way to restart the game, and you're ready to build out the logic that handles advancing to the next level.

Advancing to the Next Level

To keep track of when the player has caught all of the gloop drops and is ready to advance to the next level, you'll need two more variables: one to track the number of drops expected, and one to track the number of drops caught.

In the GameScene.swift file, add the following two properties below the line that creates the numberOfDrops property:

```
var dropsExpected = 10
var dropsCollected = 0
```

You'll use these new properties to determine when the player completes the level. Since you know the first level has 10 drops, you can set the initial value of dropsExpected to 10.

You also need to update the value of the dropsExpected property based on the current level. In the spawnMultipleGloops() method, below the switch level statement that resets numberOfDrops, add the following code:

```
// Reset and update the collected and expected drop count
dropsCollected = 0
dropsExpected = numberOfDrops
```

With this code, the dropsCollected property value is reset to 0, and the value in dropsExpected is set to the same value as numberOfDrops. However, you still need to increase this number when a drop is collected.

In the didBegin(_: method, add the following code below the sprite.collected() line:

```
dropsCollected += 1
```

The next step is to check whether or not the player collected all of the drops. Scroll down to the spawnGloop() method, and below that method, add the following two methods; you'll use these to determine when the player passes the level, and what to do when that happens:

```
func checkForRemainingDrops() {
  if dropsCollected == dropsExpected {
    nextLevel()
  }
}
// Player PASSED level
func nextLevel() {
  let wait = SKAction.wait(forDuration: 2.25)
  run(wait, completion:{[unowned self] in self.level += 1
                        self.spawnMultipleGloops()})
}
```

The first method verifies that the dropsCollected equals the dropsExpected. The second method, which is called by the first method once dropsCollected == dropsExpected, increases the value in the level property by 1, and then it runs an action that calls spawnMultipleGloops().

Before you can start using your new methods, you need to take a small detour and learn about frame updates, commonly known as *the game loop*.

Use the Game Loop to Apply Game Logic

In SpriteKit, the game loop is handled with a series of frame-cycle events. These events, in the order in which they occur, are as follows:

1. The update(_:) method is called. This method gets called once per every frame and is the main method you'll use to execute your game logic.

2. SKScene evaluates the actions. At this point, your scene processes all of the actions it needs to process.

3. The didEvaluateActions() method is called. This method gets called after all of the actions for the frame are processed.

4. SKScene simulates physics. At this point, your scene processes all of the physics on nodes with attached physics bodies.

5. The didSimulatePhysics() method is called. This method gets called after all of the physics for the frame are processed.

6. SKScene applies the constraints. At this point, your scene processes all of the constraints it needs to process.

7. The didApplyConstraints() method is called. This method gets called after all of the constraints for the frame are processed.

8. The didFinishUpdate() method is called. After everything is processed, this method gets called.

9. SKView finally renders the scene.

You can either override the frame-cycle methods to provide game logic, or you can skip implementing these methods entirely. If you don't implement these methods, SpriteKit will only render the scene when something within it changes, improving energy efficiency and overall performance. Generally, though, you'll find that most of the time you need to implement the update(_:) method, which is what you'll do now.

Add the following method to the GameScene class.

```
override func update(_ currentTime: TimeInterval) {
  checkForRemainingDrops()
}
```

Build and run the project. Do your best to catch all 10 drops that fall in Level 1. Notice that the level increases more than once and you're bombarded with gloop drops as shown in the image on page 107.

The reason for this strange behavior is because of how the update(_:) method works. Recall that the update(_:) method gets called once per frame. So, if that's the case, which it is, checkForRemainingDrops() is getting called more than it *should*, which also means nextLevel() is getting called too often. Don't believe it?

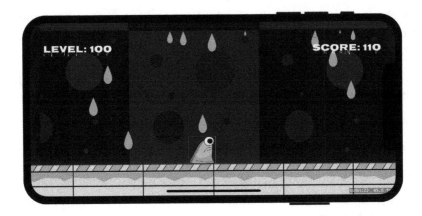

Add the following temporary print statement to the update(_:) method:

```
print("""
        \(currentTime): dropsCollected: \(dropsCollected)
        | dropsExpected: \(dropsExpected)
    """)
```

This method, which uses a *multiline string literal*, will print the values of currentTime, dropsCollected, and dropsExpected each time the update(_:) method runs.

Build and run the project and do your best to catch the first 10 gloop drops. After you catch that last drop, look at the Xcode console. Notice the number of times you see the statement dropsCollected: 10 | dropsExpected: 10. Your console may show different timestamps for currentTime, but you'll see something similar to this:

```
318486.760389749: dropsCollected: 10 | dropsExpected: 10
318486.796953599: dropsCollected: 10 | dropsExpected: 10
318486.86138900503: dropsCollected: 10 | dropsExpected: 10
318486.91907901: dropsCollected: 10 | dropsExpected: 10
318486.93574567704: dropsCollected: 10 | dropsExpected: 10
318486.95241234405: dropsCollected: 10 | dropsExpected: 10
318486.969079011: dropsCollected: 10 | dropsExpected: 10
318486.985745678: dropsCollected: 10 | dropsExpected: 10
318487.002412345: dropsCollected: 10 | dropsExpected: 10
```

To fix this problem, you have at least two options:

- Add a new property to track the current game state and use that value to determine whether or not to call the checkForRemainingDrops() method.

- Modify the code and move the game logic out of the update(_:) method.

In this chapter, you will implement both options to see the differences, but you will end up using only the second one because it provides a small bump in performance.

Add a new property named playingLevel to the GameScene class and give it a default value of false:

```
var playingLevel = false
```

Then, at the end of the spawnMultipleGloops() method, set playingLevel to true:

```
playingLevel = true
```

Finally, update the checkForRemainingDrops() method so that it checks the value of playingLevel, like so:

```
func checkForRemainingDrops() {
  if playingLevel == true {
    if dropsCollected == dropsExpected {
      playingLevel = false
      nextLevel()
    }
  }
}
```

With this change, the only time the nextLevel() method gets called is when the player is *actively* playing a level (in other words, playingLevel == true).

Build and run the project. Notice that after you catch the first 10 drops, the nextLevel() gets called only once, and the second level starts without issue.

While this first option works fine, it might make more sense to go with option two and get the added performance benefits that come along with *not* implementing the frame-cycle method.

Comment out the new code you just added; this includes the declaration of the playingLevel property and the updates to both the spawnMultipleGloops() method and the checkForRemainingDrops() method. While you're commenting out code, also comment out the update(_:) method you added earlier.

Now, scroll down to the didBegin(_:) method, and below the score += level line, add a call to checkForRemainingDrops():

```
// Verify the object is a collectible
if let sprite = body as? Collectible {
  sprite.collected()
  dropsCollected += 1
  score += level
➤ checkForRemainingDrops()
}
```

Thanks to this small change, the only time the call to checkForRemainingDrops() happens is after the player catches a drop. Before you made this change, there was a lot of unnecessary code executing *for every frame*, which could impact performance. While this isn't so much of a problem with a game like Gloop Drop, you can imagine how larger, more complex games could feel the strain on their resources.

Before ending this chapter, you'll look at one more thing: using attributed strings with the SKLabel class.

Use Attributed Strings with Labels

Attributed strings in SpriteKit work very much the same as they do in UIKit. With attributed strings, you can add additional attributes such as font styles and kerning. In this case, you're using an attributed string to provide a line break in a multiline label while also keeping the text centered—something the SKLabelNode class can't seem to do natively.

In the GameScene.swift file, add the following method below the setupLabels() method; you'll use this method to display a message in the middle of the screen:

```swift
func showMessage(_ message: String) {
  // Set up message label
  let messageLabel = SKLabelNode()
  messageLabel.name = "message"
  messageLabel.position = CGPoint(x: frame.midX, y: player.frame.maxY + 100)
  messageLabel.zPosition = Layer.ui.rawValue
➤ messageLabel.numberOfLines = 2
➤
➤ // Set up attributed text
➤ let paragraph = NSMutableParagraphStyle()
➤ paragraph.alignment = .center
➤
➤ let attributes: [NSAttributedString.Key: Any] = [
➤   .foregroundColor: SKColor(red: 251.0/255.0, green: 155.0/255.0,
➤                             blue: 24.0/255.0, alpha: 1.0),
➤   .backgroundColor: UIColor.clear,
➤   .font: UIFont(name: "Nosifer", size: 45.0)!,
➤   .paragraphStyle: paragraph
➤ ]
➤
➤ messageLabel.attributedText = NSAttributedString(string: message,
➤                                                  attributes: attributes)

  // Run a fade action and add the label to the scene
  messageLabel.run(SKAction.fadeIn(withDuration: 0.25))
  addChild(messageLabel)
}
```

The highlighted code shows the bits related to attributed strings. Here, you set the paragraph style using the NSMutableParagraphStyle and the .center option, which centers the text. You then build an array with this attribute, along with some other font-related and color attributes. Finally, you set the attributedText property on the messageLabel node.

Now that you've got a way to show a message to the player, it's time to add a method to hide that same message. Below the showMessage(_:) method, add the following code:

```
func hideMessage() {
  // Remove message label if it exists
  if let messageLabel = childNode(withName: "//message") as? SKLabelNode {
    messageLabel.run(SKAction.sequence([SKAction.fadeOut(withDuration: 0.25),
                                        SKAction.removeFromParent()]))
  }
}
```

This method uses the SKNode childNode(withName:) method to check for a node with a matching name. In this case, message. The // is part of an advanced search routine that specifies that searching should be performed recursively across the entire node tree, beginning at the root node. If it finds a match, it then runs a sequence of actions to fade out and then remove the node from its parent, in this case, the scene.

With your two new methods in place, it's time to use them.

At the end of the didMove(to:) method, add the following code:

```
// Show message
showMessage("Tap to start game")
```

And, in the spawnMultipleGloops() method, add the following code to the end of that method:

```
// Hide message
hideMessage()
```

You're almost done. In the gameOver() method, add the following code at the top of that method:

```
// Show message
showMessage("Game Over\nTap to try again")
```

Finally, in the nextLevel() method, add this at the top:

```
// Show message
showMessage("Get Ready!")
```

Build and run the program and watch in awe as messages fade in and out as you progress through the game.

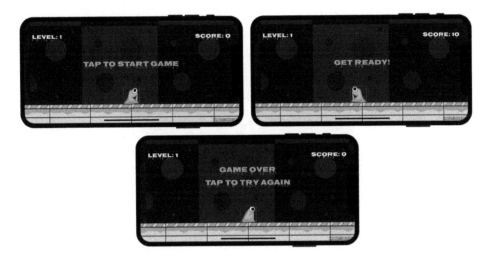

Next Steps

In this chapter, you got to play around with the SKLabelNode class as you added labels to the game scene to display the player's current level and score, complete with a custom font, which you added to the project. You also saw what it took to use the NSAttributedString class with an SkLabelNode object, and you even dipped your toes into the logic of the game loop.

In the next chapter, you'll continue building Gloop Drop by adding a little juice to the game like particle effects, visual effects, and of course, music and sound.

CHAPTER 6

Juicing Your Games with Sound and Effects

In the previous chapter, you worked with the SKLabelNode class and added some labels to the scene to keep the player informed of things like the current level and score. You also learned about the game loop and how you can leverage the like soframe-cycle methods to implement your game logic. Gloop Drop is fully functional at this point, but it's missing something: *game juice.*

Game juice is a common term used within the game development community. When you add *juice* to your game (aka, *juicing*), what you're doing is improving the overall look and feel of your game. For example, you might add subtle audio and visual effects or tweak certain aspects of the user controls.

Although juicing casts a wide net, the primary goal is always to enhance gameplay and set the emotional tone for your game, such as fear for a horror game or action-packed fun for an arcade game.

In this chapter, you'll get warmed up by adding sound effects and background music. After that, you'll move on to tweaking some of the visual effects and animation sequences—this is where you'll learn how to add a scrolling background to make a continuous flow of gloop beneath the player. From there, you'll add a little more juice using SpriteKit's Particle System and emitter nodes to make the flow of gloop a little more interesting.

To begin, open the gloopdrop project in Xcode.

Before you start adding juice, you need to remove the debug view options to get a better idea of what players will see when they play the game.

In the Project Navigator, select the GameViewController.swift file to open it in the Source Editor. Find the viewDidLoad() method and update the view options, like so:

Using the Starter Project

You may continue using your project from the previous chapter, or you can use the starter project located in the projects/begin folder included with the code resources for this chapter. Either option is fine; the only benefit to using the starter project is that you won't get stuck going forward if you missed an earlier step.

There's also an ending project for this chapter that includes all of the code and resources you'll be adding here. The end project is located in the projects/end folder included with the code resources for this chapter.

```
// Set the view options
view.ignoresSiblingOrder = false
view.showsPhysics = false
view.showsFPS = false
view.showsNodeCount = false
```

This change removes the blue physics bodies outlines, along with the FPS and node counts that show up in the bottom-right corner of the game.

With those view options out of the way, you're ready to get started.

Add Sound Effects

Creating an immersive game experience can make the difference between a game that users play versus one that they toss into the trash. One way to keep players interested is to incorporate sound effects that tap into their emotions. For example, the sound effects you'll be using for Gloop Drop are included with the project source files, but you also have the option of sourcing your own sound assets, as you saw in Gather Your Resources, on page xxvi.

Your first order of business is to add the sound effects resources you'll use with Gloop Drop.

Adding Resources for the Sound Effects

In keeping with the idea of an organized project, you'll create a separate group to hold the sound resources. Drag the resources/Sounds folder into the Project Navigator, as shown in the image on page 115.

When prompted, ensure that the Copy items if needed and Add to targets options are both checked. Also, verify that the option to Create groups is selected. Once these options are set, click Finish.

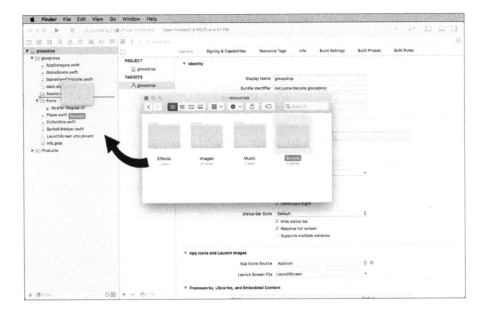

When you drag the folder into the Project Navigator, Xcode will create a new group named Sounds that contains the following six files: bubbles.mp3, collect.wav, miss.wav, blob_mumble-1.wav, blob_mumble-2.wav, and blob_mumble-3.wav.

You'll use these files to add sound effects to the game.

Creating Actions to Play Sound

Currently, when Blob catches a drop, it's a bit underwhelming—he catches the drop and it disappears. Missing a drop is also underwhelming.

To make these events more interesting, you'll use actions to play two sound effects: one when Blob catches a drop (collect.wav), and one when he misses a drop (miss.wav).

Open the Collectible.swift file and add the following two properties:

```
private let playCollectSound = SKAction.playSoundFileNamed("collect.wav",
                                        waitForCompletion: false)
private let playMissSound = SKAction.playSoundFileNamed("miss.wav",
                                        waitForCompletion: false)
```

Here, you're creating two actions that you'll use later to play the individual sound files. By setting the waitForCompletion parameter to false, you're telling SpriteKit to ignore the length of the audio file and to consider the action to have completed immediately. Alternatively, you can set this option to true, making the duration of the action the same length as the audio playback.

When to Wait for Completion

The waitForCompletion property can get a little confusing, and you may be wondering when you might consider using a value of true rather than false. One such instance would be if you're running a sequence of actions and you need an action to run *after* the audio file is done playing.

With the preloaded actions in place, you're ready to update the methods responsible for collecting and missing the drops.

Still inside the Collectible.swift file, find the collected() method and update it to match the following code:

```
func collected() {
  let removeFromParent = SKAction.removeFromParent()
  let actionGroup = SKAction.group([playCollectSound, removeFromParent])
  self.run(actionGroup)
}
```

Next, update the missed() method to match this:

```
func missed() {
  let removeFromParent = SKAction.removeFromParent()
  let actionGroup = SKAction.group([playMissSound, removeFromParent])
  self.run(actionGroup)
}
```

These changes give you some additional experience working with grouped and sequenced actions, which you first learned about in Chain Actions Together to Create a Sequence, on page 56. The new grouped actions play the appropriate audio file and remove the node from the scene simultaneously.

Build and run the project, but don't forget to turn up the volume so that you can hear the different sounds when you catch and miss the drops.

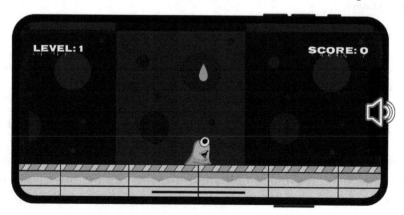

For short, incidental sound effects—like the ones you just added—actions work well. But when you're working with longer-running audio files, like background music or ambient noise, it's better to use the SKAudioNode class.

Add Background Music

The SKAudioNode class is a subclass of SKNode. With this class, you can build a robust audio node capable of 3D spatial audio effects, independent volume control, stereo balance, and special effects like speeding up or slowing down the playback rate. With these added capabilities, you can create some interesting effects like adjusting the playback of a car's engine roar as it goes faster and slower.

When you add an audio node directly to the scene, or as a child on another node, you're able to run sound-related actions on that node such as play(), pause(), and stop(). You can also run the following actions to modify some of the audio node's key properties:

Absolute Value	Relative Value
changePlaybackRate(to:duration:)	changePlaybackRate(by:duration:)
changeVolume(to:duration:)	changeVolume(by:duration:)
changeObstruction(to:duration:)	changeObstruction(by:duration:)
changeOcclusion(to:duration:)	changeOcclusion(by:duration:)
changeReverb(to:duration:)	changeReverb(by:duration:)
steroPan(to:duration:)	steroPan(by:duration:)

If you look closely, you'll notice a pattern here: the actions in that table include a to and a by variation, giving you precise control over your audio node. For example, if an audio node's volume property had a value of 1.0, you could use the changeVolume(to:duration:) method to change the value to 0.75, like so:

```
audioNode.run(SKAction.changeVolume(to: 0.75, duration: 0.0))
```

Alternatively, you could use the changeVolume(by:duration:) method to decrease the value by 0.25, like this:

```
audioNode.run(SKAction.changeVolume(by: -0.25, duration: 0.0))
```

Either way works, and which method you use all depends on what you're trying to accomplish.

In Gloop Drop, you'll add two audio nodes: one for the background music and one to add some ambient sound. But first, you need to add the resources for the music.

Adding Resources for the Background Music

Similar to what you did in Adding Resources for the Sound Effects, on page 114, drag the resources/Music folder into the Project Navigator to create a new Music group.

Don't forget to check that the Copy items if needed and Add to targets options are both checked, and that the option to Create groups is selected. Once you verify that these options are set correctly, click Finish.

You're now ready to add the background music audio node.

Setting Up the Audio Node

To get started, you'll set up a property to hold the music audio node so that you can easily access it by name.

Open the GameScene.swift file and add the following code below the line that reads var levelLabel: SKLabelNode = SKLabelNode():

```
// Audio nodes
let musicAudioNode = SKAudioNode(fileNamed: "music.mp3")
```

This code initializes an SKAudioNode object using the music.mp3 file. Another way to initialize an SKAudioNode object is to use the init(url:) method, which lets you pass in a URL instead of a filename. This URL could be either a remote resource or a local bundle resource.

The next step is to update the didMove(to:) method by adding the following code at the top of that method:

```
// Set up the background music audio node
musicAudioNode.autoplayLooped = true
musicAudioNode.isPositional = false

// Add the audio node to the scene
addChild(musicAudioNode)
```

This code not only adds the audio node to the scene but also sets two important properties: autoplayLooped and isPositional. When you set the autoplayLooped property to true, the default value, the sound will immediately play in a loop when the node gets added to the scene. The other property, isPositional, which also defaults to true, is used to alter the audio based on the listener node. You'll learn more about that in Chapter 11, Building Games with Entities and Components, on page 227.

Build and run the project. Notice how abruptly the audio plays when the scene first loads. While you *could* leave it as-is, a better user experience is to fade in the music track. For that, you'll leverage AVFoundation.

Build More Robust Sound Systems

AVFoundation is a powerful audiovisual framework for iOS, macOS, watchOS, and tvOS. With AVFoundation, you can add powerful media features to your games. In a SpriteKit scene, you have access to its audioEngine property; however, before you can use this property, you first need to import the AVFoundation framework.

Open the GameScene.swift file, and import the AVFoundation framework by adding the following line of code above the line that reads import SpriteKit:

```
import AVFoundation
```

With that import statement, you now have access to the mainMixerNode properties of the audioEngine attached to the scene.

To achieve the desired fade-in effect, you'll use the outputVolume property on the mainMixerNode to decrease the volume.

In the didMove(to:) method, add the following code at the start of the method:

```
// Decrease the audio engine's volume
audioEngine.mainMixerNode.outputVolume = 0.0
```

This code decreases the main mixer volume to 0.0. The reason you're setting the main volume to 0.0 is to effectively *mute* the audio node's sound. Remember, when an audio node's autoplayLooped property is set to true, the sound file immediately plays when the node is added to the scene.

Your next step is to use an action to set the musicAudioNode volume to 0.0, and then use some more actions to increase the audio node's volume to 0.75 gradually. You'll also reset the mainMixerNode.outputVolume back to 1.0.

Scroll down until you see the line that reads addChild(musicAudioNode). Below that line, add the following code:

```
// Use an action to adjust the audio node's volume to 0
musicAudioNode.run(SKAction.changeVolume(to: 0.0, duration: 0.0))

// Run a delayed action on the scene that fades in the music
run(SKAction.wait(forDuration: 1.0), completion: { [unowned self] in
  self.audioEngine.mainMixerNode.outputVolume = 1.0
  self.musicAudioNode.run(SKAction.changeVolume(to: 0.75, duration: 2.0))
})
```

Here, you're using a series of actions to fade in the background music after the scene starts. You're also lowering the volume to 75% so as not to over-whelm the player's audio senses with background music. The end result: you're increasing the audio node's volume from 0 to 75% over two seconds.

Build and run the project. Make sure you have your volume turned up so that you can hear the background music as it gradually fades in.

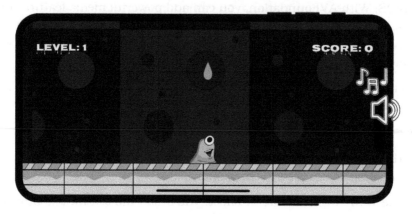

Now that you're not getting blasted with tunes when the game first loads, you can concentrate on tweaking the visual aspects of the game and adding ambient sounds.

Create an Endless Scrolling Background

Have you ever played a game where the main character stays in one spot, but the background moves from right to left, making it appear as if the player is traveling to the right? This popular technique, known as an *endless scrolling background*, isn't only for player movement—in Gloop Drop, you'll use it to create an infinite flow of gloop beneath the platform.

Adding Image Resources for the Gloop Flow

Select the Assets.xcassets asset catalog and drag the three files, flow_1@1x.png, flow_1@2x.png, and flow_1@3x.png from the resources/Images folder into the root of the Assets.xcassets asset catalog, as shown in the image on page 121.

This action creates a flow_1 image set. You'll use this image set to create an endless scrolling background.

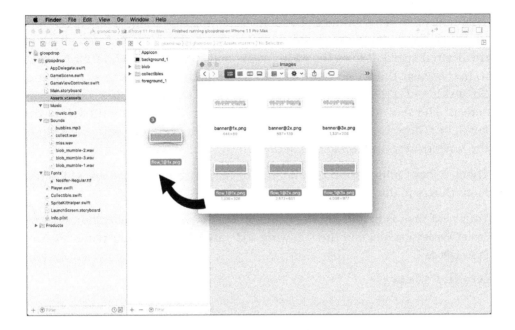

Creating Extensions for Scrolling the Background

While it's entirely possible to create a method or two inside the GameScene class to handle scrolling, you'll instead create extensions to handle it so that you can use them elsewhere in your code or in other projects.

Open the SpriteKitHelper.swift file, and to add another extension for the SKSpriteNode class, add the following code below the line that reads extension SKSpriteNode {:

```
// Used to create an endless scrolling background
func endlessScroll(speed: TimeInterval) {

  // Set up actions to move and reset nodes
  let moveAction = SKAction.moveBy(x: -self.size.width,
                                   y: 0, duration: speed)
  let resetAction = SKAction.moveBy(x: self.size.width,
                                    y: 0, duration: 0.0)

  // Set up a sequence of repeating actions
  let sequenceAction = SKAction.sequence([moveAction, resetAction])
  let repeatAction = SKAction.repeatForever(sequenceAction)

  // Run the repeating action
  self.run(repeatAction)
}
```

This code creates a sequence of actions that runs repeatedly. The first action, moveAction, takes the sprite node and moves it to the specified x-position at the desired speed. It uses the width of the node to determine how far to move it. In this case, the image width is 1336, which is the same width as the scene. So, a value of -1336 will move this sprite node to the far left, just outside the screen. The second action, resetAction, then *resets* the x-position back to the far right. These two actions endlessly repeat in a sequence with the help of the sequenceAction and repeatAction actions.

That's a lot of information to take in, but stay with me—there are still a few more things to do.

Your next task is to add a new extension for the SKNode class. Still inside the SpriteKitHelper.swift file, add the following code above the line that reads extension SKSpriteNode {:

```
extension SKNode {

    // Used to set up an endless scroller
    func setupScrollingView(imageNamed name: String, layer: Layer,
                            blocks: Int, speed: TimeInterval) {

        // Create sprite nodes; set positions based on the node's # and width
        for i in 0..<blocks {
            let spriteNode = SKSpriteNode(imageNamed: name)
            spriteNode.anchorPoint = CGPoint.zero
            spriteNode.position = CGPoint(x: CGFloat(i) * spriteNode.size.width,
                                          y: 0)
            spriteNode.zPosition = layer.rawValue
            spriteNode.name = name

            // Use the custom extension to scroll
            spriteNode.endlessScroll(speed: speed)

            // Add the sprite node to the container
            addChild(spriteNode)
        }
    }
}
```

This code is at the heart of the endless scrolling routine. You can set several options, including the image name to use for the sprite node, the z-position (layer), the number of blocks, and the speed. It then uses this information to create and add a new sprite node, which ultimately calls the endlessScroll(speed:) extension method.

With these two extensions in place, you're ready to get scrolling.

Open the GameScene.swift file and add the following code above the line that reads // MARK: - GAME FUNCTIONS:

```
// MARK: - Gloop Flow & Particle Effects
func setupGloopFlow() {
  // Set up flowing gloop
  let gloopFlow = SKNode()
  gloopFlow.name = "gloopFlow"
  gloopFlow.zPosition = Layer.foreground.rawValue
  gloopFlow.position = CGPoint(x: 0.0, y: -60)
  // Use extension for endless scrolling
  gloopFlow.setupScrollingView(imageNamed: "flow_1",
                               layer: Layer.foreground,
                               blocks: 3, speed: 30.0)

  // Add flow to scene
  addChild(gloopFlow)
}
```

This code pulls it all together by creating a new gloopFlow node to hold the scrolling background sprites. It then uses the setupScrollingView(imageNamed:layer:blocks:speed:) extension method to initiate the scroll.

To get a better idea of how this all works, look at the following image:

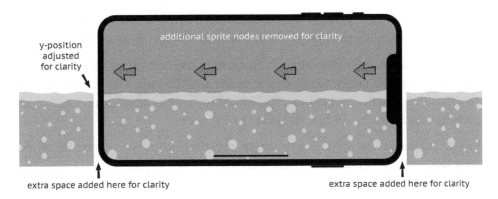

In this example, which has a few modifications added for clarity, you can see how the three images are used to show a continuous flow of gloop that moves to the left.

The last step is to call this new setupGloopFlow() method. At the bottom of the didMove(to:) method, add the following code:

```
// Set up the gloop flow
setupGloopFlow()
```

Build and run the project, and you'll see an endless flow of gooey green gloop just beneath the platform as shown in the image on page 124.

You're well on your way to making this gloop flow look good, but it's missing something: ambient sound.

Adding Ambient Sound to the Gloop Flow

Still inside the GameScene.swift file, add the following new property below the existing musicAudioNode declaration:

```
let bubblesAudioNode = SKAudioNode(fileNamed: "bubbles.mp3")
```

This code initializes another SKAudioNode object using the bubbles.mp3 file that you added in Adding Resources for the Sound Effects, on page 114.

With the musicAudioNode object, you ran an action to first lower the volume to 0.0, and then you added an action to gradually increase the volume, giving you that fade-in effect. This time, instead of adjusting the volume, you'll write an action that delays adding the node to the scene.

In the didMove(to:) method, below the action that adjusts the volume of the musicAudioNode object, add the following code:

```
// Run a delayed action to add bubble audio to the scene
run(SKAction.wait(forDuration: 1.5), completion: { [unowned self] in
  self.bubblesAudioNode.autoplayLooped = true
  self.addChild(self.bubblesAudioNode)
})
```

For reference, you'll end up with something like this:

```
// Use an action to adjust the audio node's volume to 0
musicAudioNode.run(SKAction.changeVolume(to: 0.0, duration: 0.0))

// Run a delayed action on the scene that fades in the music
run(SKAction.wait(forDuration: 1.0), completion: { [unowned self] in
  self.audioEngine.mainMixerNode.outputVolume = 1.0
  self.musicAudioNode.run(SKAction.changeVolume(to: 0.75, duration: 2.0))
})
```

```
// Run a delayed action to add bubble audio to the scene
run(SKAction.wait(forDuration: 1.5), completion: { [unowned self] in
  self.bubblesAudioNode.autoplayLooped = true
  self.addChild(self.bubblesAudioNode)
})
```

Build and run the project and listen to the sweet, sweet ambient sounds of bubbling gloop as it flows endlessly beneath the platform.

If you think adding ambient sound is cool, you're in for a real treat.

Juice Your Game with Particles

Your game is *sort of* dripping with juice now. While you could yell, "Ship it!" and call it a day, there's always more you can do when it comes to juicing your games. For example, you can use SpriteKit's Particle System to add special effects like fire, smoke, and sparks to your games—all of which are types of *particles*.

In this section, you'll get your first look at creating particles using Xcode's SpriteKit Particle Editor.

From Xcode's App menu, select File ▶ New ▶ File... or press ⌘N on your keyboard to create a new particle file. Select the iOS SpriteKit Particle File template as shown in the first image on page 126.

Your next step is to choose the options for your new particle effect. The available options are:

- Bokeh
- Fire
- Fireflies
- Magic
- Rain
- Smoke
- Snow
- Spark

Each of these options produces a different effect. Your best bet is to play with each option after learning how to create your first effect. For the gloop flow effect, choose Spark, and then click Next.

When prompted for a filename, enter GloopFlow.sks and click Create. When you're done, you'll see something like the second image on page 126.

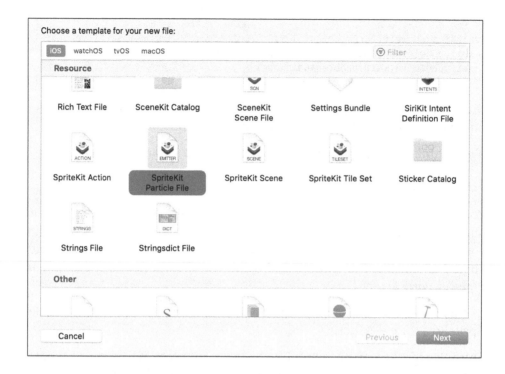

What you're looking at now is a visual representation of an SKEmitterNode object in the SpriteKit Particle Editor. For more information about this emitter node, open the Attributes inspector. To open the inspector, click the Hide or show the Inspectors button in the toolbar's upper-right corner; this button toggles the inspector's visibility.

Inside the inspector, you'll see the following options (shown side by side for clarity):

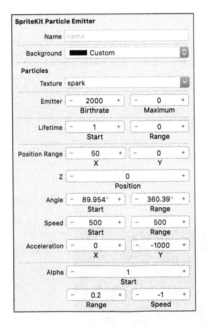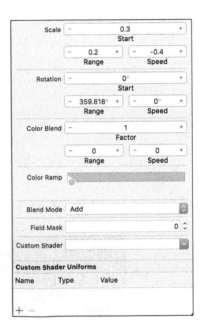

Here, you can set various options for your emitter node, like where to create the particles, how many particles to create, the translation (rotation, size, and movement) of the particles, and how they change throughout their lifetime.

Before setting any of these options for the gloop flow effect, take a few minutes to play around with each of these settings to see what effects are possible, or refer to Apple's online documentation[1] to see precisely what each option controls. As you change each property, you'll be able to see the result immediately in the preview window. When you're done playing with particles, set the options to match the settings as shown in the first image on page 128.

When you're done, your new particle emitter will look something like the second image on page 128.

---

1. https://developer.apple.com/documentation/spritekit/skemitternode/creating_particle_effects

Category	Property	Value
Emitter	Birthrate	250
	Maximum	0
Lifetime	Start	2.5
	Range	0
Position Range	X	1336
	Y	750
	Z	0
Angle	Start	89°
	Range	360°
Speed	Start	0
	Range	100
Acceleration	X	0
	Y	0
Alpha	Start	1
	Range	0.2
	Speed	-0.35

Category	Property	Value
Scale	Start	0.2
	Range	0
	Speed	0.45
Rotation	Start	0°
	Range	0°
	Speed	0°
Color Blend	Factor	1
	Range	0
	Speed	0
Color Ramp	---	#59E14B
Blend Mode	---	Alpha
Field Mask	---	0
Custom Shader	---	N/A

For information on what each property does,
please refer to the Apple documentation.

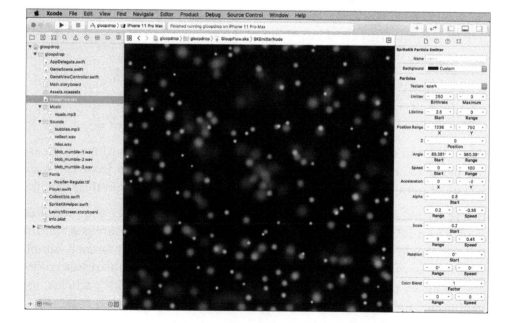

If you're having trouble getting your particles to match the ones in the book, you can copy the GloopFlow.sks file from the resources/Effects folder into your project.

Now that you have the visual component complete, your next step is to add your emitter to the game—and for that, you'll use another extension.

Update the Extension to use an Optional Emitter

Open the SpriteKitHelper.swift file and update the method signature for the setup-ScrollingView(imageNamed:layer:blocks:speed:) method, like so:

```
func setupScrollingView(imageNamed name: String, layer: Layer,
          emitterNamed: String?, blocks: Int, speed: TimeInterval) {
```

This change adds an optional parameter, emitterNamed, which you can use to pass in the filename of your emitter and create the instance of an SKEmitterNode object.

Scroll down in this same method and locate the line of code that reads spriteNode.name = name. Below that line, add the following code that sets up the SKEmitterNode object:

```
// Set up optional particles
if let emitterNamed = emitterNamed,
let particles = SKEmitterNode(fileNamed: emitterNamed) {
  particles.name = "particles"
  spriteNode.addChild(particles)
}
```

Here, you're using a *convenience initializer* to initialize the emitter node using the specified filename passed in using the emitterNamed parameter. A convenience initializer is considered a secondary, supporting initializer for a class.

You're almost done. Only one step remains: updating the call in setupGloopFlow(), which is currently generating the following error due to a mismatch in the method signature (in other words, it's expecting the emitterNode parameter, but one isn't being sent.):

```
// Use extension for endless scrolling
gloopFlow.setupScrollingView(imageNamed: "flow_1",
                  layer: Layer.foreground,          ⊗ Missing argument for parameter 'emitterNamed' in call
                  blocks: 3, speed: 30.0)
```

Open the GameScene.swift file and update the setupGloopFlow() method so that you pass in the new emitterNamed parameter, like so:

```
// Use extension for endless scrolling
gloopFlow.setupScrollingView(imageNamed: "flow_1",
                        layer: Layer.foreground,
                        emitterNamed: "GloopFlow.sks",
                        blocks: 3, speed: 30.0)
```

The error is cleared, and you're ready to test your new particle emitter.

Build and run the project and prepare to be amazed—but also annoyed because now there's a slight problem with moving Blob.

No matter how much you try, nothing gets Blob to budge from his spot. It's as if your touches are being ignored. The good news is that you can fix this by modifying how you handle the touch events.

Handle Hit-Testing and Touch Events

To fix the problem with not being able to move Blob, you first need to better understand touch events and *hit-testing*. Hit-testing in SpriteKit involves checking to see what nodes were hit during a mouse or touch event. For a node to be considered during hit-testing, its isUserInteractionEnabled property must be set to true; the default value is false for all nodes except a scene node. If a node is hit, and it's set up to ignore the interaction, the event will move on to the next closest node. The order in which nodes are tested happens in the reverse of the drawing order.

While hit-testing is undoubtedly an option, there's another way to see what node was at an intersect location.

Before you begin, you need to update the didMove(to:) method in the GameScene class. Open the GameScene.swift file and add node names to both the foreground and background sprite nodes.

First, the background:

```
background.name = "background"
```

Then, the foreground:

```
foreground.name = "foreground"
```

Now, locate the touchDown(atPoint:) method and notice the following code, which you added in Use Iterative Design to Adjust the Player's Movement, on page 66:

```
let touchedNode = atPoint(pos)
if touchedNode.name == "player" {
  movingPlayer = true
}
```

This code grabs only the first touched node. If that node's name property value matches the string player, you can move Blob; otherwise, nothing will happen. The problem is that your fancy new emitter node is now on top of the player sprite node, blocking access to it.

Modify that portion of the code to match this:

```
let touchedNodes = nodes(at: pos)
for touchedNode in touchedNodes {
  print("touchedNode: \(String(describing: touchedNode.name))")
  if touchedNode.name == "player" {
    movingPlayer = true
  }
}
```

You're now using the nodes(at:) method of the scene, which returns all *visible nodes* at the intersect point. A node is considered visible only when its isHidden property value is false, and its alpha property value is greater than zero. The alpha property controls the transparency of the node.

If you look at the following image, you'll get a better idea of where the nodes exist within the node tree:

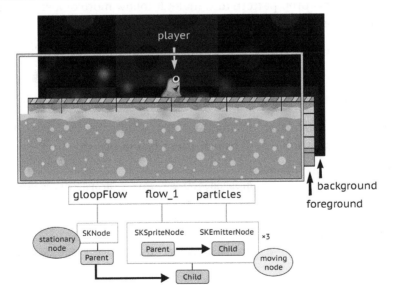

Build and run the program. Touch Blob and you'll see something like this in the console:

```
touchedNode: Optional("particles")
touchedNode: Optional("player")
touchedNode: Optional("background")
touchedNode: Optional("flow_1")
touchedNode: Optional("flow_1")
touchedNode: Optional("gloopFlow")
```

This console output shows the names of the nodes you touched and in what order the touch events were received. Because you're now checking the array of nodes using the nodes(at:) method, you'll be able to find the player node and get it moving.

Squeeze Out a Little More Juice

Before wrapping up this chapter, you're going to squeeze a little more juice out of the game. In this section, you'll tweak the drop pattern of the gloop drops for better gameplay, add juice to the catch and miss routines, give Blob a little personality, and finally, add the banner to the game.

Fixing the Drop Pattern

You may have noticed that when the drops fall from the sky, more often than not the previous drop is too far from the next drop, which makes it nearly impossible to catch everything. While you could argue that this impossibility adds to the game's challenge, it more than likely will lead to frustration instead. To fix this drop pattern and make it follow more of a snake-like pattern, you'll use a little math and some range control.

First, you need to add a new property to hold the previous drop's location.

In the GameScene.swift file, add the following new property:

```
var prevDropLocation: CGFloat = 0.0
```

Next. locate the spawnGloop() method and change the randomX property from a *constant* (let) to a *variable* (var). In other words, change this line:

```
let randomX = CGFloat.random(in:
                    dropRange.lowerLimit...dropRange.upperLimit)
```

to this:

```
var randomX = CGFloat.random(in:
                    dropRange.lowerLimit...dropRange.upperLimit)
```

You need to switch randomX from a constant to a variable because you'll be changing its value based on the previous drop location, and you can't change the value of a constant once it's been set.

Below the line you just modified, add the following code:

```
/* START ENHANCED DROP MOVEMENT
 this helps to create a "snake-like" pattern */

// Set a range
let randomModifier = SKRange(lowerLimit: 50 + CGFloat(level),
                             upperLimit: 60 * CGFloat(level))
var modifier = CGFloat.random(in:
                  randomModifier.lowerLimit...randomModifier.upperLimit)
if modifier > 400 { modifier = 400 }

// Set the previous drop location
if prevDropLocation == 0.0 {
  prevDropLocation = randomX
}

// Clamp its x-position
if prevDropLocation < randomX {
  randomX = prevDropLocation + modifier
} else {
  randomX = prevDropLocation - modifier
}

// Make sure the collectible stays within the frame
if randomX <= (frame.minX + margin) {
  randomX = frame.minX + margin
} else if randomX >= (frame.maxX - margin) {
  randomX = frame.maxX - margin
}

// Store the location
prevDropLocation = randomX

/* END ENHANCED DROP MOVEMENT */
```

A lot of stuff is going on with this code, but it's not as complicated as it may seem. Essentially, what you're doing here is clamping (restricting) the randomness to keep the drops within a certain range of each other, while also keeping them within the scene's visible frame.

Build and run the project and notice how much smoother the drop pattern is and how it now follows a snake-like pattern.

Adding Numbers to the Drops

Another nice tweak for the drop pattern is to add the current number of the drop. For that, you'll add a child label node to the drop sprite node.

Still inside the spawnGloop() method, and below the line that reads /* END ENHANCED DROP MOVEMENT */, add the following code:

```
// Add the number tag to the collectible drop
let xLabel = SKLabelNode()
xLabel.name = "dropNumber"
xLabel.fontName = "AvenirNext-DemiBold"
xLabel.fontColor = UIColor.yellow
xLabel.fontSize = 22.0
xLabel.text = "\(numberOfDrops)"
xLabel.position = CGPoint(x: 0, y: 2)
collectible.addChild(xLabel)
numberOfDrops -= 1 // decrease drop count by 1
```

When you add a child node, keep in mind that its position is relative to its parent, which is why you're using xLabel.position = CGPoint(x: 0, y: 2). This position places the label node in the center and slightly above its parent.

Build and run the project again and you'll see little yellow labels above each drop. Watch as they count down to 1.

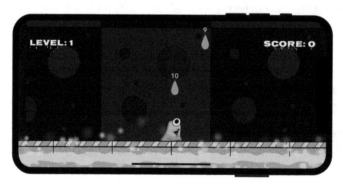

Tweaking the Catch Routine

Those labels above the drops look really neat, don't they? Let's also add a label node above the player sprite node. This label node will show up when the player catches a drop, but you won't add it as a child node of the player sprite node. Instead, you'll add it directly to the scene.

In the GameScene.swift file, locate the didBegin(_:) method. After the line that reads checkForRemainingDrops(), add the following code:

```
// Add the 'chomp' text at the player's position
let chomp = SKLabelNode(fontNamed: "Nosifer")
chomp.name = "chomp"
chomp.alpha = 0.0
chomp.fontSize = 22.0
chomp.text = "gloop"
```

```
chomp.horizontalAlignmentMode = .center
chomp.verticalAlignmentMode = .bottom
chomp.position = CGPoint(x: player.position.x, y: player.frame.maxY + 25)
chomp.zRotation = CGFloat.random(in: -0.15...0.15)
addChild(chomp)

// Add actions to fade in, rise up, and fade out
let fadeIn = SKAction.fadeAlpha(to: 1.0, duration: 0.05)
let fadeOut = SKAction.fadeAlpha(to: 0.0, duration: 0.45)
let moveUp = SKAction.moveBy(x: 0.0, y: 45, duration: 0.45)
let groupAction = SKAction.group([fadeOut, moveUp])
let removeFromParent = SKAction.removeFromParent()
let chompAction = SKAction.sequence([fadeIn, groupAction, removeFromParent])
chomp.run(chompAction)
```

This code creates a label node and then runs some actions to fade in the label, move it upward, and then fade it out. Alternatively, you could have created a new method with this code and then called that new method.

Build and run the project and watch as little labels that read "gloop" appear and disappear as you catch the drops.

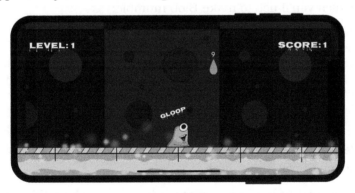

Tweaking the Miss Routine

Have you noticed that when you miss a drop, its landing feels a little stiff? Let's tweak the miss routine to give the drops a little squishiness when they hit the platform.

Open the Collectible.swift file and update the missed() method to match this:

```
func missed() {
  let move = SKAction.moveBy(x: 0, y: -size.height/1.5, duration: 0.0)
  let splatX = SKAction.scaleX(to: 1.5, duration: 0.0) // make wider
  let splatY = SKAction.scaleY(to: 0.5, duration: 0.0) // make shorter

  let actionGroup = SKAction.group([playMissSound, move, splatX, splatY])
  self.run(actionGroup)
}
```

This code uses two scale actions to squish the sprite node, giving it a more realistic appearance when it hits the platform.

Making Blob Mumble

You're getting down to the wire now. Let's give Blob some personality and make him randomly mumble.

Open the Player.swift file, and above the walk() method, add the following new method, which you'll use to make Blob mumble:

```
func mumble() {
  let random = Int.random(in: 1...3)
  let playSound = SKAction.playSoundFileNamed("blob_mumble-\(random)",
                                    waitForCompletion: true)
  self.run(playSound, withKey: "mumble")
}
```

This code uses a random number between 1 and 3 to load one of the blob_mumble-?.wav audio files, where ? represents the number 1, 2, or 3. It then uses an action to play the sound.

With the new method in place, you're ready to use it. Open the GameScene.swift file and locate the spawnMultipleGloops() method. Above the line that reads player.walk(), add the following line of code that calls the newly created method:

```
player.mumble()
```

Build and run the project—and let's get ready to mumble. (I hope you read that in your best announcer voice.)

Adding the Banner

Your main game scene is just about complete, but it's missing something: a banner with the game's name.

Select the Assets.xcassets asset catalog and drag the three files, banner@1x.png, banner@2x.png, and banner@3x.png from the resources/Images folder into the root of the Assets.xcassets asset catalog to create a banner image set, which you'll use for the banner.

Now, open the GameScene.swift file and locate the didMove(to:) method. Below the line that reads addChild(foreground), add the following code to get the banner added to the scene:

```
// Set up the banner
let banner = SKSpriteNode(imageNamed: "banner")
banner.zPosition = Layer.background.rawValue + 1
banner.position = CGPoint(x: frame.midX, y: viewTop() - 20)
banner.anchorPoint = CGPoint(x: 0.5, y: 1.0)
addChild(banner)
```

Build and run the project and you'll see the new banner located at the top of the screen in the center.

Making the Drops Radioactive

The SKEffectNode is a class not many SpriteKit developers use. While this class can render its children into a separate buffer and apply some elegant node effects using *Core Image* filters, the rumors about its poor performance, coupled with its complexity, keep some developers from using it. For these reasons, you won't spend too much time learning about SKEffectNode objects in this book.

Open the Collectible.swift file, and at the end of the init(collectibleType:) method, add the following code:

```
// Add glow effect
let effectNode = SKEffectNode()
effectNode.shouldRasterize = true
addChild(effectNode)
effectNode.addChild(SKSpriteNode(texture: texture))
effectNode.filter = CIFilter(name: "CIGaussianBlur",
                             parameters: ["inputRadius":40.0])
```

This code creates an SKEffectNode object and sets its shouldRasterize property to true. When you set this property to true, you generally gain a bump in performance as it caches the filtered image; however, with a cached image, you'll use more memory and take a hit with the initial render time. You then add the new effect node to the collectible sprite. But because effect nodes operate on their child nodes, you also need to create a new sprite node on which to apply the effects—in this case, the CIGaussianBlur effect.

Build and run the project and you will see a faint glow around the top of each drop.

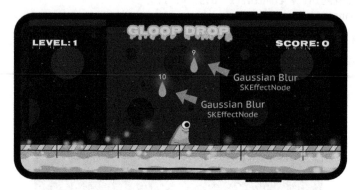

This was just a small taste of what effect nodes can accomplish. For more information on the SKEffectNode class,[2] the CIFilter class,[3] and Core Image,[4] refer to Apple's online documentation.

Challenge Project

You've come along way since starting this book. You learned how to create scenes using different types of nodes. You added actions to these nodes to make them come alive. You played with physics and collision detection. And you even added some neat audiovisual effects. You're now ready to take what you've learned and give it a go on your own.

Included with this chapter in the challenge folder are a few resources and a completed "challenge" project. Your task is to add the additional resources, add a new particle effect, and set up an action that makes a little spaceship with a robot in it fly across the scene at random intervals. You'll also add a little something to the player node to make it easier to move and see Blob.

---

2.   https://developer.apple.com/documentation/spritekit/skeffectnode
3.   https://developer.apple.com/documentation/coreimage/cifilter
4.   https://developer.apple.com/documentation/coreimage

Try to do this challenge on your own. If you get stuck, review the completed challenge project for help. You can also use the completed project to compare your solution. When you're done, you'll end up with something like this:

The challenge resources also include a challenge.md file that provides step-by-step instructions.

Next Steps

In this chapter, you learned what game juice is and how you can *juice* your game by adding tweaks to its audio and visual effects. You started by playing incidental sound effects using actions. Then you quickly skilled up and built a more robust sound system using the SKAudioNode and AVFoundation classes to play background music and ambient sound. You also dipped a toe into the power of the SKEffectNode class and the SpriteKit Particle System to squeeze a little more juice out of your game.

For now, you'll take a break from Gloop Drop as you work through the next part of the book, where you'll level up your spectacular SpriteKit skills and build your first scene with the SpriteKit Scene Editor.

Part II

Use the Scene Editor to Build Games

Discover the benefits of using the Scene Editor by building Val's Revenge, a game that shares similar gameplay to Gauntlet, another classic arcade game by Atari Games.

In Val's Revenge, you control the main character, Val, as she works her way through each dungeon level looking for a way out while also avoiding the beasts who roam the floors.

CHAPTER 7

Building Scenes with the Scene Editor

Now that you know how to build SpriteKit games programmatically, you're ready to learn how to make games using the *Scene Editor*, Xcode's powerful visual editor for creating scenes. While it's possible to create your entire game in code, having access to a visual editor can help speed up your game's development time.

With the Scene Editor, not only can you create your game scenes visually, but you can also reuse and share these scenes throughout your game by using *reference nodes*. You'll learn more about reference nodes in Use Reference Nodes in Your Scene, on page 181, but for now, imagine you have an enemy monster or a *heads-up-display (HUD)* that you want to share across multiple levels. (A HUD is a transparent or semi-transparent overlay that provides information to the players, such as their score or health stats.) With reference nodes, you can do that.

In this chapter, you'll step away from Gloop Drop, the game you built in Part I, Build Your First Game with SpriteKit, on page 1, and you'll focus on creating another game: *Val's Revenge*. The image on page 144 is a preview of the new game you'll be building.

Val's Revenge is a game that shares similar gameplay to that of *Gauntlet*, another popular arcade game from Atari. Recreating this 1985 classic hack and slash dungeon crawl makes for the perfect pairing of fun while learning your way around the Scene Editor. So, what are you waiting for? Let's head into the dungeon.

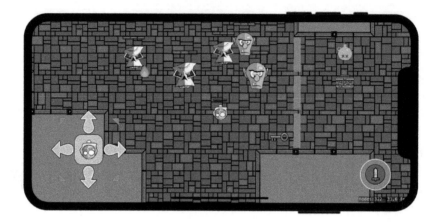

Create the Project

Before you can jump into the fun of building scenes with the Scene Editor, you need to create a new project. Launch Xcode and create a new project using the iOS Game template, like so:

For the Product Name, enter valsrevenge. Set the Team, Organization Name, and Organization Identifier to match your Apple developer information.

Set the Language to Swift and the Game Technology to SpriteKit.

Be sure to enable the option to Integrate GameplayKit, which gives you access to the APIs you'll use in this project.

Finally, disable both the Include Unit Tests and Include UI Tests options if you're on Xcode 11, or the Include Tests option if you're on Xcode 12; either way, you won't be running tests on this project, so you can disable those options.

When you're done entering all of the information, click Next.

Choose your save location and verify that the Create Git repository on my Mac option is not enabled.

Once you confirm all of the information, click Create to create the new project. If you need additional information about this process, see Create the Project, on page 3 for more details.

With the new project ready and waiting, it's time to clean up the default template by removing the code and objects you won't be using in Val's Revenge.

Clean Up the Default Template

Switch to the GameScene.swift file and remove the label and spinnyNode properties; you won't be using these. Leave the remaining properties as they are.

Next, remove all of the code in the sceneDidLoad() method, leaving only the line that reads self.lastUpdateTime = 0; you'll be using that property later.

Finally, clean up the touch event functions:

- Locate and remove all of the code in the touchDown(atPoint:), touchMoved(toPoint:), and touchUp(atPoint:) methods.

- Remove the if statement inside the touchesBegan(_:with:) method.

In Clean Up the Default Template, on page 8, you removed the Actions.sks and GameScene.sks files; however, with this project, you'll be using the GameScene.sks file, so don't delete it; instead, delete (move to trash) only the Actions.sks file.

Xcode 12 and Universal Screen-Size Support

At the time of this writing, it looks as if some key settings that enable universal support are not set when using Xcode 12. If you're using Xcode 12, you'll need to add a plist entry for Launch screen interface file base name. You can either add this entry and set its value to Main or create a custom LaunchScreen.storyboard file and set its value to LaunchScreen instead.

Xcode 12 and Universal Screen-Size Support

Alternatively, you can set this option using the drop-down list in the App Icons and Launch Images section of the General tab of the target settings. Either way, you must use an Xcode storyboard to provide a launch screen if you intend to accommodate different screen sizes. Xcode 11 automatically sets this option for you.

Now that you have the project cleaned up and the unnecessary boilerplate code cleared out, the next step is to add the assets.

Add the Assets

As you learned in Add Image Assets, on page 17, the best place to store your image assets is in the asset catalog; this is true even when building scenes with the Scene Editor.

In the Project Navigator, select the Assets.xcassets file.

Now, open Finder and drag the three files from the resources/grass/ folder into the root view of Assets.xcassets, like so:

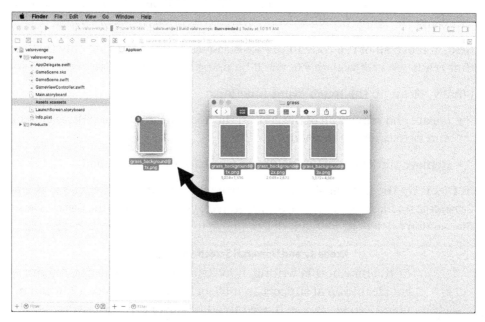

Next, create a new sprite atlas and name it player_val. While you're here, create another new sprite atlas and name this second one controller. Remove the default Sprite image sets from each atlas.

Once again, open Finder. This time, drag all of the files from the player_val and controller folders into their respective sprite atlases. When you're done, your asset catalog will look like this:

With the image assets added, it's time to start building out your first scene using the Scene Editor and the *Object Library*. You'll be using the Object Library to create and manage nodes and other content related to your scene.

Add Nodes Using the Object Library

In Add the Background, on page 19, you added a background image to the game scene by creating a new background sprite node. You then added that node as a child node of the game scene; you did all of that in code.

However, this time around, you'll create and add a background node to the node tree using the Object Library, and you'll set its options using the Attributes Inspector. But first, it's time for a quick tour.

Touring the Scene Editor

From within the Project Navigator, select the GameScene.sks file. Files with the .sks file extension are known as SpriteKit scene files. This particular scene file is what gets loaded from the GameViewController.swift file. You'll learn more about how that works in Configure the View and Load the Scene, on page 157.

When you select the GameScene.sks file, it opens in the Scene Editor and looks something like the image on page 148.

To see the entire scene, you may need to zoom out depending on the size of your monitor. You can control the zoom level in a few ways: from Xcode's App menu, select Editor ▶ Zoom In or Editor ▶ Zoom Out; you can also use the hotkeys, ⌘+ and ⌘-. Alternatively, you can use the + and - buttons, located near the bottom-right corner of the main editor window.

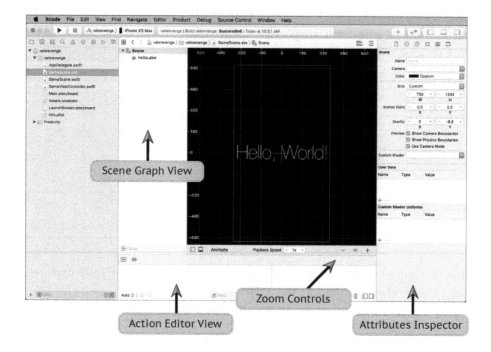

Scene Graph View

Action Editor View

Zoom Controls

Attributes Inspector

The Scene Editor includes the *Scene Graph View* where you can see all of the objects within the scene—essentially, this is where you'll find the node tree. The *Action Editor View* is where you can set up actions and animations, and of course, the various inspectors are off to the right, including the Attributes Inspector, which is where you'll spend most of your time building your scenes and setting up your nodes' properties.

As you work with different nodes, the Attributes Inspector will change accordingly. For example, see the image on page 149 for three types of nodes and their corresponding attributes.

Take a few minutes to look around.

Now that you know the lay of the land, so to speak, it's time to get building.

Adjusting the Scene Size

The first thing you can do is remove the helloLabel node since you won't be using it in Val's Revenge. From the Scene Graph View, select the helloLabel node and either right-click on the node and select Delete, or press the delete key on your keyboard.

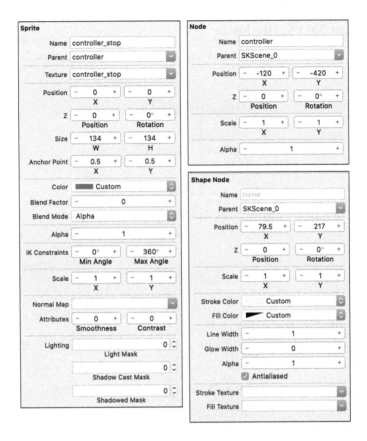

Next, you'll change the size of the scene. For Gloop Drop, you set the scene size through code; however, you can set the size right here because you're using the Scene Editor to build this scene.

With the Scene selected, look at the Attributes Inspector. Notice the scene's size is set to 750 × 1334 (width × height); this is the default scene size and represents the iPhone 8's native display size.

Unlike Gloop Drop, which is designed to support landscape orientation only, Val's Revenge is designed to support both landscape and portrait orientations, with a focus on portrait mode. You'll learn more about that in Add Support for All Devices and Orientations, on page 184, but for now, change the scene size to 1024 × 1336.

You're ready to add your first sprite node.

Adding Your First Sprite Node

Click the + button to open the Object Library; you'll find that button in the top-right corner of the editor:

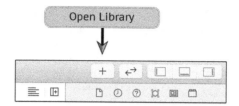

When you click the + button, the following window appears:

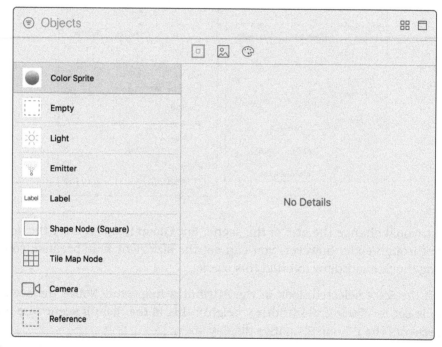

This is the library. More specifically, the Object Library, which is the interface you'll use to add new nodes and other scene-related content to the scene. You can also access the Media Library and the Color Library using the same + button.

The Case of the Disappearing Window

Have you noticed that the library window isn't docked or persistent? To keep the library open in a persistent window, hold down the ⌥ key as you click the + button.

For the background sprite node, you'll add a new Color Sprite object. Drag the Color Sprite object from the library onto the scene (don't worry about placement, just drag it anywhere onto the scene), like so:

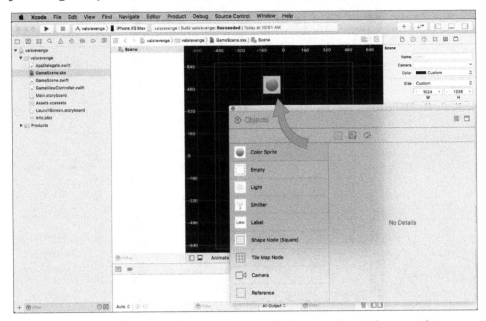

When you let go, you'll end up with a red square somewhere within your scene, like this:

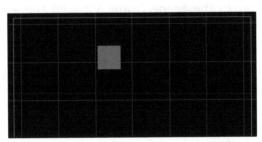

You'll also see the new SKSpriteNode in the Scene Graph View. You can either select the sprite node from the Scene Graph View or single-click the red square to select it. Now, shift your eyes to the Attributes Inspector; it's here where you can set nearly all of the same options for your nodes that you set in code. For example, you can set its texture, position, size, and more.

Let's give it a try.

In the Attributes Inspector, you'll see a Name field. In this field, enter background and press return. While you're here, also set the Texture to grass_background and the Position to X: 0, Y: 0; leave the other settings as they are.

If everything works as expected, your editor will show you something like this:

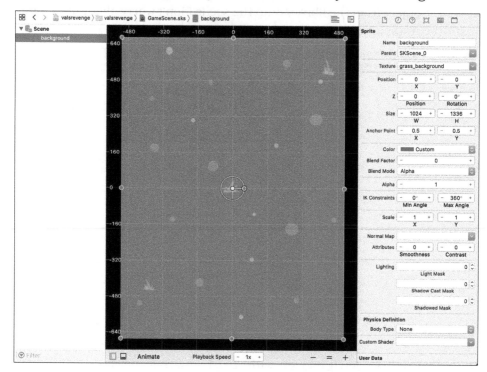

Shift your eyes over to the Scene Graph View on the left. Notice how the SKSpriteNode now reads background and shows a small image representing the node's grass texture.

If you were to do this same thing in code, you might have done something like this:

```
// Set up background
let background = SKSpriteNode(imageNamed: "grass_background")
background.name = "background"
background.position = CGPoint(x: 0, y: 0)
addChild(background)
```

Although using the Scene Editor gives you roughly the same results, it's important to understand that using the Scene Editor doesn't actually create any code for you; it's just another way to build scenes and interact with the SpriteKit framework.

It's time to test your scene. Switch the active scheme destination to the iPhone 11 Pro Max. Then, build and run the project as shown in the image on page 153.

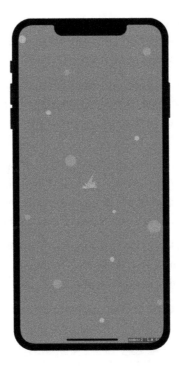

Fantastic, you now have the greenest grass in the neighborhood, but it's looking a little bare. Let's add some lawn ornaments. No, not really, but you can add a few more nodes to the scene.

Adding Other Nodes

Before you start adding more nodes to the scene, lock the background node. To lock a node, select it in the Scene Graph View and either right-click and select Locked from the context menu, or click the little lock icon to the right of the text, like so:

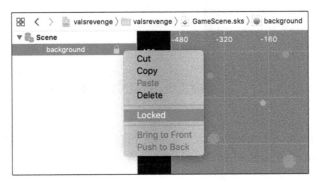

Locking nodes is a great way to prevent unintentional changes to a node; this is especially useful when dealing with the background node, which tends to get in the way when you're clicking around the scene.

With the background node locked, you're ready to add another Color Sprite. This time, set the new node's Name, Texture, and Position to player, player-val-head_0, and X: 0, Y: 0, respectively. This new sprite represents Val, the main character in Val's Revenge.

Next, you'll build the on-screen directional pad (D-pad) controller. This controller is what the player will use to move Val around the scene. Add another object, but this time instead of adding a Color Sprite, add an Empty object. When you drop it on the scene, you'll see it listed as an SKNode in the node tree.

Select the SKNode in the Scene Graph View and set its Name to controller and its Position to X: -120, Y: -420. You'll use this new, empty node as a container to hold the sprite nodes that make up the D-pad.

Return to the Object Library and drag five Color Sprite objects into the controller node, like so:

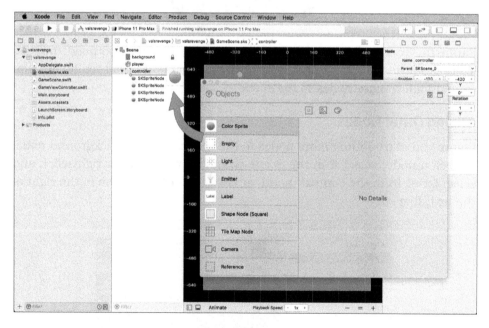

Set the properties of the five SKSpriteNode objects as shown in the image on page 155, from top to bottom.

Name	Position (X, Y)
controller_stop	0, 0
controller_left	-120, 0
controller_right	120, 0
controller_up	0, 120
controller_down	0, -120

Now, set the Texture for the controller_stop node to controller_stop; set the textures of the remaining nodes inside the controller node to controller_arrow_lg. You can multi-select the remaining nodes to make it easier.

If you think something looks a little off, you're right. All the arrows are pointing in the same direction:

This shouldn't be a surprise because you're using the same image asset for all four arrow nodes. While this helps you save on system resources, you need to rotate some of these nodes to make them look right.

Starting with the controller_right node, set the Rotation to 180°; you'll find this setting in the Attributes Inspector. Move down to the controller_up node and set its Rotation to 270°. Finally, select the controller_down node and set its Rotation to 90°. The nice thing about using the Scene Editor for this is that you don't need to worry about converting degrees to radians like you do when setting the zRotation property directly in code.

All right, you're almost done setting up the scene. Add another Color Sprite, but do *not* place it inside the controller node. Instead, drag it anywhere onto the scene. Alternatively, you can drag it directly to the Scene Graph View, placing it either above or below (but not inside) the controller node. Once you have the new Color Sprite added to the scene, set the following options in the Attributes Inspector:

- Name: button_attack
- Texture: button_attack
- Position: X: 200, Y: -420

Build and run the project.

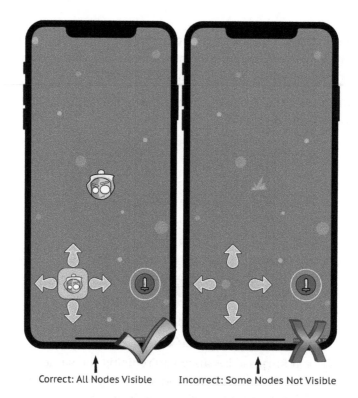

Correct: All Nodes Visible   Incorrect: Some Nodes Not Visible

Does your scene look like the one pictured on the left or on the right? Are you missing some sprite nodes? Maybe you don't see the player or part of the controller? Perhaps the Attack button is missing?

(If your scene matches the image on the left, consider yourself lucky—but understand that you can't rely on luck when it comes to scene rendering.)

The problem here is that all of the nodes share the same zPosition value, in this case, 0. Remember, you first learned about the zPosition property in Control Render Order with Z-Position, on page 37.

When multiple nodes share the same zPosition, the render order is arbitrary and can change with each launch, which means you have two choices: set all of the z-positions for all of the nodes or change the setting on the view that tells SpriteKit to ignore the sibling order.

While it's possible to set a node's z-position using the Scene Editor, for now, you'll change the view's configuration instead, and you'll do it right before loading the scene.

Configure the View and Load the Scene

In the Project Navigator, select the GameViewController.swift file to open it in the Source Editor. Locate and review the viewDidLoad() method. It looks like this:

```
override func viewDidLoad() {
  super.viewDidLoad()

  // Load 'GameScene.sks' as a GKScene. This provides gameplay-related content
  // including entities and graphs
  if let scene = GKScene(fileNamed: "GameScene") {

    // Get the SKScene from the loaded GKScene
    if let sceneNode = scene.rootNode as! GameScene? {

      // Copy gameplay-related content over to the scene
      sceneNode.entities = scene.entities
      sceneNode.graphs = scene.graphs

      // Set the scale mode to scale to fit the window
      sceneNode.scaleMode = .aspectFill

      // Present the scene
      if let view = self.view as! SKView? {
        view.presentScene(sceneNode)

        view.ignoresSiblingOrder = true

        view.showsFPS = true
        view.showsNodeCount = true
      }
    }
  }
}
```

Some of this code in this method may look a little familiar, such as the line that reads view.ignoresSiblingOrder = true. This code is what dictates, in part, how the scene renders. Change that line to read:

```
view.ignoresSiblingOrder = false
```

By setting this property to false, each node's render order within the scene won't be arbitrary anymore; instead, the scene will render its nodes in the order in which they appear in the node tree. In this case:

- background

- player

- controller, along with its five children: controller_stop, controller_left, controller_right, controller_up, and controller_down

- button_attack

While you were updating the viewDidLoad() method, did you happen to notice this code:

```
if let scene = GKScene(fileNamed: "GameScene")
```

which is sort of equivalent to this (something you saw earlier in the book):

```
if let scene = SKScene(fileNamed: "GameScene")
```

The only difference is that the first example uses a GKScene object rather than an SKScene object, which is what you used for Gloop Drop.

If you recall, in Create Your First SpriteKit Scene, on page 13, you were creating the GameScene like this:

```
// Create the view
if let view = self.view as! SKView? {

  // Create the scene
  let scene = GameScene(size: view.bounds.size)

  // Set the scale mode to scale to fill the view window
  scene.scaleMode = .aspectFill

  // Set the background color
  scene.backgroundColor =  UIColor(red: 105/255,
                                   green: 157/255,
                                   blue: 181/255,
                                   alpha: 1.0)

  // Present the scene
  view.presentScene(scene)

  // Set the view options
  view.ignoresSiblingOrder = false
  view.showsPhysics = false
  view.showsFPS = true
  view.showsNodeCount = true
}
```

For Val's Revenge, you'll be using more GameplayKit features, so it makes sense to use the GKScene object instead. You'll learn more about GameplayKit and the GKScene class in Part III, Scale Your Games with GameplayKit, on page 225.

There's one more thing: the fileNamed parameter is stuffed with the name (minus the extension, .sks) of the scene you just built:

```
if let scene = GKScene(fileNamed: "GameScene")
```

As you might have guessed, this parameter is how you load the scene using a scene file.

Build and run the project—multiple times—and you'll see all of your nodes, every time.

Next Steps

In this chapter, you got your feet wet with the Scene Editor. You added a few nodes and set their properties using the Attributes Inspector. You also modified the view and corresponding code that loads the scene, so now you're able to render content predictably. In the next chapter, you'll keep working on Val's Revenge as you begin to work with the physics engine in the Scene Editor while building out the controller that moves the player.

CHAPTER 8

Using the Scene Editor to Add Physics

In the previous chapter, you started building your first scene with the Scene Editor. You learned how to add nodes and set up their properties using the Attributes Inspector. During this process, you added the background node, the player node, and several other nodes that make up the D-pad controller and the Attack button.

But using the Scene Editor doesn't mean you get to ignore the code part of game development. You still need to write the code that drives the logic of your game.

In this chapter, you'll concentrate on building out the functionality and movement of the player. As you work through this chapter, you'll learn how to set up physics using the Scene Editor and how to connect your code with the scenes you create. By the end, you'll be able to move the player around the scene and launch a fierce attack thanks to your epic coding skills.

Write Code to Interface with the Scene

In Configure the View and Load the Scene, on page 157, you learned how to load a scene file through code. If you recall, loading a scene file takes place in the viewDidLoad() method of the GameViewController.swift file and looks like this:

```
if let scene = GKScene(fileNamed: "GameScene")
```

But loading the scene is only half of the story—you still need to write the code that interfaces with the objects within the scene, for example, the player node. In this section, you'll concentrate on making that connection.

To begin, open the valsrevenge project in Xcode.

Using the Starter Project

You may continue using your project from the previous chapter, or you can use the starter project located in the projects/begin folder included with the code resources for this chapter. Either option is fine; the only benefit to using the starter project is that you won't get stuck going forward if you missed an earlier step.

There's also an ending project for this chapter that includes all of the code and resources you'll be adding here. The end project is located in the projects/end folder included with the code resources for this chapter.

Creating the Player Class

The goal here is to hook up the player node and the controller nodes and get the player moving around using the D-pad. Rather than place this code into the GameScene.swift file, you'll create a separate file to hold the Player class. If you need a refresher on how to create files in Xcode, refer to Create the Player Class, on page 32, otherwise, create a new Swift file, name it Player.swift, and add the following code to set up the class and the two main method stubs:

```
import SpriteKit

enum Direction: String {
  case stop
  case left
  case right
  case up
  case down
}

class Player: SKSpriteNode {
  func move(_ direction: Direction) {
    print("move player: \(direction.rawValue)")
  }
  func stop() {
    print("stop player")
  }
}
```

This code sets up an enum that holds the different directions the player can move. It also sets up the Player class and two stub methods: one to move the player and one to stop the player.

Now that you've got the Player class set up, you need a way to connect this class to the player sprite node you added to the scene in Adding Other Nodes, on page 153.

Using a Custom Class in the Scene Editor

Return to the GameScene.sks file. Select the player node and switch to the Custom Class Inspector—it's the second inspector from the right.

Notice how the Custom Class defaults to the standard SKSpriteNode class. Instead of using that class, you'll use the new custom Player class you just created. To make the switch, enter Player into the Custom Class field, like so:

With the player node now using the custom Player class, you're ready to write the code that connects the nodes in your scene to the properties and objects you create in your code.

Finding the Player Node from the Game Scene

In Use Attributed Strings with Labels, on page 109, you saw how you can use the childNode(withName:) method to check for a node with a matching name. Once again, you'll use that method to locate the player node.

In the Project Navigator, select the GameScene.swift file to open it in the Source Editor.

First, add a new property for the player node:

```
private var player: Player?
```

Next, add an override for the didMove(to:) method, and inside that method, place the following code to initialize the new property (add it below the sceneDidLoad() method):

```
override func didMove(to view: SKView) {
  player = childNode(withName: "player") as? Player
  player?.move(.stop)
}
```

If you recall, the last time you used the childNode(withName:) method, you did so using an *advanced search*. This time, however, you do a *simple search* that looks for any node that has the name player—and exists as a direct child of (in this case) the Scene node. Alternatively, you can use the class name instead, like this:

```
player = childNode(withName: "Player") as? Player
```

Either way, the search finds and returns the player node you added in the GameScene.sks file. For more information about the different types of search options, refer to Searching the Node Tree[1] in Apple's documentation.

Build and run the project. Look at the console and you'll see the "move player: stop" statement:

Excellent. Your player sprite is recognized in your code, and you're ready to implement the controller movement. For that, you'll use the physics engine.

Add Physics to the Player

You can move players (and enemies) around the scene in many ways. In Gloop Drop, you used actions. In Val's Revenge, you'll use the physics engine to move Val, the main character of the game. But before you can do that, you first have to set up a physics body for the player sprite node.

In Chapter 4, Working with Physics and Collision Detection, on page 69, you learned the ins and outs of using the physics engine, including how to write code to set up the different physics bodies and properties. Now it's time to learn how to set up physics using the Scene Editor.

Open the GameScene.sks file and select the player sprite node. Look at the Attributes Inspector and scroll down to the Physics Definition section. Switch the Body Type from None to Bounding Circle. Notice the blue outline around the player sprite (enhanced here, for clarity) and the different options available in the inspector for this physics body as shown in the image on page 165.

For the most part, these settings are a 1:1 match to the properties you can access in code. For example, Dynamic is a match for physicsBody?.isDynamic and Allows Rotation is a match for physicsBody?.allowsRotation.

Also, the blue outline that represents the physics body doesn't exactly include the entire sprite; that's okay, though, because it covers enough of the sprite that it won't make too much of a difference during actual gameplay.

---

1. https://developer.apple.com/documentation/spritekit/sknode/searching_the_node_tree

Physics Body

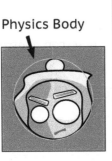

For the player node, you need to make several changes:

Disable (deselect) the Allows Rotation and Affected By Gravity options; you don't want the player sprite to rotate or fall away into nothingness.

Also, set the Friction, Restitution, Lin. Damping, and Ang. Damping to 0; movement should be smooth and consistent.

Finally, set the Category Mask to 1, the Collision Mask to 0, the Field Mask to 0, and the Contact Mask to 0; you'll return to some of these settings later, but for now, these will do.

You learned about most of these properties and settings in A Closer Look at Physics Bodies, on page 73. However, if you're curious about why the mask values are set to 4294967295—the default value in the Scene Editor—this max value indicates that the physics body will interact with *every* physics body within the scene.

Setting the Preview Options for the Scene

 If you don't see the blue outline of the physics body in the Scene Editor, check your scene's preview settings. Select the Scene node in the Scene Graph View, and in the Attributes Inspector, verify that the Show Physics Boundaries option is enabled.

Now that you have the player node's physics body set up, you're ready to hook up the on-screen controller.

Move the Player Using Physics

Using physics to move bodies is a quick and effective way to build a controller. To move the player using physics and the on-screen controller, you need to act on certain touch events.

Open the GameScene.swift file and update the touchDown(:atPoint) method:

```
func touchDown(atPoint pos : CGPoint) {
  let nodeAtPoint = atPoint(pos)
  if let touchedNode = nodeAtPoint as? SKSpriteNode {
    if touchedNode.name?.starts(with: "controller_") == true {
      let direction = touchedNode.name?.replacingOccurrences(
        of: "controller_", with: "")
      player?.move(Direction(rawValue: direction ?? "stop")!)
    }
  }
}
```

Here, you're checking to see which node was touched using the prefix of the node's name as a filter. You're then calling the move(_:) method on the player node and passing in the direction that matches the text after the "_" character in the node's name, for example, "left" or "right."

At the moment, though, the move(_:) method in the Player class doesn't do much, so you'll need to fix that. You'll also need to update the stop() method. Open the Player.swift file and update both the move(_:) and stop() methods, like so:

```
func move(_ direction: Direction) {
  print("move player: \(direction.rawValue)")
  switch direction {
  case .up:
    self.physicsBody?.velocity = CGVector(dx: 0, dy: 100)
    //self.physicsBody?.applyImpulse(CGVector(dx: 0, dy: 100))
    //self.physicsBody?.applyForce(CGVector(dx: 0, dy: 100))
  case .down:
    self.physicsBody?.velocity = CGVector(dx: 0, dy: -100)
  case .left:
    self.physicsBody?.velocity = CGVector(dx: -100, dy: 0)
  case .right:
    self.physicsBody?.velocity = CGVector(dx: 100, dy: 0)
  case .stop:
    stop()
  }
}
func stop() {
  self.physicsBody?.velocity = CGVector(dx: 0, dy: 0)
}
```

With this code, you're using the physicsBody?.velocity property to move the player in the direction indicated in the direction parameter. In the case of stopping the player, the stop() method stops all motion by setting the velocity back to 0 in all directions.

Build and run the project. Notice how the player moves around when you tap the controller. If you tap any of the arrows, the player is sent in that direction; if you tap the center of the controller, the player stops.

Using the player's velocity, the movement is smooth and consistent. But what if you wanted something a little different? Maybe you're building a game that includes a rocket ship with thrusters? For that, you might want a burst of energy with a gradual slow down.

If you look at the code you just added, you'll see two lines are commented out:

```
//self.physicsBody?.applyImpulse(CGVector(dx: 0, dy: 100))
//self.physicsBody?.applyForce(CGVector(dx: 0, dy: 100))
```

Uncomment each of those lines (one at a time) to see how force and impulse work differently; just don't forget to comment them out again when you're done playing around.

You now have a semi-decent working controller, but it does have a slight problem. Well, two problems, which you're about to address.

Making a Better Controller

You almost have the perfect-working controller. The problem, however, is that when you lift your finger from the screen (and stop touching the arrows), the player continues to move.

Sure, you could just get the player to stop moving by touching the center area of the controller, but that's not a great gameplay experience or very intuitive. A better solution is to make the player stop the moment you stop touching the screen.

In the Project Navigator, select the GameScene.swift file and modify the touchUp(atPoint:) method to match this:

```
func touchUp(atPoint pos : CGPoint) {
  let nodeAtPoint = atPoint(pos)
  if let touchedNode = nodeAtPoint as? SKSpriteNode {
    if touchedNode.name?.starts(with: "controller_") == true {
      player?.stop()
    }
  }
}
```

Build and run the project. This time the player stops when you stop touching the arrows. That's great, but there's still another problem: if you drag your finger over to another arrow, the player doesn't change directions. You can fix this by modifying the touchMoved(:toPoint) method, like this:

```
func touchMoved(toPoint pos : CGPoint) {
  let nodeAtPoint = atPoint(pos)
  if let touchedNode = nodeAtPoint as? SKSpriteNode {
    if touchedNode.name?.starts(with: "controller_") == true {
      let direction = touchedNode.name?.replacingOccurrences(
        of: "controller_", with: "")
      player?.move(Direction(rawValue: direction ?? "stop")!)
    }
  }
}
```

Build and run the project again. The player now moves continuously in all four directions, switching when necessary, and then stops when you lift your finger. As an added bonus, you can even do a neat swiping maneuver over the controller to "lock" the player's current direction for continuous movement without needing to hold the direction arrow down.

Your controller is a lot better now, but at the moment, the player can only travel in four directions. For better gameplay and maneuverability, you'll add some diagonal movement, making this an 8-way controller.

Adding Additional Directions

To support an 8-way controller, you'll need to add four new values to the Direction enum. In the Project Navigator, select the Player.swift file and add the following values to the Direction enum:

```
case topLeft
case topRight
case bottomLeft
case bottomRight
```

These new direction options will handle the diagonal movement for the player.

The next step is to update the case statement in the move(_:) method to include these new directions:

```
case .topLeft:
  self.physicsBody?.velocity = CGVector(dx: -100, dy: 100)
case .topRight:
  self.physicsBody?.velocity = CGVector(dx: 100, dy: 100)
case .bottomLeft:
  self.physicsBody?.velocity = CGVector(dx: -100, dy: -100)
case .bottomRight:
  self.physicsBody?.velocity = CGVector(dx: 100, dy: -100)
```

Finally, you need to update the scene to show the diagonal arrows. Switch to the GameScene.sks file and drag four new Color Sprite objects into the controller node. Set all of these new nodes to the same Texture: controller_arrow_sm.

Now, set the following options:

Name	Position (X, Y)	Rotation
controller_topLeft	-100, 100	315°
controller_topRight	100, 100	225°
controller_bottomLeft	-100, -100	45°
controller_bottomRight	100, -100	135°

When you're done, the updated controller and node tree will look like the image on page 170.

Moving the player around the scene in eight different directions is a great way to avoid the in-game monsters, but the object of the game isn't for Val to run away. What she needs is a way to attack.

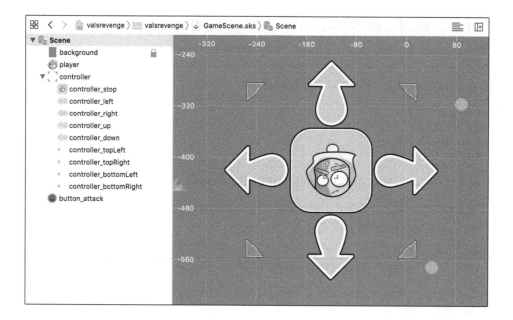

Connect the Attack Button

The last thing you'll do in this chapter is write the code that handles the player's attack routine—in this case, Val's knife throw—which should happen when the player taps the Attack button.

In the Project Navigator, select the GameScene.swift file and modify the touchDown(:_) method to match the following (you'll get a message about the missing attack() method, but for now, ignore the error):

```
func touchDown(atPoint pos : CGPoint) {
  let nodeAtPoint = atPoint(pos)
  if let touchedNode = nodeAtPoint as? SKSpriteNode {
    if touchedNode.name?.starts(with: "controller_") == true {
      let direction = touchedNode.name?.replacingOccurrences(
        of: "controller_", with: "")
      player?.move(Direction(rawValue: direction ?? "stop")!)
    } else if touchedNode.name == "button_attack" {
      player?.attack()
    }
  }
}
```

Once again, you're checking the node name. If it matches button_attack, you're calling the player's attack() method, which you still need to write.

Open the Player.swift file and add the following code:

```
func attack() {
  let projectile = SKSpriteNode(imageNamed: "knife")
  projectile.position = CGPoint(x: 0.0, y: 0.0)
  addChild(projectile)
}
```

This is a good start, but at this point, you have no surefire way (pun intended) to know in which direction the player is currently facing. For that, you can add a new property to the Player class (add it just above the move(_:) method):

```
private var currentDirection = Direction.stop
```

You'll use this new property to store the last known direction of the player. To do that, you need to update the move(_:) method by adding the following code at the end of the method:

```
if direction != .stop {
  currentDirection = direction
}
```

This saves the last known direction of the player, even after the player stops moving.

Finally, go back to the attack() method and update it to match this (the new code is highlighted):

```
    func attack() {
      let projectile = SKSpriteNode(imageNamed: "knife")
      projectile.position = CGPoint(x: 0.0, y: 0.0)
      addChild(projectile)
➤     var throwDirection = CGVector(dx: 0, dy: 0)
➤
➤     switch currentDirection {
➤     case .up:
➤       throwDirection = CGVector(dx: 0, dy: 300)
➤     case .down:
➤       throwDirection = CGVector(dx: 0, dy: -300)
➤     case .left:
➤       throwDirection = CGVector(dx: -300, dy: 0)
➤     case .right, .stop: // default pre-movement (throw right)
➤       throwDirection = CGVector(dx: 300, dy: 0)
➤     case .topLeft:
➤       throwDirection = CGVector(dx: -300, dy: 300)
➤     case .topRight:
➤       throwDirection = CGVector(dx: 300, dy: 300)
➤     case .bottomLeft:
➤       throwDirection = CGVector(dx: -300, dy: -300)
➤     case .bottomRight:
➤       throwDirection = CGVector(dx: 300, dy: -300)
➤     }
```

➤
➤   ```
➤   let throwProjectile = SKAction.move(by: throwDirection, duration: 0.25)
➤   projectile.run(throwProjectile,
➤   completion: {projectile.removeFromParent()})
     }
     ```

Build and run the project. Move the player around in a few different directions and tap the Attack button. Great, the knife travels in the right direction, but it looks a little weird since it's always pointing up.

Val's knife points in the wrong direction

You can fix this visual problem by setting the rotation of the projectile node. Update the case statement in the attack() method to match the following code:

```
switch currentDirection {
case .up:
  throwDirection = CGVector(dx: 0, dy: 300)
  projectile.zRotation = 0
case .down:
  throwDirection = CGVector(dx: 0, dy: -300)
  projectile.zRotation = -CGFloat.pi
case .left:
  throwDirection = CGVector(dx: -300, dy: 0)
  projectile.zRotation = CGFloat.pi/2
case .right, .stop: // default pre-movement (throw right)
  throwDirection = CGVector(dx: 300, dy: 0)
  projectile.zRotation = -CGFloat.pi/2
```
```

```
case .topLeft:
  throwDirection = CGVector(dx: -300, dy: 300)
  projectile.zRotation = CGFloat.pi/4
case .topRight:
  throwDirection = CGVector(dx: 300, dy: 300)
  projectile.zRotation = -CGFloat.pi/4
case .bottomLeft:
  throwDirection = CGVector(dx: -300, dy: -300)
  projectile.zRotation = 3 * CGFloat.pi/4
case .bottomRight:
  throwDirection = CGVector(dx: 300, dy: -300)
  projectile.zRotation = 3 * -CGFloat.pi/4
}
```

Build and run the project again. This time, notice that Val's knife throwing looks more natural than it did before, thanks to the rotation of the knife.

Ah, if only it was that easy to level-up your knife-throwing skills. C'est la vie.

Next Steps

In this chapter, you gave the player the ability to move Val, the main character of the game, using the on-screen D-pad controller. You did this by adding physics to the player node using the Scene Editor, and then connecting that node through code with multiple methods to move and stop the player. You also added code to connect the Attack button, giving Val the ability to defend herself against the enemies you'll soon be adding.

Now that you know your way around the Scene Editor and how it meshes with your code, you'll extend your skills even more.

In the next chapter, you'll spend some time playing with two more useful nodes: camera nodes and reference nodes. Not only will you learn how to make reusable content, but also you'll discover how to follow the player around using a camera node (you may have noticed that if you move the player too far, she disappears). You'll also finish up the work required to make this game look good on all devices in all orientations.

Operating the Camera and Using References Nodes

In the previous two chapters, you spent most of your time in the Scene Editor creating a new world and adding a player to explore it. The trouble is, once that player ventures out too far beyond the edges of the screen, she's gone—poof!

In this chapter, you'll discover how to keep the player visible as she moves around the scene. You might think that using constraints is the way to go, but that limits the area the player can explore. That's not to say you won't use constraints to set a boundary around the edges of the world—you will—but first, you need to find a way that allows the player to roam beyond the viewable display while also keeping her visible at all times.

But that's not all you'll be doing in this chapter. You'll also modify the project so that it supports portrait and landscape orientations across all devices. At the moment, there are a few problems:

- The player sprite appears much larger when you rotate the device.
- The on-screen controls disappear when you rotate the device.
- The on-screen controls show up in different places on different devices.

As you work through this chapter, you'll also discover new ways of structuring your code by taking the existing examples from Gloop Drop and refactoring them for improvement, such as using computed properties rather than full-blown methods to return values. So, what are you waiting for? The show's about to begin.

Add a Camera to Track the Player

Have you ever watched a movie that has a great storyline, but the director, for whatever reason, makes poor camera decisions? Maybe the camera is too close to an actor or object, or perhaps it's too low in the scene. The point is: if a scene isn't shot well, the story could get lost, and the audience might lose interest. Well, the same holds true for game scenes.

Currently, the way the game is set up now, the player can walk right out of the scene, which is not a great "feature" for an exciting new game. To correct this problem, you'll add a camera node to the scene and use the SKCameraNode class to direct it through code.

The SKCameraNode class is another base node that's available in SpriteKit. Because the camera node is simply another type of node, you can set the usual properties like position, scale, and rotation. But to use a camera node, you first need to add it to the scene.

To begin, open the valsrevenge project in Xcode.

Using the Starter Project

You may continue using your project from the previous chapter, or you can use the starter project located in the projects/begin folder included with the code resources for this chapter. Either option is fine; the only benefit to using the starter project is that you won't get stuck going forward if you missed an earlier step.

There's also an ending project for this chapter that includes all of the code and resources you'll be adding here. The end project is located in the projects/end folder included with the code resources for this chapter.

In the Project Navigator, select the GameScene.sks file to open the file in the Scene Editor.

Using the Object Library (⇧⌘L), drag a Camera node into the Scene Graph View, placing it just below the button_attack node, while also taking care not to make it a child of the button, as shown in the image on page 177.

Because you're dragging the object directly into the Scene Graph View, the node's position will already be set to (x: 0, y: 0), saving you an extra step. (If you already dragged the node into the scene, don't worry—you can still set its position using the Attributes Inspector.)

Double-click the SKCameraNode object in the Scene Graph View and change its name to primaryCamera.

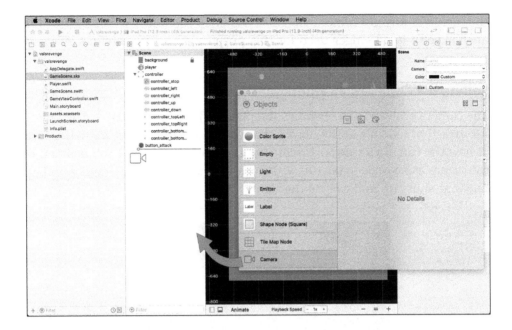

Now that you have the camera added to the scene, the next step is to tell the scene to use it. In the Scene Graph View, select the Scene object and set the Camera field in the Attributes Inspector to primaryCamera, like this:

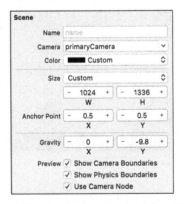

While you're there, look at the Preview section in the Attributes Inspector; this is where you can enable or disable the Show Camera Boundaries option. When this option is enabled, you'll see a thin white line that indicates the scene's visible area—in other words, the camera's *viewport*. You may need to zoom out (⌘-) to see the full scene.

In Set Position, Coordinates, and Anchor Points, on page 20, you saw how a node's anchor point can affect its position by changing its origin. When it comes to the scene, though, its anchor point also controls what's visible on the screen at any given moment. However, once you add a camera node, the anchor point is no longer used for this purpose, and the camera's viewport takes over.

Setting the Camera's Viewport

The camera's viewport determines the player's *field of view (FoV)*. The FoV is the area that's visible to the player at any given moment. To get a better idea of how the camera's viewport relates to the player's FoV, set the position of the primaryCamera node to (x: 100, y: 100), and you'll see a thin white boundary line that shifts up and over to the right:

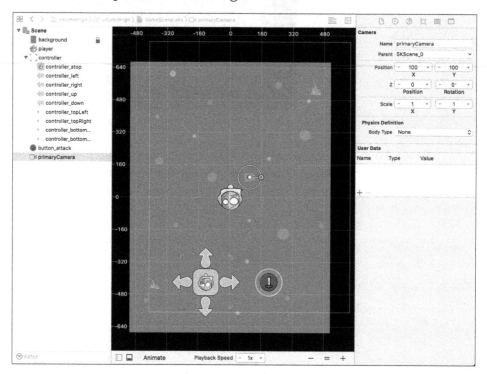

Congratulations, you've just *changed* the camera's viewport. To understand how this change affects the FoV (what the player sees), build and run the project to the Phone 11 Pro Max simulator.

If you were to make a side-by-side comparison with the different camera settings, you'd see something like the image on page 179.

Notice how the entire scene shifts to the left when the camera position is moved to the right.

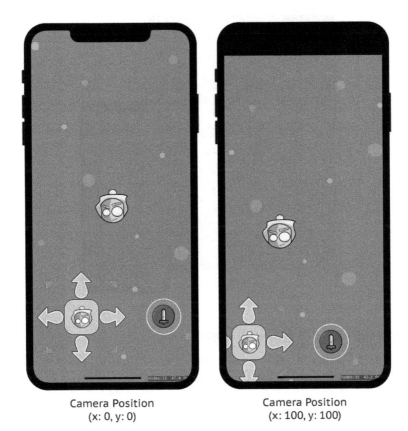

Camera Position
(x: 0, y: 0)

Camera Position
(x: 100, y: 100)

The interesting thing about the camera node is that its xScale, yScale, and zRotation properties all have the inverse effect on *every* object within the scene—not
just the child nodes of the camera. For example, if you were to set the scale
of the primaryCamera node to (x: 0.5, y: 0.5), you'd see something like the image
on page 180.

Notice how the smaller camera scale creates a smaller FoV, making everything
look much bigger and closer to the screen—this is sort of like the familiar
warning that "objects in mirror are closer than they appear."

If you haven't done so already, reset the primaryCamera node's properties back
to the following:

- Position: (x: 0, y: 0)
- Scale: (x: 1, y: 1)

With those properties reset, you're ready to write the code that *directs* the
camera to follow the player around.

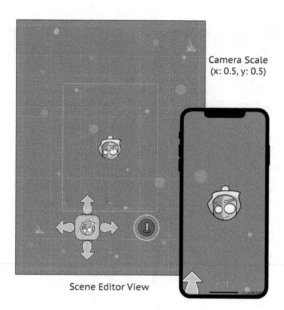

Camera Scale
(x: 0.5, y: 0.5)

Scene Editor View

Directing the Camera Through Code

In the Project Navigator, select the GameScene.swift file to open the file in the Source Editor. Below the didMove(to:) method, add the following new method:

```swift
func setupCamera() {
  guard let player = player else { return }
  let distance = SKRange(constantValue: 0)
  let playerConstraint = SKConstraint.distance(distance, to: player)

  camera?.constraints = [playerConstraint]
}
```

The setupCamera() method first verifies that the player node exists, and then it sets a ranged distance constraint between the camera node and the player node. You first learned about constraints and ranges in Use Constraints to Limit Movement, on page 46. Here, you're using the constraint to keep the camera node *firmly attached* to the player node.

The next step is to add a call to this new method at the end of the didMove(to:) method, like so:

```swift
override func didMove(to view: SKView) {
  player = childNode(withName: "player") as? Player
  player?.move(.stop)

➤ setupCamera()
}
```

The highlighted code shows your new addition.

If you were to build and run the project now (you're welcome to try), and then move the player up using the D-pad controller, you'd notice that the player stays visible. However, as she moves up the scene, the on-screen controls scroll off the bottom and out of view:

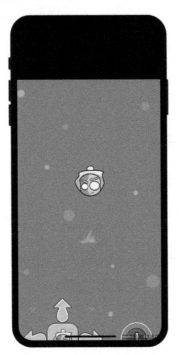

You'll fix this problem soon enough, but first, let's get the D-pad controller and the Attack button into their own reference nodes to make fixing this problem a little easier.

Use Reference Nodes in Your Scene

The SpriteKit framework includes a special kind of node known as a reference node, which is backed by the SKReferenceNode class. You create and use these nodes in your scenes when you want to *reference* the content saved in a different archived .sks file.

With reference nodes, you can share content across multiple scenes without having to worry about unnecessary duplication. Because Val's Revenge will undoubtedly include more than one level (scene), using reference nodes for certain content makes sense.

In the next section, you'll use reference nodes to build a simple 8-way D-pad controller and the Attack button. Later, in Build Better On-Screen Controls, on page 308, you'll modify these controls to make them more robust, allowing the player to move and fire using 360° of rotation.

Creating the D-pad Controller Reference Node

Create a new file (⌥⌘N) using the iOS SpriteKit Scene template:

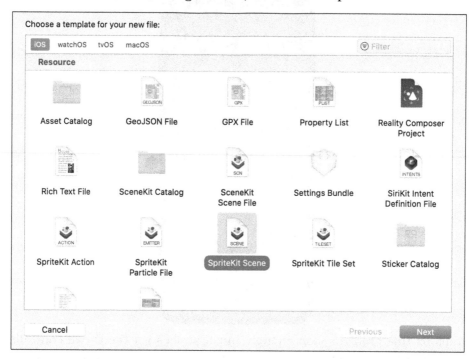

Click Next and name the file Controller.sks. When the new file opens in the Scene Editor, you're ready to get started.

In the Attributes Inspector, set the Size of the empty scene to (w: 350, h: 350) and the Anchor Point to (x: 0, y: 0). Great, you've just set the scene's origin to the lower-left corner, making it easier to place the controller in the lower-left corner of the game scene.

It doesn't make sense to recreate the wheel, er, the controller, so you'll copy the objects from the existing game scene into this new controller scene.

Switch to the GameScene.sks file. In the Scene Graph View, right-click the controller node and select Copy. Right-click again, and this time select Delete to remove the node from the scene.

Go back to the Controller.sks file, right-click the Scene object in the Scene Graph View, and select Paste.

At this point, you probably won't see the pasted node in the editor, but that's okay—make sure it's selected in the Scene Graph View. Then, in the Attributes Inspector, set the node's Position to (x: 175, y: 175), and change the Name from controller to controller_main. When you're done, your new controller scene will look like this:

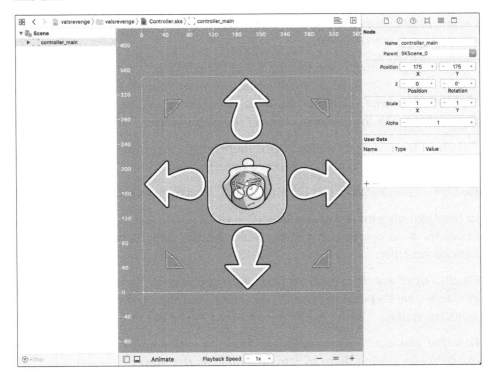

Save the Controller.sks file—this is a very important step or you won't be able to select this file as a reference—and then head back to the GameScene.sks file. Once there, open the Object Library and drag a Reference node onto the scene.

In the Attributes Inspector, set the reference node's Position to (x: -295, y: -595) and its Name to controller.

You also need to select the archived .sks file this node uses as its reference. To set the reference, go to the Reference drop-down list (located just above the Position settings), and select the Controller scene you just created.

At this point, the scene doesn't look all that different. However, by using a reference node, you just made this game more scalable and easier to manage and maintain—especially when it comes to adding new levels and their corresponding scenes.

Let's do the same thing with the Attack button.

Creating the Attack Button Reference Node

In the interest of time—and because you just finished creating a reference node for the D-pad controller—the steps in this section are condensed.

Create another new file using the iOS Resource, SpriteKit Scene template, and this time, name it AttackButton.sks.

In the Attributes Inspector, set the Size of the empty scene to (w: 140, h: 140) and the Anchor Point to (x: 1, y: 0), similar to what you did for the controller. This sets the scene's origin to the lower-*right* corner, making it easier to place the button in the lower-*right* corner of the game scene.

Switch to the GameScene.sks file. Once there, copy, then delete the button_attack node since you'll be using a reference node instead.

Go back to the AttackButton.sks file and paste the button_attack node into the scene.

In the Attributes Inspector, set the button_attack node's Position to (x: -70, y: 70). Leave its Name set to button_attack. Save the file and then go back to the GameScene.sks file.

Finally, drag another Reference node into the scene. Name the new node attackButton, set its position to (x: 270, y: -490), and choose the AttackButton scene as its reference.

Now that you have the controller and button nodes set up as references, you can focus on getting them to remain visible as the player moves around the scene regardless of device type or orientation.

Add Support for All Devices and Orientations

While not technically a heads-up display (HUD), the D-pad controller and Attack button share a similar quality in that they need to be visible at all times. At the moment, however, once the player moves beyond a certain point, the on-screen controls disappear.

One way to fix this "player movement/control visibility" problem—and the one generally recommended by Apple—is to make the HUD content a child of the camera node. That fix would look something like the image on page 185 in the Scene Graph View.

While this isn't a bad idea, it does limit what you're able to do, so you'll learn another way.

But this "player movement/control visibility" problem isn't the only problem you need to fix. Build and run the program—partly to make sure everything still works properly with your new reference nodes, but more important, to see these secondary problems firsthand.

When the game launches, don't move the player; instead, rotate the device so that its orientation is landscape. Notice how the controls "fall off" the bottom of the screen. But that's not all. Also notice how much larger the player sprite appears—neither trait will earn your game a 5-star rating.

But don't worry—you'll correct all of these problems, starting with the rotation issues.

Creating a Custom Protocol to Detect Rotation Changes

The view controller is, for the most part, responsible for handling rotations. A more accurate explanation, and the one that Apple uses in its documentation, is that "rotations are treated as a change in the size of the view controller's view and are therefore reported using the viewWillTransition(to:with:) method."

In other words, when you rotate your device, the bounds of the view that's attached to the view controller changes. And in response to that change, the view updates the positions of its subviews. When those updates are done, the view controller calls the viewDidLayoutSubviews() method. If you need to make additional changes to the layout, you can override this method; but to do so, you need a way for the view controller to interact with your scene.

The first step is to create a new, custom protocol on the GameViewController class. You first learned about protocols in Configure the Physics Contact Delegate, on page 82. The only difference here is that you're creating a custom proto-col—the same rules apply, but you're in charge.

In the Project Navigator, select the GameViewController.swift file to open the file. At the top of the file, below the import statements and before the class decla-ration, add the following code:

```
protocol GameViewControllerDelegate {
  func didChangeLayout()
}
```

This code creates a custom protocol and required method for the GameViewCon-troller class; you'll use this protocol later when you edit the GameScene class to adopt it.

Next, you need to override the viewDidLayoutSubviews() method and call the did-ChangeLayout() method on the delegate of the game view controller. Below the viewDidLoad() method, add the following code:

```
override func viewDidLayoutSubviews() {
  super.viewDidLayoutSubviews()

  guard
      let skView = self.view as? SKView,
      let gameViewControllerDelegate = skView.scene as?
              GameViewControllerDelegate else { return }

  gameViewControllerDelegate.didChangeLayout()
}
```

This code first verifies that the view is an SKView and that it's acting as a dele-gate for the game view controller. Once confirmed, it then calls the didChange-Layout() method on the delegate.

You're done creating the custom protocol; now, you just need to use it.

Using the Custom Protocol

Open the GameScene.swift file and change the class declaration from class GameScene: SKScene { to:

```
class GameScene: SKScene, GameViewControllerDelegate {
```

After changing the declaration, you'll (almost immediately) see the following error message (but don't let Xcode automatically fix it):

```
class GameScene: SKScene, GameViewControllerDelegate {

  var entities = [GKEntity]()      ⊗ Type 'GameScene' does not conform to protocol 'GameViewControllerDelegate'      ⊗
  var graphs = [String : GKGraph]()    Do you want to add protocol stubs?                                          Fix
```

Rather than have Xcode automatically add the protocol method for you, you'll add it yourself, giving you more control over where within the file the code gets added (Xcode adds it immediately below the class declaration).

For slightly better code organization, add the following protocol method *below* the didMove(to:) method:

```
func didChangeLayout() {

}
```

This method, although empty, clears the error, and you're ready for the final steps: fixing the player's size on rotation, and keeping the controls on-screen despite the device's orientation.

And yes, you could have accomplished the same thing by adding an extension at the end of the GameScene.swift file (like you did in Configure the Physics Contact Delegate, on page 82), but it's always good to know how to handle things in more than one way—it makes you, and your code, adaptable.

Resize the Player Node on Device Rotation

In Setting the Camera's Viewport, on page 178, you learned about the camera's viewport and how certain camera settings, like its position and scale, have an inverse effect on how the scene renders. Armed with that information, you can solve the problem of the resizing player.

Still inside the GameScene.swift file, add the following code to the didChangeLayout() method:

```
let w = view?.bounds.size.width ?? 1024
let h = view?.bounds.size.height ?? 1336

if h >= w { // portrait, which matches the design
  camera?.setScale(1.0)
} else {
  camera?.setScale(1.25) // helps to keep relative size
  // larger numbers results in "smaller" scenes
}
```

This code first checks the height and width of the view using default values if needed; it then adjusts the scale of the camera to *shrink* the size of the nodes within its view.

You could argue that it makes equal sense to adjust only the player sprite, but then what happens when you start adding more game objects? You'd have to loop through each object and resize it. Why go through all of that when you can accomplish the same thing by setting the camera's scale?

Build and run the project. Rotate the device and notice how much closer in size that the player sprite is when it is in landscape orientation than it was previously:

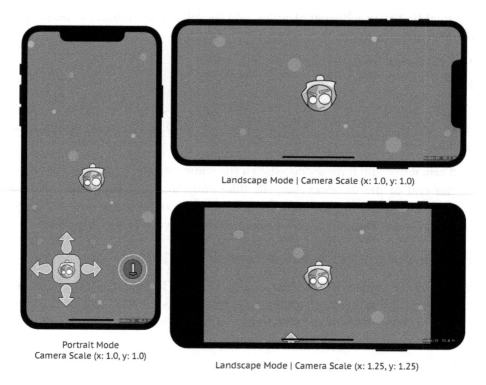

Landscape Mode | Camera Scale (x: 1.0, y: 1.0)

Portrait Mode
Camera Scale (x: 1.0, y: 1.0)

Landscape Mode | Camera Scale (x: 1.25, y: 1.25)

Now that you have the player sprite respecting its size on rotation, you're ready to tackle the final problem: disappearing controls.

Lock the Location of the On-Screen Controls

At the moment, when you switch from portrait to landscape mode, the on-screen controls are located outside of the camera's viewport. The same is true when the player navigates beyond the view. You will fix both of these problems now.

Creating an Extension to Find the View's Edges

You first need to implement something similar to what you did in Working with Different Screen Sizes, on page 91 to help you find the edges of the view. However, instead of making an extension that uses *methods* to return values, you'll create an extension that uses *computed properties*, as they're more efficient and help to produce cleaner, more succinct code.

Create a new file using the iOS Swift File template. Name this new file SKScene+
ViewProperties.swift and replace its contents with the following code:

```
import SpriteKit

extension SKScene {

  var viewTop: CGFloat {
    return convertPoint(fromView: CGPoint(x: 0.0, y: 0)).y
  }

  var viewBottom: CGFloat {
    guard let view = view else { return 0.0 }
    return convertPoint(fromView: CGPoint(x: 0.0,
                                          y: view.bounds.size.height)).y
  }

  var viewLeft: CGFloat {
    return convertPoint(fromView: CGPoint(x: 0, y: 0.0)).x
  }

  var viewRight: CGFloat {
    guard let view = view else { return 0.0 }
    return convertPoint(fromView: CGPoint(x: view.bounds.size.width,
                                          y: 0.0)).x
  }
}
```

You'll use these four computed properties to help locate the four corners of
the view (the visible screen area). What's nice about this code is that it works
across all devices, for all orientations—and now that you have it packaged
neatly in this tiny extension, you can use it with all of your SpriteKit projects,
without the worry of extra bloat.

What's in a Name?

You can name your files in many ways, particularly when it comes
to extending existing functionality. In Gloop Drop, you created a
SpriteKitHelper.swift file where you added all of your SpriteKit extensions. While this approach isn't necessarily a problem, it can get
difficult to maintain a file that includes many unrelated methods,
enums, and extensions.

With Val's Revenge being a much bigger game, it makes sense to
start thinking in terms of larger scope. One way to accomplish
this is to adopt a common naming convention that uses the pattern
ExtendedType+Functionality.swift. With this pattern, you're able to
quickly see that you're dealing with an extension on a certain
class.

Now that you have the extension ready to go, you can use it to help resolve the placement issues with on-screen controls.

Using the Four Corners Extension

Switch back to the GameScene.swift file and add a new method below the update(_:) method:

```
func updateControllerLocation() {
  let controller = childNode(withName: "//controller")
  controller?.position = CGPoint(x: viewLeft, y: viewBottom)

  let attackButton = childNode(withName: "//attackButton")
  attackButton?.position = CGPoint(x: viewRight, y: viewBottom)
}
```

This new method updates the location of the on-screen controls using the extension's properties (viewLeft, viewRight, and viewBottom). That's great, but you still need to call this method—and timing is everything.

You may think the best place to call the updateControllerLocation() method is within the update() method (because it's called every frame), but that won't work. If you attempt to update the on-screen controls within the update() method, the on-screen controls will have a sort of bouncy lag. (You're welcome to try it out because it's difficult to explain what it looks like.)

Instead, you'll call the updateControllerLocation() method from within another frame-cycle function: didFinishUpdate(). Place the following code above the updateControllerLocation() method:

```
override func didFinishUpdate() {
  updateControllerLocation()
}
```

Here, you're overriding the didFinishUpdate() method to avoid the bouncy lag.

The didFinishUpdate() method comes in handy whenever you need to update nodes or logic *after* the scene finishes all of the steps required to process animations. For more information about the frame-cycle functions, read Apple's online documentation.[1]

Build and run the project as shown in the image on page 191.

Things are starting to look better: when you rotate the device and move the player around the scene, the controls stay put. But there's still something wrong: the controls are way too close to the screen's edges.

---

1. https://developer.apple.com/documentation/spritekit/skscene/responding_to_frame-cycle_events

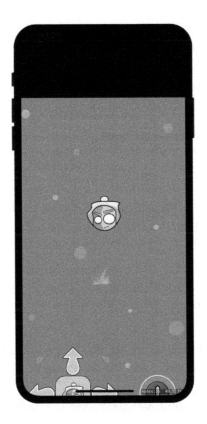

Using Safe Areas and Margins for Better Placement

When your game supports multiple devices with different view sizes, it's important to keep in mind exactly where you're placing content. Thoughtful placement becomes especially important when you're placing content near the edges of the view, and even more so when you're dealing with the iPhone X and its infamous "notch."

Right now, the on-screen controls are way too close to the edge. To fix this problem, you'll use margins and safe areas.[2]

Still inside the GameScene.swift file, add a new property to store a hard-coded margin value:

```
let margin: CGFloat = 20.0
```

Regardless of the device or its orientation, you want to always include this margin, and always use the same value.

---

2. https://developer.apple.com/documentation/uikit/uiview/positioning_content_relative_to_the_safe_area

Now, modify the updateControllerLocation() method to use this new margin property. The updated method looks like this:

```
func updateControllerLocation() {
  let controller = childNode(withName: "//controller")
  controller?.position = CGPoint(x: (viewLeft + margin),
                                 y: (viewBottom + margin))

  let attackButton = childNode(withName: "//attackButton")
  attackButton?.position = CGPoint(x: (viewRight - margin),
                                   y: (viewBottom + margin))
}
```

Here, you're adding (or subtracting, in the case of the right side) the view's extension property values and the margin value. You're then using the sum of their respective values to reposition your on-screen controls.

This change gets you part of the way there, but now you need to make sure you're placing the content within the safe areas of the view—you don't want content to get covered by the iPhone X's "notch" or the home control indicator (the line at the bottom of the iPhone X's screen).

Open the SKScene+ViewProperties.swift file. At the end of the extension, below the code for the viewRight property, add the following new property:

```
var insets: UIEdgeInsets {
  return UIApplication.shared.delegate?.window??.safeAreaInsets ?? .zero
}
```

The safeAreaInsets property helps you determine the safe area of your view by applying the insets in this property to the view's bounds rectangle. You'll do that next.

Go back to the GameScene.swift file, and for the last time in this chapter, update the updateControllerLocation() method to match this:

```
func updateControllerLocation() {
  let controller = childNode(withName: "//controller")
  controller?.position = CGPoint(x: (viewLeft + margin + insets.left),
                                 y: (viewBottom + margin + insets.bottom))

  let attackButton = childNode(withName: "//attackButton")
  attackButton?.position = CGPoint(x: (viewRight - margin - insets.right),
                                   y: (viewBottom + margin + insets.bottom))
}
```

Here, you're adding (once again subtracting, in the case of the right side) the values of the safe area insets within your existing calculation.

Before you build and run the project, let's do one more thing. Open the GameScene.sks file and drag the on-screen controls to their respective edges, like so:

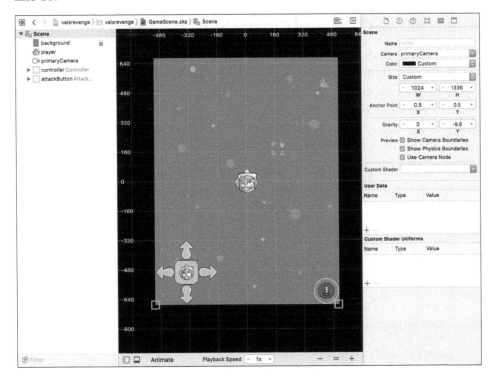

While this step isn't necessary, it does help to keep the scene free of clutter.

Build and run the project.

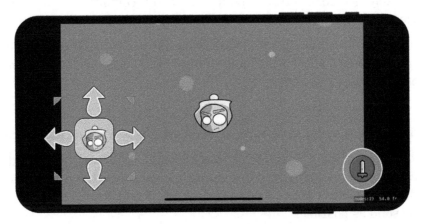

At this point, the player moves around the scene, the camera follows, and the controls are essentially pinned to the edges regardless of view size or device orientation. However, there's a bit more refactoring you can do.

Refactor the Code and Clean Up the Project

In Creating a Custom Protocol to Detect Rotation Changes, on page 185, you created a custom protocol to help detect when the view changes and the layout updates device rotation. While there's nothing wrong with how you've done it, there is some room for improvement: you can move the GameViewControllerDelegate declaration and supporting protocol methods that are currently saved in the GameScene.swift file to its own file.

Create a new file using the iOS Swift File template. Name this new file GameScene+ViewUpdates.swift and replace its contents with the following code:

```
import SpriteKit

extension GameScene: GameViewControllerDelegate {

  func didChangeLayout() {
    let w = view?.bounds.size.width ?? 1024
    let h = view?.bounds.size.height ?? 1336

    if h >= w { // portrait, which matches the design
      camera?.setScale(1.0)
    } else {
      camera?.setScale(1.25) // helps to keep relative size
      // larger numbers results in "smaller" scenes
    }
  }
}
```

You'll likely get some errors about redundant conformance and invalid redeclaration, but that's okay. You'll take care of those errors next.

Open the GameScene.swift file. Find and delete the didChangeLayout() method and change the GameScene class declaration from class GameScene: SKScene, GameViewControllerDelegate { to:

```
class GameScene: SKScene {
```

Build and run the project to make sure everything is working as expected.

By making small improvements to your code along the way, you'll find that you can quickly test things without getting too deep. In other words, it's okay to write "inefficient" code as a proof of concept, provided you clean it up later and as soon as possible.

Next Steps

You accomplished a lot in this chapter. You saw how the camera affected not only the player's FoV but also how the scene's content changes in relation to the camera's properties. You added reference nodes for the on-screen controls, making it easier to share and maintain content between your different scene files. You even worked out a way to make Val's Revenge look good in both portrait *and* landscape modes. Finally, you leveled-up your coding skills by learning new ways to solve old problems. But you're not done yet. There is much more to do and learn.

In the next chapter, you'll take Val's Revenge to the next level by building an even bigger world with tile maps.

Extending Your Game World with Tile Maps

With a game like Val's Revenge, players need to have a lot of room to explore. Although it's possible to build a gigantic scene using one, two, or even three or more background images, there's a more efficient and scalable way to create scenes worthy of exploration: *tile maps*.

With tile maps, you can build large, elaborate scenes using a grid of predefined images, or *tiles*, such as what you see here:

Whether you're building a side-scrolling platformer game or a top-down adventure game, tile maps give you greater control and flexibility over the landscape while also using less resources.

In this chapter, you'll add two tile map nodes to Val's Revenge, giving the player some much-needed room to explore the scene.

Create a Bigger World with Tile Map Nodes

Like other nodes in SpriteKit, the SKTileMapNode class is a subclass of the SKNode class, which means you can set the usual node properties like position and name. You can also run actions and use shaders[1] on these nodes. More important, though, you can define a tile set object using the SKTileSet class.

A tile set object stores an array of related tile groups. A tile group (SKTileGroup) can contain either a single tile (SKTileDefinition) or an array of tile group rules (SKTileGroupRule). A tile's definition, along with the group rules, define how the tiles are placed within a tile map node.

Confused? I'm not surprised. The rabbit hole of tile maps and supporting classes can get pretty deep, especially when you travel down that hole using code. But there's good news: you don't have to build your maps using code. Instead, you can use a combination of the Scene Editor and the *Tile Map Editor*—but first, you need to add some assets.

Adding the Assets

To begin, open the valsrevenge project in Xcode.

> ### Using the Starter Project
>
> You may continue using your project from the previous chapter, or you can use the starter project located in the projects/begin folder included with the code resources for this chapter. Either option is fine; the only benefit to using the starter project is that you won't get stuck going forward if you missed an earlier step.
>
> There's also an ending project for this chapter that includes all of the code and resources you'll be adding here. The end project is located in the projects/end folder included with the code resources for this chapter.

In the Project Navigator, select the Assets.xcassets asset catalog and create a new sprite atlas (click the + button at the bottom of the Outline View and select New Sprite Atlas). Name the new atlas tiles_grass and delete the empty Sprite image set.

---

1. https://developer.apple.com/documentation/spritekit/skshader

Xcode 12 and Sprite Atlas Creation

 In Xcode 12, the New Sprite Atlas option does not exist. To create a new sprite atlas, click the + button at the bottom of the Outline View and select AR and SceneKit ▶ Sprite Atlas.

Open Finder and drag the contents from the resources/tiles_grass folder into the newly created sprite atlas, like so:

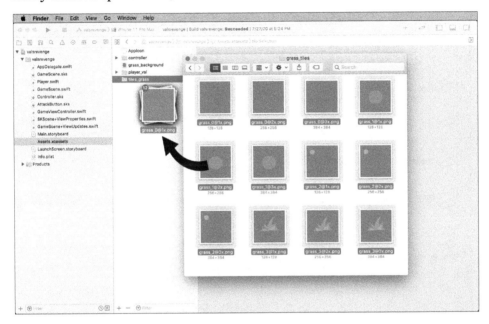

Now that you've added the images to the asset catalog, you're ready to set up your first tile set.

Setting up Your First Tile Set

Create a new file (⌘N). Select the iOS SpriteKit Tile Set template, as shown in the first image on page 200.

Click Next, and then using the Tile Set template drop-down list, select the Empty Tile Set option, as shown in the second image on page 200.

After making your selection, click Next.

Name the new file MainTileSet.sks, and verify that the Group and Targets options are both set to valsrevenge. Once confirmed, click Create.

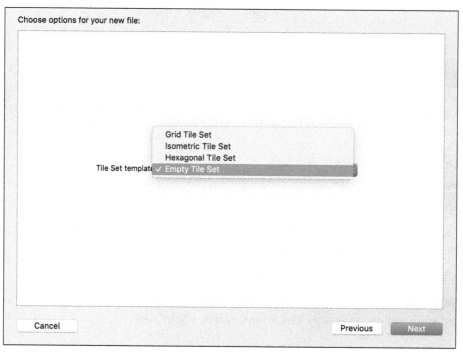

You now have your first empty tile set aptly named Tile Set. Using the disclosure indicators, expand the Tile Set and new tile group objects, and you'll see a single Tile object:

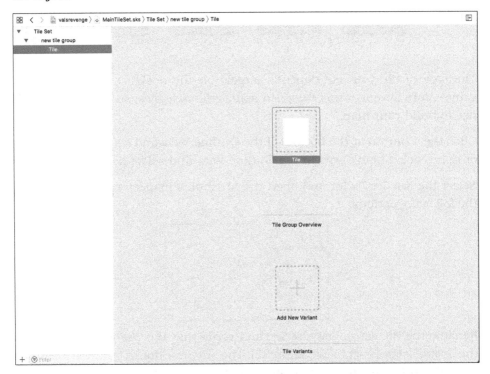

You can either rename what's here or delete the default entries and start anew. Let's remove what's here and start fresh.

Select the Tile Set entry. Then, right-click and choose Remove Selected Items from the context menu, like this:

Excellent, you're ready to begin making your own tile set.

In Xcode, you can use four types of tiles to build your tile map: Grid, Isometric, Hexagonal Flat, and Hexagonal Pointy. Each tile type has a different shape as shown in the image on page 202.

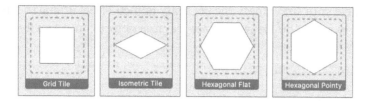

The type of tile you use depends largely on the design and style of your game—Val's Revenges was designed using grid-style tiles, so that's what you'll use to build your map.

Click the + button at the bottom of the Outline View and select New Grid Tile Set or right-click a blank area in the Outline View and select New ▶ Grid Tile Set.

Select the New Grid Tile Set and open the Attributes Inspector. Here, you'll see the following options:

Rename the tile set to Grass Tile Set, and verify that the Type is set to Grid and the Default Tile Size is set to (w: 32, h: 32). The size here doesn't matter too much since it'll automatically update once you select the tile's texture.

The next step is to add a new single tile group. With the Grass Tile Set selected in the Outline View, either right-click and select New ▶ Single Tile Group or use the + button at the bottom of the Outline View and select New Single Tile Group.

Expand the tile set and the newly created tile group. Rename the new group to Grass and the Tile group rule to Base. Great, you're essentially back where you started, but now you know how to add additional tile sets, groups, and rules.

Open the Media Library (⇧⌘L). Find and drag the grass_0 asset into the empty Base slot. You'll use this tile for the grass. But having a solid green background for grass would be kind of boring, so you'll add a little variety by adding new variants.

To create additional tile variants, drag the other grass tile resources (grass_1, grass_2, and grass_3) into the Add New Variant slot. A new slot will appear after you add each new variant. When you're done, the image on page 203 shows what you'll end up with.

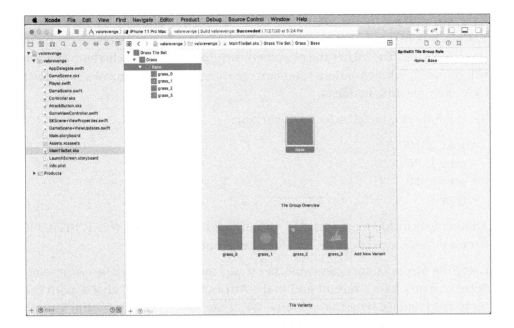

Select the grass_0 tile variant, and in the Attributes Inspector, you'll see this:

Here, you can set up the properties for your tile, including its Placement Weight. The placement weight determines how likely a tile will get placed when you're "painting" tiles. The higher the placement weight, the more likely that variation will get used. With variations, you can create more realistic scenes that don't look like repeating patterns.

Set the following weights for each variant:

- grass_0: 100
- grass_1: 20
- grass_2: 10
- grass_3: 5

Another way to add more variants without adding more resources is to enable the Flip Vertically, Flip Horizontally, and/or Rotation options.

Using the Media Library, drag another grass_2 asset into the Add New Variant slot. Select the new grass_2 variant and in the Attributes Inspector, enable both the Flip Vertically and Flip Horizontally options. While you're there, also set the Name to grass_2_alt and the Placement Weight to 8.

When you're done, you'll have the following five grass tile variants:

With your Grass Tile Set in place, you're ready to create your first tile map node. But first, save the MainTileSet.sks file (⌘S).

Create a Tile Map Node

In the Project Navigator, select the GameScene.sks file. (You may want to zoom out so that you can see the entire scene in the Scene Editor.)

Open the Object Library (⇧⌘L) and drag a new Tile Map Node into the Scene Graph View, as shown in the image on page 205.

Select the Tile Map Node in the Scene Graph View and look at the Attributes Inspector. Set the tile map node's Name to Grass Tile Map and its Position to (x: 0, y: 0).

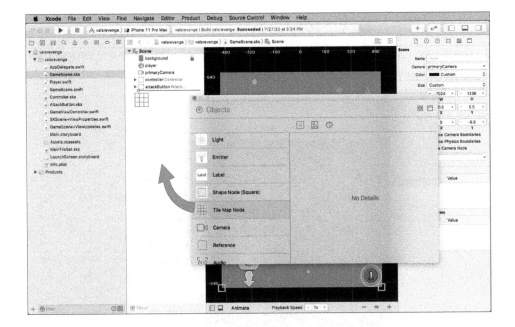

You'll see some other familiar settings like the Anchor Point and Scale, which you won't need to change, but just below those settings you'll see some new options:

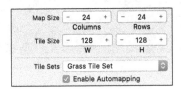

The Tile Sets drop-down list is where you select the tile set this map node will use. A tile map node can only pull tiles from a single tile set. In this case, you only created one tile set, Grass Tile Set, so select that one from the drop-down list if it's not already selected.

Before you start adding tiles to your new tile map node, hide the current "grass" background by hovering the mouse pointer over the background node in the Scene Graph View and clicking the small eye icon that appears to the right of the lock icon.

Perfect, you're ready to edit the map node using the Tile Map Editor.

Use the Tile Map Editor

In the Scene Graph, right-click the Grass Tile Map and select the Edit Tile Map from the context menu; this action takes you into the Tile Map Editor, which looks like this:

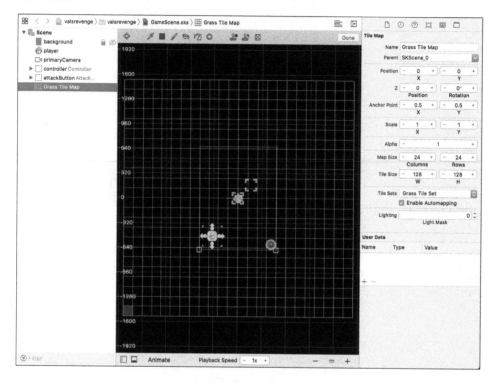

The Tile Map Editor is a powerful tool for painting your tiles onto a tile map node. With this editor, you have the option of automatically filling the map node with tiles from its corresponding tile set or individually selecting and painting tiles from the set.

Before you get into the nitty-gritty of painting tiles, let's quickly go over the toolbar.

If you've ever used a drawing and painting application, you're likely familiar with how most of these tools work. In order from left to right, you have the tools as shown in the first image on page 207.

Click the Randomize tool a few times and watch as random grass tiles are placed within the map. When you're done, you'll end up with a random painting of grass tiles that almost certainly looks different than the example as shown in the second image on page 207.

Tool Name	Description
◆ Hand	When selected, you're able to pan around the scene.
🖉 Eyedropper	Use this tool to select a tile on the map, causing the currently selected brush to switch to that type of tile.
■ Select Tile	Use this to select the tile to use when painting tiles. This selection tool changes depending on your automapping setting.
✎ Brush	Switch to this tool when you're ready to start painting tiles.
🖌 Flood Fill	Use this tool to quickly fill a space with the currently selected tile.
▨ Erase	Switch to this tool when you need to erase a tile.
◉ Select Brush Size	If you want to paint larger areas at one time, you can increase the size of your brush. (Generally, it's easier to paint with the smallest brush size, which is equal to the size of one tile.)
🏵 Create Stamp	As you begin to make more elaborate maps, you may want to reuse certain paintings. You can use this tool to create a stamp for later reuse.
🏵 Select Stamp	Similar to the Select Tile tool, this tool lets you select a previously saved stamp.
▨ Randomize	This tool lets you quickly paint a tile map node using random selection.
Done Done	Clicking this button closes the editor.

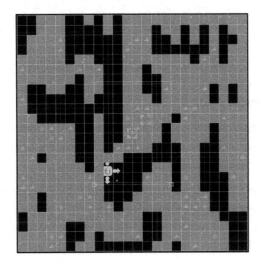

Switch to the Brush tool and paint in the missing tiles, filling every column and row with a random grass tile. (You can also try using the Flood Fill tool on the larger areas.)

The keyword here is random. Click the Select Tile tool and you'll see a single option, the Grass tile:

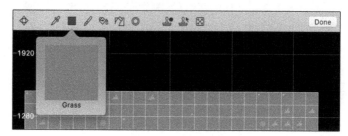

When the Enable Automapping option is enabled, the tile variant used is random. However, if you'd like a little more control over tile selection, you can disable automapping.

To disable the automapping option, remove the check mark in the Enable Automapping option (you'll find this option in the Attributes Inspector immediately below the Tile Sets drop-down list). Now, click the Select Tile tool once again, and this time, you'll see something more like this:

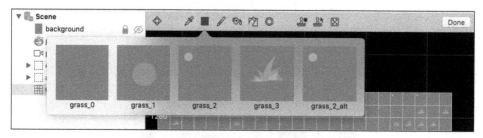

Having the ability to turn automapping on and off gives you greater control when you want more or less randomization or when you want to paint a specific tile at a certain location.

Before you build and run the project, you may have noticed that Val and the controllers are now nowhere to be found. That's because the grass tile map node is on top of the controllers and player nodes.

While you're painting your tiles, having the map node above all the other nodes makes it easier to see what you're painting, but you'll need to move the map node to where it belongs before moving on to the next step. To do that, drag the Grass Tile Map node above the player node in the Scene Graph, like the image on page 209.

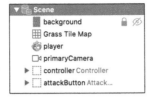

Build and run the project. You can now move the player around in all directions.

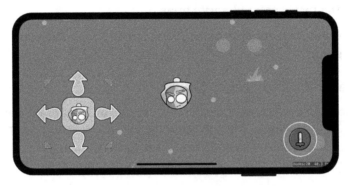

Notice how the player now has a lot more space to walk around and explore. While this is better than before, walking around an empty meadow, as lovely as it may be, isn't exactly the most exciting game. Let's liven things up with a dungeon.

Add a Dungeon Tile Map

You just finished creating a single tile with multiple variations. Now it's time to up your game a bit by creating a tile group that uses adjacency rules for placement. With adjacency rules, you can create a map that looks a little more natural and less boxy using an 8-way adjacency group:

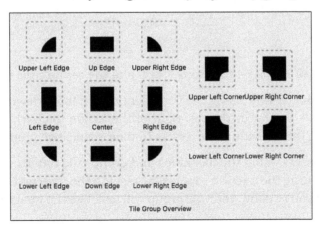

Tile Group Overview

But before you can create this new group, you need to add some more assets.

Adding the Dungeon Tile Assets

In the Project Navigator, select the Assets.xcassets asset catalog. Once there, create a new sprite atlas and name it tiles_dungeon. Don't forget to delete the default Sprite image set.

Open Finder and drag all of the image resources from the resources/tiles_dungeon folder into the newly created sprite atlas.

With the new sprite atlas in place, you're ready to build your first 8-way adjacency group.

Creating an 8-Way Adjacency Group

Switch back to the MainTileSet.sks file. To create an 8-way adjacency group, right-click an open area in the Outline View and select New Grid Tile Set. After that, select the New Grid Tile Set item (to highlight it), then right-click and select New 8-Way Adjacency Group. The two-step process looks like this:

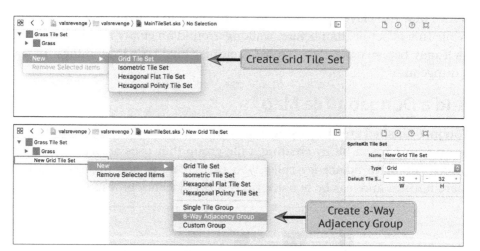

Rename the New Grid Tile Set to Dungeon Tile Set and the new tile group to Dungeon Floor.

Open the Media Library using the persistent option (hold down the ⌥ key as you click the + button in the top-right of the Xcode toolbar); this makes it easier to drag the individual tile assets to their respective group rule.

Drag all 13 assets using the filenames and group rule names as your guide. For example, drag the lower_left_edge media asset to the Lower Left Edge group rule space. When you're done, your tile group will look like the image on page 211.

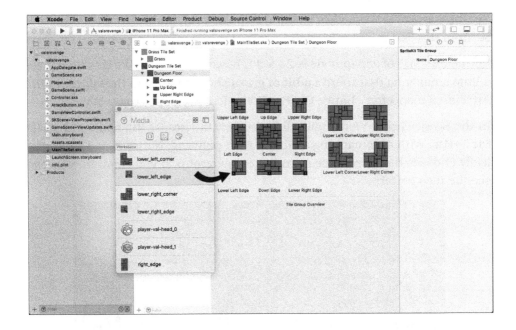

You may have noticed an asset named center_alt. Drag this asset into the Add New Variant spot of the Center tile. When you're done, the Center Tile Group Overview will look like this:

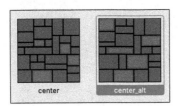

Select the center tile, and in the Attributes Inspector, set the Placement Weight to 5. Select the center_alt tile and set its Placement Weight to 3. When you're done making these changes, save the file. Remember, the Placement Weight determines how likely one tile over another is used when painting the map—the higher the number, the more likely it'll be used.

With your dungeon floor tiles set up, you're ready to build a new map node.

Adding the Dungeon Tile Map Node

In the Project Navigator, switch to the GameScene.sks file and add a new tile map node. Name this new map node Dungeon Tile Map.

Set the Dungeon Tile Map node's position to (x: 0, y: 0), and select the Dungeon Tile Set from the Tile Sets drop-down list.

The default size of a map node is 24 × 24; however, you'll make this map node a little smaller so that there's a bit of grass showing around the edges. In the Attributes Inspector, change the Map Size to (columns: 23, rows: 23).

In the Scene Graph View, right-click the new Dungeon Tile Map node and select Edit Tile Map. With automapping enabled, start painting. Notice how it automatically chooses the correct tile from the 8-way group. If you zoom in, you can see the tiles better:

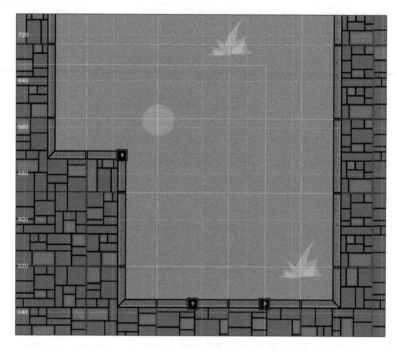

You're welcome to paint your scene any way you'd like. Mine looks like the first image on page 213.

After you're done painting your dungeon, don't forget to move the Dungeon Tile Map node above the player node in the Scene Graph. Once you've done that, build and run the project.

Everything looks good, but the character and the controls feel a little too big, as shown in the second image on page 213. Let's reduce their size by setting the x/y scale for the controller and attackButton nodes to 0.75 and the player node to 0.4. You can set the scale using the Attributes Inspector.

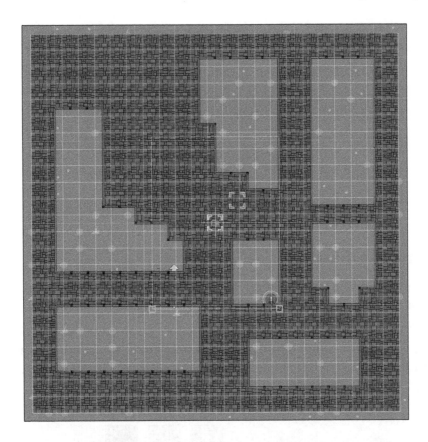

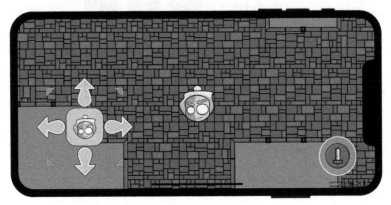

Build and run the project again, and notice that this time the sizes look a lot better as shown in the image on page 214.

The dungeon is starting to look good, but it could use a little something—how about some animated flames?

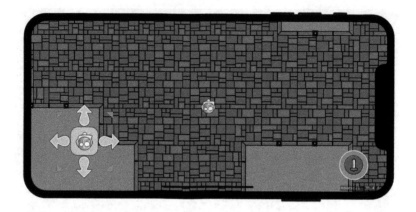

Animating Tiles

In the Project Navigator, select the Assets.xcassets asset catalog and create another new sprite atlas. Name this one tiles_animated and remove the empty Sprite image set.

Open Finder and drag all of the image assets from the resources/tiles_animated folder into the tiles_animated atlas. When you're done, you'll end up with something like this:

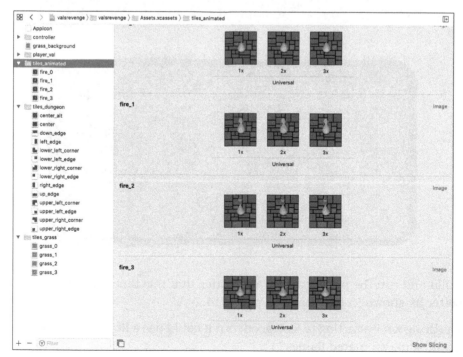

Switch to the MainTileSet.sks file—you're about to add another Center variant.

Expand the Dungeon Tile Set and then the Dungeon Floor. Select the Center tile (it may already be selected from when you added the center_alt variant).

Open the Media Library and drag the fire_0 image asset into the Add New Variant empty space. Select the fire_ tile variant and open the Attributes Inspector.

Using the Media Library, drag the other fire assets (fire_1, fire_2, and fire_3) into the Textures area, like so:

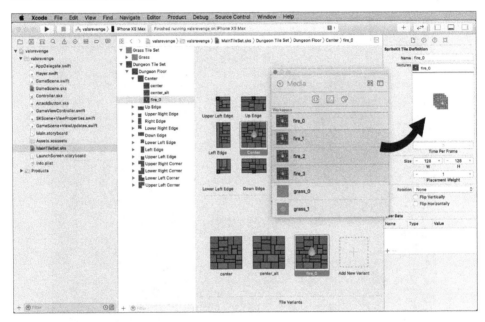

In the Attributes Inspector, you'll see a Time Per Frame setting, which is currently set to 0. Change this value to 0.25 to represent 0.25 seconds per frame, and you'll see a fire animation appear as it cycles through all four frames in the order they appear in the Textures area:

fire_0   fire_1   fire_2   fire_3

Add Multiple Variants at Once

If you're looking to speed up your development, you can add multiple static or animated tiles by selecting multiple assets from the Medial Library and dragging them into the Add New Variant slot. You'll then get prompted to Create multiple new definitions or Create new animated definition with a default Time Per Frame of 0.5.

Save the file and then switch back to the GameScene.sks file. You'll see something like this:

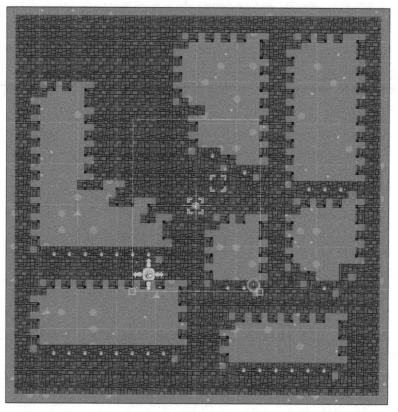

The problem here (and I'm not sure if this is a bug or what) is that any time you make changes to the underlying tile set, regardless of the automapping setting, the tile map that uses that tile set gets wonky. To correct the problem, toggle the Enable Automapping setting on the Dungeon Tile Map node, which will correct and reset the map.

Once the map returns to what it once was before, you're ready to make your edits—in this case, you'll add some fire tiles and you'll set up the edges of the dungeon floor.

Right-click the Dungeon Tile Map node and select Edit Tile Map. Now, disable the automapping option, and you'll be able to select the individual tile definitions using the Select Tile tool:

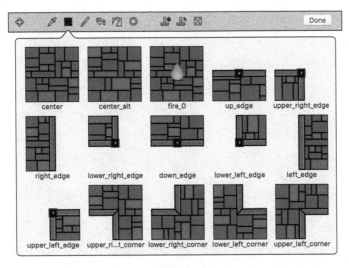

Start by adding a few random fire tiles around the dungeon floor. When you're done with that, you're ready to add the outside edges.

For the outside edges, you'll use the following eight tiles for the top, bottom, and corner edges:

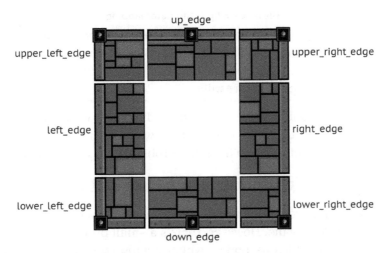

The image on page 218 shows how my updated map looks, with a portion of the map zoomed in so that you can better see the edges.

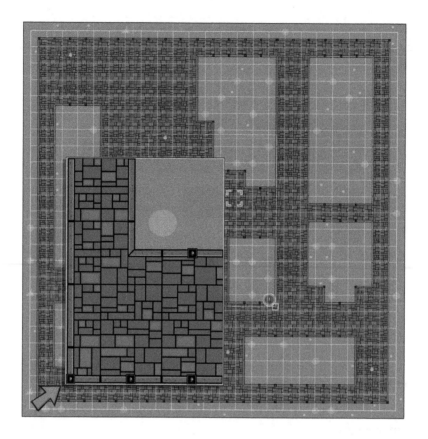

Tile Maps, Edges, and Automapping

 When mixing automapping and manual mapping, always start with automapping enabled. Otherwise, when you switch from manual to automapping modes, your pre-existing tiles may change, causing unexpected results.

If you were to build and run the project now, the player would be able to walk through walls. While this nifty talent works well for ghosts, the fearless Val doesn't need this ability, so you'll fix that problem next using physics bodies.

Configure Physics Bodies Using User Data

To keep the player from leaving the dungeon, you'll set up physics bodies around the dungeon walls. However, there's a small problem: tile map nodes do not expose their tiles as nodes, which means you can't assign physics bodies to the individual tiles. Instead, you'll use custom *user data*, more specifically, the userData property of the SKNode class.

The userData property of the SKNode class is an NSMutableDictionary that you can use to store custom values known as "user data." These custom values can include integers, floats, booleans, and strings. You can either set these up in code or, more conveniently, using the Scene Editor and the Attributes Inspector (there's a User Data section near the bottom).

For Val's Revenge, you'll set up two custom values:

- bodySize: Indicates the size of the physics body to use.
- bodyOffset: Specifies the offset to use for the body.

The question now is, "Where do you set up these values and how does it all work?"

Working with User Data and Tiles

In the Project Navigator, select the MainTileSet.sks file. With the Attributes Inspector open, expand the Left Edge tile group rule and select the left_edge tile definition inside.

At the bottom of the Attributes Inspector, you'll see the User Data section, which looks like this:

Click the + button in the lower-left corner to add a new entry. Set the Name to bodySize and switch the Type to String. For the Value, enter {20,128}.

With this user data entry, you're specifying that the body size will be (w: 20, h: 128). So why are you setting a body size?

To better understand, look at the following image:

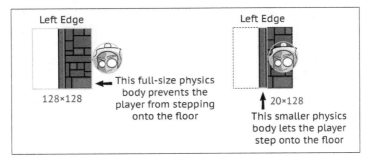

Notice that each tile is 128 × 128—including the alpha area of the tile. If you set the physics body's size using the full size of the tile, the player wouldn't be able to get close to the wall, as you can see in the image on the left. However, if you reduce the physics body size to 20 × 128, the player can get closer to the wall, as shown in the image on the right. Remember, when you add a physics body to a node, it defaults to placing that body in the center of the node. So when you resize the body, it'll resize from both directions, keeping the body in the center of the node.

Now the left_edge tile definition is set up, select the right_edge tile definition inside the Right Edge tile group rule, and add a new user data entry of bodySize, String, {20,128}. Once again, you're specifying the body size will be (w: 20, h: 128).

The left and right edges are now set up. Next, you need to set up the top and bottom edges. You'll use essentially the same settings, but instead of specifying a body size of (w: 20, h: 128), you need to use a size of (w: 128, h: 20), which will shrink the top and bottom of the physics body.

Select the up_edge tile definition inside the Up Edge tile group rule. This time, add a new user data entry of bodySize, String, {128,20}. Do the same for the down_edge tile definition inside of the Down Edge tile group rule.

For the four corner edges, you'll create a square body instead. Individually select the upper_right_edge, lower_right_edge, lower_left_edge, and upper_left_edge tile definitions, and for each one, add a new user data entry of bodySize, String, {84,84}.

The main outside dungeon walls are now set up. But there's still a matter of the inner walls, more specifically, the upper_right_corner, lower_right_corner, lower_left_corner, and upper_left_corner.

Remember, when you add a physics body to a node, it places that body in the center of the node. For these inner corner pieces, you'll need to use an offset. To understand why, look at the following image:

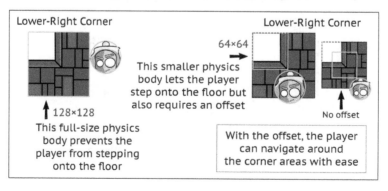

Notice that without the offset, the player wouldn't be able to step onto the floor. But this is where it might get a little complicated because you need to move the offset up or down and left or right depending on which tile you're setting up. For example, with the Lower Right Corner, you need to move the offset up and over to the left using (x: -32, y: 32).

First, to make it easier, add a bodySize user data string value of {64,64} for the four corners. Then, go back and add a new bodyOffset string value for each one, taking special note of which values are positive and which are negative:

- upper_right_corner: {-32,-32}
- lower_right_corner: {-32,32}
- lower_left_corner: {32,32}
- upper_left_corner: {32,-32}

Excellent, you now have the user data set up for your tile definitions, and you're ready to write the code to read that data.

Setting up the Physics Body Code

Setting up the user data is only the first step in getting physics bodies added to the tile map. The next step is to write some code to read that data. While there are many ways to read the data and write the code, you'll create a new SKTileMapNode extension to keep things clean and reusable.

Create a new file (⌘N) using the iOS Swift File template. Name the new file SKTileMapNode+Physics.swift and replace its contents with the following code:

```
import SpriteKit

extension SKTileMapNode {

}
```

This sets up a new extension for the SKTileMapNode class. Inside this new extension, you'll add two new methods:

```
func setupEdgeLoop() {
  let mapPoint = CGPoint(x: -frame.size.width/2,
                         y: -frame.size.height/2)
  let mapSize = CGSize(width: frame.size.width,
                       height: frame.size.height)
  let edgeLoopRect = CGRect(origin: mapPoint, size: mapSize)

  // Set up physics body
  physicsBody = SKPhysicsBody(edgeLoopFrom: edgeLoopRect)
```

```
// Adjust default values
physicsBody?.affectedByGravity = false
physicsBody?.allowsRotation = false
physicsBody?.isDynamic = false

physicsBody?.categoryBitMask = 2
}
```

This first extension method, when called, creates an edge-loop physics body around the tile map node using a value of 2 for the categoryBitMask property. You first learned about physics categories and masks in Configure Physics Categories, on page 79. The difference here is that instead of using an enum, you're setting this property using a raw value of 2.

Hardcoding the Default Category Value

 For simplicity, the categoryBitMask property is using a hardcoded default value of 2.

Below the method you just added, add the following code:

```
func setupMapPhysics() {
  let halfWidth = CGFloat(numberOfColumns) / 2.0 * tileSize.width
  let halfHeight = CGFloat(numberOfRows) / 2.0 * tileSize.height

  for col in 0..<numberOfColumns {
    for row in 0..<numberOfRows {
      if let td = tileDefinition(atColumn: col, row: row) {

        if let bodySizeValue = td.userData?.value(forKey: "bodySize")
          as? String {

          let x = CGFloat(col) *
            tileSize.width - halfWidth + (tileSize.width/2)
          let y = CGFloat(row) *
            tileSize.height - halfHeight + (tileSize.height/2)

          let bodySize = NSCoder.cgPoint(for: bodySizeValue) // {x,y}
          let pSize = CGSize(width: bodySize.x, height: bodySize.y)

          let tileNode = SKNode()
          tileNode.position = CGPoint(x: x, y: y)

          if let bodyOffsetValue = td.userData?.value(forKey: "bodyOffset")
            as? String {

            let bodyOffset = NSCoder.cgPoint(for: bodyOffsetValue)
            tileNode.physicsBody =
              SKPhysicsBody(rectangleOf: pSize,
                        center: CGPoint(x: bodyOffset.x, y: bodyOffset.y))
          } else {
            tileNode.physicsBody = SKPhysicsBody(rectangleOf: pSize)
          }
```

```
        // Adjust default values
        tileNode.physicsBody?.affectedByGravity = false
        tileNode.physicsBody?.allowsRotation = false
        tileNode.physicsBody?.isDynamic = false

        tileNode.physicsBody?.categoryBitMask = 2

        // Add node
        addChild(tileNode)
      }
    }
  }
}
}
```

There's a lot going on with this code, so take a moment to read through it. It's okay if you don't understand it fully. The key takeaways include:

- Looping through the tile definitions using the numberOfColumns and numberOfRows properties of the SKTileMapNode class.

- Reading the values stored in the userData property of the tileDefinition at the specified row and column.

- Using the bodySize and bodyOffset values to set the physics body properties.
  - If the bodySize value is not present, no action is taken.
  - If the bodySize value is present, the bodyOffset and bodyCategory values are read, along with the bodySize value, and all three are used to create the physics body.

Now that you have the extension methods in place, you're ready to use them to read the user data for each tile definition and set up the corresponding physics body.

In the Project Navigator, select the GameScene.swift file. Jump to the didMove(to:) method and add the following code:

```
let grassMapNode = childNode(withName: "Grass Tile Map") as? SKTileMapNode
grassMapNode?.setupEdgeLoop()
```

```
let dungeonMapNode = childNode(withName: "Dungeon Tile Map") as? SKTileMapNode
dungeonMapNode?.setupMapPhysics()
```

This code uses optional chaining to execute the extension methods on the two tile map nodes.

The last thing to do is update the player node's collision mask so that it reacts when hitting one of the wall bodies.

Updating the Player's Collision Mask

Open the GameScene.sks and select the player node. In the Attributes Inspector, set the Collision Mask value to 2, which is the value you used for the categoryBitMask property of your tile map node bodies.

Build and run the project, and notice how the player reacts to the dungeon's walls. Also notice the animated flames that you added earlier.

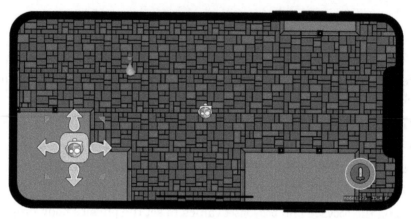

Thanks to tile maps, you now have a bigger world for your player to explore—and thanks to user data, you have a way to identify tiles and set up physics bodies, making it possible for the player to step right up to the edge of a wall but not go through it. Pretty neat, right?

Next Steps

In this chapter, you took a deep dive into the world of tile maps. Not only did you create tile maps and add physics bodies using custom user data, you also set up tile variations to make your maps more interesting—including an animated tile. But something's missing: monsters, keys, treasures, and loot. That's right—the stuff that makes dungeon-crawler games fun. So, strap yourself in, because in the next part of the book, you'll add all of these things.

Part III

Scale Your Games with GameplayKit

Build smarter, more scalable games using Game-playKit. Find out how to create believable characters by adding autonomous creatures to Val's Revenge.

Building Games with Entities and Components

How you plan and design your game's architecture is crucial to its maintainability and scalability. As you begin building bigger games, it's imperative that you consider the project's file organization and how you plan to manage the different game objects and classes within your game.

In this chapter, you'll continue working with the Val's Revenge game. You'll start by reorganizing the project, and then you'll implement an Entity-Component design pattern.

The *Entity-Component* design pattern, also known as *Entity Component System (ECS)*, is a common architecture in game design. This type of architecture pattern uses a *composition-based* design pattern rather than an *inheritance-based* design pattern. The difference between the two is often confusing, especially when you're first starting out.

With *entities* and *components*, you need to consider what a object *does* rather than what a object *is*. To get a better idea of how composition-based design differs from inheritance-based design, consider the following example:

Suppose you have two types of monsters in your game, each having slightly different traits: one monster can shoot at the player and move, whereas the other monster can only shoot.

In this example, if you were to use an inheritance-based design pattern, you might create a base Monster class with a few shared properties like spriteNode, maxHealth, and currentHealth. You might also create two additional subclasses, one for each type of monster. In the end, you might end up with something like the diagram shown on page 228.

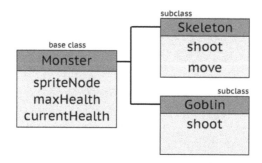

Here, the base Monster class handles the three shared properties, and each subclass handles its specific functionality: the Skeleton subclass includes both a shoot() and move() method, whereas the Goblin subclass includes only a shoot() method.

This is just one example of how you might design your monster classes. You could instead put a single shoot() method in the base Monster class, letting both the Skeleton and Goblin classes share this single method. But what happens when you add more monsters with more traits?

Do you add these traits to the base Monster class, or do you make new subclasses for each new monster type—and if so, what functionality will the base Monster class offer over its subclassed counterparts?

As you might have already guessed, the more monsters and traits you add, the more *monstrous* and out of hand your code can get.

Don't get me wrong; there isn't anything inherently bad with the inheritance-based design pattern; however, a composition-based design pattern can (and does) offer more reusability and scalability while also being somewhat more comfortable to maintain.

Using the same example of having multiple monsters with different traits, let's look at how you might build your game using a composition-based design pattern instead:

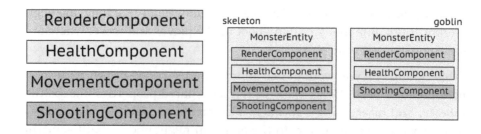

Here, you create a separate *component* for each trait or ability you want to include in your game. You also create a single Monster *entity*. You then add the desired components to your entities at runtime. (You can also remove components at runtime, making this design pattern even more powerful.)

I won't mince words with you; using entities and components seems a little counter-intuitive, confusing, and not worth the trouble at first, but the more you use this design pattern, the more you'll see how powerful and valuable it is—not only when designing and building your games, but also with scalability and ease of use.

However, to begin using the Entity-Component architecture to your advantage, you first need to do a little project housekeeping.

Organize the Project

Up until now, you've been adding files and building Val's Revenge with very little consideration to the project's overall organization. While you may think this isn't a problem—I mean, it's only a sample game, right?—keeping things organized (regardless of the "what for") helps reduce confusion and frustration, especially when working on your own games. In other words, it doesn't matter if you're learning how to use a game framework or building a full-fledged dungeon crawler—you should follow the same best practices for project organization regardless.

To begin, open the valsrevenge project in Xcode.

Using the Starter Project

You may continue using your project from the previous chapter, or you can use the starter project located in the projects/begin folder included with the code resources for this chapter. Either option is fine; the only benefit to using the starter project is that you won't get stuck going forward if you missed an earlier step.

There's also an ending project for this chapter that includes all of the code and resources you'll be adding here. The end project is located in the projects/end folder included with the code resources for this chapter.

Additional Note: You can skip the next two sections entirely and use the project in the projects/begin/organized folder, which includes all of the new groups, sprite atlases, and resources you'll be adding in the next two sections. If you choose this option, please skip to the Create Your First Component section.

In the Project Navigator, select the valsrevenge group and create a new group (⌥⌘N). Name this new group Extensions, and then move the SKScene+ViewProperties.swift, GameScene+ViewUpdates.swift, and SKTileMapNode+Physics.swift files into the newly created group.

Just above the Extensions group, create another new group (⌥⌘N) and name this one Reference Nodes. Move the Controller.sks and AttackButton.sks files into the newly created Reference Nodes group.

You're almost done, hang in there—you have two more groups to create. Name the first new group Scenes and place it above the Reference Nodes group. Move the GameScene.sks and GameScene.swift files into the new Scenes group.

Finally, create the last new group, naming it Tile Sets, and then move the Main-TileSet.sks into the Tile Sets group.

To further organize your project, move the GameViewController.swift file and the Assets.xcassets catalog above the Tile Sets group. When you start adding additional resources, like music and sound files, having all of the audio and visual assets grouped at the top of the project, along with the main view controller, is helpful.

Excellent, you're ready to add some resources.

Add the Resources

Rather than have you jump in and out of Finder over the next few chapters, you'll add all of the necessary resources for this part of the book, making things a little easier to follow.

First, below the Assets.xcassets catalog, create two more groups. Name one Music and the other Sounds.

In the Project Navigator, select the Assets.xcassets catalog and add four new sprite atlases (click the + button at the bottom of the Outline View and select New Sprite Atlas). Name these new atlases as follows:

- collectibles
- health
- monster_goblin
- monster_skeleton

Xcode 12 and Sprite Atlas Creation

In Xcode 12, the New Sprite Atlas option does not exist. To create a new sprite atlas, click the + button at the bottom of the Outline View and select AR and SceneKit ▶ Sprite Atlas.

When you're done creating these new atlases, don't forget to delete all of the default Sprite image sets Xcode creates.

Next, open Finder and navigate to the resources folder for this chapter. In Finder, switch to the list view, like this (it's easier to drag multiple files into the project when Finder is in list view mode):

Finally, drag all of the resources from Finder into their respective places within your project. For example, drag all of the files from the collectibles folder into the collectibles sprite atlas, and all of the files in the sounds folder into the Sounds group.

When you drag the reference nodes, sound, and music files into their respective groups, be sure that Copy items if needed is checked, Create groups is selected, and the valsrevenge option is checked in the Add to targets box.

When you're done, your project will look like this:

Fantastic, you've got your project organized, and the resources added—you're officially ready to get your hands dirty with entities and components.

Create Your First Component

The first component you'll make is a health component. The health component is a way to track the number of health points an entity has remaining.

To make a component using the GameplayKit framework, you need to subclass the GKComponent superclass (which is another way of referring to the base class or parent class).

Each component represents a single "trait" or "ability" that you can add to an entity, and an entity represents one of your game objects. The nice thing about components is that you can reuse and add them to any type of entity. For example, you can create a single health component that both your player and monsters can share.

Creating the Health Component

In the Project Navigator, below the Extensions group, create a new group (⌥⌘N) and name it Components.

Inside the new Components group, create a new file (⌘N) using the iOS Swift File template. Name the new file HealthComponent.swift, and replace its contents with the following code:

```swift
import SpriteKit
import GameplayKit

class HealthComponent: GKComponent {

  override func didAddToEntity() {

  }

  override func willRemoveFromEntity() {

  }

  override func update(deltaTime seconds: TimeInterval) {

  }

  override class var supportsSecureCoding: Bool {
    true
  }
}
```

This code represents a standard implementation of a GameplayKit component. Let's have a closer look at your new health component.

The first two methods, didAddToEntity() and willRemoveFromEntity(), are useful for when you need to take some kind of action when adding or removing a component from an entity; this can include things like setting up the health component or altering the color of the player sprite as she gains or loses a power-up.

The third method, update(deltaTime:), is useful for when you need to make periodic updates to your entities and components. This method works in conjunction with the scene's update method and is useful for when you want to update certain entities and/or components with specific game logic, such as simulating monster AI.

You can use two types of update patterns with entities and components: *per-entity* and *per-component*.

With per-entity updates, the entity is responsible for updating its components. You accomplish these updates by looping through all of the entities within a scene, calling the update(deltaTime:) method on each one. This, in turn, calls the update(deltaTime:) method on the attached components:

```swift
// Update entities
for entity in self.entities {
  entity.update(deltaTime: dt)
}
```

With per-component updates, you set up a component system using a GKComponentSystem object. The component system is then responsible for handling the updates. When you use a components system, you can target specific components and then update them in a deliberate and deterministic order rather than looping through the entities within a scene:

```
// Set up the component system
let system = GKComponentSystem(componentClass: MonsterComponent.self)

// Set up the monster entity
let monster = MonsterEntity()

// Either explicitly add a type of component to the system
monster.addComponent(GeneratorComponent())

// Or find a specific component inside of an entity, and add it that way
system.addComponent(foundIn: monster)

// Update the system
system.update(deltaTime: dt)
```

Val's Revenge uses a per-entity design pattern when updating the components.

The remaining code, which isn't actually part of the GKComponent class, is a static Boolean value indicating whether or not this component supports secure coding. Because you'll be using your components with archived scene files, you need to override the supportsSecureCoding type property and return a value of true. Failure to override this property will cause loading problems with your scenes, typically resulting in an empty gray screen.

When you first add a health component to an entity, you'll need to set up and add the health meter reference node. The health meter reference node is one of the resource files you added in Add the Resources, on page 230. For reference (no pun intended), the HealthMeter.sks file looks like this:

Adding the Health Meter Reference Node

With the HealthComponent.swift file open in the Source Editor, add the following code to the didAddToEntity() method:

```
guard let node = entity?.component(ofType: GKSKNodeComponent.self)?.node
  else {
  return
}
```

```
if let healthMeter = SKReferenceNode(fileNamed: "HealthMeter") {
  healthMeter.position = CGPoint(x: 0, y: 100)
  node.addChild(healthMeter)
}
```

This code first checks that a SpriteKit node is present before attempting to add a child reference node to itself.

Save the HealthComponent.swift file, and then in the Project Navigator, select the GameScene.sks file to open it in the Scene Editor.

To prevent any accidental node movement, lock the Grass Tile Map and the Dungeon Tile Map.

In the Scene Graph View, select the player node. Click the button to show the inspectors and then switch to the Component Inspector, which looks like this:

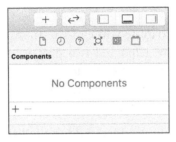

The Component Inspector is where you can add and remove your components. When you add components to a node using the Scene Editor, Xcode automatically creates the GKSKNodeComponent object for you. This object manages the relationship between the node and the entity property of the node to which the component is attached.

Click the + button to reveal the list of available components. For now, there's only one, the HealthComponent. Select the HealthComponent item from the list to add it to the player node, like this:

Build and run the project, you'll see Val now has a health meter above her head:

This is a great start, but there's a lot more you need to do, such as configuring the health meter's initial settings.

Configuring the Health Meter

You'll eventually add monsters to your game, and those monsters will also require a health meter, so it makes sense to build the health component with shareability and flexibility in mind.

In the Project Navigator, select the HealthComponent.swift file to, once again, open it in the Source Editor.

Below (and inside) the class declaration, add the following code:

```
@GKInspectable var currentHealth: Int = 3
@GKInspectable var maxHealth: Int = 3
```

The @GKInspectable is an attribute you can use to expose a property within the Scene Editor. Here, you're exposing two properties you can use to set the current health and maximum health for any node you attach this health component to, which gives you more flexibility with regard to the amount of health you can set up per entity.

Below the properties you just added, add the following two lines of code:

```
private let healthFull = SKTexture(imageNamed: "health_full")
private let healthEmpty = SKTexture(imageNamed: "health_empty")
```

Here, you're setting up the two textures you'll use to represent when a health bar is full versus when it's empty.

Next, you will need a way to determine which texture to use depending on how much health an entity has remaining. For that, you can use a small helper method. Add the following new method below the didAddToEntity() method:

```
func setupBar(at num: Int, tint: SKColor? = nil) {
  guard let node = entity?.component(ofType: GKSKNodeComponent.self)?.node
    else {
      return
  }
  if let health = node.childNode(withName: ".//health_\(num)")
    as? SKSpriteNode {
    if currentHealth >= num {
      health.texture = healthFull
      if let tint = tint {
        health.color = tint
        health.colorBlendFactor = 1.0
      }
```

```
    } else {
      health.texture = healthEmpty
      health.colorBlendFactor = 0.0
    }
  }
}
```

Once again, you're verifying that a node exists, and then you're using that node to find the corresponding health bar node within the reference node. You're also making it possible to set a tint color for the health bar, providing even more flexibility.

Finally, add one more new method to the health meter component, placing it above the setupBar(at:tint:) method:

```
func updateHealth(_ value: Int, forNode node: SKNode?) {
  currentHealth += value

  if currentHealth > maxHealth {
    currentHealth = maxHealth
  }
  if let _ = node as? Player {
    for barNum in 1...maxHealth {
      setupBar(at: barNum, tint: .cyan)
    }
  } else {
    for barNum in 1...maxHealth {
      setupBar(at: barNum)
    }
  }
}
```

You'll use this function to update the health meter as needed, for example, when setting up the entity's initial health points or when the health points decrease or increase during gameplay. Notice that you're passing in .cyan as the tint color when the node is a Player node.

Now that you have this handy helper method and update routine in place, it's time to put them to use. In the didAddToEntity() method, below the line that reads node.addChild(healthMeter), add the following line of code:

```
updateHealth(0, forNode: node)
```

For reference, the updated didAddToEntity() method looks like this:

```
override func didAddToEntity() {
  guard let node = entity?.component(ofType: GKSKNodeComponent.self)?.node
    else {
      return
  }
```

```
  if let healthMeter = SKReferenceNode(fileNamed: "HealthMeter") {
    healthMeter.position = CGPoint(x: 0, y: 100)
    node.addChild(healthMeter)

    updateHealth(0, forNode: node)
  }
}
```

Excellent, the health bar will now update once this component is added to an entity. Save this file and then switch back to the GameScene.sks file.

Once again, in the Scene Graph View, select the player node and this time, notice that in the Components Inspector, you now have some new options:

What you're seeing are the inspectable properties you set up earlier in the HealthComponent class. For the player node, enter the number 3 for both the currentHealth and maxHealth properties. (You could also leave the maxHealth and currentHealth fields blank, letting them use their default values of 3; however, it's generally best to be explicit when setting the component properties.)

Updating Components in the Scene Editor

Working with components and their properties inside the Scene Editor is quite powerful; however, the integration between GameplayKit and the Scene Editor has a few glitches, especially when the underlying component changes or the value of one of its properties changes.

Should you find that components and nodes aren't behaving as expected—for example, the value you set isn't being recognized—try removing and re-adding the component or the node to resolve the problem.

Now that you have a fully customizable health component, it's time to try it out with a monster.

Creating Your First Monster

Drag a new Color Sprite into the scene. In the Attributes Inspector, set the following options:

- Name: monster
- Texture: skeleton_0
- Scale: (X: 0.75, Y: 0.75)

With the monster node still selected, switch to the Components Inspector and add a new HealthComponent. Set both the currentHealth and maxHealth property values to 2.

Build and run the project. Notice that Val and the Skeleton monster each have their own health component attached, and each with its own configuration:

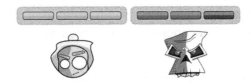

Now that you have your first component set up and know how to add it to a node using the Scene Editor, you're ready to find out how to add this same component to an entity through code.

Create Your First Entity

An entity, as it relates to the Entity-Component architecture, is any game object within your game. This can include things like the player, the monsters, the collectibles, and even the projectiles—but typically, not something like the background.

With GameplayKit, you can either use a generic GKEntity object or create a new GKEntity subclass. For Val's Revenge, you'll create a new subclass.

In keeping with your new project organization, create a new group (⌥⌘N) above the Components group and name this new group Entities.

Although the Player class isn't *technically* an entity (it's an SKSpriteNode), drag the Player.swift file into the newly created Entities group. By placing the Player.swift file into the Entities group, you are keeping up with your overall project organization.

Inside the Entities group, create a new file (⌘N) using the iOS Swift File template. Name this new file MonsterEntity.swift and replace its contents with the following code:

```
import SpriteKit
import GameplayKit

class MonsterEntity: GKEntity {

  init(monsterType: String) {
    super.init()

  }

  required init?(coder: NSCoder) {
    super.init(coder:coder)
  }
}
```

This code creates a new MonsterEntity class with an initialization method that takes a single string input parameter with a name of monsterType. You'll use this parameter to specify the monster type, which as of now, is either a skeleton or a goblin.

Because a GameplayKit entity is *not* a SpriteKit sprite node, and therefore does not include a visual representation of itself, you need to create a new component to render the sprite.

Inside the Components group, create another new file (⌘N) using the iOS Swift File template. Name this new file RenderComponent.swift and replace its contents with the following code:

```
import SpriteKit
import GameplayKit

class RenderComponent: GKComponent {
  lazy var spriteNode: SKSpriteNode? = {
    entity?.component(ofType: GKSKNodeComponent.self)?.node as? SKSpriteNode
  }()

  init(node: SKSpriteNode) {
    super.init()
    spriteNode = node
  }

  init(imageNamed: String, scale: CGFloat) {
    super.init()

    spriteNode = SKSpriteNode(imageNamed: imageNamed)
    spriteNode?.setScale(scale)
  }
```

```
  override func didAddToEntity() {
    spriteNode?.entity = entity
  }
  required init?(coder: NSCoder) {
    super.init(coder:coder)
  }
  override class var supportsSecureCoding: Bool {
    true
  }
}
```

Once again, you're grabbing the entity's node, except this time, you're returning that node as an SKSpriteNode object and storing it in the spriteNode property.

Now that you have a monster entity and a way to render a sprite for it, it's time to create a monster generator. (Because what good is a dungeon if it's not filled with monsters, right?)

For your monster generator, you'll build another component.

Build a Monster Generator

The monster generator is what you'll use to periodically spawn new monsters of a certain type at specific locations within the dungeon.

In the Project Navigator, select the Components group, and inside that group, create a new file (⌘N) using the iOS Swift File template. Name the new file GeneratorComponent.swift and replace its contents with the following code:

```
import SpriteKit
import GameplayKit

class GeneratorComponent: GKComponent {

  override func didAddToEntity() {

  }
  override class var supportsSecureCoding: Bool {
    true
  }
}
```

Because you won't be overriding any of the other standard methods in this component, you can omit them.

Also, because you'll be doing a lot with components—both in code and by way of the Scene Editor—it makes sense to create an extension to better manage the underlying node of the entity.

Creating a Component Extension

You may have noticed that in the health component you created in Create Your First Component, on page 232, there was some duplicated code—specifically in regard to verifying that an underlying node exists. Rather than recreating the wheel in every component you make, you'll create a GKComponent extension to handle it for you.

Inside the Extensions group, create a new file (⌘N) using the iOS Swift File template. Name this new file GKComponent+Node.swift and replace its contents with the following code:

```
import SpriteKit
import GameplayKit

extension GKComponent {
  var componentNode: SKNode {
    if let node = entity?.component(ofType: GKSKNodeComponent.self)?.node {
      return node
    } else if let node = entity?.component(ofType:
      RenderComponent.self)?.spriteNode {
      return node
    }

    return SKNode()
  }
}
```

Here, you're creating an extension on the GKComponent class that returns either the node from the GKSKNodeComponent object or the node from the RenderComponent class. Thanks to this extension, it won't matter if you're referring to a component that's been added through code or one that's been added by way of the Scene Editor.

You can now modify the health component you made earlier to use this new componentNode property. In the Project Navigator, select the HealthComponent.swift file and update the didAddToEntity() method to match the following:

```
override func didAddToEntity() {
  if let healthMeter = SKReferenceNode(fileNamed: "HealthMeter") {
    healthMeter.position = CGPoint(x: 0, y: 100)
    componentNode.addChild(healthMeter)

    updateHealth(0, forNode: componentNode)
  }
}
```

Also, update the setupBar(at:tint:) method to match this:

```
func setupBar(at num: Int, tint: SKColor? = nil) {
  if let health = componentNode.childNode(withName: ".//health_\(num)")
    as? SKSpriteNode {
    if currentHealth >= num {
      health.texture = healthFull
      if let tint = tint {
        health.color = tint
        health.colorBlendFactor = 1.0
      }
    } else {
      health.texture = healthEmpty
      health.colorBlendFactor = 0.0
    }
  }
}
```

If you'd like, you can also remove or comment out the two empty override methods (willRemoveFromEntity() and update(deltaTime:)') since you won't be needing or using them.

Getting Back to Your Generator

Switch back to the GeneratorComponent.swift file and add the following inspectable properties (remember, like other properties, these properties go inside the class below the declaration):

```
@GKInspectable var monsterType: String = "skeleton"
@GKInspectable var maxMonsters: Int = 10

@GKInspectable var waitTime: TimeInterval = 5
@GKInspectable var monsterHealth: Int = 3
```

You'll use these new properties to set up the type and strength of the monsters the generator will spawn. These properties also determine how many monsters each generator will produce and how often it spits them out.

The next step is to write the method that creates each monster, so add the following new method to the GeneratorComponent class:

```
func spawnMonsterEntity() {
  let monsterEntity = MonsterEntity(monsterType: monsterType)
  let renderComponent = RenderComponent(imageNamed: "\(monsterType)_0",
    scale: 0.65)
  monsterEntity.addComponent(renderComponent)

  if let monsterNode =
    monsterEntity.component(ofType: RenderComponent.self)?.spriteNode {
    monsterNode.position = componentNode.position
    componentNode.parent?.addChild(monsterNode)

    monsterNode.run(SKAction.moveBy(x: 100, y: 0, duration: 1.0))
```

```
    let healthComponent = HealthComponent()
    healthComponent.currentHealth = monsterHealth
    monsterEntity.addComponent(healthComponent)
  }
}
```

Here, you're creating a monster entity and then adding to it the two components, HealthComponent and RenderComponent, using the addComponent(_:) method of the GKEntity class. You're also using an action to move the monster a little to the right after it spawns. You'll eventually attach some AI logic to your monsters in Chapter 13, Planning Routes and Creating Believable AI, on page 277 to get them moving on their own, but for now, this move will get them out of the way of the generator.

Now that you have a method to spawn monsters, you can call that method when the generator component is added to an entity. However, because you want the generator to spawn multiple monsters, you'll use a repeating action to call the new spawnMonsterEntity() method.

Add the following code in the didAddToEntity() method:

```
let wait = SKAction.wait(forDuration: waitTime)
let spawn = SKAction.run { [unowned self] in self.spawnMonsterEntity() }
let sequence = SKAction.sequence([wait, spawn])

let repeatAction: SKAction?
if maxMonsters == 0 {
  repeatAction = SKAction.repeatForever(sequence)
} else {
  repeatAction = SKAction.repeat(sequence, count: maxMonsters)
}

componentNode.run(repeatAction!, withKey: "spawnMonster")
```

With this method, you're using the value in the maxMonsters property to determine how many times to call the spawnMonsterEntity() method. Note, however, that if the value is 0, you call the spawnMonsterEntity() method indefinitely. (Although, you probably don't want to make too many generators that continually spit out monsters. Resources are a valuable thing, and you don't want to needlessly overload your player's device.)

Save the file and then switch to the GameScene.sks file to open it in the Scene Editor.

Select the monster node and add your new generator component. For now, don't worry about setting any of the values in this component. Because you've set up default values in the GeneratorComponent class, the component will automatically use the following settings:

- monsterHealth: 3
- maxMonsters: 10
- monsterType: skeleton
- waitTime: 5

Build and run the project. Notice that every five seconds, the monster generator spawns a new skeleton monster with a health of 3. After 10 monsters, the generator stops.

You're making great progress, but the monster generators could use a little animation to help bring them to life and set them apart from the regular (soon to be roaming) monsters.

Animate the Monsters

To help distinguish your monster generators from standard monsters, you'll create an animation component, which you'll use to animate the monsters. First you'll create an extension to help build the textures. Then, you'll build out the animation component and define the different types of animations.

Creating an Animation Extension

In Load the Textures, on page 34, you built a small helper method to help load textures for animation. This time around, however, you'll create an extension method for the SKTexture class instead. Extensions are generally preferred as they tend to be more reusable than helper methods that can easily get buried within the underbelly of your code.

In the Project Navigator, and inside the Extensions group, create a new file (⌘N) using the iOS Swift Filetemplate. Name the new file SKTexture+LoadTextures.swift and replace its contents with the following:

```
import SpriteKit

extension SKTexture {
  static func loadTextures(atlas: String, prefix: String,
                           startsAt: Int, stopsAt: Int) -> [SKTexture] {

    var textureArray = [SKTexture]()
    let textureAtlas = SKTextureAtlas(named: atlas)
    for i in startsAt...stopsAt {
      let textureName = "\(prefix)\(i)"
      let temp = textureAtlas.textureNamed(textureName)
      textureArray.append(temp)
    }

    return textureArray
  }
}
```

This code should look familiar to you since you used something similar in Gloop Drop. In case it doesn't (or if you forgot how it works), you're essentially looping through the input values to build an array of textures that you'll use for the animation.

Excellent, you now have a handy way of loading textures. It's time to put this method to good use in a new animation component.

Creating an Animation Component

Inside the `Components` group, create a new file (⌘N) using the iOS Swift File template. Name the new file AnimationComponent.swift and replace its contents with the following:

```
import SpriteKit
import GameplayKit

// MARK: - COMPONENT CODE STARTS HERE

class AnimationComponent: GKComponent {

  override func didAddToEntity() {

  }

  override class var supportsSecureCoding: Bool {
    true
  }
}
```

This code sets you up with a base starting point for your new animation component.

However, before you get into the finer implementation details, let's use a struct to define exactly what an animation is.

At the top of this file (and below the import statements), add the following:

```
struct Animation {
  let textures: [SKTexture]
  var timePerFrame: TimeInterval

  let repeatTexturesForever: Bool
  let resizeTexture: Bool
  let restoreTexture: Bool

  init(textures: [SKTexture],
       timePerFrame: TimeInterval = TimeInterval(1.0 / 5.0),
       repeatTexturesForever: Bool = true, resizeTexture: Bool = true,
       restoreTexture: Bool = true) {

    self.textures = textures
    self.timePerFrame = timePerFrame
    self.repeatTexturesForever = repeatTexturesForever
```

```
    self.resizeTexture = resizeTexture
    self.restoreTexture = restoreTexture
  }
}
```

Here, you're setting up a handful of properties that define an animation; this includes properties like the texture array, the time per frame, and how often to repeat the animation. But before you can complete and use the animation component, you need to specify the different types of animation for your game objects.

Defining the Game Objects

Inside the Entities group, create another new file (⌘N) using the iOS Swift File template. Name this new file GameObjects.swift and replace its contents with the following code:

```
import SpriteKit
import GameplayKit

enum GameObjectType: String {

  // Monsters
  case skeleton
  case goblin
}

struct GameObject {

  static let defaultGeneratorType = GameObjectType.skeleton.rawValue
  static let defaultAnimationType = GameObjectType.skeleton.rawValue

  static let skeleton = Skeleton()
  static let goblin = Goblin()

  struct Goblin {
    let animationSettings = Animation(textures:
      SKTexture.loadTextures(atlas: "monster_goblin",
                     prefix: "goblin_", startsAt: 0, stopsAt: 1))
  }

  struct Skeleton {
    let animationSettings = Animation(textures:
      SKTexture.loadTextures(atlas: "monster_skeleton",
                     prefix: "skeleton_", startsAt: 0, stopsAt: 1),
                     timePerFrame: TimeInterval(1.0 / 25.0))
  }
}
```

This uses the new SKTexture extension to create some static properties that hold information about your game objects, including its animation type. As your game grows, you can add additional properties and objects here, keeping everything you need about your game objects in one place.

Below the code you just added, yet still inside the GameObject struct, add the following code:

```
static func forAnimationType(_ type: GameObjectType?) -> Animation? {
  switch type {
  case .skeleton:
    return GameObject.skeleton.animationSettings
  case .goblin:
    return GameObject.goblin.animationSettings
  default:
    return nil
  }
}
```

This code defines a static method that you can use to grab an object's animation set up.

Switch back to the AnimationComponent.swift file and then add the following new property:

```
@GKInspectable var animationType: String = GameObject.defaultAnimationType
```

You can use this property to define the animation type, setting the default property to whatever string value you defined in the GameObjects.swift file—in this case, skeleton.

Scroll down a bit, and in the didAddToEntity() method, add the following code:

```
guard let animation =
  GameObject.forAnimationType(GameObjectType(rawValue: animationType)) else {
    return
}

let textures = animation.textures
let timePerFrame = animation.timePerFrame
let animationAction = SKAction.animate(with: textures,
                                       timePerFrame: timePerFrame)

if animation.repeatTexturesForever == true {
  let repeatAction = SKAction.repeatForever(animationAction)
  componentNode.run(repeatAction)
} else {
  componentNode.run(animationAction)
}
```

This code uses the static method to retrieve and build the desired game object's animation.

Notice the animationType inspectable property? If you recall, in the GeneratorComponent class, you had a monsterType inspectable property where you set its default string value to skeleton. Rather than hardcode that value (hardcoding should be avoided when possible), you can now update this property to use your new defaultGeneratorType that you created in the GameObject struct—again, keeping all of your game objects and related setup in one place.

Switch to the GeneratorComponent.swift file and replace the following line:

```
@GKInspectable var monsterType: String = "skeleton"
```

with this one instead:

```
@GKInspectable var monsterType: String = GameObject.defaultGeneratorType
```

With this change, you make it much easier to change your default generator type in the future. For example, suppose you initially wanted skeleton monsters as the default monster type. You might create multiple components and/or other code where you'd hardcode skeleton for the value, as you previously did here. Then suppose, some time later in the future, you decide that a ghost monster would have been a better choice. In that case, you'd have to update all of those hardcoded values. However, by creating a single default type and using that instead, you only need to update your value in one spot.

Adding the Monster Generators to the Scene

All right, it's time to get the monster generators added to the scene.

Save the GeneratorComponent.swift file and switch back to the GameScene.sks file. Remove the monster node and add two new Color Sprite nodes. Switch to the Attributes Inspector, and set up the two sprite nodes like so:

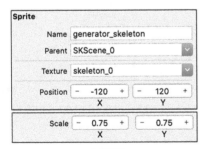
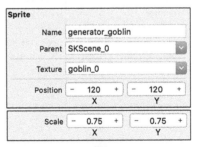

Setting Up the Monster Generators

The final step is to add the components to each of the monster generator nodes. Val is a warrior at heart, so she'll need quite a few monsters to give her a worthy challenge. Switch to the Components Inspector, and with the generator_goblin node selected, add the following components with the following settings:

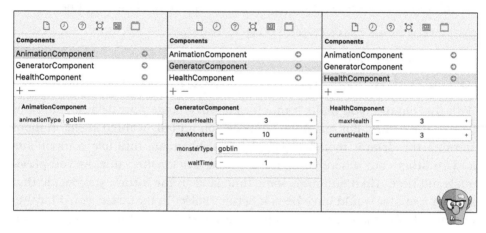

Switch to the generator_skeleton node and add its components with the following settings:

Build and run the project. You'll notice that each monster generator spits out its monsters, each with its own health indicator. You'll also see that the generators are now animated with blinking eyes.

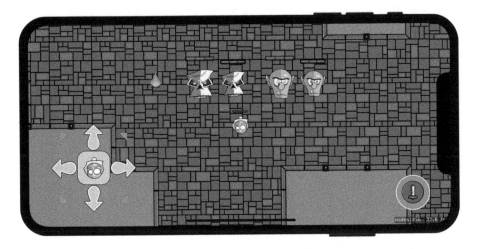

Next Steps

In this chapter, you brought some much-needed organization to your project, and you started working with the Entity-Component design pattern using the GameplayKit framework. With this design pattern, you're able to better manage your code while also providing yourself with the flexibility to extend your game with new monsters without completely re-writing your code.

In the next chapter, you'll do a little more work with entities and components as you start to build out some additional player logic.

Using States and State Machines

In the previous chapter, you started using the Entity Component System (ECS) architecture. As you were learning about this popular game design pattern, you built four separate components for the Val's Revenge game.

In this chapter, you'll pick up where you left off, adding two more components: one to handle collectible items, and one to manage the physics bodies. You'll also begin to add more gameplay- and game state–related logic, such as what happens when players find treasure and food, or what happens when they pick up keys that Val can use to unlock doors.

Game State and the State Pattern

 Finding the definition of *game state* isn't that easy. Not because it's a made-up term—that's not it at all. The problem is that game state is actually part of a larger design pattern known as the *state pattern*, which is closely related to the concept of a *finite-state machine (FSM)*. Using the state pattern, you're able to track the state of an object—in other words, the way something is with respect to its attributes. For example, whether or not the game is in progress.

Traditionally, game developers would manage game state and state-related logic using a series of if statements. For example, in the GameScene class, you might add code similar to this:

```
if gameInProgress == true {
  // do this
} else {
  // do this instead
}
```

Although this sort of code works—in fact, you used something similar in Restarting the Game, on page 101—you do have another option: use *states* and *state machines*.

With states and state machines, you're able to define distinct states within your game, such as if the game is in progress or not. You can then set up and use state machines to handle moving between the different states, giving you more control of what happens when exiting and entering the different states. More important, you can define what occurs when your game is currently in one state versus another.

With GameplayKit, you use the GKState and GKStateMachine superclasses to create and manage your game states. In Val's Revenge, you'll create a player state machine to track when players have keys in their inventory versus when they do not. You'll use this information to determine whether or not Val can unlock the dungeon doors that stand in her way of fortune and glory.

Now that you have an idea of what you'll be doing in this chapter, it's time to jump into the code, starting with setting up the different game states.

Create the Player States

Val has a lot going on—keeping the dungeon free and clear of monsters isn't easy, ya know? The least you can do is help her keep track of her keys.

To begin, open the valsrevenge project in Xcode.

Using the Starter Project

You may continue using your project from the previous chapter, or you can use the starter project located in the projects/begin folder included with the code resources for this chapter. Either option is fine; the only benefit to using the starter project is that you won't get stuck going forward if you missed an earlier step.

There's also an ending project for this chapter that includes all of the code and resources you'll be adding here. The end project is located in the projects/end folder included with the code resources for this chapter.

In the Project Navigator, select the valsrevenge group and create a new group (⌥⌘N). Name this new group States and move it above the Entities group.

Inside of the newly created States group, create a new file (⌘N) using the iOS Swift File template. Name the new file PlayerStates.swift.

For this project, and to keep things somewhat simplified, you will use a single file to store the player states. As you add more states to your game or build states that contain a lot of code, you may decide to create a separate file for each one. Replace the contents of the PlayerStates.swift file with the following code:

```
import GameplayKit

class PlayerHasKeyState: GKState {

}

class PlayerHasNoKeyState: GKState {

}
```

Here, you are declaring two separate states using the GKState superclass, each representing a possible game state for the player: one for when Val has a key in her possession, and one for when she does not. With these two states, you will have more precise control over the state-dependent game logic.

With the two player states stubbed out, you're ready to add the rest of the code. Update the code in the PlayerStates.swift file to match the following:

```
import GameplayKit

class PlayerHasKeyState: GKState {
  override func isValidNextState(_ stateClass: AnyClass) -> Bool {
    return stateClass == PlayerHasKeyState.self ||
      stateClass == PlayerHasNoKeyState.self
  }

  override func didEnter(from previousState: GKState?) {
    print(" Entering PlayerHasKeyState")
  }

  override func willExit(to nextState: GKState) {
    // print("Exiting PlayerHasKeyState")
  }

  override func update(deltaTime seconds: TimeInterval) {
    // print("Updating PlayerHasKeyState")
  }
}
class PlayerHasNoKeyState: GKState {
  override func isValidNextState(_ stateClass: AnyClass) -> Bool {
    return stateClass == PlayerHasKeyState.self ||
      stateClass == PlayerHasNoKeyState.self
  }

  override func didEnter(from previousState: GKState?) {
    print("Entering PlayerHasNoKeyState")
  }
```

```
  override func willExit(to nextState: GKState) {
    // print("Exiting PlayerHasNoKeyState")
  }
  override func update(deltaTime seconds: TimeInterval) {
    // print("Updating PlayerHasNoKeyState")
  }
}
```

There's quite a bit of code here, so let's break it down:

The isValidNextState(_:) method in each state tells the state machine whether or not the state it's trying to enter is valid. In this case, a player going from either state into the other (or itself) is allowed, so you return both states in each method.

Although you're not doing much with the didEnter(from:) and willExit(to:) methods, you can use these to run state-dependent game logic when entering and/or exiting a specific state. For example, let's say players can only keep keys for a certain length of time. In that case, you may want to start a timer in the didEnter(from: method that automatically exits the PlayerHasKeyState after that time expires. That's not the plan for this game, but it is possible. Instead, you're just printing a message to the console when entering the different states. (You normally wouldn't override these methods if you weren't using them.)

Finally, there's the update(deltaTime:) method. With this method, you can execute per-frame, state-dependent game logic while the state machine is in *this* state—whatever the state may be at the time of the update. For example, using the same example from earlier, you could use this method to track the elapsed time since entering the PlayerHasKeyState state to automatically exit to the PlayerHasNoKeyState state after a specific amount of time has passed. (Again, you normally wouldn't override this method if you weren't using it.)

With the player states ready and waiting, it's time to set up a state machine to handle them.

Set Up the Player State Machine

In GameplayKit, you use the GKStateMachine superclass to create state machines. A state machine holds the list of possible states, the current state, and some logic for moving between the states.

For Val's Revenge, you'll create a player state machine that controls the player's state, specifically for tracking when players have a key versus when they don't.

In the Project Navigator, switch to the Player.swift file. Below the line that reads import SpriteKit, add the following new import statement to import the GameplayKit framework:

```
import GameplayKit
```

Next, you need a property to hold the state machine for the Player class. Add the following code at the top of the Player class, just above the currentDirection property declaration:

```
var stateMachine = GKStateMachine(states: [PlayerHasKeyState(),
                                            PlayerHasNoKeyState()])
```

This code creates a single state machine, initialized with the two player states you created earlier.

The next step is to set the initial state for the player state machine. In Creating the Player Class, on page 162, you created the bare minimum required to get the Player class working. Since you're adding the player sprite node using the Scene Editor, you can override the init(coder:) method and set the default state there. Above the move(_:) method, add the following new method to the Player class:

```
// Override this method to allow for a class to work in the Scene Editor
required init?(coder: NSCoder) {
  super.init(coder: coder)

  stateMachine.enter(PlayerHasNoKeyState.self)
}
```

(While you're here, comment out the print() statement in the move(_:) method.)

There's not much going on with this code: you're using the enter(_:) method of the GKStateMachine class to enter the specified state: PlayerHasNoKeyState. It makes sense to start Val without a key, giving her the immediate challenge of finding one so that she can explore deeper into the dungeon.

Build and run the project. Look at the console and you'll see something like this:

```
Entering PlayerHasNoKeyState
```

With this confirmation, you now know you have a new initialization method that gets called when the player node is added to the scene. This same method also sets the initial state of the player; however, you still need to define the collectible items—for that, you'll create a new collectible component.

Add a New Collectible Component

You first learned about components in Create Your First Component, on page 232. With components, the focus is on what a "thing" does versus what it is.

You might believe that this focus lets you off the hook for thinking about what things are, but that isn't the case; you still need to consider how you'll be using your components.

In Val's Revenge, there are three kinds of collectible items (types):

Key   Food   Treasure

Each type serves a useful purpose:

- Key: Collect keys to unlock dungeon doors
- Food: Collect food to increase Val's health (up to her maximum)
- Treasure: Collect treasure for bragging rights

Similar to what you did in Creating an Animation Component, on page 246, you'll create a single file to hold the collectible component and the corresponding collectible struct that defines the collectible properties.

Creating the Collectible Struct

In the Components group, create a new file (⌘N) using the iOS Swift File template. Name the new file CollectibleComponent.swift and replace the contents with the following code:

```
import SpriteKit
import GameplayKit

struct Collectible {
  let type: GameObjectType

  let collectSoundFile: String
  let destroySoundFile: String

  let canDestroy: Bool

  init(type: GameObjectType, collectSound: String,
       destroySound: String, canDestroy: Bool = false) {
    self.type = type

    self.collectSoundFile = collectSound
    self.destroySoundFile = destroySound

    self.canDestroy = canDestroy
  }
}
```

This code sets up the new Collectible struct and its initializer with a default value for the canDestroy property. In addition to this property, the struct also includes properties for the collectible type and the collected and destroyed sound filenames—in other words, what sounds the player will hear when Val picks up or destroys a collectible.

Before you finish this new component, you need to set up the collectible game objects. Before moving on to the next section, save the file.

Adding the Collectible Game Objects

Switch to the GameObjects.swift file. Inside the GameObjectType enum, and below the line that reads case goblin, add the following code:

```
// Collectibles
case key
case food
case treasure
```

These are the three collectible types you'll be using in Val's Revenge.

Next, you'll use the Collectible struct to set up and store the collectible settings for each type. In the GameObject struct, add the following code below the Skeleton struct:

```
struct Key {
  let collectibleSettings = Collectible(type: .key,
                                        collectSound: "key",
                                        destroySound: "destroyed")
}

struct Food {
  let collectibleSettings = Collectible(type: .food,
                                        collectSound: "food",
                                        destroySound: "destroyed",
                                        canDestroy: true)
}

struct Treasure {
  let collectibleSettings = Collectible(type: .treasure,
                                        collectSound: "treasure",
                                        destroySound: "destroyed")
}
```

This code configures the collectible settings for the three different collectible types; this includes which sound file to use when the player either picks up or destroys a collectible item. (In Add the Resources, on page 230, you added some project resources; some of those resources included the sound files you're using here.)

Scroll up a little, and just above the Goblin struct, add the following code:

```
static let key = Key()
static let food = Food()
static let treasure = Treasure()
```

This code creates the static instances of your three collectible types, making it possible to refer to them later so that you can retrieve their individual settings.

Now scroll back down, and below the forAnimationType(_:) method, add the following new method:

```
static func forCollectibleType(_ type: GameObjectType?) -> Collectible? {
  switch type {
  case .key:
    return GameObject.key.collectibleSettings
  case .food:
    return GameObject.food.collectibleSettings
  case .treasure:
    return GameObject.treasure.collectibleSettings
  default:
    return nil
  }
}
```

This static method, like the forAnimationType(_:) method before it, grabs the settings for the specified collectible type.

Finally, below the line that reads:

```
static let defaultAnimationType = GameObjectType.skeleton.rawValue
```

add the following code:

```
static let defaultCollectibleType = GameObjectType.key.rawValue
```

This code sets the default collectible type, making it easier to maintain your code, especially if you want to change the default collectible type later. With everything in place, you're ready to create the collectible component so that you can define the collectibles in the game and on the map.

Creating the Collectible Component

Switch back to the CollectibleComponent.swift file and add the following code below (and outside of) the Collectible struct:

```
// MARK: - COMPONENT CODE STARTS HERE

class CollectibleComponent: GKComponent {

  @GKInspectable var collectibleType: String =
    GameObject.defaultCollectibleType
  @GKInspectable var value: Int = 1

  private var collectSoundAction = SKAction()
  private var destroySoundAction = SKAction()
  private var canDestroy = false

}
```

Here, you're creating the necessary properties for the collectible component. Notice that two of these properties are inspectable, meaning you'll have access to them in the Scene Editor.

Get More Control in the Scene Editor

In Val's Revenge, the canDestroy property is not something you can modify on the fly while you're building your scene. You can, however, change this behavior by changing the code to use a @GKInspectable property instead. There is no right or wrong here as to which properties you expose in the Scene Editor—it's really just a matter of what makes the most sense for your game.

Next, inside the new CollectibleComponent class, add the following code:

```
override func didAddToEntity() {
  guard let collectible =
    GameObject.forCollectibleType(GameObjectType(rawValue: collectibleType))
    else {
      return
  }

  collectSoundAction =
    SKAction.playSoundFileNamed(collectible.collectSoundFile,
                              waitForCompletion: false)

  destroySoundAction =
    SKAction.playSoundFileNamed(collectible.destroySoundFile,
                              waitForCompletion: false)

  canDestroy = collectible.canDestroy
}
func collectedItem() {
  componentNode.run(collectSoundAction, completion: {
    self.componentNode.removeFromParent()
  })
}

func destroyedItem() {
  if canDestroy == true {
    componentNode.run(destroySoundAction, completion: {
      self.componentNode.removeFromParent()
    })
  }
}

override class var supportsSecureCoding: Bool {
  true
}
```

Here, the didAddToEntity() method preloads two sound actions using the filenames stored in the collectSoundFile and destroySoundFile properties. You preload these actions so that there's no delay when you first play the sounds (which happens in the collectedItem() and destroyedItem() methods).

At this point, you might be tempted to start adding the collectible items to your map. While I appreciate your enthusiasm, you're missing two key components (no pun intended): a way to add physics bodies to your nodes, and a way to handle contacts. Because, as of right now, there's no way for the player to collect keys, food, and treasure, much less open any doors.

Configure the Physics Bodies

In Chapter 8, Using the Scene Editor to Add Physics, on page 161, you used the Scene Editor to add a physics body to the player node. However, as you start to build out Val's Revenge, keeping track of the physics categories can (and will) get a little tricky. While it's entirely possible to use only the Scene Editor, setting up the physics bodies like you did for the player node, you have another option: use components and extensions.

Unlike the physics code you wrote in Configure Physics Categories, on page 79, where you simply set up a single enum to hold the physics categories using a UInt32 type, you'll instead expand that idea and use a combination of String enums and protocols. You'll also create and use a new physics component to set up your physics bodies.

To make this solution more robust, you won't handle the collisions directly in the GameScene class; instead, you'll build out a separate GameScene extension to further keep your project code organized.

There's a lot to do. Let's start with setting up the physics categories.

Mapping and Designing Your Physics Categories

Before you start writing physics-related code—well, any code, really—it's always nice to have a plan. The plan, here, is to use seven physics categories, like so:

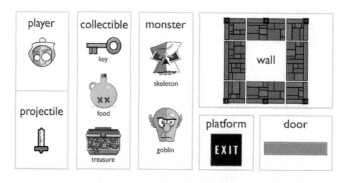

Each category represents some "object" within your game—and now that you know what's what, you're ready to begin writing some code.

Setting up and Configuring the Physics Categories

Inside the Components group, create a new file (⌘N) using the iOS Swift File template. Name the new file PhysicsComponent.swift and replace its contents with the following code:

```
import SpriteKit
import GameplayKit

enum PhysicsCategory: String {
  case player
  case wall
  case door
  case monster
  case projectile
  case collectible
  case exit
}setting up and

enum PhysicsShape: String {
  case circle
  case rect
}
```

Here, you're setting up two String enums: one for the physics body category, and one for the physics body shape. You'll use the raw values specified here when setting up your game objects. These values will then be used to determine which category an object belongs to, and what shape to use for its physics body.

For this type of setup to work, you need a new struct that conforms to the OptionSet protocol.[1] OptionSets are well-suited for working with bit masks. You also need the struct to implement the Hashable protocol[2] as is required when working with sets. (Note: The OptionSet and Hashable protocols are quite powerful; if you're not familiar with them, reading through the Apple documentation may provide some valuable insight.)

Below the PhysicsShape enum, add the following code:

```
struct PhysicsBody: OptionSet, Hashable {
  let rawValue: UInt32

}
```

---

1. https://developer.apple.com/documentation/swift/optionset
2. https://developer.apple.com/documentation/swift/hashable

This code is the beginning of your PhysicsBody struct—the heart of your physics bodies and collision detection solution. Notice your new struct conforms to both the Hashable and OptionSet protocols.

Inside the new PhysicsBody struct, and below the line that reads let rawValue: UInt32, and the following options:

```
static let player       = PhysicsBody(rawValue: 1 << 0) // 1
static let wall         = PhysicsBody(rawValue: 1 << 1) // 2
static let door         = PhysicsBody(rawValue: 1 << 2) // 4
static let monster      = PhysicsBody(rawValue: 1 << 3) // 8
static let projectile   = PhysicsBody(rawValue: 1 << 4) // 16
static let collectible  = PhysicsBody(rawValue: 1 << 5) // 32
static let exit         = PhysicsBody(rawValue: 1 << 6) // 64
```

You'll notice that these options perfectly align with the case statements in the PhysicsCategory struct. While having the case statements and options match isn't necessarily a requirement, it does make it a little easier when setting up your component.

The next step is to define how the physics categories will interact with one another, in other words, which categories will collide and which will simply participate in contact checking. Below the last option in the list, and still within the PhysicsBody struct, add the following code:

```
static var collisions: [PhysicsBody: [PhysicsBody]] = [
  .player: [.wall, .door],
  .monster: [.wall, .door]
]

static var contactTests: [PhysicsBody: [PhysicsBody]] = [
  .player: [.monster, .collectible, .door, .exit],
  .wall: [.player],
  .door: [.player],
  .monster: [.player, .projectile],
  .projectile: [.monster, .collectible, .wall],
  .collectible: [.player, .projectile],
  .exit: [.player]
]
```

Using the collisions property, you make it so that both the player and the monsters will collide with the walls and doors instead of passing through them. Using the contactTests property, you define which bodies will trigger a message for the physics contact delegate. The next three properties you're about to add will tie this solution together. Below the contactTests property, add the following code:

```
var categoryBitMask: UInt32 {
  return rawValue
}
```

```
var collisionBitMask: UInt32 {
  let bitMask = PhysicsBody
    .collisions[self]?
    .reduce(PhysicsBody(), { result, physicsBody in
      return result.union(physicsBody)
    })
  return bitMask?.rawValue ?? 0
}
var contactTestBitMask: UInt32 {
  let bitMask = PhysicsBody
    .contactTests[self]?
    .reduce(PhysicsBody(), { result, physicsBody in
      return result.union(physicsBody)
    })
  return bitMask?.rawValue ?? 0
}
```

Here, you return the raw value for the category. Because each of the physics bodies will get assigned to only one category, you can keep your code somewhat simple by returning a single value. For the other two properties—contactTestBitMask and collisionBitMask—you use reduce and union to return the values. With reduce, you can reduce an array of values into a single value. You then use union to generate and return the final value.

The final piece of this puzzle is to create the static method for retrieving the correct body. Below the contactTestBitMask property, add the following code:

```
static func forType(_ type: PhysicsCategory?) -> PhysicsBody? {
  switch type {
  case .player:
    return self.player
  case .wall:
    return self.wall
  case .door:
    return self.door
  case .monster:
    return self.monster
  case .projectile:
    return self.projectile
  case .collectible:
    return self.collectible
  case .exit:
    return self.exit
  case .none:
    break
  }

  return nil
}
```

You've seen code like this before—this is the static method you'll use to fetch and return the correct physics body.

At last, you're ready to create the physics component, which you'll use to assign physics bodies to your game objects.

Creating the Physics Component

Still inside the PhysicsComponent.swift file, and just below (and outside of) the PhysicsBody struct, add the following code:

```
// MARK: - COMPONENT CODE STARTS HERE

class PhysicsComponent: GKComponent {

  @GKInspectable var bodyCategory: String = PhysicsCategory.wall.rawValue
  @GKInspectable var bodyShape: String = PhysicsShape.circle.rawValue

  override func didAddToEntity() {
    guard let bodyCategory =
      PhysicsBody.forType(PhysicsCategory(rawValue: bodyCategory)),
      let sprite = componentNode as? SKSpriteNode else {
        return
    }

    let size: CGSize = sprite.size

    if bodyShape == PhysicsShape.rect.rawValue {
      componentNode.physicsBody = SKPhysicsBody(rectangleOf: size)
    } else if bodyShape == PhysicsShape.circle.rawValue {
      componentNode.physicsBody = SKPhysicsBody(circleOfRadius: size.height/2)
    }

    componentNode.physicsBody?.categoryBitMask =
      bodyCategory.categoryBitMask
    componentNode.physicsBody?.collisionBitMask =
      bodyCategory.collisionBitMask
    componentNode.physicsBody?.contactTestBitMask =
      bodyCategory.contactTestBitMask

    componentNode.physicsBody?.affectedByGravity = false
    componentNode.physicsBody?.allowsRotation = false
  }
  override class var supportsSecureCoding: Bool {
    true
  }
}
```

Here, you set up the component with two @GKInspectable properties; you'll use the values of these two properties to set up the physics body category and shape. You then proceed to set up the body using those values.

Now that you have a component that you can attach to your entities, you're ready to build the GameScene extension that handles contacts and collisions.

Add a Physics Contact Extension

Inside the Extensions group, create a new file (⌘N) using the iOS Swift File template. Name the new file GameScene+PhysicsContact.swift and replace its contents with the following:

```
import SpriteKit

extension GameScene: SKPhysicsContactDelegate {
  func didBegin(_ contact: SKPhysicsContact) {
    let collision = contact.bodyA.categoryBitMask
      | contact.bodyB.categoryBitMask

    switch collision {
    default:
      break
    }
  }
}
```

This code is the start of your physics contact manager.

To keep the code organized and make it easier to see what contacts are taking place, you'll use code comments. Add the following code just *above* the line that reads default::

```
// MARK: - Player | Collectible
case PhysicsBody.player.categoryBitMask |
 PhysicsBody.collectible.categoryBitMask:
  let playerNode = contact.bodyA.categoryBitMask ==
    PhysicsBody.player.categoryBitMask ?
      contact.bodyA.node : contact.bodyB.node

  let collectibleNode = contact.bodyA.categoryBitMask ==
    PhysicsBody.collectible.categoryBitMask ?
      contact.bodyA.node : contact.bodyB.node

  // TODO: ADD CODE TO HANDLE PLAYER COLLECTION

  // MARK: - Player | Door
case PhysicsBody.player.categoryBitMask | PhysicsBody.door.categoryBitMask:
  let playerNode = contact.bodyA.categoryBitMask ==
    PhysicsBody.player.categoryBitMask ?
      contact.bodyA.node : contact.bodyB.node

  let doorNode = contact.bodyA.categoryBitMask ==
    PhysicsBody.door.categoryBitMask ?
      contact.bodyA.node : contact.bodyB.node

// TODO: ADD CODE TO HANDLE PLAYER OPENING DOOR
```

With this code, you're checking to see which bodies made contact, but you aren't actually doing anything—yet.

Look at the jump bar and the code:

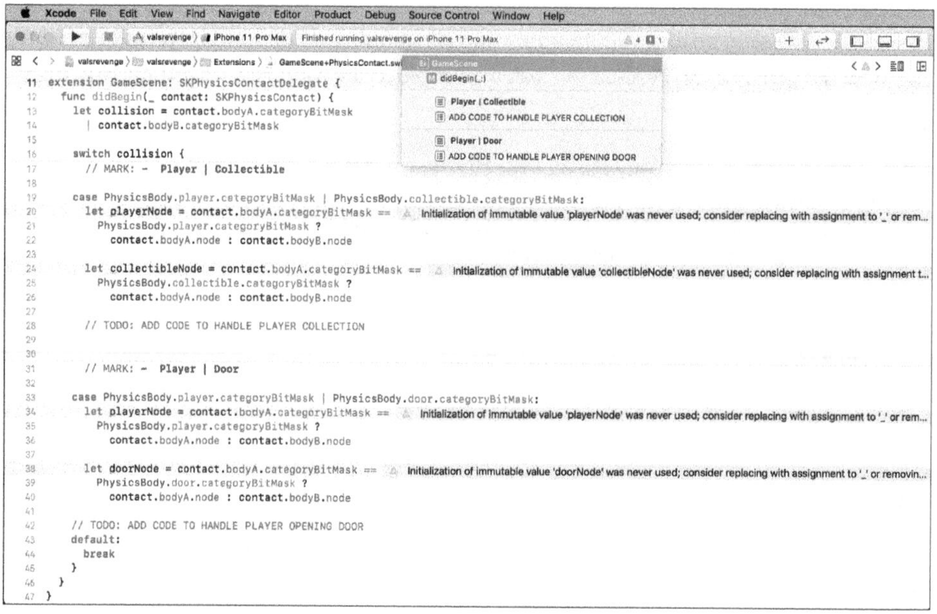

Here, you're using code comments to help visually organize your code, making it easier to maintain. As you add more contact detection code, it'll be easier to find using these comments. Of course, things will be even easier to see once you take care of those warnings, which you'll do next.

Adding New Functionality to the Player Class

There are certainly different ways to design and implement your game's Entity-Component design pattern. With Val's Revenge, you'll keep things somewhat simple. In this case, since Val is the only character who can collect and use items, you'll add some new methods in the Player class to handle these actions. Open the Player.swift file and add the following new properties:

```
private var keys: Int = 0 {
  didSet {
    print("Keys: \(keys)")
    if keys < 1 {
      stateMachine.enter(PlayerHasNoKeyState.self)
    } else {
      stateMachine.enter(PlayerHasKeyState.self)
    }
  }
}
```

```
private var treasure: Int = 0 {
  didSet {
    print("Treasure: \(treasure)")
  }
}
```

You'll use these two properties to track how many keys Val has in her pockets and how much treasure she's collected. For now, you'll just print this information to the console. Notice that you're using the didSet property observer on the keys property to handle updating the player state machine depending on how many keys Val has in her inventory.

With these properties in place, you're ready to add the method that handles item collection. Below the init(coder:) method, add the following code:

```
func collectItem(_ collectibleNode: SKNode) {
  guard let collectible = collectibleNode.entity?.component(ofType:
    CollectibleComponent.self) else {
    return
  }

  collectible.collectedItem()

  switch GameObjectType(rawValue: collectible.collectibleType) {
  case .key:
    // print("collected key")
    keys += collectible.value

  case .food:
    // print("collected food")
    if let hc = entity?.component(ofType: HealthComponent.self) {
      hc.updateHealth(collectible.value, forNode: self)
    }
  case .treasure:
    // print("collected treasure")
    treasure += collectible.value

  default:
    break
  }
}
```

This is the method you will call when the player makes contact with a collectible item.

Next, you need a method to run when Val unlocks a door. Add the following code below the collectItem(_:) method:

```
func useKeyToOpenDoor(_ doorNode: SKNode) {
  // print("Use key to open door")

  switch stateMachine.currentState {
  case is PlayerHasKeyState:
    keys -= 1

    doorNode.removeFromParent()
    run(SKAction.playSoundFileNamed("door_open",
                              waitForCompletion: true))
  default:
    break
  }
}
```

With this code, you first confirm that the player state machine is in the proper state for unlocking doors. If so, you remove the door node and play the sound action. (You copied the "door_open" sound when you copied the other resources.)

Now that you have methods available to call when certain physics bodies make contact, you can finish up the physics contact extension and get rid of those pesky warnings.

Finishing the Physics Contact Extension

Switch back to the GameScene+PhysicsContact.swift file. Locate the line that reads:

```
// TODO: ADD CODE TO HANDLE PLAYER COLLECTION
```

and replace it with this code:

```
if let player = playerNode as? Player, let collectible = collectibleNode {
  player.collectItem(collectible)
}
```

Next, replace the following line of code:

```
// TODO: ADD CODE TO HANDLE PLAYER OPENING DOOR
```

with this code:

```
if let player = playerNode as? Player, let door = doorNode {
  player.useKeyToOpenDoor(door)
}
```

Excellent, your physics contact extension is ready for use, and you're almost ready for testing. But first, you need to give Val some items to pick up and some doors to unlock.

Place Collectibles and Doors

Switch to the GameScene.sks file to open it in the Scene Editor. Once there, add three new sprite nodes with the following settings.

First, start with the key:

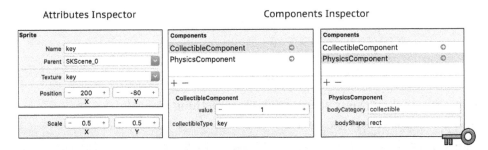

Next, add some food:

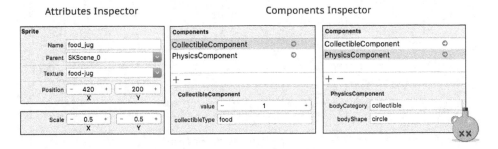

Finally, give Val some treasure:

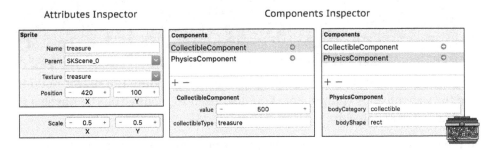

With the items in place, you're ready to add some doors—three, actually—so drag three more sprite nodes into the scene. Set them up, as shown in the image on page 272.

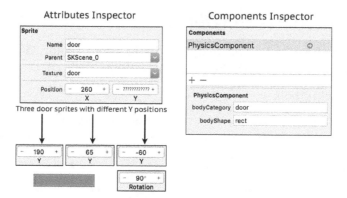

When you're done, your scene will look something like this:

Before you build and run the project, you need to update the player node to use the new physics component. You also need to modify the tile physics to use the new wall category.

In the Scene Graph View, select the player node and switch to the Attributes Inspector. In the Physics Definition section, set the Body Type to None. Once you have that done, switch to the Components Inspector and add the Physics Component, setting the bodyCategory to player and the bodyShape to circle.

Save the GameScene.sks file and then switch to the SKTileMapNode+Physics.swift file. Once there, replace the following line of code:

```
physicsBody?.categoryBitMask = 2
```

with this code instead:

```
physicsBody?.categoryBitMask = PhysicsBody.wall.categoryBitMask
physicsBody?.collisionBitMask = PhysicsBody.wall.collisionBitMask
physicsBody?.contactTestBitMask = PhysicsBody.wall.contactTestBitMask
```

Scroll down a bit, and then switch this line of code:

```
tileNode.physicsBody?.categoryBitMask = 2
```

with this code:

```
tileNode.physicsBody?.categoryBitMask =
  PhysicsBody.wall.categoryBitMask
tileNode.physicsBody?.collisionBitMask =
  PhysicsBody.wall.collisionBitMask
tileNode.physicsBody?.contactTestBitMask =
  PhysicsBody.wall.contactTestBitMask
```

Fantastic, now all of your game objects are set up using the new physics categories.

Last, but certainly not least, you need to tell the GameScene class that it is now responsible for handling the physics. Switch to the GameScene.swift file, and at the end of the didMove(to:) method, add the following line of code:

```
physicsWorld.contactDelegate = self
```

Build and run the project. Before you run off and collect the key, try to go "through" one of the doors first. You shouldn't be able to get through any of them because they're "locked." Once you confirm that's working, collect the key (notice the sound), and then try to go through the door again. This time, the door should unlock and disappear. Go into the now unlocked area and collect the treasure and the food.

(Oh, and don't worry about those monsters. They can't harm you—yet.)

As you're collecting items, you'll see something like the following in the console, which confirms everything is working as expected:

```
Entering PlayerHasNoKeyState
Keys: 1
Entering PlayerHasKeyState
Keys: 0
Entering PlayerHasNoKeyState
Treasure: 500
```

Before wrapping up this chapter, you need to add the necessary code to handle what happens when Val accidentally shoots a collectible whose canDestroy property is set to true.

Add Code to Destroy Collectibles

Switch back to the Player.swift file, and in the attack() method, above the line that reads var throwDirection = CGVector(dx: 0, dy: 0), add the following code:

```
// Set up physics for projectile
let physicsBody = SKPhysicsBody(rectangleOf: projectile.size)

physicsBody.affectedByGravity = false
physicsBody.allowsRotation = true
physicsBody.isDynamic = true

physicsBody.categoryBitMask = PhysicsBody.projectile.categoryBitMask
physicsBody.contactTestBitMask = PhysicsBody.projectile.contactTestBitMask
physicsBody.collisionBitMask = PhysicsBody.projectile.collisionBitMask

projectile.physicsBody = physicsBody
```

This sets the projectile's physics body to use the projectile category.

Next, back in the GameScene+PhysicsContact.swift file, add the code necessary to handle the contacts between the projectile and collectible categories:

```
// MARK: - Projectile | Collectible

case PhysicsBody.projectile.categoryBitMask |
  PhysicsBody.collectible.categoryBitMask:
  let projectileNode = contact.bodyA.categoryBitMask ==
    PhysicsBody.projectile.categoryBitMask ?
      contact.bodyA.node : contact.bodyB.node

  let collectibleNode = contact.bodyA.categoryBitMask ==
    PhysicsBody.collectible.categoryBitMask ?
      contact.bodyA.node : contact.bodyB.node

  if let collectibleComponent =
    collectibleNode?.entity?.component(ofType: CollectibleComponent.self) {
    collectibleComponent.destroyedItem()
  }
  projectileNode?.removeFromParent()
```

Build and run the project. Try shooting the key, the treasure, and the food. Notice you're able to shoot and destroy only the food.

Next Steps

In this chapter, you made a little more headway with the Val's Revenge game. You added some additional components and extensions, making it possible for Val to collect or destroy items and unlock doors.

You also worked a bit with states and state machines by adding a simple player state machine with two distinct states. Although it may not be evident now, states and state machines are a great way to manage your game states and keep your code clean and concise, which is especially important for larger, more complex games. You'll see more evidence of this in the next chapter as you get to work on adding some much-needed AI and pathfinding to to your dungeon monsters.

Planning Routes and Creating Believable AI

In the previous chapter, you continued your work with entities and components as you learned about and added states and state machines to Val's Revenge.

In this chapter, you'll keep working with the GameplayKit framework as you code autonomous life into Val's pesky dungeon "pets" by giving them the ability to think and act on their own. You'll also add a little more challenge to the game by making one of the collectible items move around. You'll do all of this using two other GameplayKit features:

- *Agents, goals, and behaviors.* With agents, goals, and behaviors you're able to give your entities some autonomy. For example, you might set up a pathfinding goal to automatically avoid obstacles or a goal that tracks the player's location so that her enemies know where to stage an attack.

  Think of the *agent* as the brains of the entity. In GameplayKit, the agent is responsible for managing the entity's *goals* and *behavior* using the GKGoal and GKBehavior classes. You'll learn more about each of these classes in this chapter.

- *Pathfinding.* Pathfinding is the ability to navigate the game map. In other words, finding a route from Point A to Point B. Before frameworks like GameplayKit came around, developers had to implement complicated algorithms—such as Dijkstra's algorithm or one of its variants like A*—to help with pathfinding. Both of these algorithms work well, but they're not always easy to code or understand. However, with GameplayKit's pathfinding features, mapping your game worlds is considerably easier using the GKGraph class or one of its specialized subclasses, GKGridGraph, GKObstacleGraph, or GKMeshGraph.

Before you "navigate" your way through AI and pathfinding (that's a terrible joke, I know), let's discuss how you'll be using these features in Val's Revenge, and what needs to happen before you can begin.

Modify the Monster Generator

In Build a Monster Generator, on page 241, you set up a monster generator component that spawns monsters based on its set up, such as how many monsters per generator and how often they spawn. When a generator spawns a monster, you fire off an action that moves the new monster slightly to the right, stopping a few pixels away from the generator.

As you might have guessed, monsters who don't move pose very little threat or challenge for Val—she is a warrior after all, and she deserves better. To solve this problem, you'll set up some goals and behaviors to help the monsters track Val, but only when she has keys in her pocket. You'll know when she does thanks to the state machine you set up in the previous chapter.

But moving monsters still won't be enough of a challenge for Val, so you'll also set up pathfinding on the Key collectible, making it move around the scene on a set path.

With all of these new challenges ahead, Val (and the player) will need a moment to get ready for battle. In other words, you don't want the monsters to start spawning right away. Instead, you'll wait until the player starts the game. As it turns out, you don't know when the player has actually started the game, so you'll need to work on fixing that first.

Setting up the Main Game States and State Machine

As you learned in Chapter 12, Using States and State Machines, on page 253, states and state machines help you track the status (or state) of something. In this case, you want to track when the player starts the game. Sure, you could use a boolean flag to track whether the game is in progress, but because you have some fancy new knowledge about states and state machines, let's put it to good use.

To begin, open the valsrevenge project in Xcode.

In the Project Navigator, select the States group and create a new file (⌘N) using the iOS Swift File template.

Using the Starter Project

You may continue using your project from the previous chapter, or you can use the starter project located in the projects/begin folder included with the code resources for this chapter. Either option is fine; the only benefit to using the starter project is that you won't get stuck going forward if you missed an earlier step.

There's also an ending project for this chapter that includes all of the code and resources you'll be adding here. The end project is located in the projects/end folder included with the code resources for this chapter.

Name the new file MainGameStates.swift and replace the contents of the file with the following code:

```
import GameplayKit

class PauseState: GKState {

  override func isValidNextState(_ stateClass: AnyClass) -> Bool {
    return stateClass == PlayingState.self
  }
}

class PlayingState: GKState {

  override func isValidNextState(_ stateClass: AnyClass) -> Bool {
    return stateClass == PauseState.self
  }
}
```

Here, you're creating two new states; you'll use these to keep track of when the player starts the game.

Switch to the GameScene.swift file and add a new property, placing it above the lastUpdateTime property:

```
let mainGameStateMachine = GKStateMachine(states: [PauseState(),
                                                    PlayingState()])
```

This code creates the main game state machine, setting it up to use the two states you just created.

Next, you need to set the state machine's initial state. In the didMoveTo(_:) method, add the following code at the top:

```
mainGameStateMachine.enter(PauseState.self)
```

With the initial game state set, you're ready to add the code that controls when to start and stop the generators.

Starting and Stopping the Generators

Switch to the GeneratorComponent.swift file and add a new property:

```
var isRunning = false
```

You'll use this property to track when the generator is actively spawning monsters.

Next, create two new method stubs, placing them above the spawnMonsterEntity() method:

```
func startGenerator() {

}
func stopGenerator() {

}
```

You'll use these two methods to start and stop the generators.

Because you don't want the generators to immediately spawn monsters, move all of the code from the didAddToEntity() method into the new startGenerator() method. Also, set the isRunning property to true. The updated method looks like this:

```
func startGenerator() {
➤    isRunning = true

    let wait = SKAction.wait(forDuration: waitTime)
    let spawn = SKAction.run { [unowned self] in self.spawnMonsterEntity() }
    let sequence = SKAction.sequence([wait, spawn])

    let repeatAction: SKAction?
    if maxMonsters == 0 {
      repeatAction = SKAction.repeatForever(sequence)
    } else {
      repeatAction = SKAction.repeat(sequence, count: maxMonsters)
    }

    componentNode.run(repeatAction!, withKey: "spawnMonster")
}
```

The highlighted line is the "new" code where you set the isRunning property to true. The rest of the code is from the didAddToEntity() method, which should now be empty.

Next, update the stopGenerator() method to match the following:

```
func stopGenerator() {
  isRunning = false
  componentNode.removeAction(forKey: "spawnMonster")
}
```

Here, you're setting the isRunning property back to false and removing the action responsible for spawning monsters.

Finally, add an override for the update(deltaTime:) method, placing it below the spawnMonsterEntity() method:

```
override func update(deltaTime seconds: TimeInterval) {
  if let scene = componentNode.scene as? GameScene {
    switch scene.mainGameStateMachine.currentState {
    case is PauseState:
      if isRunning == true {
        stopGenerator()
      }
    case is PlayingState:
      if isRunning == false {
        startGenerator()
      }
    default:
      break
    }
  }
}
```

This code overrides the component's update(deltaTime:) method, which is a per-frame update, and uses the main game state machine's current state to decide when it should spawn monsters. Remember, generators won't spawn monsters until the player starts the game. So, now you need a way to start the game.

For simplicity, you'll start the game when the player touches the scene, regardless of the touch location. Another option would be to add a "Play" or "Start" button, but for this example, simply touching the scene works.

Switch back to the GameScene.swift file and locate the touchDown(atPoint:) method. Add the following line of code at the top:

```
mainGameStateMachine.enter(PlayingState.self)
```

Build and run the game, but don't immediately "start" the game—wait for a moment before touching the scene. Notice how the monsters won't start spawning until after the first touch.

Thanks to the new state machine, you'll have a much easier time knowing when the game is in play. Now it's time to get those monsters thinking for themselves.

Use Agents, Goals, and Behaviors

To give monsters some autonomy, you'll use a combination of agents, goals, and behaviors. Consider the agent as the brains behind the entity, and the goals and behaviors as the driving forces behind its decision making.

You can create an agent for 2D space using the GKAgent2D class. Because this class is a subclass of the GKComponent class, you can use a component system to handle its updates. Using a component system works well when you have lots of entities or for games with complex object graphs (which you'll add in Using the Navigation Graph Editor, on page 293). In doing so, you guarantee that all of the entities using this component will get updated at the same time, so let's get one added.

Creating a Component System

Still inside the GameScene.swift file, add a new property below the graphs property:

```
let agentComponentSystem = GKComponentSystem(componentClass: GKAgent2D.self)
```

This code creates a new agentComponentSystem property to hold the agent component system; notice it's set up to manage only GKAgent2D components.

You also need to ensure that this system takes part in the update routine. In the GameScene class's update(_:) method, just below the for-in loop that updates the entities, add the following code:

```
// Update the component systems
agentComponentSystem.update(deltaTime: dt)
```

Now that you have the new component system ready, you're ready to build the brains behind the baddies, which includes implementing an agent's protocol methods through delegation.

Delegating an Agent's Responsibilities

The agent has two primary responsibilities: the first is to update the agent's position to match the attached node's position; the second is to update the node's position to match the agent's position—essentially, keeping the two objects in sync. These two responsibilities are handled through delegation, specifically with the GKAgentDelegate protocol.

The GKAgentDelegate protocol includes two methods: agentWillUpdate(_:) and agent-DidUpdate(_:). To make it easier for your component to conform to these methods, you'll add a new SKNode extension to handle them.

Creating an Extension to Help with Delegation

Inside the Extensions group, create a new file (⌘N) using the iOS Swift File template. Name the new file SKNode+AgentDelegate.swift and replace its contents with the following code:

```
import SpriteKit
import GameplayKit

extension SKNode: GKAgentDelegate {

  // Update the agent position to match the node position
  public func agentWillUpdate(_ agent: GKAgent) {

    guard let agent2d = agent as? GKAgent2D else {
      return
    }
    agent2d.position = vector_float2(Float(position.x),
                                     Float(position.y))

  }

  // Update the node position to match the agent position
  public func agentDidUpdate(_ agent: GKAgent) {
    guard let agent2d = agent as? GKAgent2D else {
      return
    }

    position = CGPoint(x: CGFloat(agent2d.position.x),
                       y: CGFloat(agent2d.position.y))

  }
}
```

This is the code responsible for keeping the agent and the node in sync. Notice that you're downcasting the GKAgent object to a GKAgent2D object. You need this downcast because the GKAgent class does not include any positional information, and without it, you wouldn't know how to update neither the agent nor the node. For 2D worlds like those in SpriteKit, you use the GKAgent2D class. (For 3D worlds, you use the GKAgent3D class.)

With the SKNode extension complete, you're finally ready to create the agent component.

Creating the Agent Component

In the Project Navigator, select the Components group and create a new file (⌘N) using the iOS Swift File template. Name the new file AgentComponent.swift and replace its contents with the following code:

```
import SpriteKit
import GameplayKit
```

```swift
class AgentComponent: GKComponent {
  let agent = GKAgent2D()
  override func didAddToEntity() {

  }
  override class var supportsSecureCoding: Bool {
    true
  }
}
```

You've see this code before: it's the start of a new component. Notice the agent property. This is the agent object that's responsible for the entity to which this component is attached. It's also the object you'll be adding to the component system you created in Creating a Component System, on page 282.

Inside the didAddToEntity() method, add the following code:

```swift
guard let scene = componentNode.scene as? GameScene else {
  return
}
// Set up the goals and behaviors
let wanderGoal = GKGoal(toWander: 1.0)
agent.behavior = GKBehavior(goal: wanderGoal, weight: 100)

// Set the delegate
agent.delegate = componentNode

// Constrain the agent's movement
agent.mass = 1
agent.maxAcceleration = 125
agent.maxSpeed = 125
agent.radius = 60
agent.speed = 100

// Add the agent component to the component system
scene.agentComponentSystem.addComponent(agent)
```

Notice the highlighted code:

- The GKGoal class is responsible for establishing one or more goals for an agent, for example, a goal that causes an agent to wander around aimlessly.

- The GKBehavior class (and the agent's behavior property) is what you use to add goals to an agent's overall behavior, giving each one a weighted value (essentially setting a priority level when more than one goal is set up).

Goals and behavior are divided into four distinct categories:

- *General movement*, which includes seeking another agent, fleeing an agent, reaching a target speed, and wandering around.

- *Avoidance and interception* for when you need to find another agent or hide from one.

- *Flocking behavior* so that your agents can travel in packs or maintain their distance from another group of agents.

- *Path-following*, which tells your agents to follow and/or stay on a set path.

With this code, you set up a simple wander goal. Later in this chapter, you'll set up another goal that tracks the player, but only when Val has keys in her pocket.

Continuing on with the rest of this code, look at the property settings for the agent property. In addition to setting the componentNode object as the delegate, these five properties constrain the agent's movement. You can tweak their values to achieve the desired effect. For example, if you want to introduce a little resistance in how fast an agent responds to its goals, you could increase the mass property.

For more information on how an agent's properties affect its goals, please refer to the online documentation[1] or use the Quick Help Inspector to get more information about each property by clicking on the property in the Source Editor and opening the Quick Help Inspector:

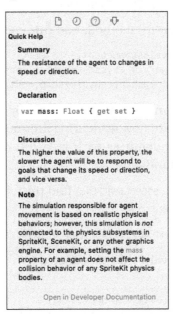

Finally, you add the agent (not the custom component) to the agent system ensuring that it participates in the update routine.

That's all of the code you need for this component to work. Now it's time to add it to the monster entities.

Add Agents to Monsters

Switch to the GeneratorComponent.swift file. In the spawnMonsterEntity(), add the following code below the line that reads monsterEntity.addComponent(healthComponent):

```
let agentComponent = AgentComponent()
monsterEntity.addComponent(agentComponent)
```

While you're here, also add the physics component not only to the monsters being spawned, but also to the generator itself. By adding the physics component here, you won't need to worry about adding it to your generators when you add them to the scene using the Scene Editor, saving you an additional step.

Below the code you just added, add the following code:

```
let physicsComponent = PhysicsComponent()
physicsComponent.bodyCategory = PhysicsCategory.monster.rawValue
monsterEntity.addComponent(physicsComponent)
```

Then, inside the didAddToEntity() method, add this code:

```
let physicsComponent = PhysicsComponent()
physicsComponent.bodyCategory = PhysicsCategory.monster.rawValue
componentNode.entity?.addComponent(physicsComponent)
```

Build and run the program, then start the game by moving the player. Notice how all of the monsters are now wandering around. Pretty neat, right? Well, except for the lack of randomness with regard to the spawn location. Let's make that a little more random.

Still inside the GeneratorComponent.swift file, find the following line (located in the spawnMonsterEntity() method):

```
monsterNode.run(SKAction.moveBy(x: 100, y: 0, duration: 1.0))
```

Remove it and replace it with this code instead:

```
// Initial spawn movement
let randomPositions: [CGFloat] = [-50,-50,50]
let randomX = randomPositions.randomElement() ?? 0
monsterNode.run(SKAction.moveBy(x: randomX, y: 0, duration: 1.0))
```

Here, you're grabbing a random element from the randomPositions array, giving a slight advantage to the -50 value by including that value twice in the array.

Build and run the project again. This time around, watch as the monsters shoot out in different directions—remember, though, you need to touch the scene to start the game.

A game with wandering monsters is certainly more challenging, but a game with monsters that actively hunt the player is *even more* challenging. However, for that to happen, the player also requires an agent.

Add an Agent to the Player

Rather than use the same agent component for the player that you're using for the monsters, you'll add an agent property directly to the Player class.

Switch to Player.swift file and add a new property, placing it directly above the currentDirection property:

```
var agent = GKAgent2D()
```

Next, inside the init(coder:) method, and at the end of that method, set the delegate for your new agent:

```
agent.delegate = self
```

Because you created an SKNode extension to handle the agent delegate methods, you're able to set the Player class as the delegate without having to add those methods here. Remember, the Player class is a subclass of the SKSpriteNode class, which, itself, is a subclass of the SKNode class.

All right, switch back to the AgentComponent.swift file and add a new lazy property:

```
lazy var interceptGoal: GKGoal = {
  guard let scene = componentNode.scene as? GameScene,
    let player = scene.childNode(withName: "player") as? Player else {
      return GKGoal(toWander: 1.0)
  }
  return GKGoal(toInterceptAgent: player.agent, maxPredictionTime: 1.0)
}()
```

Here, you're getting the player node (and subsequently its agent) from the scene. You're then creating and returning a GKGoal object designed to intercept another agent; in this case, the player's agent. If for some reason the player object is nil, you return a simple wander goal instead.

Now it's time to add this new goal to the monster's agent behavior.

Use Multiple Goals

The thing about AI and autonomy is that once you give an object a little freedom, it's no longer subject to your direct commands. Instead, it's designed to think and act on its own. Sure, you may give it a goal, and it will attempt to meet that goal, but you're no longer the one in charge.

Earlier, you "asked" the monsters to wander around by giving them a goal. So far, so good. The next goal you have for them is to chase Val, but only if she has a set of keys.

Still inside the AgentComponent.swift file, locate the following line:

```
agent.behavior = GKBehavior(goal: wanderGoal, weight: 100)
```

and replace it with this one:

```
agent.behavior = GKBehavior(goals: [wanderGoal, interceptGoal],
                            andWeights: [100, 0])
```

Now, instead of setting the agent's behavior with one goal, you're using two. Also notice that each goal has a weight associated with it. The weight determines a goal's priority: the higher the number, the more of a priority it is for the agent.

Here, the wander goal has a much higher weight (100 vs 0), which means this agent (the monster) is more likely to wander than it is to track the other agent (Val)—at least at first.

Remember, the "behavior" you want your monsters to achieve is that when Val has keys in her pocket, they're *more likely* to chase her than when she doesn't have keys. I use the phrase *more likely* because the agents are responsible for the thinking, not you. Your job was to give them a set of goals; their job is to figure out what to do and where to travel based on those goals—and what better way to handle that logic than in the component's update(deltaTime:) method, which you'll need to override, of course.

Below the didAddToEntity() method, add the following code:

```
override func update(deltaTime seconds: TimeInterval) {
  guard let scene = componentNode.scene as? GameScene,
    let player = scene.childNode(withName: "player") as? Player else {
      return
  }

  switch player.stateMachine.currentState {
  case is PlayerHasKeyState:
    agent.behavior?.setWeight(100, for: interceptGoal)
```

```
    default:
      agent.behavior?.setWeight(0, for: interceptGoal)
      break
  }
}
```

This code checks the current state of the player.stateMachine object using the following logic: when Val has keys, you increase the weighted value of the intercept goal to match the wander goal; when she doesn't have keys, you decrease that value back to 0. A value of 0 almost guarantees the agent will ignore the goal completely.

Before you can test this new monster behavior, you first need to have the player's agent participate in the update routine so that the monster agents know what to do and where to go.

Add the Player Agent to the Component System

Switch to the GameScene.swift file and look at the didMove(To:) method. Notice there's a lot of player-related code stuffed into this method. Let's tidy up this method by moving the player-related code into its own set-up method.

Below the setupCamera() method, add the following code:

```
func setupPlayer() {
  player = childNode(withName: "player") as? Player

  if let player = player {
    player.move(.stop)
    agentComponentSystem.addComponent(player.agent)
  }
}
```

Essentially, this is the same code that's currently in the didMove(to:) method with one exception: you're adding the player.agent component to the agent component system so that it participates in the update routine.

You're almost done and ready to test. In the didMove(to:) method, remove the following two lines of code:

```
player = childNode(withName: "player") as? Player
player?.move(.stop)
```

and replace them with this one-liner instead:

```
setupPlayer()
```

Excellent, the didMove(to:) method is cleaner, but there's still one more thing you need to do: get the monster entities to participate in the updates.

Add the Monster Entities to the Scene's Entities Array

Switch to the GeneratorComponent.swift, and at the bottom of the spawnMonsterEntity() method, after the line that reads monsterEntity.addComponent(physicsComponent), add the following code:

```
if let scene = componentNode.scene as? GameScene {
  scene.entities.append(monsterEntity)
}
```

This code adds the "spawned" monster entity to the scene's entities array, which you need to do so that the attached components participate in the update routine. This update takes place in the GameScene's update(_:) method, which looks like this:

```
// Update entities
for entity in self.entities {
  entity.update(deltaTime: dt)
}
```

Fantastic, you're ready to test the new monster agent goals.

Build and run the project, but don't pick up the key right away. Give the monsters some time to wander around first. After a short while, pick up the key and watch how some of the monsters' attentions turn to Val. (Don't worry, the monsters still can't hurt Val, but you're about to work on that next.)

Update Physics for Monsters and Projectiles

At the moment, Val and the monsters who hunt her don't take on any damage when hit. The reason this is happening is because the GameScene+PhysicsContact.swift file isn't set up to handle the contacts between the player and the monsters or the monsters and the projectiles.

Switch to the GameScene+PhysicsContact.swift file, and inside of the switch statement (above the line that reads // MARK: - Projectile | Collectible), add the following code:

```
  // MARK: -  Player | Monster
case PhysicsBody.player.categoryBitMask |
  PhysicsBody.monster.categoryBitMask:
  let playerNode = contact.bodyA.categoryBitMask ==
    PhysicsBody.player.categoryBitMask ?
      contact.bodyA.node : contact.bodyB.node

  if let healthComponent =
    playerNode?.entity?.component(ofType: HealthComponent.self) {
    healthComponent.updateHealth(-1, forNode: playerNode)
  }
```

This code takes care of the contacts between the monsters' physics bodies and the player's physics body. Notice that when these two bodies make contact, the player takes a hit by way of calling the updateHealth(_:forNode:) method on the HealthComponent class.

You also need to add the code to handle when the monsters get hit with Val's knives, so add the following code above the code you just added:

```
// MARK: -  Projectile | Monster
case PhysicsBody.projectile.categoryBitMask |
  PhysicsBody.monster.categoryBitMask:
  let monsterNode = contact.bodyA.categoryBitMask ==
    PhysicsBody.monster.categoryBitMask ?
      contact.bodyA.node : contact.bodyB.node

  if let healthComponent =
    monsterNode?.entity?.component(ofType: HealthComponent.self) {
    healthComponent.updateHealth(-1, forNode: monsterNode)
  }
```

Similar to the monster/player contact code you added, this code sends the health update (the hit) to the monster node rather than to the player node, resulting in -1 to its current health.

Build and run the project. Notice the monster generators, spawned monsters, and Val all lose health points when they're hit. This new functionality is great, but it's still a little flat: there's very little indication that a hit has occurred, and the "entities" stick around long after they're dead. Time to fix both issues by building a better health component.

Build a Better Health Component

In the Project Navigator, select the HealthComponent.swift file and add two new properties:

```
private var hitAction = SKAction()
private var dieAction = SKAction()
```

You'll use these properties to preload the actions needed to handle hits and "deaths" for both the monsters and the player. While you can preload these actions in other ways, you'll opt for simplicity over versatility.

In the didAddToEntity() method, add the following code below the line that reads updateHealth(0, forNode: componentNode):

```
if let _ = componentNode as? Player {
  hitAction = SKAction.playSoundFileNamed("player_hit",
                                    waitForCompletion: false)
```

```
    let playSound = SKAction.playSoundFileNamed("player_die",
                                        waitForCompletion: false)
    dieAction = SKAction.run {
      self.componentNode.run(playSound, completion: {
        // TODO: Add code to restart the game
        // but for now, reset the player's health
        self.currentHealth = self.maxHealth
      })
    }
  } else {
    hitAction = SKAction.playSoundFileNamed("monster_hit",
                                        waitForCompletion: false)

    let playSound = SKAction.playSoundFileNamed("monster_die",
                                        waitForCompletion: false)
    dieAction = SKAction.run {
      self.componentNode.run(playSound, completion: {
        self.componentNode.removeFromParent()
      })
    }
  }
}
```

This code determines if the attached node is a player or something else—presumably a monster. If the node is a player, you define one set of actions; whereas if it's something else, such as a monster, you define an entirely different set of actions.

The next step is to run those actions at the appropriate time. In the update-Health(_:forNode:) method, above the line that reads if let _ = node as? Player {, add the following code:

```
// Run hit or die actions
if value < 0 {
  if currentHealth == 0 {
    componentNode.run(dieAction)
  } else {
    componentNode.run(hitAction)
  }
}
```

Because you're using this method to also set the initial value of the health bar, you need to ensure this call to updateHealth(_:forNode:) is a result of a hit. You do this by making sure the value amount is less than zero. If it is, you then check to see if the monster (or player) is still alive by checking the value in the currentHealth property.

Build and run the project. Notice how the monsters make a sound with every hit; they also disappear when they're out of health. Val also makes noise when she's hit, but she never dies (at least not yet—you'll deal with that in the next chapter).

Your final task for this chapter is to implement pathfinding using navigation graphs. Specifically, you'll give Val a little challenge by moving the Key collectible along a set path.

Add Pathfinding to Your Game

Pathfinding is a big topic, so it won't be possible to cover everything. However, this section aims to give you enough information to get started with it.

You started this project in Configure the View and Load the Scene, on page 157, in which you were instructed to pay little attention to the GameplayKit-related code, including the GKScene's graphs property.

The graphs property contains the list of the pathfinding graph objects managed by the scene, in other words, the navigation graphs you add to the scene using the Scene Editor.

At the moment, your scene doesn't contain any navigation graphs, so the first step is to add one and to learn how the Navigation Graph Editor works.

Using the Navigation Graph Editor

Switch to the GameScene.sks file. Now, open the Object Library (⇧⌘L) and look for the Navigation graph object:

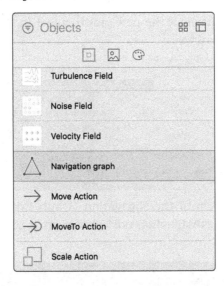

Drag the Navigation graph object onto the scene. Note that you can't drag this object into the Scene Graph View—you can only drag it onto the scene:

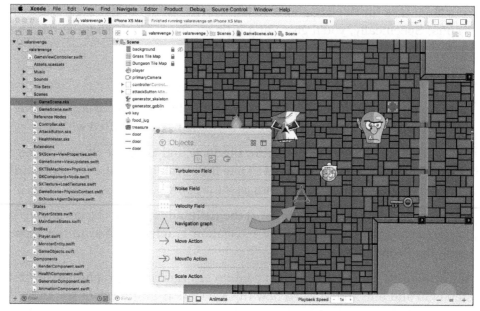

Place this object near the player node, setting its position to (X: -75, Y: -60). You can use the Attributes Inspector to set the position, although its exact position is irrelevant. (Using the Attributes Inspector, you can also set the graph's name; although, for this example, the default name of Graph is fine.)

To edit the graph, right-click the new graph object in the Scene Graph View and select Edit Navigation Graph:

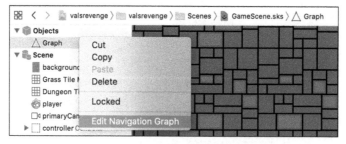

This action takes you into the Navigation Graph Editor. You know you're there because a black "instruction box" shows up at the bottom of the Scene Editor:

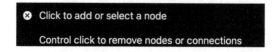

To select a node, click on it. Selected nodes look like this:

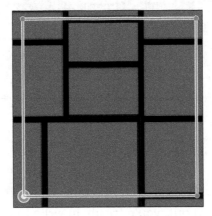

To move a node's position, first select it, then drag it around. However, you must make this three distinct actions:

- Click to select the node.
- Click the same node again to indicate your desire to reposition the node.
- While still holding down the mouse button, drag the node to its new location.

To remove a node—contrary to the on-screen instructions—you need to right-click it; this action deletes the node immediately. There is no undo, so be careful.

To add a new node, left-click anywhere within the scene. You can either add a stand-alone node or a node that is joined to another node using a connection. Connections define available and acceptable paths, so orphaned nodes are not something you will typically need or use.

To move around the scene—and this is the tricky part—you need to left-click a node to select it, but don't let go of the mouse button. Instead, continue to hold it down while moving the mouse in the direction you want to move around the scene.

To exit the editor, click the X button in the black instruction box.

I won't lie: editing a graph using the Scene Editor is a little frustrating. But once you get the hang of it, it's not too bad.

Spend the next few minutes mapping out a path for the Key collectible. Try to go through the generators so that you can test obstacle avoidance. One example of what you might do is shown on page 296.

With your path mapped out, you're ready to write the code necessary that'll tell the Key to follow the path.

Following the Navigation Path

Save the GameScene.sks file and switch to the GameScene.swift file. At the bottom of the file, but still inside the GameScene class, add the following method:

```
func startAdvancedNavigation() {

  // Check for a navigation graph and a key node
  guard let sceneGraph = graphs.values.first,
    let keyNode = childNode(withName: "key") as? SKSpriteNode else {
      return
  }

  // Set up the agent
  let agent = GKAgent2D()

  // Set up the delegate and the initial position
  agent.delegate = keyNode
  agent.position = vector_float2(Float(keyNode.position.x),
                                 Float(keyNode.position.y))

  // Set up the agent's properties
  agent.mass = 1
  agent.speed = 50
  agent.maxSpeed = 100
  agent.maxAcceleration = 100
  agent.radius = 60

  // Find obstacles (generators)
  var obstacles = [GKCircleObstacle]()

  // Locate generator nodes
  enumerateChildNodes(withName: "generator_*") {
    (node, stop) in
```

```
    // Create compatible obstacle
    let circle = GKCircleObstacle(radius: Float(node.frame.size.width/2))
    circle.position = vector_float2(Float(node.position.x),
                                    Float(node.position.y))
    obstacles.append(circle)
  }

  // Find the path
  if let nodesOnPath = sceneGraph.nodes as? [GKGraphNode2D] {

    // Show the path (optional code)
    for (index, node) in nodesOnPath.enumerated() {
      let shapeNode = SKShapeNode(circleOfRadius: 10)
      shapeNode.fillColor = .green
      shapeNode.position = CGPoint(x: CGFloat(node.position.x),
                                   y: CGFloat(node.position.y))

      // Add node number
      let number = SKLabelNode(text: "\(index)")
      number.position.y = 15
      shapeNode.addChild(number)

      addChild(shapeNode)
    }
    // (end optional code)

    // Create a path to follow
    let path = GKPath(graphNodes: nodesOnPath, radius: 0)
    path.isCyclical = true

    // Set up the goals
    let followPath = GKGoal(toFollow: path, maxPredictionTime: 1.0,
                            forward: true)
    let avoidObstacles = GKGoal(toAvoid: obstacles, maxPredictionTime: 1.0)

    // Add behavior based on goals
    agent.behavior = GKBehavior(goals: [followPath, avoidObstacles])

    // Set goal weights
    agent.behavior?.setWeight(0.5, for: followPath)
    agent.behavior?.setWeight(100, for: avoidObstacles)

    // Add agent to component system
    agentComponentSystem.addComponent(agent)
  }
}
```

There's a lot of code here, so take a moment to look through it. Some of it looks familiar, like the agent-, goal-, and behavior-related code, but look at the code that locates the generator nodes and follows the path. Pay close attention to the circle property where you create a GKCircleObstacle obstacle. This is where you create an obstacle for the agent to avoid, which happens to be right where the generators are placed.

Next, in the didMove(to:) method, add the following code at the bottom of that method:

```
startAdvancedNavigation()
```

Build and run the program. Notice how the Key follows the set path while also avoiding the generators. Also notice how when Val destroys a generator, the Key continues to avoid where the generator once stood. For this example, that's fine, but you may decide to write some additional code to remove an obstacle once its been destroyed.

Also, I had you add all of this pathfinding code into the main GameScene class; your challenge (should you choose to accept it) is to refactor this code and turn it into a reusable component.

Before you begin this challenge, there are two things to consider:

- First, the scene graph isn't immediately available, so you'll need to implement a starting and stopping routine similar to what you did with the monster generator, letting you delay the start of the routine.

- Second, I never told you how to "pause" an agent. Here's a hint: an agent can't do its work if it has no delegate.

If you get stuck on this challenge, you can find one possible solution in the challenge folder for this chapter's resources along with a Challenge.md file that gives you a brief overview of the steps you need to take to solve this challenge. Good luck, and have fun.

Next Steps

In this chapter, you learned how to make your game entities think and move on their own. You also improved your knowledge of GameplayKit by adding more components and learning about (and adding to your game) agents, goals, and behaviors. With these new features, you're able to add AI into your games, including the ability to follow a path and avoid obstacles.

In the next part of the book, you'll continue working on Val's Revenge. First, you'll add some animations to the player node using the Action Editor, and then you'll work on building better on-screen controls (while also fixing a small problem in which the spawned monsters end up underneath these very same controls). After that, you'll finish out the game by adding more scenes and a way for the player to load a previously saved game.

Part IV

Enhance the Player's Experience

Get ready to boost the player's experience by adding a few final details to Val's Revenge, including better controls, more scenes, and a way to save the player's progress.

Using the Action Editor and Enhancing Gameplay

You're making great progress with Val's Revenge. You started by building a small, simple scene using the Scene Editor. You then added reference nodes and tile maps, making it easier to share content between scenes, and making it possible to build larger scenes while also keeping resources at a minimum.

You also improved your game development skills (and your game) by learning about GameplayKit and adding components, entities, states, and state machines to Val's Revenge. You even gave life to your entities by adding little "brains" to them using agents, goals, and behaviors.

In this chapter, you'll strengthen your game development skills as you begin to add small enhancements to Val's Revenge, such as adding a player heads-up display and building better controls. You'll also learn how to add and modify actions using the *Action Editor*. The Action Editor is tool available in the Scene Editor that helps you build your actions without writing any code. So, what are you waiting for? Let's get to it.

Use the Action Editor to Add Actions

In Chapter 2, Adding Animation and Movement with Actions, on page 27, you learned about one of the most powerful features in SpriteKit: actions. But you haven't yet had a chance to play with them in the Scene Editor. Let's change that by having you add a subtle blink to Val's eye using the Action Editor rather than using the animation component you created in Animate the Monsters, on page 245.

To begin, open the valsrevenge project in Xcode.

Using the Starter Project

You may continue using your project from the previous chapter, or you can use the starter project located in the projects/begin folder included with the code resources for this chapter. Either option is fine; the only benefit to using the starter project is that you won't get stuck going forward if you missed an earlier step.

There's also an ending project for this chapter that includes all of the code and resources you'll be adding here. The end project is located in the projects/end folder included with the code resources for this chapter.

In the Project Navigator, select the GameScene.sks file to open it in the Scene Editor. Then, select the player node in the Scene Graph View.

To open (or hide) the Action Editor, click the Show/Hide button as shown in the following image:

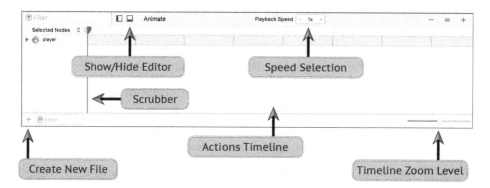

This editor is where you define your scene's actions. Take a moment to get familiar with its interface. Notice the drop-down list above the player node—it's currently set to Selected Nodes. Your other options include All Nodes and Nodes with Actions. You can use this drop-down list to minimize the actions shown in the editor at any give moment, which is helpful in reducing clutter.

There's also a timeline scrubber and a way to zoom in and out on the timeline. You can also create new action files here should you decide to store your actions in a separate file. This is useful for when you create an action that might be shared with more than one node. You won't be doing that for Val's Revenge, but it is something you can do for your games.

Now that you know your way around, it's time to add your first action: giving Val a more natural-looking blink versus her current "death stare."

Adding a New Action

To add a new action, open the Object Library (⇧⌘L) and scroll through the list until you get to the available actions:

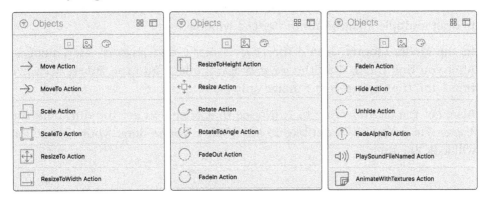

At the very bottom of the list, you'll see AnimateWithTextures Action. Drag this action into the first frame of the player node's animation timeline, like so:

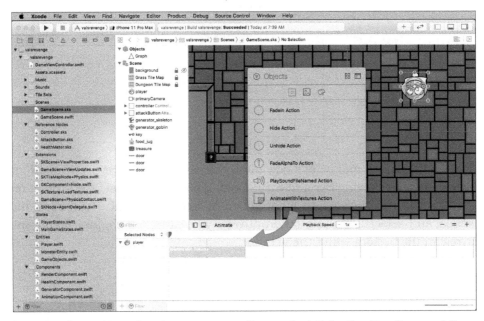

To get information about your new action, select it in the timeline and then open the Attributes Inspector.

Like other scene objects, the options in the Attributes Inspector change depending on the type of object you're inspecting. For the AnimateWithTextures Action, you can set the following options: Start Time, Duration, Resize, Restore, and Textures.

To give Val a subtle blink, you'll use two images and six frames with a total duration of two seconds. This action will also repeat on an endless loop.

Open the Object Library in a persistent window (⌥⇧⌘L) and then switch to the Media Library. (Using the persistent window mode makes it a little easier to drag multiple images into the Textures window.)

In the Media Library, locate the player-val-head_0 and player-val-head_1 images. After you find them, drag the player-val-head_0 image into the Textures area five times and the player-val-head_1 image only once.

Also, set the Duration value to 2. (Notice that once you set the duration, the Animate with Textures block doubles in size.) When you're done, your new action will look like this:

The next step is to make Val's new blink animation loop (forever) throughout the entire game, giving her a natural-looking blink; otherwise, the animation cycle would run once, then stop, which is hardly natural. Right-click the action and select Create Loop (alternatively, you can click the small rotating arrow in the bottom left of the action):

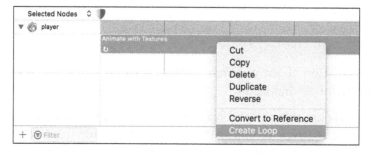

A small Looping window pops up:

From there, you can select the infinity sign to indicate that this action should run forever.

Do you see that little X button in the Looping window? You may think this button closes the Looping window, except it doesn't; instead, this button removes any looping options you've set up.

To close the Looping window, click anywhere outside of it. But, before you do, take note of the + and - buttons: these buttons increase or decrease the number of times the action runs; for example, suppose you wanted a character to swing a sword three times, then stop. You'd set this Looping option to 3.

All right, you're ready to test your new action, but don't be too quick to build and run the project—you can test your actions right here in the Scene Editor.

Testing Actions in the Scene Editor

To save yourself some time, you can test your actions right in the Scene Editor.

Look at the Action Editor bar. Do you see the Animate button to the right of the Action Editor Show/Hide button? You can use that button to test your actions. Here's how it works:

When you click the Animate button, the Action Editor bar turns blue, indicating that the scene actions are running. You can then start and stop the actions with the Play/Pause button:

To return to the "edit" mode, click the Layout button.

If everything looks good, you're ready to test your new action either on your device or using the Simulator app. Regardless of which route you take, build and run the project and take a closer look at Val (but don't blink, else you might miss hers):

Thanks to the infinity loop on the Animate with Textures action, you'll see Val blink every now and again, giving her a much more natural look—although her previous "death stare" was also kind of cool.

Wrapping up Actions in the Scene Editor

In this example, you added a single action to the player node; but you're not limited to just one. If you'd like, you can add multiple actions to a single node, or you can add one or more actions to the other nodes, too—whatever you need for your games. For example, you could add a dragon that not only blinks but also sends out a puff of smoke every so often.

Although this was a only a simple example, there's a lot more you can do with actions in the Scene Editor, so take a moment to play around with it for a bit. When you're ready, move on to the next section, where you'll add a heads-up display to keep player keenly aware of how much treasure they've collected and how many keys Val has in her pocket.

Add the Player's Heads-Up Display

What better way to keep a player informed than with a heads-up display (HUD). With a HUD, you're able to display important information about the game in a way that is always visible to the player without "getting in the way" of the gameplay. At the moment, the player has no way of knowing how many keys Val has in her pocket or how much treasure she's acquired.

In Adding New Functionality to the Player Class, on page 268, you added two properties—keys and treasure—to help keep track of these important things. You'll use these properties with your new HUD.

A lot of the code you're about to write should be familiar to you since you've seen similar examples in previous chapters. So, to keep things moving along, the code explanations will be kept to a minimum unless there's a new concept to learn.

Building the Player HUD

In the Project Navigator, select the Player.swift file and add three new properties to the Player class, placing them just above the keys property:

```
var hud = SKNode()
private let treasureLabel = SKLabelNode(fontNamed: "AvenirNext-Bold")
private let keysLabel = SKLabelNode(fontNamed: "AvenirNext-Bold")
```

Next, you need to build the HUD node. Add a new method just below the init?(coder:) method:

```
func setupHUD(scene: GameScene) {
  // Set up the treasure label
  treasureLabel.text = "Treasure: \(treasure)"
  treasureLabel.horizontalAlignmentMode = .right
  treasureLabel.verticalAlignmentMode = .center
  treasureLabel.position = CGPoint(x: 0, y: -treasureLabel.frame.height)
  treasureLabel.zPosition += 1

  // Set up the keys label
  keysLabel.text = "Keys: \(keys)"
  keysLabel.horizontalAlignmentMode = .right
  keysLabel.verticalAlignmentMode = .center
  keysLabel.position = CGPoint(x: 0,
                    y: treasureLabel.frame.minY - keysLabel.frame.height)
  keysLabel.zPosition += 1

  // Add the labels to the HUD
  hud.addChild(treasureLabel)
  hud.addChild(keysLabel)

  // Add the HUD to the scene
  scene.addChild(hud)
}
```

This method takes one argument: the scene. It then builds the HUD using the two labels and corresponding properties. Finally, this method adds the hud node to the calling scene.

You also need to update the exiting keys and treasure properties so that they keep their respective labels up to date. Starting with the keys property, find the line that reads:

```
print("Keys: \(keys)")
```

and replace it with this:

```
keysLabel.text = "Keys: \(keys)"
```

Do the same thing for the treasure property. Find this line:

```
print("Treasure: \(treasure)")
```

and replace it with this one:

```
treasureLabel.text = "Treasure: \(treasure)"
```

The next step is to call this method from the scene and make sure the HUD stays "pinned" to the view's upper-right corner.

Adding the HUD to the Scene

Switch to the GameScene.swift file. First, in the setupPlayer() method, after the line that reads if let player = player {, add the following code:

```
player.setupHUD(scene: self)
```

Then, just below the updateControllerLocation() method, add the following new method:

```
func updateHUDLocation() {
  player?.hud.position = CGPoint(x: (viewRight - margin - insets.right),
                                 y: (viewTop - margin - insets.top))
}
```

Finally, in the didFinishUpdate() method, make a call to the new method you just created by adding the following code:

```
updateHUDLocation()
```

Build and run the project and you'll see the player now has a heads-up display, pinned to the upper-right portion of the view:

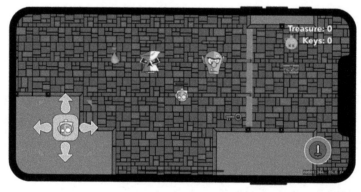

Before you stop the build, collect the key and the treasure chest, and watch how the labels stay up to date with the latest stats. If everything works as expected, you're ready for the next task: build better on-screen controls.

Build Better On-Screen Controls

In Chapter 8, Using the Scene Editor to Add Physics, on page 161, you created a simple 8-way D-pad controller and an Attack button. While those controls work okay (except for the z-position problem, where newly spawned monsters show up on top of the controls), you're about to make them much better by giving the player the ability to move and fire with a full 360° of rotation.

Prepping for the New Controls

In the Project Navigator, select the GameScene.sks file to open it up in the Scene Editor.

From the Scene Graph View, select and delete both the controller and the attackButton reference nodes.

To keep your project free of clutter, remove the two corresponding SKS files: Controller.sks and AttackButton.sks. When prompted, move both of these files to the trash.

The next step is to add the resources for the new controls.

Adding and Updating Controller Resources

Back in the Project Navigator, select the Assets.xcassets asset catalog, and in the controller sprite atlas, find and delete the button_attack and controller_stop image sets. Again, you want to keep your project free of unnecessary clutter. You won't be using these resources, so there's no need to keep them around; you will, however, need to add the new resources.

Open Finder, then navigate to the resources folder for this chapter. Inside that folder you'll find six image files and a Controller.sks file.

Drag the six image files into the controller sprite atlas to create two new image sets, controller_attack and controller_stick:

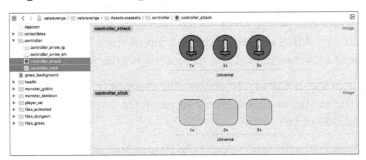

While you're still in Finder, drag the new Controller.sks file into the Reference Nodes group in the Project Navigator. Don't forget to verify that the Copy items if needed and Add to targets options are both checked. Also make sure that the option to Create groups is selected.

This new controller file replaces the old one you deleted earlier. Let's take a minute to review what's new.

Touring Your New Controller File

In the Project Navigator, select the new Controller.sks file and you'll see your new scene archive in the Scene Editor, like so:

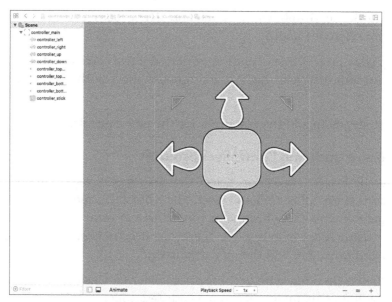

There are two notable differences between this new scene and the old one:

- The image on the controller stick is blank. Because you'll be using this file for both the attack controller and the movement controller, you'll need a way to let the player know which one does what. You'll make this distinction by adding a sprite node on top of the blank stick node: one to represent movement, and one to represent attack.

- The anchor point is set to center the content. Having the anchor point set to the center makes it easier to place the controller on either the left or right side of the scene.

Your next task is to write (and update) the code to support your new controller file.

Creating the Controller Class

In the Project Navigator, select the Reference Nodes group and create a new file (⌘N) using the iOS Swift File template. Name the new file Controller.swift and replace its contents with the following code:

```
import SpriteKit

class Controller: SKReferenceNode {

}
```

This code is the start of your new Controller class.

For this new controller to work as both a movement controller and an attack controller, you need to set up a few properties. Add the following code to your new class:

```
private var isMovement: Bool!

private var attachedNode: SKNode!
private var nodeSpeed: CGFloat!

private var base: SKNode!
private var joystick: SKSpriteNode!
private var range: CGFloat!

private var isTracking: Bool = false
```

You'll use these properties to help set up and operate your controller.

The next step is to add the initializers for your new class. Below the properties you just added, add the following code:

```
// MARK: -  Controller init

convenience init(stickImage: SKSpriteNode?,
                 attachedNode: SKNode, nodeSpeed: CGFloat = 0.0,
                 isMovement: Bool = true,
                 range: CGFloat = 55.0, color: SKColor = .darkGray) {

  self.init(fileNamed: "Controller")

  // TODO: Add set up code here
}
override init(fileNamed fileName: String?) {
  super.init(fileNamed: fileName)
}
required init?(coder aDecoder: NSCoder) {
  fatalError("init(coder:) has not been implemented")
}
```

Here, you're setting up a convenience initializer and two other initialization methods: one that overrides the superclass initializer, and one that handles the required init(code:) method. Overriding the superclass initializer is necessary, otherwise you'll get the following error:

```
Convenience initializer for 'Controller' must delegate (with 'self.init')
rather than chaining to a superclass initializer (with 'super.init')
```

With the initializers in place, it's time to add the code to set up the controller and its main properties, starting with the joystick. As you add this code, I won't provide much explanation until the end.

In the convenience initialization method, replace the line of code that reads:

```
// TODO: Add set up code here
```

with the following code:

```
// Set up joystick
joystick = childNode(withName: "//controller_stick") as? SKSpriteNode
joystick.zPosition += 1
if let stickImage = stickImage {
  joystick.addChild(stickImage)
}
```

After that, add the code that sets up the inner base of the joystick.

Set up the inner base:

```
// Set up inner base shape
base = joystick.childNode(withName: "//controller_main")

let innerBase = SKShapeNode(circleOfRadius: range * 2)
innerBase.strokeColor = .black
innerBase.fillColor = color
base.addChild(innerBase)
```

Then, set up the constraints for the joystick:

```
// Lock joystick to base
let rangeX = SKRange(lowerLimit: -range, upperLimit: range)
let rangeY = SKRange(lowerLimit: -range, upperLimit: range)
let lockToBase = SKConstraint.positionX(rangeX, y: rangeY)
joystick.constraints = [lockToBase]
```

Finally, add the code that sets the remaining properties:

```
// Set the other properties
self.range = range

self.attachedNode = attachedNode
self.nodeSpeed = nodeSpeed

self.isMovement = isMovement
```

Take a moment to get familiar with the code you just added. Notice that you're using some of the arguments in the initialization method to set up the joystick; for example, you're using the object in the stickImage argument to add a new sprite node on top of the joystick. You're also using the values stored in the range and color arguments to set up the base of the joystick. The range value establishes the radius, or range the player will have when moving the joystick.

Also, because you're adding the base node *after* adding the other nodes, you increase the joystick node's zPosition property by +1, ensuring that it shows *above* (*on top of*) the base node.

You're almost done with the set up. There's just one more thing to do: create the methods responsible for setting the controller for the left or right side of the view.

Below the initialization methods, add the following code:

```
func anchorRight() {
  scene?.anchorPoint = CGPoint(x: 1, y: 0)
  base.position = CGPoint(x: -175.0, y: 175.0)
}

func anchorLeft() {
  scene?.anchorPoint = CGPoint(x: 0, y: 0)
  base.position = CGPoint(x: 175.0, y: 175.0)
}
```

With this code, you modify the anchorPoint property and set the position property of the base node according to which side the controller will appear.

If you're not a fan of showing the arrows on your controllers, you can add methods to hide them.

Add the following method to hide the large arrows:

```
func hideLargeArrows() {
  if let node = childNode(withName: "//controller_left")
    as? SKSpriteNode {
    node.isHidden = true
  }

  if let node = childNode(withName: "//controller_right")
    as? SKSpriteNode {
    node.isHidden = true
  }

  if let node = childNode(withName: "//controller_up")
    as? SKSpriteNode {
    node.isHidden = true
  }

  if let node = childNode(withName: "//controller_down")
    as? SKSpriteNode {
    node.isHidden = true
  }
}
```

And then add the following method to hide the small arrows:

```
func hideSmallArrows() {
  if let node = childNode(withName: "//controller_topLeft")
    as? SKSpriteNode {
    node.isHidden = true
  }
```

```
  if let node = childNode(withName: "//controller_topRight")
    as? SKSpriteNode {
    node.isHidden = true
  }

  if let node = childNode(withName: "//controller_bottomLeft")
    as? SKSpriteNode {
    node.isHidden = true
  }

  if let node = childNode(withName: "//controller_bottomRight")
    as? SKSpriteNode {
    node.isHidden = true
  }
}
```

These two methods give you just a bit more flexibility with these controls.

All right, with that set up out of the way, you're ready to add your new controllers to the main game scene.

Adding New Controllers to the Scene

To keep track of your new controller nodes, you'll set up two new properties. Switch to the GameScene.swift file and add a new property for the movement controller, placing it just above the sceneDidLoad() method:

```
lazy var controllerMovement: Controller? = {
  guard let player = player else {
    return nil
  }

  let stickImage = SKSpriteNode(imageNamed: "player-val-head_0")
  stickImage.setScale(0.75)

  let controller =  Controller(stickImage: stickImage, attachedNode: player,
                              nodeSpeed: 4, isMovement: true,
                              range: 55.0,
                              color: SKColor(red: 59.0/255.0,
                                             green: 111.0/255.0,
                                             blue: 141.0/255.0,
                                             alpha: 0.75))
  controller.setScale(0.65)
  controller.zPosition += 1

  controller.anchorLeft()
  controller.hideLargeArrows()
  controller.hideSmallArrows()

  return controller
}()
```

Below the controllerMovement property, add another new property, this time for the attack controller:

```
lazy var controllerAttack: Controller? = {
  guard let player = player else {
    return nil
  }

  let stickImage = SKSpriteNode(imageNamed: "controller_attack")
  let controller =  Controller(stickImage: stickImage, attachedNode: player,
                               nodeSpeed: 25, isMovement: false,
                               range: 55.0,
                               color: SKColor(red: 160.0/255.0,
                                              green: 65.0/255.0,
                                              blue: 65.0/255.0,
                                              alpha: 0.75))
  controller.setScale(0.65)
  controller.zPosition += 1

  controller.anchorRight()
  controller.hideLargeArrows()
  controller.hideSmallArrows()

  return controller
}()
```

The two controller properties you just added are nearly identical, with a few slight differences. Take a closer look to see if you can spot the differences. Here's a couple of hints: visually, they're a little different, and each one is anchored to a different side.

Also, notice that you're setting each of the controller's zPosition property to +1. The default value is zero, so, naturally, the result is a zPosition value of 1. This value ensures that your controllers will stay on top of the other content, including the monsters your generators are making.

Alternatively, you can modify the view's ignoresSiblingOrder property from false to true. If you go that route, you'll need to also set up an enum to control the scene's rendering order. For a refresher on rendering order and z-Position, please refer to the aside on page 40.

Okay, you're ready to add the new controllers to the scene. In the setupPlayer() method, add the following code at the end:

```
if let controllerMovement = controllerMovement {
  addChild(controllerMovement)
}

if let controllerAttack = controllerAttack {
  addChild(controllerAttack)
}
```

Finally, modify the updateControllerLocation() method to match this:

```
func updateControllerLocation() {
  controllerMovement?.position =
    CGPoint(x: (viewLeft + margin + insets.left),
            y: (viewBottom + margin + insets.bottom))

  controllerAttack?.position =
    CGPoint(x: (viewRight - margin - insets.right),
            y: (viewBottom + margin + insets.bottom))
}
```

Build and run the project.

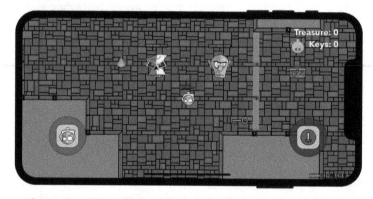

Make sure the controllers show up in the correct location, but don't touch either one—you're just checking for placement; if you touch any part of the controller, the game will crash because you haven't finished writing the code for your new Controller class. But before you can finish that class, you first need to update the Player class and remove the old movement code (which is now partially responsible for causing the crash).

Updating the Player Class

Switch to the Player.swift file. First, remove the Direction enum and the currentDirection property. Also, remove the move(_:), stop(), and attack() methods.

With a decluttered Player class, you're ready to refactor it. Start by adding the following new properties, placing them above the hud property:

```
var movementSpeed: CGFloat = 5

var maxProjectiles: Int = 1
var numProjectiles: Int = 0

var projectileSpeed: CGFloat = 25
var projectileRange: TimeInterval = 1

let attackDelay = SKAction.wait(forDuration: 0.25)
```

You'll use these properties to control the player's movement speed and attack power. Speaking of the player's attack power, you need a new attack method that can handle the full 360° of rotation.

At the bottom of the Player class, add this new attack method:

```
func attack(direction: CGVector) {
    // Verify the direction isn't zero and that the player hasn't
    // shot more projectiles than the max allowed at one time
    if direction != .zero && numProjectiles < maxProjectiles {

        // Increase the number of "current" projectiles
        numProjectiles += 1

        // Set up the projectile
        let projectile = SKSpriteNode(imageNamed: "knife")
        projectile.position = CGPoint(x: 0.0, y: 0.0)
        projectile.zPosition += 1
        addChild(projectile)

        // Set up the physics for the projectile
        let physicsBody = SKPhysicsBody(rectangleOf: projectile.size)

        physicsBody.affectedByGravity = false
        physicsBody.allowsRotation = true
        physicsBody.isDynamic = true

        physicsBody.categoryBitMask = PhysicsBody.projectile.categoryBitMask
        physicsBody.contactTestBitMask = PhysicsBody.projectile.contactTestBitMask
        physicsBody.collisionBitMask = PhysicsBody.projectile.collisionBitMask

        projectile.physicsBody = physicsBody

        // Set the throw direction
        let throwDirection = CGVector(dx: direction.dx * projectileSpeed,
                                      dy: direction.dy * projectileSpeed)

        // Create and run the actions to attack
        let wait = SKAction.wait(forDuration: projectileRange)
        let removeFromScene = SKAction.removeFromParent()

        let spin = SKAction.applyTorque(0.25, duration: projectileRange)
        let toss = SKAction.move(by: throwDirection, duration: projectileRange)

        let actionTTL = SKAction.sequence([wait, removeFromScene])
        let actionThrow = SKAction.group([spin, toss])

        let actionAttack = SKAction.group([actionTTL, actionThrow])
        projectile.run(actionAttack)

        // Set up attack governor (attack speed limiter)
        let reduceCount = SKAction.run({self.numProjectiles -= 1})
        let reduceSequence = SKAction.sequence([attackDelay, reduceCount])
        run(reduceSequence)
    }
}
```

Look through the code you just added. For the most part, it should make sense. You're first making sure the player's attack is possible by checking both the direction and the number of projectiles allowed at once. If everything passes the test, you go through the rest of the method, launching the attack and resetting the numProjectiles property once it's complete.

That's it for the Player class. Next, you need to update the Controller class to handle the player's movement—or more accurately, the node that's "attached" to the controller.

Adding Movement Methods to the Controller

Before you add the methods for the new Controller class, you're going to create a new extension to help with some CGFloat operations that will help you clamp the numbers to a minimum and maximum value.

In the Project Navigator, select the Extensions group and create a new file (⌘N) using the iOS Swift File template. Name the new file CGFloat+Extensions.swift and replace the contents of the file with the following code:

```
import CoreGraphics

extension CGFloat {
  func clamped(v1: CGFloat, v2: CGFloat) -> CGFloat {
    let min = v1 < v2 ? v1 : v2
    let max = v1 > v2 ? v1 : v2

    return self < min ? min : (self > max ? max : self)
  }
  func clamped(to r: ClosedRange<CGFloat>) -> CGFloat {
      let min = r.lowerBound, max = r.upperBound
      return self < min ? min : (self > max ? max : self)
  }
}
```

You'll use this new extension and its methods in the Controller class to help clamp the range between two values so that the controller's movement is restricted to the specified range of values.

(Note: I've included two variations of *essentially* the same method; one uses two arguments, and one uses a ClosedRange argument. You may include either one or both.)

Now, switch to the Controller.swift file and add the following code at the bottom of the class (don't worry about the error you're about to get, you'll fix that in a moment):

```
// MARK: -  Controller Methods
func beginTracking() {
  isTracking = true
}

func endTracking() {
  isTracking = false
  joystick.position = .zero
  moveAttachedNode(direction: .zero)
}
```

Here, you've added the beginTracking() and endTracking() methods, where you set the isTracking property value according to whether or not the player is using the controller. In the endTracking() method, you also reset the positions to zero.

Next, add the method stubs for the main controller functions (which clears the error):

```
func moveJoystick(pos: CGPoint) {

}

func moveAttachedNode(direction: CGVector) {

}

func otherAction(direction: CGVector) {

}
```

Perfect, you're ready to populate those methods.

In the moveJoystick(pos:) method, add the following code:

```
// Store the location
var location = pos

// Verify the player is using the on-screen controls
if isTracking == true {
  location = base.convert(pos, from: self.scene!)
}

// Move the joystick node
let xAxis = CGFloat(location.x.clamped(to: -range...range))
let yAxis = CGFloat(location.y.clamped(v1: -range, v2: range))
joystick.position = CGPoint(x: location.x, y: location.y)

// Call the appropriate method based on the controller type
if isMovement {
  moveAttachedNode(direction: CGVector(dx: xAxis, dy: yAxis))
} else {
  otherAction(direction: CGVector(dx: xAxis, dy: yAxis))
}
```

This code is responsible for moving the joystick node.

Next, you need to add the code that moves the player node (the attached node). In the moveAttachedNode(direction:) method, add the following code:

```
attachedNode?.physicsBody?.velocity =
  CGVector(dx: CGFloat(direction.dx * nodeSpeed),
           dy: CGFloat(direction.dy * nodeSpeed))
```

Finally, add the following code in the otherAction(direction:) method:

```
// If the player exists, launch its attack
guard let player = attachedNode as? Player else {
  return
}
```

```
player.attack(direction: direction)
```

You're almost done. But, because the Direction enum no longer exists, the GameScene.swift file is bursting with errors. Time to fix that.

Cleaning up the Game Scene Errors

Switch to the GameScene.swift file. The first error shows up in the setupPlayer() method. Go ahead and remove the line causing the error:

```
player.move(.stop)
```

Next, remove all of the code in the touchDown(atPoint:) method except the following line:

```
mainGameStateMachine.enter(PlayingState.self)
```

Likewise, remove all of the code inside of the touchMoved(toPoint:) and touchUp(atPoint:) methods.

When you're done, you'll end up with the following touch-related code (and no errors):

```
func touchDown(atPoint pos : CGPoint) {
  mainGameStateMachine.enter(PlayingState.self)
}

func touchMoved(toPoint pos : CGPoint) {

}

func touchUp(atPoint pos : CGPoint) {

}
```

With the errors cleared, you're ready for the next step: connecting the controllers.

Connecting the Controllers

Still inside the GameScene class, find and update the two controller properties so that they use the new Player movement and speed properties.

Here's the updated controllerMovement initialization:

```
let controller = Controller(stickImage: stickImage, attachedNode: player,
                            nodeSpeed: player.movementSpeed,
                            isMovement: true, range: 55.0, color: .darkGray)
```

And here's the updated controllerAttack initialization:

```
let controller = Controller(stickImage: stickImage, attachedNode: player,
                            nodeSpeed: player.projectileSpeed,
                            isMovement: false, range: 55.0, color: .gray)
```

The highlighted code shows the changes.

You're almost done, but there's still the matter of tracking touches and knowing which controller the player is using.

To help with this tracking, you'll set up two new properties in the GameScene class.

Place the following new properties above the controllerMovement property:

```
private var leftTouch: UITouch?
private var rightTouch: UITouch?
```

Now that you have a way to store the player's touch, you can use this information to determine which controller's methods to call. But first, you need to update the touch methods.

(Note: You're going to get some errors while you add the next bit of code, but you can ignore them because they'll all go away once your done.)

Locate and update the touchDown(atPoint:) method so that it matches the following:

```
func touchDown(atPoint pos : CGPoint, touch: UITouch) {
  mainGameStateMachine.enter(PlayingState.self)

  let nodeAtPoint = atPoint(pos)

  if let controllerMovement = controllerMovement {
    if controllerMovement.contains(nodeAtPoint) {
      leftTouch = touch
      controllerMovement.beginTracking()
    }
  }

  if let controllerAttack = controllerAttack {
```

```
    if controllerAttack.contains(nodeAtPoint) {
      rightTouch = touch
      controllerAttack.beginTracking()
    }
  }
}
```

Here, you're updating more than just the code inside of the method; you're also updating its signature so that you can capture the touch object, saving that object to either the leftTouch or rightTouch property.

Next, update the touchMoved(toPoint:) method to match this:

```
func touchMoved(toPoint pos : CGPoint, touch: UITouch) {
  switch touch {
  case leftTouch:
    if let controllerMovement = controllerMovement {
      controllerMovement.moveJoystick(pos: pos)
    }
  case rightTouch:
    if let controllerAttack = controllerAttack {
      controllerAttack.moveJoystick(pos: pos)
    }
  default:
    break
  }
}
```

Again, you're updating the code and the method signature to capture the touch object. And becauase you now know which touch object made the call, you know which controller to move.

Finally, update the touchUp(atPoint:) method to match this:

```
func touchUp(atPoint pos : CGPoint, touch: UITouch) {
  switch touch {
  case leftTouch:
    if let controllerMovement = controllerMovement {
      controllerMovement.endTracking()
      leftTouch = touch
    }
  case rightTouch:
    if let controllerAttack = controllerAttack {
      controllerAttack.endTracking()
      rightTouch = touch
    }
  default:
    break
  }
}
```

All right, time to update the override touch methods so that they account for the new arguments in the methods they each call. Modify them to match the following:

```
override func touchesBegan(_ touches: Set<UITouch>, with event: UIEvent?) {
  for t in touches {self.touchDown(atPoint: t.location(in: self), touch: t)}
}

override func touchesMoved(_ touches: Set<UITouch>, with event: UIEvent?) {
  for t in touches {self.touchMoved(toPoint: t.location(in: self), touch: t)}
}

override func touchesEnded(_ touches: Set<UITouch>, with event: UIEvent?) {
  for t in touches {self.touchUp(atPoint: t.location(in: self), touch: t)}
}

override func touchesCancelled(_ touches: Set<UITouch>, with event: UIEvent?) {
  for t in touches {self.touchUp(atPoint: t.location(in: self), touch: t)}
}
```

Whew, that was a lot of work, but you're ready for the big reveal.

Build and run the project. If you have a physical device, this is a great time to build your project to that instead of the simulator.

Start the game, then move Val around using the left stick while also moving the right stick to throw knives—all the while moving and attacking using 360° of rotation.

Pretty nice, right?

Not only do these updated controls improve your game, but should you decide to support external controllers, you will be in a better place (code-wise) to do so.

Supporting External Game Controllers

 This chapter's resources include some external game controller code in the extras folder. Sadly, there wasn't enough room in this book to cover this topic directly, but I wanted to supply the code for you should you decide to include this type of support. To help get you started, that folder also includes a readme.md file.

Next Steps

You're getting really close to the finishing Val's Revenge. In this chapter, you added some much-needed enhancements to the player's overall gaming experience, especially with regard to the on-screen controls.

Specifically, you learned how to define scene actions using the Action Editor, make the actions run in an infinite loop, and test the actions. You also created a heads-up display to inform the player about the latest stats related to the game—in this case, keys and treasure. Finally, you built controls that allow the player to move and fire with a full 360° of rotation and set yourself up to support external controllers in the future.

In the next chapter, you'll add the final touches to Val's Revenge, including more scenes and a way to save and load the game.

Adding More Scenes and Saving the Game

Using a single game scene is not uncommon, especially for smaller games like Gloop Drop, the game you built in Part I, Build Your First Game with SpriteKit, on page 1. With a single scene, game developers can place all of the game content and supporting methods in a handful of classes, so that when the first (and only) game scene loads, the player can tap the screen (or maybe a certain button) to start the game.

There's nothing wrong with using a single scene for your game, but when you're working on larger games, such as Val's Revenge, you'll likely want to include multiple scenes like a title scene, a "game over" scene, and perhaps more than one game scene that represents a different level within your game.

However, as your game grows, so will the expectations of your players, such as the expectation of being able to save their progress. Imagine how frustrating it would be for players if every time they made a wrong choice, they had to start the game back at the beginning.

In this chapter, you'll work on taking Val's Revenge to the next level—quite literally—by adding new scenes and new levels to the game. You'll also add a way for players to save and load their progress.

So, what are you waiting for? It's time to get to work.

Add New Scenes

At the moment, Val's Revenge uses a single game scene. Although it's entirely possible to stuff more content and logic into this game scene, you'll take a different approach by creating two separate classes—TitleScene and GameOver-Scene—each using their own scene file. The benefit of multiple scenes and classes is that your game-related logic is kept separate from the other logic. Why is this important?

Suppose you had a menu scene or a settings scene where players were able to make certain selections or change options, like the game's sound settings or whether or not the player prefers left-sided or right-sided controls. Now imagine if you stuffed the code necessary to support these two scenes inside of the GameScene class. Before you know it, you'd have a massive class that does way too much and will, no doubt, be difficult to maintain.

To avoid these massive, over-bloated classes, you're betting off creating multiple classes and scenes, which is what you will do here. To help speed up this process, some of the work has already been done for you; you just need to add the resources to your project and make a few changes to the existing code.

Adding the Resources

To begin, open the valsrevenge project in Xcode.

Using the Starter Project

You may continue using your project from the previous chapter, or you can use the starter project located in the projects/begin folder included with the code resources for this chapter. Either option is fine; the only benefit to using the starter project is that you won't get stuck going forward if you missed an earlier step.

There's also an ending project for this chapter that includes all of the code and resources you'll be adding here. The end project is located in the projects/end folder included with the code resources for this chapter.

In the Project Navigator, select the Assets.xcassets asset catalog and create a new sprite atlas (click the + button at the bottom of the Outline View, and select New Sprite Atlas). Name the new atlas game_ui and delete the empty Sprite image set.

Xcode 12 and Sprite Atlas Creation

In Xcode 12, the New Sprite Atlas option does not exist. To create a new sprite atlas, click the + button at the bottom of the Outline View and select AR and SceneKit ▶ Sprite Atlas.

Open Finder and drag the contents from this chapter's resources/game_ui folder into the newly created sprite atlas; you'll end up with the new image sets as shown on page 327.

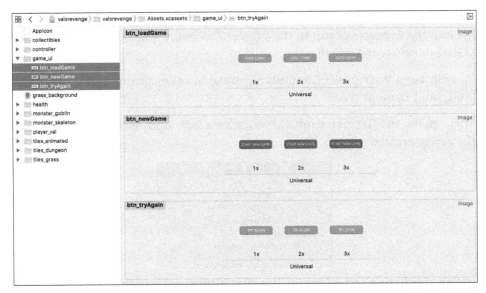

Next, open the resources/backgrounds folder and drag the contents of that folder directly into the root of the asset catalog. When you're done, you'll have two more image sets:

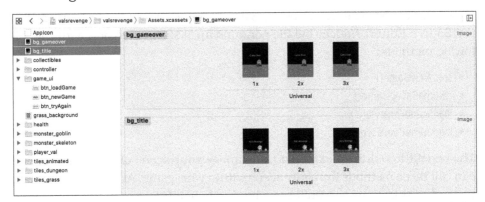

With the image sets in place, you're ready to add the new scenes and the scene manager. The scene manager is an SKScene extension to help load your scenes. As you add these files, don't forget to verify that the Copy items if needed and Add to targets options are both checked. Also make sure that the option to Create groups is selected.

Still in Finder, open the resources/scenes folder and drag the four files from that folder into the Scenes group in the Project Navigator, placing them below the GameScene.swift file.

Finally, open the resources/extensions folder and drag the SKScene+SceneManager.swift file into the Extensions group in the Project Navigator, placing it just below the SKScene+ViewProperties.swift file.

To help keep your project organized, make another group inside the Scenes group and name it Code.

Then, place the GameScene.swift, GameOverScene.swift, and TitleScene.swift files into the newly created group:

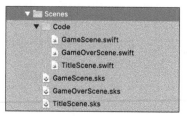

Before moving on, let's look at the new scenes and review the code in the SKScene+SceneManager.swift file.

Touring the New Scenes and the Scene Manager

In the Project Navigator, select the SKScene+SceneManager.swift file to open it in the Source Editor. Notice this file contains an SKScene extension with the following methods:

- startNewGame()
- resumeSavedGame()
- loadSceneForLevel(_:)
- loadGameOverScene()

The benefit to using an extension to manage your scene changes is that you can call these methods from any scene within your game. As you work through the rest of this chapter, you'll see why this is helpful.

While you're here, let's examine the methods in this file from the bottom up, starting with the loadGameOverScene() method:

```
func loadGameOverScene() {
  print("Attempting to load the game over scene.")

  // Create actions to load the game over scene
  let wait = SKAction.wait(forDuration: 0.50)
  let block = SKAction.run {
    if let scene = GameOverScene(fileNamed: "GameOverScene") {
      scene.scaleMode = .aspectFill

      self.view?.presentScene(scene, transition:
        SKTransition.doorsOpenHorizontal(withDuration: 1.0))
```

```
    } else {
      print("Can't load game over scene.")
    }
  }

  // Run the actions in sequence
  run(SKAction.sequence([wait, block]))
}
```

This small method uses SpriteKit actions to load the game over scene, which looks like this:

The two buttons you see here will either start a new game or let the player try again (or in other words, load the previously saved game). The method responsible for starting a new or previously saved game looks like this:

```
func touchDown(atPoint pos : CGPoint) {
  let nodeAtPoint = atPoint(pos)
  if newGameButton.contains(nodeAtPoint) {
    startNewGame()
  } else if loadGameButton.contains(nodeAtPoint) {
    resumeSavedGame()
  }
}
```

You'll find this method in both the GameOverScene and TitleScene classes. The only difference between these two scenes are how they look, not how they function.

Here's a look at the title scene for comparison:

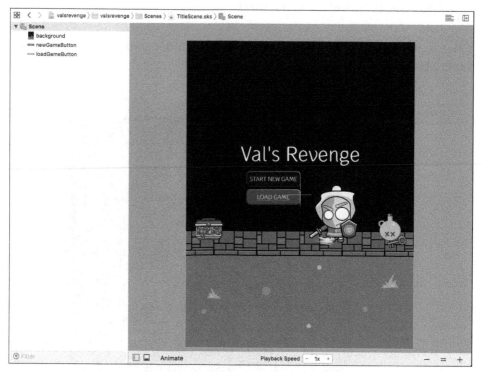

The next method in the SKScene+SceneManager.swift file (from the bottom up) is the loadSceneForLevel(_:) method:

```
func loadSceneForLevel(_ level: Int) {
  print("Attempting to load next scene: GameScene_\(level).")

  // Play sound
  run(SKAction.playSoundFileNamed("exit", waitForCompletion: true))

  // Create actions to load the next scene
  let wait = SKAction.wait(forDuration: 0.50)
  let block = SKAction.run {

    // Load 'GameScene_xx.sks' as a GKScene
    if let scene = GKScene(fileNamed: "GameScene_\(level)") {

      // Get the SKScene from the loaded GKScene
      if let sceneNode = scene.rootNode as! GameScene? {

        // Copy gameplay-related content over to the scene
        sceneNode.entities = scene.entities
        sceneNode.graphs = scene.graphs
```

```
      // Set the scale mode to scale to fit the window
      sceneNode.scaleMode = .aspectFill

      // Present the scene
      self.view?.presentScene(sceneNode, transition:
        SKTransition.doorsOpenHorizontal(withDuration: 1.0))

      // Update the layout
      sceneNode.didChangeLayout()
    }
  } else {
    print("Can't load next scene: GameScene_\(level).")
  }
}

// Run the actions in sequence
run(SKAction.sequence([wait, block]))
}
```

This code should look familiar as it's almost what's being used now in the
GameViewController.swift file to load the initial game scene. The difference is that
you're passing in the level so that the correct scene file gets loaded depending
on which level the player is about to begin.

The remaining methods—startNewGame() and resumeSavedGame()—are, for the
most part, empty. But they won't be for long. Your job, with a little guidance,
is to finish out those methods. But first, you need to get the title scene
working.

Present the Title Scene

You've already seen the title scene for Val's Revenge, now it's time to let the
player see it. For that to happen, you'll need to make some adjustments to
the existing code.

Switch to the GameViewController.swift file and update the viewDidLoad() method to
match this:

```
override func viewDidLoad() {
  super.viewDidLoad()

  // Create the view
  if let view = self.view as! SKView? {

    // Create the scene
    let scene = TitleScene(fileNamed: "TitleScene")

    // Set the scale mode to scale to fill the view window
    scene?.scaleMode = .aspectFill

    // Present the scene
    view.presentScene(scene)
```

```
    // Set the view options
    view.ignoresSiblingOrder = false
    view.showsPhysics = false
    view.showsFPS = false
    view.showsNodeCount = false
  }
}
```

With this update, instead of loading the game scene as the initial scene, you're now loading the title scene. Before you build and run the project, let's get the first game scene working, too.

Load the First Game Scene

As you learned earlier, the loadSceneForLevel(_:) method in the SKScene+SceneManager.swift file is responsible for loading the correct game scene depending on the level the player is about to begin. It does so using the following code:

```
GKScene(fileNamed: "GameScene_\(level)")
```

The value stored in the level argument determines which game scene file to load; for example, the GameScene_1.sks file represents Level 1, the GameScene_2.sks file represents Level 2, and so on. Of course, none of these files exist right now, so you'll need to make at least one—and the easiest way to do so is to rename what you already have.

In the Project Navigator, select the GameScene.sks file and rename it GameScene_1.sks. *(Note: Do not rename the GameScene.swift file; leave that as it is.)*

Build and run the project and you'll see the new title scene, as shown on page 333. After a moment or two, tap the Start New Game button to start a new game, which then loads the first scene.

With the title scene working, you're ready to work on the code necessary to present the game over scene.

Present the Game Over Scene

In Create Your First Component, on page 232, you created a health component to monitor an entity's health. Later, in Build a Better Health Component, on page 291, you enhanced this component by giving it the ability to run certain actions when an entity takes a hit or runs out of health. At the time, you weren't ready to implement all of the actions for the player—now you are.

↑ Title Scene

Game Scene ↓

Switch to the HealthComponent.swift file, and in the didAddToEntity() method, replace the following code:

```
// TODO: Add code to restart the game
// but for now, reset the player's health
self.currentHealth = self.maxHealth
```

with this code:

```
self.componentNode.scene?.loadGameOverScene()
```

Excellent, this small change takes care of loading the game over scene when Val has to call it quits due to her lack of health. The reason it's such a small change is because you're leveraging the SKScene extension you added to the project.

Build and run the project again. This time let the monsters attack Val until she can't fight any more, thus ending the game, as shown on page 334. When the game over scene appears, tap the Start New Game button to start a new game.

Game Scene ↓

↑ Game Over Scene

Excellent, now you have a reason for players to *really* avoid those monsters.

The next thing you need to do is provide a way for players to exit the map into another level; however, before you can do that, you first need a way to track what level players are on. You also need a way to track how many keys Val has in her pocket and how much treasure she has collected. In other words, you need a way to save and load game data.

Save and Load Game Data

Saving and loading game data is essential for games like Val's Revenge. Players don't want to spend a lot of time progressing through a game if their progress isn't saved.

But saving and loading game data isn't something you can take lightly. You need to consider *what* data to save and *how* to save it.

For a game like Val's Revenge, you'll need to save the current level, the number of keys collected, and how much treasure the player found. Because you don't want nefarious users to "break into" this saved data and make changes, you will securely store it to the file system rather than using NSUserDefaults.[1]

1.   https://developer.apple.com/documentation/foundation/nsuserdefaults

To help speed things up, you'll be adding a pre-made GameData class.

Open Finder and in the resources folder for this chapter, you'll see a GameData.swift file. Drag that file into the Project Navigator, placing it just below the GameViewController.swift file. Don't forget to verify that the Copy items if needed and Add to targets options are both checked. Also make sure that the option to Create groups is selected.

The GameData.swift file is small, but it packs a lot of punch. If you don't already have it open in the Source Editor, open it now.

First, notice that the GameData class contains the following properties (ignoring the static property for a moment):

```
// MARK: - Properties
var level: Int = 1

var keys: Int = 0
var treasure: Int = 0
```

These three properties are, essentially, all you need to worry about when saving and restoring the player's game.

Saving and restoring game data doesn't have to be painstaking—especially, if that data supports the Encodable and Decodable protocols; something you can specify by using the Codable type alias.[2] However, because the Player class itself does not conform to these two protocols, and making it do so would be quite the undertaking, you're creating a smaller, more focused class to handle only the game data your player needs. For more information on the Codable type alias, please review Apple's online documentation.[3]

Below those three properties, you will see a static property with the following code:

```
// Set up a shared instance of GameData
static let shared: GameData = {
  let instance = GameData()

  return instance
}()
```

This code sets up the shared instance property. You'll use this property to access the other property values, such as GameData.shared.keys.

---

2.   https://developer.apple.com/documentation/swift/codable
3.   https://developer.apple.com/documentation/foundation/archives_and_serialization/encoding_and_decoding_cus-
      tom_types

Next, you'll see the methods that make up the GameData class. The two key methods are saveDataWithFileName(_:) and loadDataWithFileName(_:). One method is responsible for writing the data, and the other method is responsible for reading that data.

Here's how it works:

The saveDataWithFileName(_:) method converts the GameData object into a file that looks something like this:

```
// !!! BINARY PROPERTY LIST WARNING !!!
//
// The pretty-printed property list below has been created
// from a binary version on disk and should not be saved as
// the ASCII format is a subset of the binary representation!
//
{   "$archiver" = "NSKeyedArchiver";
    "$objects" = ( "$null", <62706C69 73743030 D3010203 04050555 6C657665
6C546B65 79735874 72656173 75726510 01100008 0F151A23 25000000 00000001
01000000 00000000 06000000 00000000 00000000 00000000 27> );
    "$top" = { root = false; };
    "$version" = 100000;
}
```

What's nice about storing the data using NSKeyedArchiver is that the data is unreadable by humans, because (in reality) the raw file looks something more like this:

```
                          gamedata.json
bplist00'
X$versionY$archiverT$topX$objectsÛt_NSKeyedArchiver–    ṬṛọọṭÃ¢

U$nullOMbplist00"UlevelTkeysXtreasure#%'$)27ILQSV\
```

By storing the game data in this format, you lesson the risk of nefarious players cracking that data and increasing their stats.

Now, take a closer look at the loadDataWithFileName(_:) method. Inside of that method, you'll see (in part) the following code:

```
let gd = try PropertyListDecoder().decode(GameData.self, from: data)

// Restore data (properties)
level = gd.level

keys = gd.keys
treasure = gd.treasure
```

This code is where the stored values get read back into the GameData object's properties. This processing happens after the code uses NSKeyedUnarchiver to re-assemble the data.

You're welcome to look around the rest of the file; however, before you can use the GameData class, you first need to modify the AppDelegate.swift file.

Updating the App Delegate to Load Data

Switch to the AppDelegate.swift file, and in the application(_:didFinishLaunchingWithOptions:) method, just before the line that reads return true, add the following line of code:

```
GameData.shared.loadDataWithFileName("gamedata.json")
```

This code uses the shared instance of the GameData object to load the player's game data. Now that you have a way to load that data, you're ready to use that data to populate the keys and treasure properties in the Player class.

Updating the Player Class to Use Saved Data

Switch to the Player.swift file and update the keys and treasure properties to use the data from the GameData object as their default values, like so:

```
private var keys: Int = GameData.shared.keys {
  didSet {
    keysLabel.text = "Keys: \(keys)"
    if keys < 1 {
      stateMachine.enter(PlayerHasNoKeyState.self)
    } else {
      stateMachine.enter(PlayerHasKeyState.self)
    }
  }
}
private var treasure: Int = GameData.shared.treasure {
  didSet {
    treasureLabel.text = "Treasure: \(treasure)"
  }
}
```

Perfect, the properties are now using the stored data as their defaults, which will come in handy when you load your game scenes; however, because these properties are private, you need a public method to access them, so add the following code, placing it just above the init(coder:) method:

```
func getStats() -> (keys: Int, treasure: Int) {
  return (self.keys, self.treasure)
}
```

With this method, you're returning both the keys property and the treasure property, both of which are part of the Player class.

The next step is to modify the startNewGame() and resumeSavedGame() methods to keep these properties up to date.

Modifying the Scene Manager

Switch to the SKScene+SceneManager.swift file and update the startNewGame() and resumeSavedGame() to match the following:

```
func startNewGame() {
  // Reset saved game data
  GameData.shared.level = 1

  GameData.shared.keys = 0
  GameData.shared.treasure = 0

  // Load level
  loadSceneForLevel(GameData.shared.level)
}
func resumeSavedGame() {
  loadSceneForLevel(GameData.shared.level)
}
```

In the first method, you're "resetting" the values stored in the GameData object when the player starts a new game. In the second method, you're "using" one of the properties to resume a previously saved game.

Finally, switch to the GameScene.swift, and in the sceneDidLoad() method, add the following code:

```
GameData.shared.saveDataWithFileName("gamedata.json")
```

This codes triggers the method that saves the data, and it does so each time players advance to the next level, making it possible for players to "try again" should they fail to complete the level.

Before you can test the new saving and loading routine, you first need to:

- Add a way for players to get to the next level.
- Create and add more levels.

Let's start by adding a way for players to get to the next level.

Exit the Map and Load the Next Scene

As cool-looking as your game scene is right now, players will quickly get bored if they have to keep playing the same level. To add a little challenge to the game, and to make it more interesting, you can add multiple levels.

At the moment, Val's Revenge has only one level and no way for players to even reach another level. You're about to change that.

Adding an Exit Node

Switch to the GameScene_1.sks file and add a new Color Sprite to the scene. With the newly added sprite selected, open the Attributes Inspector. Name the new sprite exit, set its Texture to exit and its position to (X: 630, Y: 200).

Switch to the Components Inspector and add the PhysicsComponent component with the following settings:

- bodyCategory: exit
- bodyShape: rect

Also, drag the player node to the bottom of the Scene Graph View so that it appears on top of the exit node when the player moves over it.

When you're done, your scene will look like this:

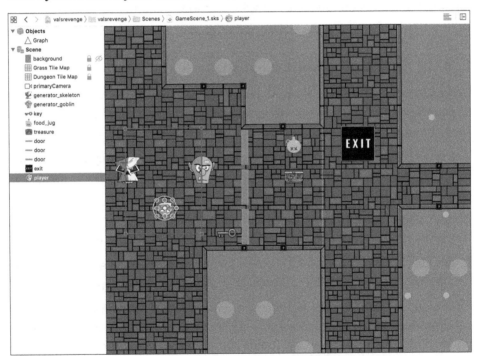

Next, you need to modify the extension that handles the physics contacts so that the game scene knows what to do when the player moves over the exit.

Updating the Physics Contact Extension

Switch to the GameScene+PhysicsContact.swift file, and above the line that reads default:, add the following code:

```
// MARK: - Player | Platform
case PhysicsBody.player.categoryBitMask | PhysicsBody.exit.categoryBitMask:
  let playerNode = contact.bodyA.categoryBitMask ==
    PhysicsBody.player.categoryBitMask ?
      contact.bodyA.node : contact.bodyB.node
  // Update the saved stats
  if let player = playerNode as? Player {
    GameData.shared.keys = player.getStats().keys
    GameData.shared.treasure = player.getStats().treasure
  }
  // Load the next level
  GameData.shared.level += 1
  loadSceneForLevel(GameData.shared.level)
```

With this code, you're saving the player's stats to the GameData object and then loading the next scene using the loadSceneForLevel(_:) method.

There's only one more thing left to do: create more game scenes.

Create Additional Game Scenes

To create your new game scenes, you'll be using the naming convention of GameScene_#.sks where the # symbol represents the level number. You already have GameScene_1.sks, so the next scene to create is GameScene_2.sks.

You're welcome to create the new scenes on your own or copy the examples in the resources/levels folder. The examples are all very similar with one exception: the exit is in a slightly different spot.

Should you choose to copy the pre-made scenes, simply drag the files into the Scenes group in the Project Navigator and you'll be ready to go.

If, however, you'd rather make the new levels yourself, there's something you can do to help speed up the process: use custom Xcode templates.

To create a new Xcode template, copy the AGFT Book folder from the resources/levels/template folder into your ~/Library/Developer/Xcode/Templates/File Templates folder. This step creates a new Xcode template, which you can then access from the New File window, as shown on page 341.

Build and run the project to check out your new levels.

The last thing you'll be working on in this chapter is adding music to the game levels.

Support 3D Spatial Audio Effects

Wouldn't it be neat to have the background music get louder as the player approaches the exit? (Yeah, I thought so, too.) One of the neat things you can do with SpriteKit and the SKAudioNode class is support 3D spatial audio effects, such as using positional sound based on where a *listener* node is located.

The listener node is an instance property on an SKScene object. Typically, you'd set the camera or player node to be the scene's listener. In Val's Revenge, you'll set the player node as the listener.

Switch to the GameScene.swift file. Below the setupPlayer() method, add the following code:

```
func setupMusic() {
  let musicNode = SKAudioNode(fileNamed: "music")
  musicNode.isPositional = false

  // Make the audio node positional
  // so that the music gets louder as
  // the player gets closer to the exit
  if let exit = childNode(withName: "exit") {
    musicNode.position = exit.position
    musicNode.isPositional = true
    listener = player
  }

  addChild(musicNode)
}
```

This code first makes sure there's an exit node available within the scene. If so, it sets the position of the SKAudioNode object to match the exit node. It also sets the player node to the scene's listener.

Of course, you'll need to call this method from somewhere, and because you're relying on the player node to exist, it makes sense to call it from the setupPlayer() method. Add the following code to the setupPlayer() method:

```
setupMusic()
```

Build and run the project. Notice how when you get closer to the exit, the music gets louder, and when you get farther away, so does the sound of the music.

Next Steps

Well, you've reached the end of your journey with Val's Revenge. In this chapter, you learned how to add new scenes and how to save and load player data. You also learned how to use positional sound by adding some background music that gets louder as the player gets closer to the exit.

There's a lot more you can do with Val's Revenge:

- You can refactor the code to add certain components through code rather than the Scene Editor, which could help speed up the process of building new scenes. For example, if the scene requires that every entity needs a set of components, it might make sense to create a new entity subclass that adds those components on initialization.

- You can add additional features like having the monsters drop treasure after Val destroys them.

- And, of course, you can add new monsters and levels.

At this point, you're limited only by your imagination.

With Val's Revenge complete, you'll continue your Apple game development experience by working with GameKit on another game—one that incorporates social interaction. But don't worry about Val. She's more than capable of slaying a few monsters on her own while you work on the next game.

Part V

Build Social Games with GameKit

Social games are a great way to build a community. Discover what's possible using Game Center and GameKit by adding leaderboards, achievements, matchmaking, and challenges to an existing game called Hog Dice—a player versus player dice game.

Adding Leaderboards and Achievements

Social gaming is nothing new—people have been playing online games together for quite a while now. When you stop to think about it, social gaming is a great way to build a community around your game, which can help make your game more popular on the App Store.

But social gaming was a lot more complicated to set up than it is today. Players needed to find a way to connect with other players, and game developers often had to create a robust back-end system to handle the gameplay and synchronization of data.

Today, however, social gaming is a lot easier thanks to Apple's *Game Center* network and *GameKit* framework. Game Center is Apple's social gaming network. With Game Center, players can compare leaderboard ranks, earn achievements, and enjoy multiplayer gaming experiences. With GameKit, developers can make all of that possible.

In this chapter, you'll learn how to add Game Center support to an already fully-playable mobile dice game. Introducing Hog Dice, shown in the following image:

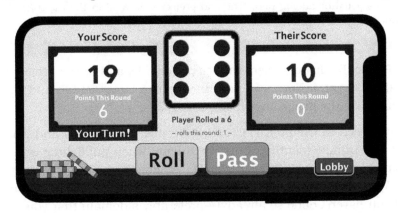

You'll start by adding the Game Center capability and the GameKit framework. You'll then set up an app in App Store Connect, along with some sandbox tester accounts. After that, you'll set up a "most wins" leaderboard and a "first win" achievement for this game, and then you'll return to Xcode to finish up.

The Game of Hog Dice

 In Hog Dice, players take turns rolling a single die. As each player rolls, the player's score increases by the number shown on the die. The first player to 25 wins. Players can roll as many times as they want, but if they roll a 1, they'll lose the points they've rolled that turn.

Now, if you jumped ahead to Use App Store Connect to Add a New App, on page 429 so that you could finish building Gloop Drop while learning about monetization, you'll notice many of the same things, like screenshots and explanations. Don't worry, though; it's only a few pages. Besides, it never hurts to review something you already know. With that in mind, you're ready to add the Game Center capability to Hog Dice.

Add Game Center Capability Using Xcode

To enable Game Center in Hog Dice, you need to add the Game Center capability to the Xcode project and target.

Open the hog project in Xcode.

> ### Using the Starter Project
>
> The starter project is located in the projects/begin folder included with the code resources for this chapter.
>
> There's also an ending project for this chapter that includes all of the code and resources you'll be adding here. The end project is located in the projects/end folder included with the code resources for this chapter.

In the Project Navigator, select the hog project file, and in the Project Editor, select the hog target. Now, switch to the Signing & Capabilities tab and you'll see something like the image shown on page 347.

As you learned in Chapter 1, Creating Scenes with Sprites and Nodes, on page 3, the Bundle Identifier must be unique when publishing a project to the App Store. Because the Bundle ID, net.justwritecode.hogdice, already exists on my Apple developer account, be sure to change the Bundle ID to something else (if you haven't done so already)—preferably a domain that you own.

With the Bundle ID set to something unique, the next step is to add the Game Center capability.

Before you begin, verify that you have the Automatically manage signing option enabled. When that option is enabled, Xcode will handle setting up the profiles, app IDs, and certificates you'll need to successfully publish to the App Store.

To add a new capability, click the + Capability button in the top-left corner of the Project Editor window, and you'll see something like this:

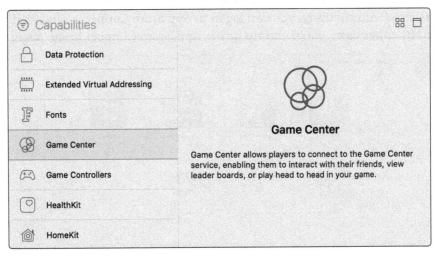

Here, you can select the capability you wish to add. Scroll down to the Game Center capability and double-click the row to add that capability. Because the Automatically manage signing option is enabled, Xcode creates the necessary profiles, apps IDs, and certificates needed to work with and support Game Center.

If everything went as expected, you'll see the Game Center capability listed at the bottom of the Signing & Capabilities tab.

Your next task is to set up the app in App Store Connect.

Use App Store Connect to Add a New App

To work with Game Center, you first need to set up an app in App Store Connect. Log in to your Apple Developer[1] account, and you'll see something like this:

On the left side of the screen (listed with the other Program Resources), click App Store Connect. Alternatively, you can log in to App Store Connect using its direct link.[2] In either case, you'll end up at the App Store Connect home page:

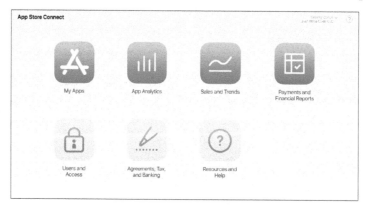

Before moving forward, you may first need to accept the agreements,[3] specifically the *Paid Applications agreement*. You also may need to enter the tax

---

1. https://developer.apple.com/account
2. https://appstoreconnect.apple.com/login
3. https://help.apple.com/app-store-connect/#/deva001f4a14

and banking information for the account holder. Once you have signed the agreements, you can add users and assign roles.

Adding a Sandbox Tester Account

To test Game Center features, you need at least one user account and one sandbox tester account.[4] With a single sandbox tester account, you can test your leaderboards and achievements. However, you'll need at least two or more sandbox tester accounts to test multiplayer games. You'll be adding multiplayer functionality in the next chapter, so be sure to set up at least two sandbox tester accounts.

Setting up users and sandbox tester accounts is not something this book covers; however, you can follow these steps as per Apple's documentation to add tester accounts:

1. Sign in to App Store Connect.
2. On the home page, click Users and Access.
3. Under Sandbox, click Testers.
4. Click "+" to set up your tester accounts.
5. Complete the tester information form and click Invite.
6. Sign out of your Apple ID on all testing devices and sign back in with your new sandbox tester account.

For more information about adding and editing users, please refer to Apple's online documentation.[5]

Now that you have the user accounts set up, you're ready to add a new app.

Adding a New App

From the App Store Connect home page, open the My Apps section. To add a new app, click the Add (+) button in the top-left corner and select New App, like so:

---

4. https://appstoreconnect.apple.com/access/testers
5. https://help.apple.com/app-store-connect/#/devdbefef011

When the New App dialog appears, enter or select the following options:

- Platform: iOS
- Name: Hog Dice
- Primary Language: English
- Bundle ID: {your bundle id}
- SKU: HOGDICE
- User Access: Full Access

Be sure to replace {your bundle id} with your Bundle ID. You may also need to change the Name and SKU values if you get an error about them already being in use.

When you're done, you'll end up with something like this:

Click the Create button to create your new app. For more information about adding apps, please refer to Apple's online documentation.[6]

If everything works, you'll see the App Information page, as shown in the image on page 351.

The next step is to add the Game Center features.

Adding Game Center Features

With the App Information page open, switch to the Features tab and you'll see the Game Center setup page. This page is where you can set up the various Game Center features.

---

6. https://help.apple.com/app-store-connect/#/dev2cd126805

Scroll down to the bottom of the screen and you'll see an area where you can add leaderboards:

Just below that, you'll see another area where you can add achievements:

To make working through this chapter a little easier, you'll add both the leaderboard and the achievement now so that you won't have to return to the portal later.

Add a Leaderboard

What better way to motivate your players than with leaderboards. With leaderboards, players can see how their scores compare with other players around the world. In a game like Hog Dice, you may have leaderboards that rank players based on how many rolls it took to win the game or who has the most wins.

Each app can have up to 500 leaderboards. You can make leaderboards *recurring*, which means they reset after a set amount of time; or you can set up *classic* leaderboards that never expire; you can also mix and match. The types of leaderboards you create depends mostly on your game and its players.

For this example, you'll set up a single "Most Wins" leaderboard that shows the players' rankings from highest (most wins) to lowest (least wins) scores.

To add a new leaderboard, click the + button immediately to the right of the text that reads Leaderboards (0). After that, you'll be prompted to select the type of leaderboard you want to add:

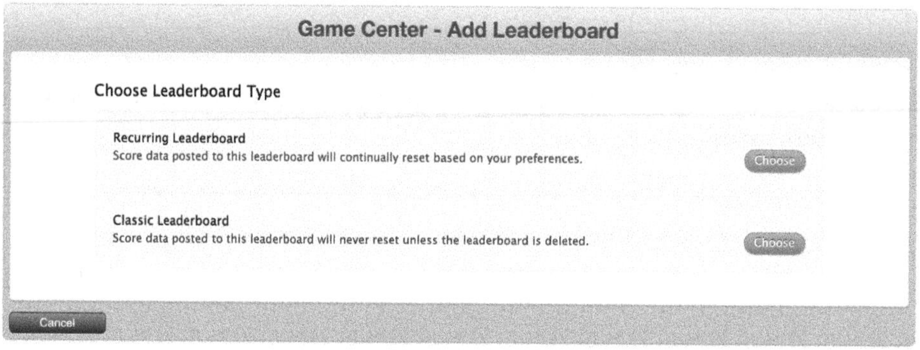

Select Classic Leaderboard by clicking the Choose button, which takes you to the Add Leaderboard page, where you can set up the following options:

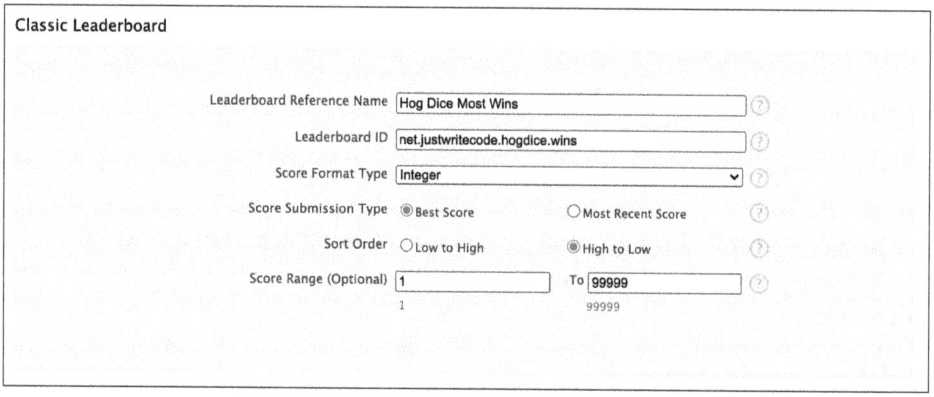

For more information on each of these settings, click the small question mark icon to the right of each option. Note that you'll need to modify the Leaderboard ID to match the Bundle ID you set up earlier. For example, {your bundle id}.wins.

The next step is to add the leaderboard's localization options to allow your game to reach a broader worldwide audience. You're welcome to set up more than one language; however, for Hog Dice, you'll set up only one: English.

Click the Add Language button to open the Add Language page. Set the language options, like so:

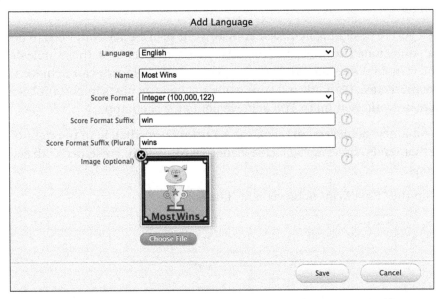

To add the leaderboard image, click Choose File and navigate to the resources folder for this chapter. Inside, you'll see two files; the one you want now is the most_wins.png file.

Once you have everything set up, click Save. You'll end up with something like this:

Click the Save button on the leaderboard setup screen to save the leaderboard and its options.

The next step is to add an achievement.

Add an Achievement

Similar to leaderboards, achievements give your players an incentive to play your game. Unlike leaderboards, though, achievements mark when players reach certain milestones within your game; for example, with Hog Dice, you'll create a "First Win" achievement that players can earn the first time they win a game.

When you're designing achievements for your own games, you need to decide what milestones to include. You also need to decide if these milestones (achievements) are hidden from the player and if players can achieve them more than once. Planning out your game's achievements is important because you're only allowed up to 100 achievements for each app.

To add a new achievement, click the + button immediately to the right of the text that reads Achievements (0). Like leaderboards, you're presented with several options.

Set up the "First Win" achievement, like so:

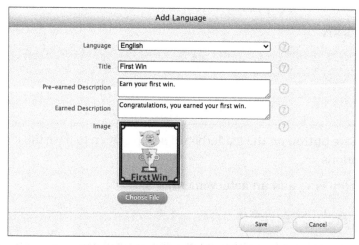

You'll need to modify the Achievement ID to match your Bundle ID, for example, {your bundle id}.first.win.

Again, like leaderboards, you need to set up the localization options. Click the Add Language button and set up the language options, like so:

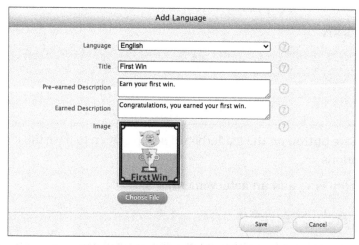

For the image, select the first_win.png file from the resources folder.

Once you have everything set up, click Save and you'll end up with something like this:

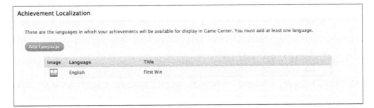

Click the Save button on the achievement setup screen to save the achievement and all of its options.

Perfect, you're done in the portal, and you're ready to return to Xcode to write the necessary code that interfaces with your new leaderboard and achievement.

Create the Game Center Helper

Switch back to the Xcode hog project, and in the Project Navigator, just below the Assets.xcassets asset catalog, create a new group (⌥⌘N). Name this group Game Center; this is where you'll put all of your Game Center–related code.

Inside the new group, create a new file (⌘N) using the iOS Swift File template. Name the new file GameKitHelper.swift and replace its contents with the following code:

```
import GameKit

class GameKitHelper: NSObject {

  // Shared GameKit Helper
  static let shared: GameKitHelper = {
    let instance = GameKitHelper()

    return instance
  }()
}
```

This code is the start of your new GameKit helper class; it sets up the shared instance property, which you'll use to access the main GameKit methods.

The next step is to authenticate the local player on the device so that they can access the Game Center features of your game.

Authenticating the Local Player

Before you can use the Game Center features, you need to authenticate the local Game Center player—and this process should happen as early as possible.

Authentication happens by setting the authentication handler on the shared instance of the GKLocalPlayer object. This object represents the authenticated Game Center player on the device. For this process, you'll use the Notification Center. With notifications,[7] you can broadcast specific information to designated observers. These observers then watch for the notifications, taking specific actions when they occur.

In this case, you'll create a custom notification that informs its observers that it's time to authenticate the player.

At the bottom of the GameKitHelper.swift file (outside the GameKitHelper class), add the following code:

```
// MARK: - NOTIFICATION EXTENSIONS

extension Notification.Name {
  static let presentAuthenticationViewController =
    Notification.Name("presentAuthenticationViewController")
}
```

The next step is to set up the property that'll hold the authentication view controller object.

Inside the GameKitHelper class, add the following new property:

```
// Game Center- & GameKit-Related View Controllers
var authenticationViewController: UIViewController?
```

And now for the fun part: adding the method that handles authentication.

Below the new authenticationViewController property, add the following code:

```
// MARK: - GAME CENTER METHODS

func authenticateLocalPlayer() {

  // Prepare for new controller
  authenticationViewController = nil

  // Authenticate local player
  GKLocalPlayer.local.authenticateHandler = { viewController, error in

    if let viewController = viewController {
      // Present the view controller so the player can sign in
      self.authenticationViewController = viewController
      NotificationCenter.default.post(
        name: .presentAuthenticationViewController,
        object: self)
      return
    }
```

---

7. https://developer.apple.com/documentation/foundation/notifications

```
  if error != nil {
    // Player could not be authenticated
    // Disable Game Center in the game
    return
  }

  // Player was successfully authenticated
  // Check if there are any player restrictions before starting the game

  if GKLocalPlayer.local.isUnderage {
    // Hide explicit game content
  }

  if GKLocalPlayer.local.isMultiplayerGamingRestricted {
    // Disable multiplayer game features
  }

  if GKLocalPlayer.local.isPersonalizedCommunicationRestricted {
    // Disable in game communication UI
  }

  // Place the access point in the upper-right corner
  // GKAccessPoint.shared.location = .topLeading
  // GKAccessPoint.shared.showHighlights = true
  // GKAccessPoint.shared.isActive = true

  // Perform any other configurations as needed
  }
}
```

There's a lot of code you're not using here, but it's code that you should know about in case you want or need to include these features in your own games; for example, you may need to restrict certain content—like multiplayer gaming or personalized communication—based on the player's Game Center preferences. Or, you may decide to include the Game Center Access Point[8] if your game's design allows for it. The Game Center Access Point is an Apple-designed interface that lets players view their Game Center profiles without leaving your game. Deciding to use (or not use) the access point depends on your game's design and, perhaps, how *important* the Game Center features are to its players. Hog Dice isn't designed to use this access point, so the code is commented out.

Now, focus on the first block of code. Notice that it's setting the authenticationViewController property and then posting the .presentAuthenticationViewController notification. This notification is what your observers will be looking for and is the mechanism you'll use to present the authentication controller.

---

8.   https://developer.apple.com/design/human-interface-guidelines/game-center/overview/access-point

Presenting the Authentication Controller

To present the Game Center authentication controller, you'll configure the main view controller to act as an observer. Switch to the GameViewController.swift file. Near the end of the file, replace the line that reads // TODO: Add Game Center Notification Handlers with the following code:

```
@objc func showAuthenticationViewController() {
  if let viewController = GameKitHelper.shared.authenticationViewController {
    present(viewController, animated: true, completion: nil)
  }
}
```

This is the code you'll call when the .presentAuthenticationViewController notification gets posted; it handles presenting the shared view controller object stored in the GameKitHelper class.

All that's left to do now is set up the GameViewController class as an observer of that notification and call the authenticateLocalPlayer() method in the GameKitHelper class.

In the viewDidLoad() method located at the top of the file, replace the two TODO comments with the following code:

```
// Add Game Center Observers
NotificationCenter.default.addObserver(
  self,
  selector: #selector(self.showAuthenticationViewController),
  name: .presentAuthenticationViewController, object: nil)

// Authenticate the Local GC Player
GameKitHelper.shared.authenticateLocalPlayer()
```

Build and run the project.

The first time you run the game, you'll be prompted to log in to the Game Center. Be sure to log in with your sandbox tester account. After a successful login, stop the project.

Build and run the project again.

Notice that this time around, the player is already logged in and authenticated.

Show the Game Center Dashboard

You already know that Hog Dice doesn't use the Game Center Access Point. However, players will still need a way to access the Game Center Dashboard because what's the point of adding Game Center features if players can't access them, right?

In Hog Dice, you'll provide a way for players to access the dashboard, leaderboards, and achievements using the following three buttons:

These three buttons are the main access points into the Game Center. The first one is located in the lobby scene, while the other two are located in the game over scene.

Using the Game Center View Controller

The first step is to create another shared view controller. Switch to the GameKitHelper.swift file and add a new property:

```
var gameCenterViewController: GKGameCenterViewController?
```

The GKGameCenterViewController class is the single user interface that displays the Game Center information.

As you did with the authentication controller, you'll use a notification to present the controller. In the Notification.Name extension, add the following code:

```
static let presentGameCenterViewController =
  Notification.Name("presentGameCenterViewController")
```

However, unlike the authentication controller, you also need to implement the GKGameCenterControllerDelegate protocol, which handles dismissing the Game Center controller. At the bottom of the GameKitHelper.swift file, just above the Notification.Name extension mark, add the following code:

```
// MARK: - DELEGATE EXTENSIONS

extension GameKitHelper: GKGameCenterControllerDelegate {
  func gameCenterViewControllerDidFinish(_ gameCenterViewController:
                                         GKGameCenterViewController) {
    gameCenterViewController.dismiss(animated: true, completion: nil)
  }
}
```

Finally, add the method that handles showing the Game Center view controller, placing it in the extension you just created:

```
// Show the Game Center View Controller
func showGKGameCenter(state: GKGameCenterViewControllerState) {
  guard GKLocalPlayer.local.isAuthenticated else { return }

  // Prepare for new controller
  gameCenterViewController = nil

  // Create the instance of the controller
  if #available(iOS 14, *) {
    gameCenterViewController = GKGameCenterViewController(state: state)
  } else {
    gameCenterViewController = GKGameCenterViewController()
    gameCenterViewController?.viewState = state
  }

  // Set the delegate
  gameCenterViewController?.gameCenterDelegate = self

  // Post the notification
  NotificationCenter.default.post(name: .presentGameCenterViewController,
                                  object: self)
}
```

Excellent, it's time to update the GameViewController class to handle presenting the Game Center view controller.

Presenting the Game Center View Controller

Switch to the GameViewController.swift file. At the bottom of the file, still inside the class, add the following code:

```
@objc func showGameCenterViewController() {
  if let viewController = GameKitHelper.shared.gameCenterViewController {
    present(viewController, animated: true, completion: nil)
  }
}
```

Then, in the viewDidLoad() method, add the observer, placing it below the one you created earlier:

```
NotificationCenter.default.addObserver(
  self,
  selector: #selector(self.showGameCenterViewController),
  name: .presentGameCenterViewController, object: nil)
```

The final piece to this puzzle is to update the button actions in the lobby and game over scenes.

Updating the Game Center Button Actions

Switch to the LobbyScene.swift file, and in the touchDown(atPoint:) method, replace the line that reads // TODO: Add code to open Game Center with the following one-liner:

```
GameKitHelper.shared.showGKGameCenter(state: .dashboard)
```

This code calls the showGKGameCenter(state:) method, passing in the GKGameCenterViewControllerState value that represents the Game Center dashboard.

Now, head over to the GameOverScene.swift file, and in its touchDown(atPoint:) method, replace the line that reads // TODO: Add code to open Leaderboards, with the following:

```
GameKitHelper.shared.showGKGameCenter(state: .leaderboards)
```

Also, replace the line that reads // TODO: Add code to open Achievements with this one:

```
GameKitHelper.shared.showGKGameCenter(state: .achievements)
```

These two lines of code open the Game Center in their respective states.

Build and run the project. On the lobby scene, tap the Game Center button and you'll see the standard Game Center dashboard:

To test the game over scene buttons, tap either the chips (on the left) or the dice (on the right) of the lobby scene. After the scene loads, tap the Leaderboards button to open the Game Center Leaderboards view:

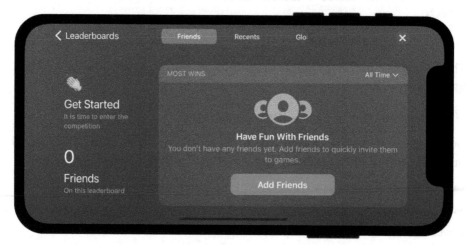

Close that view and then tap the Achievements button to open the Game Center Achievements view:

Excellent, the Game Center integration is working quite nicely, which means you're ready to add the code that reports the player's wins.

Report Score to Leaderboard

Before you jump into the code that reports scores to leaderboards, you may want to review the GameData.swift file. In this file, you'll see there's a wins property. This is the property you'll use to track the player's number of wins. If you switch to the GameOverScene.swift file, you'll see the didMove(to:) method increments this value by one every time the player wins a game. So, when you report the number of wins to the leaderboard, you'll actually be passing in the value saved in this property.

All right, let's get to it.

Switch to the GameKitHelper.swift file. First, add a new static property to hold the Leaderboard ID string, placing it at the top of the class (for easy access):

```
// Leaderboard IDs
static let leaderBoardIDMostWins = "net.justwritecode.hogdice.wins"
```

Be sure to use the ID you set up earlier, for example, {your bundle id}.hogdice.wins.

The next step is to create the method for reporting the score. Below the authenticateLocalPlayer() method, add the following code:

```
// Report Score
func reportScore(score: Int, forLeaderboardID leaderboardID: String,
                 errorHandler: ((Error?)->Void)? = nil) {
  guard GKLocalPlayer.local.isAuthenticated else { return }

  if #available(iOS 14, *) {
    GKLeaderboard.submitScore(score, context: 0,
                              player: GKLocalPlayer.local,
                              leaderboardIDs: [leaderboardID],
                              completionHandler: errorHandler ?? {
                                error in
                                print("error: \(String(describing: error))")
                              })
  } else {
    let gkScore = GKScore(leaderboardIdentifier: leaderboardID)
    gkScore.value = Int64(score)
    GKScore.report([gkScore], withCompletionHandler: errorHandler)
  }
}
```

Recently, Apple made some modifications as to how GameKit reports scores to leaderboards. Before iOS 14, GameKit used the GKScore class for reporting. However, this class is now deprecated and was replaced with a new method in the GKLeaderboard class. If you plan to support older devices, which Hog Dice does, you may want to consider using an API availability check (#available) shown in the reportScore(score:forLeaderboardID:errorHandler:) method.

Finally, you need to call this method from the game over scene. Switch to the GameOverScene.swift file, and at the end of the didMove(to:) method, replace the TODO comment with the following code:

```
// Report Score
GameKitHelper.shared.reportScore(score: GameData.shared.wins,
        forLeaderboardID: GameKitHelper.leaderBoardIDMostWins)
```

Here, you're passing in the total wins and the value stored in the static leaderBoardIDMostWins property.

Build and run the project, then play a quick game to 25. To make it easier for you to win, play a local game rather than a solo match. This way, you can play against yourself; just make sure Player One wins. Alternatively, you *could* cheat and tap the dice on the lobby scene, which forces a win. This simulator-only code was added to the existing project for testing purposes only. If you're curious what it looks like, search for #if targetEnvironment(simulator) inside the project.

When the game ends, click the Leaderboards button, and you'll see your first win listed:

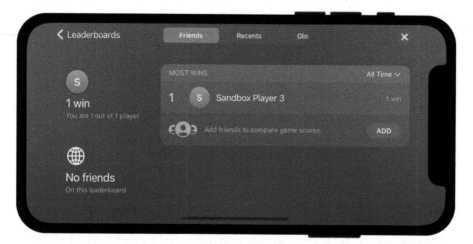

(Note that if you were playing the game beforehand, your wins were being recorded, so you may see more than one win listed here.)

You're well on your way to finishing out this chapter. There's only one more thing to do: add the code to report achievements.

Report Achievement

Achievements are slightly different in how they are reported, as they require a bit more code than leaderboard score reporting. First, switch back to the GameKitHelper.swift file.

You'll start by creating a new class. You could put this new class in a file of its own, but because there's only one achievement in Hog Dice, you'll add it to the GameKitHelper.swift file instead.

Above the delegate extension mark, add the following code:

```
// MARK: - ACHIEVEMENTS HELPER CLASS
class AchievementsHelper {
  static let achievementIdFirstWin = "net.justwritecode.hogdice.first.win"

  class func firstWinAchievement(didWin: Bool) -> GKAchievement {
    let achievement = GKAchievement(
      identifier: AchievementsHelper.achievementIdFirstWin)

    if didWin {
      achievement.percentComplete = 100
      achievement.showsCompletionBanner = true
    }
    return achievement
  }
}
```

Here, you're creating a static property to hold the Achievement ID (remember to update that value to match your Achievement ID). You're then creating a GKAchievement object and setting its properties depending on whether the player won the game.

Now, in the GameKitHelper class, just below the method that reports the player's score, add the following code:

```
// Report Achievement
func reportAchievements(achievements: [GKAchievement],
                        errorHandler: ((Error?)->Void)? = nil) {
  guard GKLocalPlayer.local.isAuthenticated else { return }

  GKAchievement.report(achievements, withCompletionHandler: errorHandler)
}
```

This is the method you'll call from the game over scene to report the player's achievements; you still need to call this method.

Switch back to the GameOverScene.swift file, and below the code that report's the score, add the following code:

```
// Get and report achievements
var achievements: [GKAchievement] = []
achievements.append(AchievementsHelper.firstWinAchievement(didWin: isWinner))
GameKitHelper.shared.reportAchievements(achievements: achievements)
```

This code creates an array of achievements and passes it into the method you created to report achievements; it also causes Xcode to complain about a missing GKAchievement type:

```
// Get and report achievements
var achievements: [GKAchievement] = []                      ⊗ Cannot find type 'GKAchievement' in scope
achievements.append(AchievementsHelper.firstWinAchievement(didWin: isWinner))
GameKitHelper.shared.reportAchievements(achievements: achievements)
```

To resolve this error, you need to import the GameKit framework. Scroll up to the top of the file and add the import statement:

```
import GameKit
```

Build and run the project, and when you win the game this time, you'll see the Achievement banner at the top of the scene:

Now, tap the Achievements button and you'll see that you earned the "First Win" achievement:

Congratulations, you're a winner—and you're well on your way to learning the inner workings of Game Center and the GameKit framework.

Next Steps

Game Center—and social gaming in general—is a big topic, and it would be nearly impossible to cover every aspect of leaderboards and achievements in a single chapter. However, this chapter gave you a chance to get familiar with Game Center and its supporting framework, GameKit. Specifically, you got to set up Game Center support, add the GameKit framework to your project, authenticate the local Game Center player, and implement a classic leaderboard and a "First Win" achievement. These examples are just the tip of the iceberg when it comes to Game Center and social gaming.

In the next chapter, you'll learn how to add another Game Center feature to Hog Dice: multiplayer gaming. With multiplayer gaming, you further increase the chances of getting more people interested in playing your game.

Creating Multiplayer Games with GameKit

Now that you have some of the basic Game Center features added to Hog Dice, you're ready to extend the game's functionality to allow for online multiplayer gaming over Game Center.

With online multiplayer Game Center games, players can enjoy playing your game with other real-life people, which can help increase the popularity of your game. Besides the bump in popularity, playing games with other humans is a lot of fun. So, if your game lends itself to player versus player gameplay, consider adding multiplayer functionality—even if it means a little more work on your part.

In Game Center, there are two types of multiplayer games: real-time and turn-based. In both cases, players can invite friends or participate in an auto-matched game with random players. In this chapter, you'll focus on auto-matched, turn-based gaming, which the following images depict:

 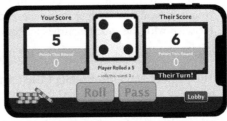

An auto-matched game occurs when Player A attempts to start a new online game. If there's already a game started by another player (Player B), and that game is looking for a spot to fill, then Player A will join Player B's game, which is already in progress. Additionally, players can have more than one multiplayer Game Center game active at any given time. The beauty of turn-based gaming is that players don't have to be connected to the Game Center during the entire game; they need to connect only when it's their turn.

Hog Dice already has what it needs to play solo games against a primitive AI system. The game also has the functionality it needs to play games against another local player on the same device. Your job is to extend this multiplayer capability to allow players to play against other Game Center players.

Request a Turn-Based Match

Before your players can start or join a multiplayer Game Center game, they first need to make a request. To set up a multiplayer game request, you can use the GKTurnBasedMatchmakerViewController class and its corresponding GKTurn-BasedMatchmakerViewControllerDelegate protocol. You can also create a custom match controller, but that goes beyond the scope of this book, so you'll stick with the standard matchmaking UI.

The GKTurnBasedMatchmakerViewController class is responsible for showing the standard interface where players can manage their multiplayer games. To present this view controller, you'll use another custom notification, similar to what you created in the previous chapter.

Preparing for the Turn-Based Matchmaker View Controller

Open the hog project in Xcode.

Using the Starter Project

You may continue using your project from the previous chapter, or you can use the starter project located in the projects/begin folder included with the code resources for this chapter. Either option is fine; the only benefit to using the starter project is that you won't get stuck going forward if you missed an earlier step.

There's also an ending project for this chapter that includes all of the code and resources you'll be adding here. The end project is located in the projects/end folder included with the code resources for this chapter.

In the Project Navigator, select the GameKitHelper.swift file to open it in the Source Editor.

First, inside the GameKitHelper class, add the following new property, placing it below the gameCenterViewController property:

```
var matchmakerViewController: GKTurnBasedMatchmakerViewController?
```

You'll use this property to store the matchmaker view controller.

Then, at the bottom of the GameKitHelper.swift file, add the new custom notification in the Notification.Name extension:

```
static let presentTurnBasedGameCenterViewController =
  Notification.Name("presentTurnBasedGameCenterViewController")
```

You'll post this notification when it's time to present the matchmaking view controller.

The final step is to add another extension that includes the required methods to support the GKTurnBasedMatchmakerViewControllerDelegate protocol.

Just above the Notification.Name extension, add the following code:

```
extension GameKitHelper: GKTurnBasedMatchmakerViewControllerDelegate {
  func turnBasedMatchmakerViewControllerWasCancelled(_ viewController:
    GKTurnBasedMatchmakerViewController) {
    viewController.dismiss(animated: true, completion: nil)
  }

  func turnBasedMatchmakerViewController(_ viewController:
    GKTurnBasedMatchmakerViewController, didFailWithError error: Error) {
    print("MatchmakerViewController failed with error: \(error)")
  }
}
```

The first method is responsible for dismissing the view controller; the second method is responsible for handling errors; both are required by the protocol. In this example, error handling is simplified by printing a message to the screen. In a production environment, it's better to inform the player when an error occurs rather than ignore it.

At this point, you are ready to work on the code that sets up the match request.

Using the Turn-Based Matchmaker View Controller

Still inside the GameKitHelper.swift file, and below the turnBasedMatchmakerViewController(_:didFailWithError:) method, add the following code:

```
// Show the Turn-Based Matchmaker View Controller (Find Match)
func findMatch() {
  guard GKLocalPlayer.local.isAuthenticated else { return }

  let request = GKMatchRequest()
  request.minPlayers = 2
  request.maxPlayers = 2
  request.defaultNumberOfPlayers = 2

  request.inviteMessage = "Do you want to play Hog Dice?"

  matchmakerViewController = nil
```

```
matchmakerViewController =
  GKTurnBasedMatchmakerViewController(matchRequest: request)
matchmakerViewController?.turnBasedMatchmakerDelegate = self

NotificationCenter.default.post(name:
  .presentTurnBasedGameCenterViewController, object: nil)
}
```

This code sets up a Game Center match request using a GKMatchRequest object. When setting up a match request, you must specify the minimum and the maximum number of players allowed for each match. For Hog Dice, that number is two.

Next, you need to modify the main game view controller to handle the presentation of the matchmaker view controller.

Switch to the GameViewController.swift file, and at the bottom of the file (still inside the class), add the following code:

```
@objc func showTurnBasedMatchmakerViewController() {
  if let viewController = GameKitHelper.shared.matchmakerViewController {
    present(viewController, animated: true, completion: nil)
  }
}
```

Like the notification handlers you added in the previous chapter, this one verifies that the matchmakerViewController property contains a value before presenting the view controller.

Finally, you need to add the corresponding observer. In the viewDidLoad() method, add the observer, placing it just below the other two observers you added in the previous chapter:

```
NotificationCenter.default.addObserver(
  self,
  selector: #selector(self.showTurnBasedMatchmakerViewController),
  name: .presentTurnBasedGameCenterViewController, object: nil)
```

That takes care of the GameViewController class. The next step is to update the lobby scene so that you can present the matchmaking view controller to the player.

Updating the Lobby Scene

Switch to the LobbyScene.swift file. In the touchDown(atPoint:) method, find and replace the line that reads // TODO: Add code to open find match with the following code:

```
GameKitHelper.shared.findMatch()
```

Build and run project to the simulator. Depending on when you last logged in to the Game Center, you may need to log in again. After you log in, tap the Find Match button and you'll see the following screen:

Hang on—don't start the game yet—you have a little more work to do.

Manage Multiplayer Matches

One of the neat things about Game Center and GameKit is that they include everything you need to set up and manage multiplayer games, well, almost everything—you need to supply the game data. However, before getting too deep into the game data, let's cover the heart of turn-based matches: the GKTurnBasedMatch object.

The GKTurnBasedMatch object is what you use to implement a turn-based match. This object, which your game never creates directly, contains important information about the match. This object uses a store-and-forward approach to share your game's match data between its match *participants*.

The GKTurnBasedMatch object has a few key properties:

- participants: Holds information about the "players" participating in the game.

- currentParticipant: This is the participant whose turn it is currently.

- matchData: Contains the game-specific data, including the details of the match and its current state.

- matchID: A unique string that identifies the match.

Before you get started using this class, it'll be helpful to extend it by adding two new properties that will make it easier to know which participant is the local player.

Extending the GKTurnBasedMatch Class

To help better manage the match data, you'll start by creating a new extension for the GKTurnBasedMatch class.

In the Extensions group, create a new file (⌘N) using the iOS Swift File template. Name the new file GameKit+Extensions.swift and replace its contents with the following code:

```
import GameKit

extension GKTurnBasedMatch {

  var localPlayer: GKTurnBasedParticipant? {
    return participants.filter({ $0.player == GKLocalPlayer.local}).first
  }

  var opponents: [GKTurnBasedParticipant] {
    return participants.filter {
      return $0.player != GKLocalPlayer.local
    }
  }
}
```

This GKTurnBasedMatch extension—well, technically, the properties it contains—makes it easier to filter the participants array. Using the GKTurnBasedParticipant objects in this array, you can separate the local player from the opponents.

Speaking of players, it's time to create a new simplified class to hold the player information.

Handling Game-Related Data

If you look at the Player.swift file, you'll see that the Player class has a lot of properties the Game Center doesn't need. Also, many of these properties do not conform to the Encodable and Decodable protocols. (You first learned about encoding and decoding in Save and Load Game Data, on page 334.) For these two reasons, you'll create a new class to support multiplayer gameplay.

In the Game Center group, create a new file (⌘N) using the iOS Swift File template. Name the new file GameCenterPlayer.swift and replace its contents with the following code:

```
class GameCenterPlayer: Codable, Equatable {

  var playerId: String
  var playerName: String

  var isLocalPlayer: Bool = false
  var isWinner: Bool = false

  var totalPoints: Int = 0
```

```
  // protocol required for `Equatable`
  static func == (lhs: GameCenterPlayer, rhs: GameCenterPlayer) -> Bool {
    return lhs.playerId == rhs.playerId && lhs.playerName == rhs.playerName
  }
  init(playerId: String, playerName: String) {
    self.playerId = playerId
    self.playerName = playerName
  }
}
```

This simplified GameCenterPlayer class gives you a smaller, more focused class to hold the player information.

Still inside the Game Center group, create another new file (⌘N) using the iOS Swift File template. Name this one GameCenterData.swift and replace its contents with the following code:

```
class GameCenterData: Codable {
  var players: [GameCenterPlayer] = []

  func addPlayer(_ player: GameCenterPlayer) {
    if let p = getPlayer(withName: player.playerName) {
      p.isLocalPlayer = player.isLocalPlayer
      p.isWinner = player.isWinner
    } else {
      players.append(player)
    }
  }

  func getLocalPlayer() -> GameCenterPlayer? {
    return players.filter({ $0.isLocalPlayer == true}).first
  }

  func getRemotePlayer() -> GameCenterPlayer? {
    return players.filter({ $0.isLocalPlayer == false}).first
  }

  func getPlayer(withName playerName: String) -> GameCenterPlayer? {
    return players.first(where: {$0.playerName == playerName})
  }

  func getPlayerIndex(for player: GameCenterPlayer) -> Int? {
    return players.firstIndex(of: player)
  }
}
```

This is the class you'll use to store the data in the GKTurnBasedMatch.matchData property.

With these two classes in place, you're ready to add the code that handles player turns and sending the game-related data.

Process Player Turns Using an Event Listener

The GKTurnBasedEventListener protocol takes care of exchanges and match-related events for turn-based games; however, you don't implement this protocol directly. Instead, you implement the GKLocalPlayerListener protocol, which inherits methods from the GKTurnBasedEventListener protocol. One of those methods is player(_:receivedTurnEventFor:didBecomeActive:).

The player(_:receivedTurnEventFor:didBecomeActive:) method gets called when it's the local player's turn. This method also gets called when:

- The current player's turn time-out is about to expire.
- The player accepts an invite from another player.
- The player's turn was passed to another player.
- The match data is saved by another player.
- The player receives a reminder about his or her turn.

As you did with the other Game Center–related actions, you'll use a custom notification to help process this turn event.

You'll start by adding a new custom notification.

Setting up a Custom Turn Event Notification

Switch to the GameKitHelper.swift file. At the bottom of the file, in the Notification.Name extension, add a new custom notification:

```
static let receivedTurnEvent = Notification.Name("receivedTurnEvent")
```

Next, just above the Notification.Name extension, add a new GameKitHelper extension:

```
extension GameKitHelper: GKLocalPlayerListener {
  func player(_ player: GKPlayer,
              receivedTurnEventFor match: GKTurnBasedMatch,
              didBecomeActive: Bool) {

    matchmakerViewController?.dismiss(animated: true, completion: nil)
    NotificationCenter.default.post(name: .receivedTurnEvent,
                                    object: match)
  }
}
```

Here, you're implementing the GKLocalPlayerListener protocol and its corresponding player(_:receivedTurnEventFor:didBecomeActive:) method. Inside this method, you're dismissing the matchmakerViewController view controller and posting your new custom notification.

Now, you just need to register the listener so that you can receive these turn events.

Registering the Listener

Still inside the GameKitHelper.swift file, find the authenticatePlayer() method, and above the line that reads if error != nil {, add the following code to register the listener:

```
else if GKLocalPlayer.local.isAuthenticated {
  GKLocalPlayer.local.register(self)
}
```

To register a listener, the local player must already be authenticated. Once authenticated, you're passing in a reference of self, indicating that the GameKitHelper class will act as the GKLocalPlayerListener object.

With your listener in place, you're ready to get into the nitty-gritty of match data.

Use Custom Match Data in Multiplayer Games

In Handling Game-Related Data, on page 374, you created the classes responsible for modeling the game's custom game-related data. For Hog Dice, that data includes two players and their scores. The next step is to use that data to manage and maintain the multiplayer game's current state.

You'll start by adding a new property to the GameKitHelper class. Below the matchmakerViewController property, add the following code:

```
// Turn-based match properties
var currentMatch: GKTurnBasedMatch?
```

You'll use this property to store the current match.

The next step is to add the "turn" methods in the new GameKitHelper extension—the one that implements the GKLocalPlayerListener protocol.

Below the player(_:receivedTurnEventFor:didBecomeActive:) method, add the following code:

```
// Is it the player's turn?
func canTakeTurn() -> Bool {
  guard let match = currentMatch else { return false }
  return match.currentParticipant?.player == GKLocalPlayer.local
}
```

You'll use this method to determine if it's the local player's turn.

Next, you need to add another method to handle when the local player ends his or her turn, so add the following code:

```
// The player's turn has ended
func endTurn(_ gcDataModel: GameCenterData,
             errorHandler: ((Error?)->Void)? = nil) {
  guard let match = currentMatch else { return }

  do {
    match.message = nil
    match.endTurn(withNextParticipants: match.opponents,
                  turnTimeout: GKExchangeTimeoutDefault,
                  match: try JSONEncoder().encode(gcDataModel),
                  completionHandler: errorHandler)
    print("Game Center Data has been sent.")
  } catch {
    print("There was an error sending the match data: \(error)")
  }
}
```

You'll call this method at the end of the local player's turn. Notice that this method calls the endTurn(withNextParticipants:turnTimeout:match:completionHandler:) instance method on the GKTurnBasedMatch object, passing in the necessary objects, such as the match's opponents (in this case, there's only one) and the custom match data.

Next, you need a method to call when the local player wins the game:

```
// The player won the game
func winGame(_ gcDataModel: GameCenterData,
             errorHandler: ((Error?)->Void)? = nil) {
  guard let match = currentMatch else { return }

  match.currentParticipant?.matchOutcome = .won

  match.opponents.forEach { participant in
    participant.matchOutcome = .lost
  }

  match.endMatchInTurn(withMatch: match.matchData ?? Data(),
                       completionHandler: {error in })
}
```

In this method, you're setting the matchOutcome property to .won for the winner (the local player) and .lost to the other participants in the match. This is an important step, otherwise the Game Center has no way of knowing when a match has ended.

Finally, you need a method for when the local player loses the game:

```
// The player lost the game
func lostGame(_ gcDataModel: GameCenterData,
              errorHandler: ((Error?)->Void)? = nil) {
  guard let match = currentMatch else { return }

  match.currentParticipant?.matchOutcome = .lost
```

```
match.opponents.forEach { participant in
  participant.matchOutcome = .won
}
match.endMatchInTurn(withMatch: match.matchData ?? Data(),
                     completionHandler: {error in })
}
```

Here, you're setting the matchOutcome property again, but this time, the local player has lost the game, which means the other player has won.

You're done with the helper file. The next step is to modify the project code to use the new methods.

Update the Game Scene to Send the Match Data

Now that you've got the methods in place to handle passing the game data back and forth between players, you need to update the rest of the project code to use those methods. You also need to add a way for players to launch a multiplayer match.

To speed up the process, use the Find Navigator to search for the TODO marks, like so:

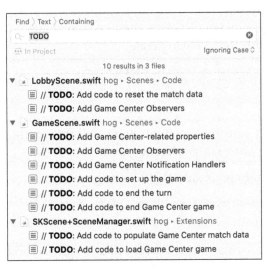

Now that you know which files need your attention, you're ready to begin.

Updating the Scene Manager

Working from the bottom up, select the second TODO listed in the SKScene+SceneManager.swift file. This will open the SKScene+SceneManager.swift file in the Source Editor, with the corresponding TODO highlighted, as shown here:

As you add the necessary code to this file, you'll receive some warnings and errors. These errors and warnings are expected, so you can ignore them for now. If the errors become too distracting, or you wish to rely on Xcode's autocomplete functionality, you can scroll up to the top of this file now and import the GameKit framework; otherwise, you'll add this import later.

The first step is to add a new method to the scene manager that handles loading multiplayer games. Replace the line that reads // TODO: Add code to load Game Center game with the following code:

```
func loadGameCenterGame(match: GKTurnBasedMatch) {
  print("Attempting to load the game scene using Game Center match data.")
}
```

This is the start of your new method. You'll call this method when the player launches a multiplayer Game Center game.

Below the print statement, add the following code:

```
match.loadMatchData(completionHandler: {(data, error) in

})
```

This code calls the loadMatchData(completionHandler:) method on the GKTurnBasedMatch object. This method is responsible for fetching the match data for the match.

Next, inside the completion handler, add the following code:

```
// Set current match data
GameKitHelper.shared.currentMatch = match

// Set up the Game Center data model
var gcDataModel: GameCenterData
```

```
// If available, use the match data to set up the model
if let data = data {
  do {
    gcDataModel = try JSONDecoder().decode(GameCenterData.self,
                                           from: data)
  } catch {
    gcDataModel = GameCenterData()
  }
} else {
  gcDataModel = GameCenterData()
}
```

Here, you're setting the GameKitHelper.shared.currentMatch property using the match object, and you're also creating the GameCenterData object either by decoding the existing data or creating new data.

Below the code you just added, and still within the completion handler, add the following code:

```
// Set up the players and mark the local player
for participant in match.participants {

}
```

This for-in loop is where you'll loop through the participants to find and set the local player.

Next, inside the for-in loop, add this code:

```
if let player = participant.player {

  // Create the gc player object
  let gcPlayer = GameCenterPlayer(playerId: player.gamePlayerID,
                                  playerName: player.displayName)

  // Check if this is the local player
  if player == GKLocalPlayer.local {
    gcPlayer.isLocalPlayer = true
  }

  // Check for a winner
  if participant.matchOutcome == .won {
    gcPlayer.isWinner = true
  }

  // Add gc player to the gc model
  gcDataModel.addPlayer(gcPlayer)
}
```

Here, you're setting up the players of the game and marking some key properties, like isLocalPlayer and isWinner.

Finally, outside the for-in loop, but still inside the completion handler, add the following code:

```
// Load the game scene
self.loadGameScene(gameType: .remoteMatch,
                   matchData: gcDataModel, matchID: match.matchID)
```

At this point, you'll get another error about "extra arguments at positions #2, #3 in call." You'll take care of that error in a moment. In the meantime—and for reference—the entire method you just added looks like this:

```
func loadGameCenterGame(match: GKTurnBasedMatch) {
  print("Attempting to load the game scene using Game Center match data.")

  match.loadMatchData(completionHandler: {(data, error) in
    // Set current match data
    GameKitHelper.shared.currentMatch = match

    // Set up the Game Center data model
    var gcDataModel: GameCenterData

    // If available, use the match data to set up the model
    if let data = data {
      do {
        gcDataModel = try JSONDecoder().decode(GameCenterData.self,
                                               from: data)
      } catch {
        gcDataModel = GameCenterData()
      }
    } else {
      gcDataModel = GameCenterData()
    }

    // Set up the players and mark the local player
    for participant in match.participants {
      if let player = participant.player {

        // Create the gc player object
        let gcPlayer = GameCenterPlayer(playerId: player.gamePlayerID,
                                        playerName: player.displayName)

        // Check if this is the local player
        if player == GKLocalPlayer.local {
          gcPlayer.isLocalPlayer = true
        }

        // Check for a winner
        if participant.matchOutcome == .won {
          gcPlayer.isWinner = true
        }
```

```
      // Add gc player to the gc model
      gcDataModel.addPlayer(gcPlayer)
    }
  }

  // Load the game scene
  self.loadGameScene(gameType: .remoteMatch,
                     matchData: gcDataModel, matchID: match.matchID)
  })
}
```

All right, time to fix the error. Do you see that little red X in the error? It looks something like this:

```
// Load the game scene
self.loadGameScene(gameType: .remoteMatch,          ⊗ Extra arguments at positions #2, #3 in call
                   matchData: gcDataModel, matchID: match.matchID)
```

Click that little red X and you're taken to the top of the file where you'll see something like this:

```
func loadGameScene(gameType: GameType) {          ① 1. 'loadGameScene(gameType:)' declared here
  print("Attempting to load the game scene.")
```

What's happening here is that you're passing in arguments that don't yet exist. To fix this problem, you need to change the method signature for func loadGameScene(gameType: GameType) { to:

```
func loadGameScene(gameType: GameType,
                   matchData: GameCenterData? = nil,
                          matchID: String? = nil) {
```

While you're here, if you didn't already add the import statement for the GameKit framework, you can add it now just below the line that reads import GameplayKit, like so:

```
import GameKit
```

Now, scroll down to the next TODO that reads // TODO: Add code to populate Game Center match data and replace it with the following two lines of code:

```
sceneNode.gameCenterData = matchData
sceneNode.gameCenterMatchID = matchID
```

You'll get another two errors about the GameScene class missing these two "members," but you'll take care of fixing that problem momentarily. For now, save the file and move on to the next batch of TODOs in the Find Navigator panel.

If you'd like, you can refresh the search results so that you're looking only at the remaining TODOs.

Updating the Lobby Scene

For now, skip the GameScene.swift file TODOs and focus on the TODOs in the LobbyScene.swift file; you'll find them in the didMove(to:) method.

Once again, you can either disregard the errors you'll get as you add the new code, or you can scroll up to the top of the LobbyScene.swift file and import the GameKit framework. Either way, you'll be reminded to import the framework later in this section.

In the didMove(to:) method, you'll see both of the TODOs in this file. Replace those TODOs with the following code:

```
// Reset current match data
GameKitHelper.shared.currentMatch = nil

// Set up GC Remote Game notification
NotificationCenter.default.addObserver(
  self,
  selector: #selector(self.processGameCenterRequest),
  name: .receivedTurnEvent, object: nil)
```

You'll get another error about a missing member, which will look something like this:

```
override func didMove(to view: SKView) {

    // Reset current match data
    GameKitHelper.shared.currentMatch = nil

    // Set up GC Remote Game notification
    NotificationCenter.default.addObserver(
      self,
      selector: #selector(self.processGameCenterRequest),
      name: .receivedTurnEvent, object: nil)
}                                    ⊗  Value of type 'LobbyScene' has no member    ⊗
                                         'processGameCenterRequest'

// MARK: — TOUCH HANDLERS
```

To fix this "missing member" error, add a new method below the didMove(to:) method:

```
@objc func processGameCenterRequest(_ notification: Notification) {
  guard let match = notification.object as? GKTurnBasedMatch else {
    return
  }

  loadGameCenterGame(match: match)
}
```

And, of course, to fix the error related to the missing GKTurnBasedMatch type, import the GameKit framework, if you haven't done so already.

Save the file and get ready to resolve the final list of TODOs in the GameScene.swift file.

Updating the Game Scene

There are six TODOs in the GameScene.swift file. This time, before you get started, import the GameKit framework:

```
import GameKit
```

Taking each TODO one at a time, replace the line that reads // TODO: Add Game Center-related properties with the following code:

```
// Multiplayer game properties
var gameCenterMatchID: String?
var gameCenterData: GameCenterData?
```

You'll use these properties to store the Game Center match data. Adding these properties also resolve the error your were getting in the SKScene+SceneManager.swift file.

Next, replace the line that reads // TODO: Add Game Center Observers, with the following code:

```
// Set up GC Remote Game notification
NotificationCenter.default.addObserver(
  self,
  selector: #selector(self.processGameCenterRequest),
  name: .receivedTurnEvent, object: nil)
```

You'll receive the following error:

```
      // Set up GC Remote Game notification
      NotificationCenter.default.addObserver(
        self,
        selector: #selector(self.processGameCenterRequest),
        name: .receivedTurnEvent, object: nil)      ⊗ Value of type 'GameScene' has no member    ⊗
  }                                                    'processGameCenterRequest'
}

// TODO: Add Game Center Notification Handlers
```

To fix that error, replace the line that reads // TODO: Add Game Center Notification Handlers with the following code:

```
@objc func processGameCenterRequest(_ notification: Notification) {
  guard let match = notification.object as? GKTurnBasedMatch else {
    return
  }
```

```
  if gameCenterMatchID == match.matchID {
    loadGameCenterGame(match: match)
  } else {
    print("Player is playing a different game.")
  }
}
```

All right, on to the next TODO.

In the setupRemoteGame() method, replace the line that reads // TODO: Add code to set up the game with the following code:

```
// Check if it's the local player's turn
if GameKitHelper.shared.canTakeTurn() == false {
  print("It's the remote player's turn.")

  // Move play to the next player in the game model
  gameModel.nextPlayer()

  // Visually disable pass and roll buttons
  rollButton.texture = rollButtonTextureDisabled
  passButton.texture = passButtonTextureDisabled
}
```

This code first verifies that it's *not* the local player's turn, and if that's the case, it moves play to the next (remote) player; otherwise, no action is needed.

Next, you need to update the players' scores. Starting with the local player, add the following code below the code you just added:

```
// Update local player scoreboard
if let localPlayer = gameCenterData?.getLocalPlayer() {
  gameModel.players[0].totalPoints = localPlayer.totalPoints
  if localPlayer.isWinner == true {
    gameModel.currentPlayerIndex = 0
    endGame()
  }
}
```

Now, the remote player:

```
// Update remote player scoreboard
if let remotePlayer = gameCenterData?.getRemotePlayer() {
  gameModel.players[1].totalPoints = remotePlayer.totalPoints
  if remotePlayer.isWinner == true {
    gameModel.currentPlayerIndex = 1
    endGame()
  }
}
```

Moving right along to the next TODO in the processEndTurnForRemoteGame() method, find the line that reads // TODO: Add code to end the turn, and replace it with this:

```
// Update the local player's stats
if let localPlayer = gameCenterData?.getLocalPlayer() {
  if let index = gameCenterData?.getPlayerIndex(for: localPlayer) {
    gameCenterData?.players[index].totalPoints =
      gameModel.players[0].totalPoints
  }
}

// Update the remote player's stats
if let remotePlayer = gameCenterData?.getRemotePlayer() {
  if let index = gameCenterData?.getPlayerIndex(for: remotePlayer) {
    gameCenterData?.players[index].totalPoints =
      gameModel.players[1].totalPoints
  }
}

// End the turn and send the data
GameKitHelper.shared.endTurn(gameCenterData!)

// Switch back to the remote player? Yes.
if GameKitHelper.shared.canTakeTurn() == false {
  // Visually disable pass and roll buttons
  rollButton.texture = rollButtonTextureDisabled
  passButton.texture = passButtonTextureDisabled
}
```

Finally, you need to add the code to the endGame() method to clear up the last
TODO. Find the line that reads // TODO: Add code to end Game Center game, and
replace it with the following code:

```
if gameType == .remoteMatch && isWinner == true {
  GameKitHelper.shared.winGame(gameCenterData!)
} else if gameType == .remoteMatch && isWinner == false {
  GameKitHelper.shared.lostGame(gameCenterData!)
}
```

Fantastic, you have everything in place, and you're ready to test the game.

Use Multiple Devices or Simulators for Testing

Testing turn-based games on the simulator can be a bit challenging. First,
there's not an easy way to get the notification of turns working, which means
you have to return to the Lobby after every turn, and then back to the game
when it's your turn. Also, you'll need two distinct sandbox tester accounts
and two instances of the build running.

Build and run the project to the iPhone 12 mini simulator. After Hog Dice
launches to the lobby scene, move the simulator out of the way and then stop
the build. Now, switch to the iPhone 12 Pro Max or another simulated device. If
you have a physical device, you can build to that, but you'll need to log in

with your sandbox tester account, which can sometimes be a pain if you're an active Game Center player on that device. Either way, you need to have two instances of the game running, and you need to be logged in with two different accounts:

It doesn't matter which player starts the game—just remember to keep track of who did. Now, with the starting player, tap the Find Match button and then tap the Start Game button to start a new game:

Roll the dice, and then tap the Pass button. Play moves to the other player, although you haven't been matched to one yet. (If you roll a 1, your turn is over and play passes automatically. If that happens, don't worry—it's okay.)

Now, on the other device (Player 2), tap the Find Match button to start a new match. This time, however, you'll notice that you're not starting a new match; instead, you're joining a game already in progress. You can tell because you'll see the score you rolled when you were acting as Player 1.

To verify that the two devices are playing the same game, go back to the first device and return to the Lobby. After it loads, tap the Find Match button:

To close the Game Center screen on the first device, tap the Done button.

Time to play some more. Return to Player 2's device, roll the dice, and then pass play back to Player 1. Once you do, tap the Find Match button on Player 1's device and you'll see it's now your turn once again:

Select the game from the list, which opens the current game and loads in the scores:

Keep playing the game until one player wins; it doesn't matter who because you'll be able to test both the winning scenario and the losing scenario at the same time.

When you win the game, go to the losing device and tap the Find Match button again. You'll see that you lost the game:

Tap into the game on the losing device. Then, return to the winning device, go back to the Lobby, and tap Find Match:

Testing turn-based gaming on the simulator is challenging but possible. And once you know game center data is successfully being transferred between devices, you're well on your way to creating multiplayer turn-based games with Game Center and GameKit.

Next Steps

In this chapter, you finished the work needed to get multiplayer games working with Hog Dice. In doing so, you learned how to start, stop, and manage turn-based games in the Game Center using GameKit. You also learned how adding the ability to play against other Game Center players can help increase your game's exposure.

Over the last two chapters, you've done a lot of work with Game Center and GameKit, but there's still a lot more to learn. Sadly, this book has only so much room. Yet, despite the enormity of this topic, you have enough to get you started with implementing Game Center features in your own games. For more information, please refer to the following two resources:

- The main Game Center site[1] on Apple's developer website.
- The official GameKit framework documentation.[2]

In the next chapter, you'll return to the Gloop Drop game, where you'll get a chance to dip your toe into the shallow end of monetization.

---

1. https://developer.apple.com/game-center
2. https://developer.apple.com/documentation/gamekit

Part VI

Bonus Content: Monetize Your Games

Use the bonus content in this part to get started with monetizing your games. Dip your toe in the shallow end of ads and in-app purchases by adding both to the Gloop Drop game.

Using Ads to Increase Revenue

While there are many reasons you might choose to make a mobile game, one reason shouldn't be overlooked: to make money. But monetizing your game, especially as an indie game developer, isn't an easy task. Luckily, though, you have some options to make it easier. One such option is *in-app advertising*.

With in-app advertising, you can show ads from multiple *ad networks*. While many ad networks are available to connect your games with paying advertisers, this chapter focuses on using Google AdMob.

Google AdMob[1] is "a mobile advertising platform that you can use to generate revenue from your app." As you might expect, Google AdMob works with the Google Mobile Ads SDK—and in this chapter, you'll work with both.

Don't Wait Until the End

 Although this chapter was saved for the end, it's important to recognize that planning your game's monetization strategy shouldn't be an afterthought. When you're thinking up a new game, its monetization strategy depends largely on the game's design and features. Game monetization is a complex and fascinating topic that could easily fill the pages of a book on its own; this chapter is meant to get you started.

Sign up for AdMob and Register Your App

The first step in working with Google AdMob is to set up an AdMob account and register an app. To create an AdMob account, you'll need a Google account and an AdSense or Google Ads account.

---

1. https://admob.google.com/home

To get started, visit the Google AdMob Get Started page.[2] Scroll down until you see the Create an AdMob account link, click that link, and you'll see a page similar to this:

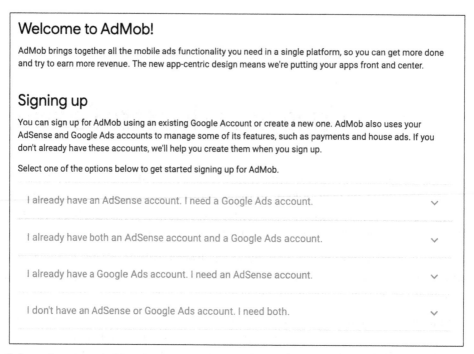

Select the option that works best for you—for example, I don't have an AdSense or Google Ads account. I need both.—and follow the on-screen instructions until you reach the end. Once you're done, you'll see something like this:

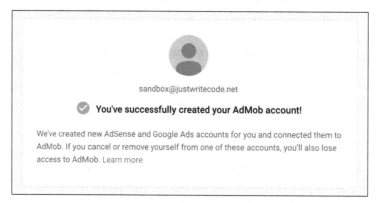

The next step is to create your app. For this exercise, you'll use Gloop Drop, the first game you built in this book.

---

2.   https://developers.google.com/admob/ios/quick-start

From the AdMob Home page, navigate to the All Apps page. If this is your first app, which it likely is, you'll see a page similar to this:

Click the ADD YOUR FIRST APP button, and follow the on-screen instructions to add your first app. You'll need to select the app's status—published or non-published—and enter the app's information, such as its name (Gloop Drop) and platform (iOS), and whether or not to enable metrics. With metrics enabled, you'll have access to additional tools and data that may help you nail down your monetization strategy.

When you're done, you'll see something similar to this message:

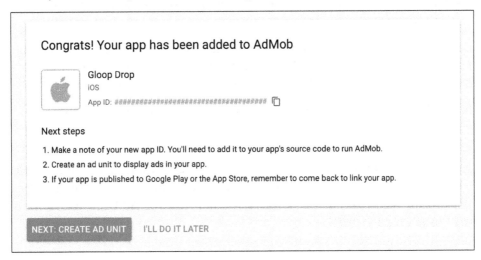

With your first AdMob app added, you're ready to create some *ad units*. An ad unit specifies the details of the ads your game will display, such as the format and type.

Create Ad Units

To create an ad unit, you first need to select an *ad format*. The ad format determines how the ads will appear in your game. Four different ad formats are available:

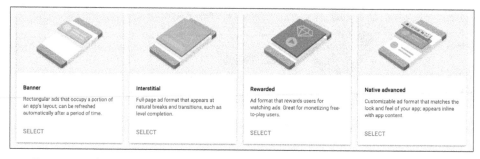

- Banner: A basic rectangular ad that typically appears at the top or bottom of the device screen.

- Interstitial: This is a full-page ad that supports video and appears during natural breaks and transitions, such as level completion.

- Rewarded: This format rewards players for watching short videos and interacting with playable ads and surveys.

- Native advanced: You can use this customizable ad format to match the look and feel of your game.

Deciding which ad format to use depends largely on the design of your game. For example, you likely wouldn't use interstitial ads if your game didn't have distinct levels, or rewarded ads if you had nothing valuable to offer.

In this book, you'll work with two ad formats: banner and rewarded.

Creating an Ad Unit for Banner Ads

To create an ad unit for banner ads, select the Banner ad format and enter the required information, such as the ad unit name and the ad format, which you already selected. For the Ad unit name enter "Banner Ad Unit" as shown in the image on page 397.

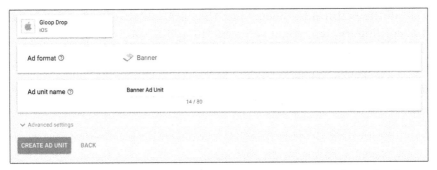

Expand the Advanced settings section. Here, you can set up the refresh options and whether or not to define a custom eCPM floor. The eCPM is the *cost per mile* or the ad revenue generated per 1,000 ad impressions. For more information, see the AdMob documentation.[3]

For this example, you'll stick with the default settings, as shown here:

If you're curious about what each setting does, click the question mark icon next to each setting to see a small pop-up that explains things:

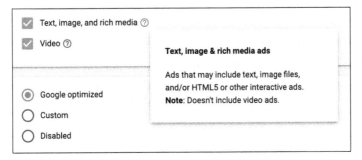

---

3.   https://developers.google.com/admob/ios/quick-start

With all of the settings in place, click the CREATE AD UNIT button. If everything went according to plan, you'll see something like this:

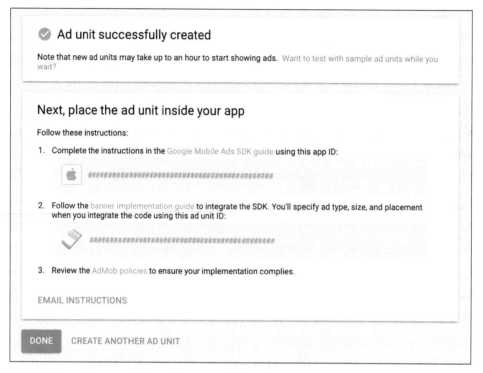

To finish setting up this ad unit, click either the DONE button or the CREATE ANOTHER AD UNIT link. (Heads-up: you'll be making another ad unit, so click the link.)

At this point, your ad unit is ready for use. However, before moving on to integrating this ad unit into your game, you'll first set up another ad unit to handle rewarded ads.

Creating an Ad Unit for Rewarded Ads

To create an ad unit for rewarded ads, select the Rewarded ad format. As before, you'll need to provide an ad unit name. You'll also need to set up the reward settings. In other words, you'll define what players will receive when they watch the ad.

Enter "Rewarded Ad Unit" for the Ad unit name, the number "1" for the reward amount, and the word "Continue" for the reward item, as shown in the image on page 399.

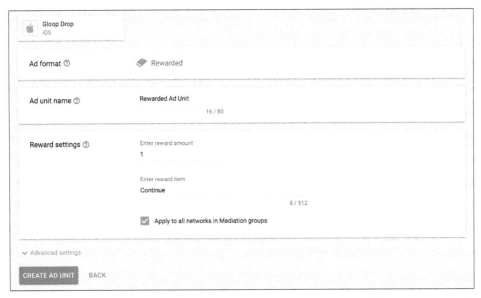

When checked, the Apply to all networks in Mediation groups option lets you serve ads from multiple sources, including the AdMob Network, third-party ad networks, and AdMob campaigns. You can keep this option enabled (which is the default setting), but this book does not cover using multiple sources or other networks.

Click the Advanced settings link. Notice the rewarded ads have a different set of options, as you can see in the following image:

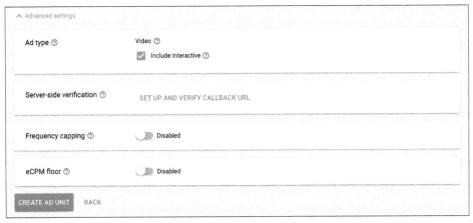

If you're curious about a setting, click the question mark icon next to the setting to learn more about it.

After confirming all of the ad unit settings, click the CREATE AD UNIT button and you'll receive the following confirmation:

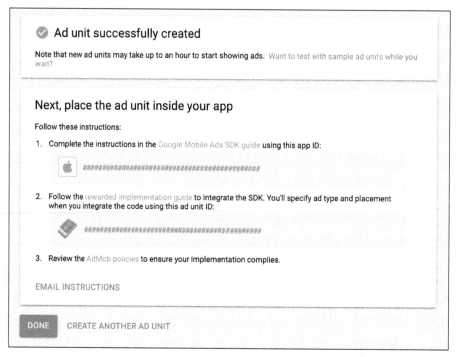

Click the DONE button and you'll see the main Ad units page, which looks something like this:

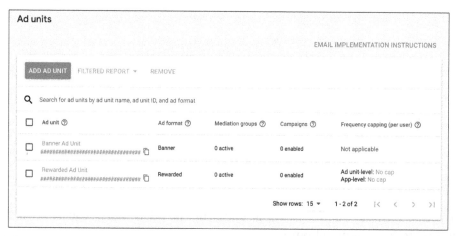

Before moving on, it's important to understand how to test ads while you're developing your game without getting your account flagged for suspicious activity.

Using Test Ad Units

While your game is in development and you're testing your code, Google encourages you to use test ads. You can use test ads in two ways:

- Use Google's sample ad units.
- Use your own ad units and enable test devices, which gives you more flexibility for testing—especially with rewarded ads.

The current sample ad unit IDs are as follows:

Ad format	Sample ad unit ID
Banner	ca-app-pub-3940256099942544/2934735716
Interstitial	ca-app-pub-3940256099942544/4411468910
Interstitial Video	ca-app-pub-3940256099942544/5135589807
Rewarded Video	ca-app-pub-3940256099942544/1712485313
Native Advanced	ca-app-pub-3940256099942544/3986624511
Native Advanced Video	ca-app-pub-3940256099942544/2521693316

You'll see these IDs used throughout the code examples in this book. You'll also see the test App ID, ca-app-pub-3940256099942544~1458002511. Google provides this ID to experiment with the SDK.

You can either use these test IDs or the ones you create with your account—provided you follow Google's recommendations for testing with your own IDs.

For more information about testing and using test ads, please refer to Google's online documentation, specifically the Test Ads section.[4]

With your AdMob app ID and ad unit IDs set up, the next step is to download the Google Mobile Ads SDK and integrate it with your Xcode project.

Download and Integrate the Google Mobile Ads SDK

To use AdMob with your iOS project, you need to download and install the Mobile Ads SDK from Google. Visit the Mobile Ads SDK (iOS) download page[5] to download the latest version.

---

4. https://developers.google.com/admob/android/test-ads
5. https://developers.google.com/admob/ios/download

From within Finder, create a new folder in the project directory and name it AdMob. Unzip the downloaded SDK and copy all of the folders extracted from the zip file into the newly created AdMob folder, like so:

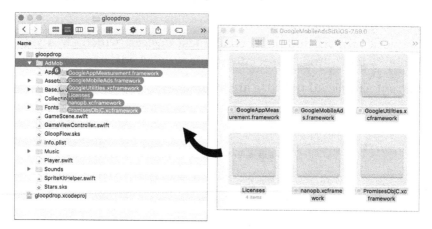

Note that copying the License folder here is optional, but you should include it somewhere within your distribution.

Once you have the folders copied, you're ready to add the frameworks to your Xcode project.

Adding the Framework

Open the gloopdrop project in Xcode.

Using the Starter Project

You may continue using your challenge project from Chapter 6, Juicing Your Games with Sound and Effects, on page 113, or you can use the starter project located in the projects/begin folder included with the code resources for this chapter. Either option is fine; the only benefit to using the starter project is that you won't get stuck going forward if you missed an earlier step.

There's also an ending project for this chapter that includes all of the code and resources you'll be adding here. The end project is located in the projects/end folder included with the code resources for this chapter.

In the Project Navigator, select the gloopdrop project file. Then, in the Project Editor, select the gloopdrop target and switch to the General tab. Scroll down until you see the Frameworks section, as shown in the image on page 403.

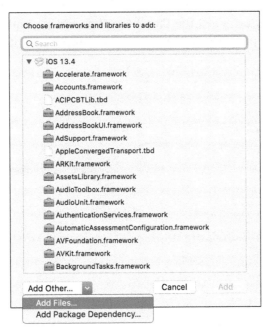

To add a new framework, click the + button in the lower-left corner.

When the Choose frameworks and libraries to add window appears, click the Add Other... drop-down list and select Add Files..., like so:

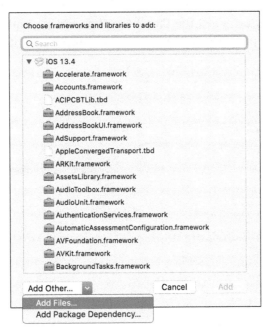

When prompted to select the frameworks to add, choose only the .framework folders, then click the Open button, as shown here:

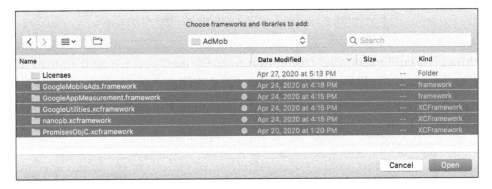

To avoid build and runtime errors, you need switch the Embed option from Embed & Sign to Do Not Embed for all of the frameworks you just added. Use the option select arrows next to each framework to make this change, like so:

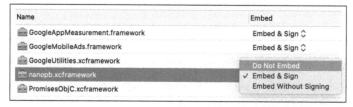

You're almost done. Switch to the Build Settings tab and scroll down until you see the Linking section. Find the Other Linker Flags setting and double-click that line to add a new property. When the pop-up appears, enter -ObjC, like this:

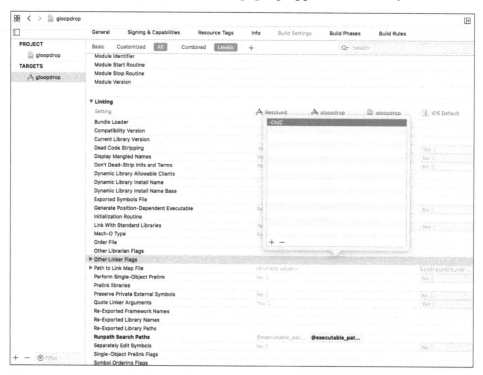

When you add (pass) the -ObjC option to the linker, you cause it to load all members of static libraries that implement any Objective-C class or category.

To verify that everything went according to plan, expand the Other Linker Flags setting. You should see something like this:

▼ Other Linker Flags	-ObjC	-ObjC
Debug	-ObjC	-ObjC
Release	-ObjC	-ObjC

The last step is to import the framework into the app delegate and initialize the SDK.

Open the AppDelegate.swift file, and below the line that reads import UIKit, add the following code to import the mobile ads framework:

```
import GoogleMobileAds
```

Then, inside the application(_:didFinishLaunchingWithOptions:) method, and just above the line that reads return true, add the following line to initialize things:

```
GADMobileAds.sharedInstance().start(completionHandler: nil)
```

Finally, open the Info.plist file. Highlight the last item in the list and click the + button to add a new entry, like so:

Key	Type	Value
▼ Information Property List	Dictionary	(18 items)
Localization native development re...	String	$(DEVELOPMENT_LANGUAGE)
Executable file	String	$(EXECUTABLE_NAME)
Bundle identifier	String	$(PRODUCT_BUNDLE_IDENTIFIER)
InfoDictionary version	String	6.0
Bundle name	String	$(PRODUCT_NAME)
Bundle OS Type code	String	$(PRODUCT_BUNDLE_PACKAGE_TYPE)
Bundle version string (short)	String	1.0
Bundle version	String	1
Application requires iPhone enviro...	Boolean	YES
Launch screen interface file base...	String	LaunchScreen
Main storyboard file base name	String	Main
	Array	(1 it...
	Boolean	YES
	Boolean	YES
▶ Supported interface orientations	Array	(2 items)
▶ Supported interface orientations (i...	Array	(2 items)
▶ Fonts provided by application	Array	(1 item)
GADApplicationIdentifier	String	ca-app-pub-3940256099942544~1458002511

Add a new key to identify the AdMob App

Enter either your AdMob App ID or Google's Test ID

For clarity, the Key name is GADApplicationIdentifier, and the Key value is ca-app-pub-3940256099942544~1458002511. The value shown here is Google's test app ID. You may use this ID or the one you set up earlier.

That's it, you're done. The Google Mobile Ads SDK is ready and waiting in your Xcode project. And while there are many ways to implement and use the SDK, you'll use a small helper file to do most of the heavy lifting.

Add the AdMob Helper File

Helper files are great. They keep your code organized—and to some degree, modular—which is why you'll be using a custom helper file here.

Open Finder and drag the AdMobHelper.swift file from the resources folder into the Project Navigator. Place it below the SpriteKitHelper.swift file, like so:

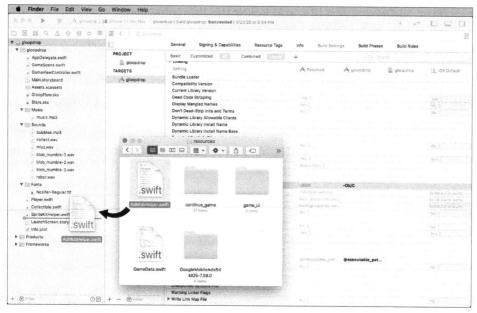

Don't forget to verify that the Copy items if needed and Add to targets options are both checked, and that the option to Create groups is selected.

Back in Xcode, open the AdMobHelper.swift file and have a look around. Yes, there's a lot of code in this file, but don't worry, what you're seeing are the delegate method stubs for handling ads. You'll learn about these methods and how to use them as you work through this chapter.

Now that you have the helper file loaded, it's time to put it to work, starting with banner ads.

Use the AdMob Helper for Banner Ads

To use the AdMob helper file, you first need to set up a struct to hold some static properties.

In the AdMobHelper.swift file, and after the import statements, add the following struct:

```swift
struct AdMobHelper {
  static let bannerAdDisplayTime: TimeInterval = 30
  static let bannerAdID = "ca-app-pub-3940256099942544/2934735716" // test id
}
```

The first property is the time, in seconds, each banner ad will remain visible on the screen. The second property holds the ad unit ID. Because you're still testing and developing the game, it's best to use the ID shown in the example. See Using Test Ad Units, on page 401 for more information about testing ads.

Ultimately, you need to extend the functionality of the GameViewController class to handle the ad functionality, so it makes sense to create an extension. Below the code you just added, add a new GameViewController extension, like this:

```
extension GameViewController {

}
```

With banner ads, you need a view to display them. To create a reusable view, you'll set up a property to hold it. The trouble is, Swift extensions don't support stored properties, which means you need to get a little creative.

Above the GameViewController extension you just added, add the following file-private property:

```
fileprivate var _adBannerView = GADBannerView(adSize: kGADAdSizeBanner)
```

Within the new GameViewController extension, add the following computed property:

```
// MARK: - Properties
var adBannerView: GADBannerView {
  get {
    return _adBannerView
  }
  set(newValue) {
    _adBannerView = newValue
  }
}
```

What you end up with is something like this:

```
fileprivate var _adBannerView = GADBannerView(adSize: kGADAdSizeBanner)

extension GameViewController {
  // MARK: - Properties
  var adBannerView: GADBannerView {
    get {
      return _adBannerView
    }
    set(newValue) {
      _adBannerView = newValue
    }
  }
}
```

Here, you're creating a file-private property, _adBannerView, that is only available to this file. You're also creating a computed property with a getter and setter. This computed property returns the value of the file-private property.

You're ready to set up the view.

Setting up the Banner Ad View

Still inside the AdMobHelper.swift file, add the following new method to the GameViewController extension:

```
// Set up Banner Ads
func setupBannerAdsWith(id: String) {

  // Set up the banner ads and the banner view
  adBannerView.adUnitID = id
  adBannerView.delegate = self
  adBannerView.rootViewController = self

  // Add the banner view to the view
  addBannerViewToView(adBannerView)

  // Start serving ads
  startServingAds(after: AdMobHelper.bannerAdDisplayTime)
}
```

This new method sets some properties of the GADBannerView object—in this case, the adBannerView you created earlier—and calls two additional methods, which you'll write now (so ignore the errors).

The first method will add the ad banner view as a subview of the GameViewController.view. It'll also set some constraint properties.

Below the setupBannerAdsWith(id:) method, add the following code:

```
// Add the ad banner to the view
func addBannerViewToView(_ bannerView: GADBannerView) {
  bannerView.translatesAutoresizingMaskIntoConstraints = false
  view.addSubview(bannerView)
  NSLayoutConstraint.activate([
      bannerView.topAnchor.constraint(equalTo: view.topAnchor),
      bannerView.centerXAnchor.constraint(equalTo: view.centerXAnchor)
  ])
}
```

The second method will make the call to start the request. Below the method you just added, add the following code:

```
// Start serving ads using a scheduled timer
func startServingAds(after seconds: TimeInterval) {
```

```
  // Start serving banner ads after XX seconds
  Timer.scheduledTimer(timeInterval: seconds, target: self,
                       selector: #selector(requestAds(_:)),
                       userInfo: adBannerView, repeats: false)
}
```

Here, you're using a scheduled timer[6] to make the call, and you're passing in the adBannerView as the userInfo object. You'll read this object later in the selector method. You still need to add this method (along with its counterpart), which is why you're seeing another error.

Below the startServingAds(after:) method, add two new methods:

```
// Start serving banner ads
@objc func requestAds(_ timer: Timer) {
  let bannerView = timer.userInfo as? GADBannerView
  let request = GADRequest()
  bannerView?.load(request)

  timer.invalidate()
}

// Hide banner
@objc func hideBanner(_ timer: Timer) {
  let bannerView = timer.userInfo as! GADBannerView
  UIView.animate(withDuration: 0.5) {
    bannerView.alpha = 0.0
  }

  timer.invalidate()
}
```

In a way, these methods—well, at least the first one—are at the heart of the helper file. In requestAds(_:), you use the object stored in timer.userInfo, which is the adBannerView, to request an ad using the load(_:) method of the GADRequest object. To put it simply: this is what loads the first (or next) ad.

The second method, hideBanner(_:), is the method you'll use to hide the banner view gracefully.

Everything is now in place to start serving banner ads.

Serving and Handling Banner Ads

The Google Mobile Ads SDK uses the delegate pattern to keep track of important events related to serving and handling ads. The AdMob helper file you added in Add the AdMob Helper File, on page 405 has the delegate method stubs you'll use to handle ads using a GameViewController extension.

---

6.   https://developer.apple.com/documentation/foundation/timer

In the AdMobHelper.swift file, locate the adViewDidReceiveAd(_:) method. This is the method that gets called when the request returns an ad, and it's within this method where you animate the banner view to show the ad.

Add the following code at the end of the adViewDidReceiveAd(_:) method:

```
adBannerView = bannerView
UIView.animate(withDuration: 0.5,
              animations: {[weak self] in self?.adBannerView.alpha = 1.0})
// Auto-hide banner
Timer.scheduledTimer(timeInterval: AdMobHelper.bannerAdDisplayTime,
                    target: self,
                    selector: #selector(hideBanner(_:)),
                    userInfo: bannerView, repeats: false)
```

This small update sets the adBannerView property and animates the banner view so that it slowly fades in once the ad is ready. It then fires off a scheduled timer, calling the hideBanner(_:) method.

Hang in there, you're almost ready to test your ads.

Open the GameViewController.swift file, and in the viewDidLoad() method, below the line that reads view.showsNodeCount = false, add this code:

```
// Set up Google AdMob
setupBannerAdsWith(id: AdMobHelper.bannerAdID)
```

Okay, are you ready for the big reveal? Build and run the project. After waiting for about a minute, you'll see your first Google test ad:

Now that you know how to work with banner ads, you're ready to move on to rewarded ads. But first, you need to set up the Continue Game feature so that you'll have a reward worthy of offering.

Add the Continue Game Feature (Player Reward)

In Creating an Ad Unit for Rewarded Ads, on page 398, you set up a rewarded ad unit that serves video ads to Gloop Drop. The idea is that when players watch one of these ads, they'll earn a reward: the ability to continue their game. At the moment, though, this Continue Game feature doesn't yet exist, so you'll need to build it, starting with a few tweaks to the UI.

Adding a Start Button

Open the Assets.xcassets asset catalog and create a new sprite atlas named game_ui. Copy the three image files—start@1x.png, start@2x.png, and start@3x.png—from the resources/game_ui folder into the newly created sprite atlas. (Don't forget to delete the default Sprite image set.)

With the new sprite atlas in place, you're ready to add a new sprite node. Open the GameScene.swift file and add the following property for the Start button sprite:

```
// Start game button
let startGameButton = SKSpriteNode(imageNamed: "start")
```

Next, you need to create a few methods to set up the sprite node and handle the actions to show and hide the button. Below the setupLabels() method, add the following new methods:

```
func setupStartButton() {
  startGameButton.name = "start"
  startGameButton.setScale(0.55)
  startGameButton.zPosition = Layer.ui.rawValue
  startGameButton.position = CGPoint(x: frame.midX, y: frame.midY)
  addChild(startGameButton)

  // Add animation
  let scaleUp = SKAction.scale(to: 0.55, duration: 0.65)
  let scaleDown = SKAction.scale(to: 0.50, duration: 0.65)
  let playBounce = SKAction.sequence([scaleDown, scaleUp])
  let bounceRepeat = SKAction.repeatForever(playBounce)
  startGameButton.run(bounceRepeat)
}

func showStartButton() {
  startGameButton.run(SKAction.fadeIn(withDuration: 0.25))
}

func hideStartButton() {
  startGameButton.run(SKAction.fadeOut(withDuration: 0.25))
}
```

The actions in the first method give the Start button a sort of pulse-like animation. The fade actions in the other two methods keep the Start button from appearing too abruptly.

While you're here, scroll down a little to the showMessage(_:) method. Locate the following line of code:

```
messageLabel.position = CGPoint(x: frame.midX, y: player.frame.maxY + 100)
```

and change it to this:

```
messageLabel.position = CGPoint(x: frame.midX,
                                y: frame.midY + startGameButton.size.height/2)
```

If you skip this change, the Start button and the message label would overlap—you can't have that, now, can you?

The next step is to update the didMove(to:) method so that it calls the newly created setupStartButton() method.

Scroll up until you see the didMove(to:) method (or use the jump bar), and find the comment // Set up User Interface. Below that comment, and after the call to setupLabels(), add the following code:

```
setupStartButton()
```

Build and run the project and you'll see the Start button pulsating just below the text.

You may have noticed that the Start button doesn't work correctly. It also doesn't disappear when you start a new game. It's time to fix that.

In the spawnMultipleGloops() method, below the call to hideMessage(), add the following code:

```
// Hide start button
hideStartButton()
```

Now, in the gameOver() method, below the line that reads popRemainingDrops(), add this:

```
// Show start button
showStartButton()
```

That change takes care of calling the methods that show and hide the Start button. Now you need to update the touch method to handle when the player taps the button.

Locate the touchDown(atPoint:) method and update it to match the following:

```swift
func touchDown(atPoint pos: CGPoint) {
  let touchedNodes = nodes(at: pos)
  for touchedNode in touchedNodes {
    // print("touchedNode: \(String(describing: touchedNode.name))")
    if touchedNode.name == "player" && gameInProgress == true {
      movingPlayer = true
    } else if touchedNode == startGameButton && gameInProgress == false {
      spawnMultipleGloops()
      return
    }
  }
}
```

This updated method simplifies how touches are handled and now includes a check to see if the touched node is the startGameButton object. If it is, you call spawnMultipleGloops(), and the game starts.

Build and run the project to check it out. If everything works, you're ready to make the next UI update: adding the Continue and Watch Ad buttons.

Adding the Continue and Watch Ad Buttons

In the Assets.xcassets asset catalog, create a new sprite atlas named continue_game. Copy all of the image files from the resources/continue_game folder into the newly created sprite atlas. (Don't forget to delete the default Sprite image set.)

Now, open the GameScene.swift file and add the following properties:

```swift
// Continue Game
let watchAdButton = SKSpriteNode(imageNamed: "watchAd")
let continueGameButton = SKSpriteNode(imageNamed: "continueRemaining-0")
let maxNumberOfContinues = 6
var numberOfFreeContinues: Int = 0

var isContinue: Bool = false
```

You'll use these properties to create the new sprites and to help maintain the status of the player's continues.

Next, you'll be adding an extension to the GameScene class that handles the Continue Game functionality. Although this isn't a requirement, it helps to keep things organized and focused.

Scroll all the way to the bottom of the GameScene.swift file and add the following block of code:

```
extension GameScene {
  func setupContinues() {
    watchAdButton.name = "watchAd"
    watchAdButton.setScale(0.75)
    watchAdButton.zPosition = Layer.ui.rawValue
    watchAdButton.position = CGPoint(x: startGameButton.frame.maxX + 75,
                                     y: startGameButton.frame.midY - 25)
    addChild(watchAdButton)

    continueGameButton.name = "continue"
    continueGameButton.setScale(0.85)
    continueGameButton.zPosition = Layer.ui.rawValue
    continueGameButton.position = CGPoint(x: frame.maxX - 75,
                                          y: viewBottom() + 60)
    addChild(continueGameButton)

    updateContinueButton()
  }

  func updateContinueButton() {
    if numberOfFreeContinues > maxNumberOfContinues {
      let texture = SKTexture(imageNamed: "continueRemaining-max")
      continueGameButton.texture = texture
    } else {
      let texture = SKTexture(imageNamed:
                              "continueRemaining-\(numberOfFreeContinues)")
      continueGameButton.texture = texture
    }
  }
}
```

There's a lot going on here, but nothing you haven't seen before.

Finally, in the in the didMove(to:) method, below the line that reads setupStartButton(), add a call to setupContinues(), like so:

```
setupContinues()
```

Build and run the project and you'll see two new buttons, as shown in the image on page 415.

Excellent, you're ready to implement the methods that handle continuing the game.

Continuing the Game

With the GameScene.swift file still open, go to the GameScene extension at the bottom of the file. Below the updateContinueButton() method, add the following new method:

```
func useContinue() {
  if numberOfFreeContinues > 0 {
    isContinue = true
    numberOfFreeContinues -= 1
    spawnMultipleGloops()
  }
}
```

You'll call this new method when the player taps the Continue button. Notice that it first checks to make sure the player has at least one continue before setting isContinue = true and calling spawnMultipleGloops(). It also decrements the numberOfFreeContinues by 1.

Now, jump to the spawnMultipleGloops() method and locate the following code:

```
// Reset the level and score
if gameInProgress == false {
  score = 0
  level = 1
}
```

and replace it with this:

```
// Reset the level and score
if gameInProgress == false && isContinue == false {
  score = 0
  level = 1
} else {
  isContinue = false
}
```

Thanks to this change, when the player continues the game, the score and level are not reset.

You now need to update how touches are handled. Jump to the touch-Down(atPoint:) method and update it to match this:

```
func touchDown(atPoint pos: CGPoint) {
  let touchedNodes = nodes(at: pos)
  for touchedNode in touchedNodes {
    // print("touchedNode: \(String(describing: touchedNode.name))")
    if touchedNode.name == "player" && gameInProgress == true {
      movingPlayer = true
    } else if touchedNode == watchAdButton && gameInProgress == false {
      // TODO: Add call to gameSceneDelegate?.showRewardVideo()
      return
    } else if touchedNode == continueGameButton && gameInProgress == false {
      useContinue()
      return
    } else if touchedNode == startGameButton && gameInProgress == false {
      spawnMultipleGloops()
      return
    }
  }
}
```

Finally, give the player one free continue. Go back to the properties section and modify the numberOfFreeContinues property to match this:

```
var numberOfFreeContinues: Int = 1 {
  didSet {
    updateContinueButton()
  }
}
```

This update gives the player one free continue and automatically calls the updateContinueButton() method whenever the value changes. The updateContinueButton() is what is responsible for changing the texture of the Continue button sprite to match the number of continues available.

Build and run the project. Score a few points and then lose the game. Instead of starting a new game, tap the Continue button to keep playing.

Update the Message Text

 At this point, you may want to update the calls to showMessage(_:) to make them more in line with the UI updates. For example, showMessage("Game Over\nStart a New Game or Continue") in gameOver() and showMessage("Tap Start to Play the Game") in didMove(to:).

Now that you've got the Continue Game functionality in place and working, you're ready to implement the rewarded ads—and for that, you'll use the AdMob helper file again.

Use the AdMob Helper for Rewarded Ads

Similar to what you did in Use the AdMob Helper for Banner Ads, on page 406, you'll modify the AdMobHelper.swift file to support your rewarded ads.

Open the AdMobHelper.swift file, and in the AdMobHelper struct, add the following new static properties:

```
static var rewardAdReady = false
static let rewardAdID = "ca-app-pub-3940256099942544/1712485313" // test
```

Once again, the example here uses the Google test ID, but you're welcome to use the ID you set up earlier—provided you follow Google's recommendations for testing ads.

Next, add the file-private property below the _adBannerView property to hold the rewarded ad object:

```
fileprivate var _rewardedAd: GADRewardedAd?
```

Finally, add the computed property to the GameViewController extension; place it below the existing adBannerView property:

```
var rewardedAd: GADRewardedAd? {
    get {
      return _rewardedAd
    }
    set(newValue) {
        _rewardedAd = newValue
    }
}
```

You're now ready to set up rewarded ads in Gloop Drop.

Setting up Rewarded Ads

Still inside the AdMobHelper.swift file, and below the hideBanner(_:) method, add the following new method that initializes the rewarded ads object:

```
// Set up Rewarded Ads
func setupRewardAdsWith(id: String) {
  AdMobHelper.rewardAdReady = false // reset the ready flag

  rewardedAd = GADRewardedAd(adUnitID: id)
  rewardedAd?.load(GADRequest()) { error in
    if let error = error {
      print("********************* \(error.localizedDescription)")
    } else {
      print("********************* Reward Ad Loaded OK!")
      AdMobHelper.rewardAdReady = true
    }
  }
}
```

Similar to how banner ads were initialized in Setting up the Banner Ad View, on page 408, this method resets the AdMobHelper.rewardAdReady static property and initializes a GADRewardedAd object. It then stores that object in the rewardedAd property.

You're almost ready to show rewarded ads, but first, you need to do a few more things.

Preparing to Show Rewarded Ads

The way rewarded ads work is that the view responsible for playing the video needs to be presented from a view controller—in this case, the GameViewController. While you can handle a request like this in a few different ways, you'll create a new custom GameScene protocol that the GameViewController will use.

Open the GameScene.swift file and add the following code to the top of the file; place it below the import statements and above the class declaration:

```
protocol GameSceneDelegate: AnyObject {
  func showRewardVideo()
}
```

This is the method you'll call from the delegate (the GameViewController).

After that, add a new property to the GameScene class, like so:

```
weak var gameSceneDelegate: GameSceneDelegate?
```

You'll use this property to store the delegate.

Finally, in the touchDown(atPoint:) method, locate the // TODO: Add call to gameSceneDelegate?.showRewardVideo() comment and remove the first part of the comment that reads // TODO: Add call to. When you're done, you'll end up with this:

```
gameSceneDelegate?.showRewardVideo()
```

This line of code routes the call to showRewardVideo() from the GameScene to the delegate. Speaking of which, you still need to set up the delegate so that you can show the rewarded ads.

Setting up the Delegate and Showing Rewarded Ads

Open the GameViewController.swift file, and below the line that reads let scene = GameScene(size:CGSize(width: 1336, height: 1024)), add this:

```
scene.gameSceneDelegate = self
```

This code sets the gameSceneDelegate property in the GameScene class, but it also throws the following error:

```
let scene = GameScene(size:CGSize(width: 1336, height: 1024))
scene.gameSceneDelegate = self

// Set the scale mode to scale
scene.scaleMode = .aspectFill
```
> ⊗ Cannot assign value of type 'GameViewController' to type 'GameSceneDelegate?'   ⊗
>
> Add missing conformance to 'GameSceneDelegate' to class 'GameViewController'   Fix

To fix that error, go to the bottom of the GameViewController.swift file and add a new extension that handles the GameScene protocol method:

```
extension GameViewController: GameSceneDelegate {
  func showRewardVideo() {
    if rewardedAd?.isReady == true {
      rewardedAd?.present(fromRootViewController: self, delegate:self)
    }
  }
}
```

This method first verifies that a rewarded ad is ready for presentation; if it is, the view controller presents it.

The only thing left to do now is update the rewarded ad delegate methods. But first, you need to add a few custom notifications.

Create Custom Notifications

Currently, there is no way for the GameScene to know when ads are getting loaded and presented to the player. You'll take care of this problem by adding some custom notifications. With notifications,[7] you can broadcast specific information to designated observers. These observers then watch for the notifications, taking specific actions when they occur.

Open the AdMobHelper.swift file and add the following block of code to the bottom of the file:

```
extension Notification.Name {
  static let userDidEarnReward = Notification.Name("userDidEarnReward")
  static let adDidOrWillPresent = Notification.Name("adDidOrWillPresent")
  static let adDidOrWillDismiss = Notification.Name("adDidOrWillDismiss")
}
```

You'll use these notifications to alert the GameScene whenever one of the ad delegate methods is called.

The next step is to post these notifications where and when appropriate.

Adding Notifications for Reward Ads

With the AdMobHelper.swift file open, go to the // MARK: - GADRewardedAdDelegate: Lifecycle Notifications section. Here, you'll see the four delegate methods for the rewarded ads. Update the first three methods to match the following:

```
/// Tells the delegate that the user earned a reward.
func rewardedAd(_ rewardedAd: GADRewardedAd, userDidEarn
                      reward: GADAdReward) {
  print("Reward received: \(reward.type) | amount: \(reward.amount).")
➤ NotificationCenter.default.post(name: .userDidEarnReward, object: reward)
}

/// Tells the delegate that the rewarded ad was presented.
func rewardedAdDidPresent(_ rewardedAd: GADRewardedAd) {
  print("Rewarded ad presented.")
➤ NotificationCenter.default.post(name: .adDidOrWillPresent, object: nil)
}
```

---

7. https://developer.apple.com/documentation/foundation/notifications

```
/// Tells the delegate that the rewarded ad was dismissed.
func rewardedAdDidDismiss(_ rewardedAd: GADRewardedAd) {
  print("Rewarded ad dismissed.")
➤  setupRewardAdsWith(id: AdMobHelper.rewardAdID)
➤  NotificationCenter.default.post(name: .adDidOrWillDismiss, object: nil)
}
```

The highlighted code shows the new notification posts in each method. Also, notice the call to setupRewardAdsWith(id: AdMobHelper.rewardAdID) in the rewardedAdDid-Dismiss(_:) method. This call forces the next rewarded ad to load.

While you're here, it makes sense to add some notifications to the banner ad delegate methods, too.

Adding Notifications for Banner Ads

With the AdMobHelper.swift file still open, go to the // MARK: - GADBannerViewDelegate: Click-Time Lifecycle Notifications section. Here, you'll see the four delegate methods for the banner ads. Update the first three methods to match the following:

```
/// Tells the delegate that a full-screen view will be presented in response
/// to the user clicking on an ad.
func adViewWillPresentScreen(_ bannerView: GADBannerView) {
  print("adViewWillPresentScreen")
➤  NotificationCenter.default.post(name: .adDidOrWillPresent, object: nil)
}

/// Tells the delegate that the full-screen view will be dismissed.
func adViewWillDismissScreen(_ bannerView: GADBannerView) {
  print("adViewWillDismissScreen")
➤  NotificationCenter.default.post(name: .adDidOrWillDismiss, object: nil)
}

/// Tells the delegate that the full-screen view has been dismissed.
func adViewDidDismissScreen(_ bannerView: GADBannerView) {
  print("adViewDidDismissScreen")
➤  NotificationCenter.default.post(name: .adDidOrWillDismiss, object: nil)
}
```

The highlighted code shows the new notification posts in each method.

In this example, you're sharing the same post notifications between rewarded ads and banner ads. In a production environment, however, it might be best to use separate notifications for each so that you can act directly and independently depending on the type of ad.

Observing Notifications

The final piece of this notification puzzle is to have the GameScene class observe and act on these notifications.

Still inside the AdMobHelper.swift file, go to the bottom of the file and add the new GameScene extension, like so:

```
extension GameScene {
  func setupAdMobObservers() {
    // Add notification observers
    NotificationCenter.default.addObserver(self,
                              selector:
                              #selector(self.userDidEarnReward(_:)),
                              name: .userDidEarnReward, object: nil)

    NotificationCenter.default.addObserver(self,
                              selector:
                              #selector(self.adDidOrWillPresent),
                              name: .adDidOrWillPresent, object: nil)

    NotificationCenter.default.addObserver(self,
                              selector:
                              #selector(self.adDidOrWillDismiss),
                              name: .adDidOrWillDismiss, object: nil)
  }

  @objc func userDidEarnReward(_ reward: GADAdReward) {
    numberOfFreeContinues += 1
  }

  @objc func adDidOrWillPresent() {
    audioEngine.mainMixerNode.outputVolume = 0.0
    watchAdButton.alpha = 0.0
  }

  @objc func adDidOrWillDismiss() {
    audioEngine.mainMixerNode.outputVolume = 1.0
  }
}
```

You could have added this extension directly to the GameScene.swift file, but it makes sense to keep it with the AdMob helper file since the methods here are related.

If you look at the last three methods, you'll see that players will earn one free continue if they finish watching the rewarded ad. You'll also see that when presenting ads, the in-game volume is muted; when the ad is finished or when the player closes it, the in-game volume is restored.

The final step is to call the setupAdMobObservers() method to get the observers loaded. The best place to make that call is within the didMove(to:) method of the GameScene.swift file.

Open the GameScene.swift file, and inside the didMove(to:) method, add the following code at the top:

```
// Set up notification observers
setupAdMobObservers()
```

While you're in this file, find the setupContinues() method, and above the line that reads addChild(watchAdButton), add the following code:

```
watchAdButton.alpha = 0.0
```

When you first set up the Watch Ad button, you left it visible. However, because the potential exists for a rewarded ad not to be ready, you need to hide the Watch Ad button until there's something to show the player.

Of course, now that you've hidden the Watch Ad button, you need a way to unhide it. Head over to the showStartButton() method and add the following code:

```
if AdMobHelper.rewardAdReady == true {
  watchAdButton.run(SKAction.fadeIn(withDuration: 0.25))
}
```

This code checks the AdMobHelper.rewardAdReady static property before slowly animating a fade-in of the Watch Ad button.

Wait, you're not done yet—you also need to hide the Watch Ad button when the game restarts. In the hideStartButton() method, add the following code:

```
if AdMobHelper.rewardAdReady == true {
  watchAdButton.run(SKAction.fadeOut(withDuration: 0.25))
}
```

With this update, the Watch Ad button will fade out when the game restarts.

Save Resources by Sharing Actions

In the updated showStartButton() and hideStartButton() methods, you're using separate actions to show or hide the buttons. You could, instead, create a single, shared SKAction object for each event and use that. For example:

```
let hideAction = SKAction.fadeOut(withDuration: 0.25)
startGameButton.run(hideAction)
if AdMobHelper.rewardAdReady == true {
  watchAdButton.run(hideAction)
}
```

You're almost ready to test rewarded ads. Open the GameViewController.swift, and in the viewDidLoad() method, below the line that reads setupBannerAdsWith(id: AdMobHelper.bannerAdID), add the following code:

```
setupRewardAdsWith(id: AdMobHelper.rewardAdID)
```

This code makes a call to setupRewardAdsWith(id:), starting your first rewarded ads request.

Whew, that was a lot. Are you ready to test things?

Build and run the project. Notice how the Watch Ad button doesn't show up anymore when you first start the game. Also take note that until a rewarded ad is loaded, the Watch Ad button won't appear. When it does, you'll be able to tap that button and watch a rewarded ad.

Make sure you watch the ad until the timer counts down, otherwise the user-DidEarnReward(_:) delegate method won't get called, and you won't earn the reward.

The final step is to save and load the number of continues the player can use. For that, you'll use a familiar custom class you created earlier.

Save and Load the Number of Continues

In Chapter 15, Adding More Scenes and Saving the Game, on page 325, you learned how to securely save and load game data by creating a custom Game-Data class. Rather than recreate the wheel, you'll copy the resource file, GameData.swift, from the resources folder into the gloopdropproject. Note that this file is a bare-bones copy of what you made earlier.

Open Finder and drag the GameData.swift file into the Project Navigator; place it below the AdMobHelper.swift file.

Go back to Xcode, open the GameData.swift file, and below the line that reads // var propertyName: type = value, add the following:

```
var freeContinues: Int = 1 {
  didSet {
    saveDataWithFileName("gamedata.json")
  }
}
```

Here, you're making sure that any time the freeContinues property value changes, you save the data. You're also setting the default value to 1.

Scroll down to the loadDataWithFileName(_:) method, and below the line that reads // propertyName = gd.propertyName, add the following:

```
freeContinues = gd.freeContinues
```

If you remember, this restores the data from the file into the corresponding object—in this case, freeContinues.

To load the data, open the AppDelegate.swift file, and in the application(_:didFinishLaunchingWithOptions:) method, above the line that reads return true, add the following code:

```
GameData.shared.loadDataWithFileName("gamedata.json")
```

Finally, you need to update the numberOfFreeContinues property in the GameScene class to use the stored data. Open the GameScene.swift file and update the numberOfFreeContinues property, like so:

```
var numberOfFreeContinues: Int {
  get {
    return GameData.shared.freeContinues
  }
  set(newValue) {
    GameData.shared.freeContinues = newValue
    updateContinueButton()
  }
}
```

The gloopdrop project is now ready to securely read and write the number of free continues the player has earned to the device's local storage.

You're ready to build and run the project.

Play a few games and watch a few ads. Sometimes close the ad before earning the reward so that you can verify that players aren't being rewarded for their impatience. Also, keep an eye on how the Continue button number changes as you earn and use continues. To test this feature thoroughly, don't forget to exit and re-launch the game to make sure the number of continues saves and loads correctly. For best results, use the App Switcher to exit the game completely.

Next Steps

This was a long chapter, but you made it to the end and you accomplished a lot, such as adding a new Continue Game feature to Gloop Drop and using helper files. You also learned how to integrate ads using Google's AdMob network and the Google Mobile Ads SDK to increase your game's revenue.

But ads aren't the only way to increase revenue. Next, you'll learn how to add in-app purchases to your game to make a few extra bucks.

Monetizing Your Games with In-App Purchases

In the previous chapter, you added banner and rewarded ads to the gloopdrop project. With ads, your games have the potential to earn a little extra revenue. But ads are not the only way to earn some extra cash. Another popular option is to sell additional in-game content through, what Apple calls, *in-app purchases*.

This additional content can be anything from extra lives and power-ups to new levels and bonus material. You can even sell virtual currency like coins and gems. Regardless of what you're selling, in-app purchases and virtual goods are a great way to further monetize your games.

There's a lot involved when it comes to setting up and designing a game that supports in-app purchases—too much to cover in a single chapter. However, the information you'll learn in this chapter will help get you started when it's time to develop your own games.

To get started, the first step is to prepare the Xcode project and target for the In-App Purchase capability.

Add In-App Purchase Capability Using Xcode

In this chapter, you'll add two types of in-app purchases to the gloopdrop project: one to remove banner ads, and one to let the player purchase additional opportunities to continue the game.

To enable in-app purchases in Gloop Drop, you need to add the In-App Purchase capability to the Xcode project and target.

Open the gloopdrop project in Xcode.

Using the Starter Project

You may continue using your project from the previous chapter, or you can use the starter project located in the projects/begin folder included with the code resources for this chapter.

Either option is fine; the only benefit to using the starter project is that you won't get stuck going forward if you missed an earlier step. Additionally, some of the print statements used in earlier chapters have been commented out. There's also an ending project for this chapter that includes all of the code you'll be adding here. The end project is located in the projects/end folder included with the code resources for this chapter.

In the Project Navigator, select the gloopdrop project file, and in the Project Editor, select the gloopdrop target. Now, switch to the Signing & Capabilities tab and you'll see something like this:

As you learned in Chapter 1, Creating Scenes with Sprites and Nodes, on page 3, the Bundle Identifier must be unique when publishing a project to the App Store. Because the Bundle ID, net.justwritecode.gloopdrop, already exists on my Apple developer account, be sure to change the Bundle ID to something else (if you haven't done so already)—preferably a domain that you own.

With the Bundle ID set to something unique, the next step is to add the In-App Purchase capability.

Before you begin, verify that you have the Automatically manage signing option enabled. When that option is enabled, Xcode will handle setting up the profiles, app IDs, and certificates you'll need to successfully publish to the App Store.

To add a new capability, click the + Capability button in the top-left corner of the Project Editor window. You'll see something like the image on page 429.

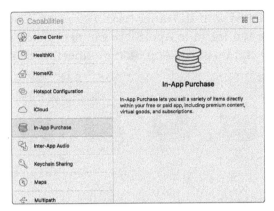

Here, you can select the capability you wish to add. Scroll down to the In-App Purchase capability and double-click the row to add that capability. Because the Automatically manage signing option is enabled, Xcode creates the necessary profiles, apps IDs, and certificates needed to work with and support in-app purchases.

If everything went as expected, you'll see the In-App Purchase capability listed at the bottom of the Signing & Capabilities tab.

Your next task is to set up the app in App Store Connect.

Use App Store Connect to Add a New App

To offer in-app purchases within your game, you first need to set up an app in App Store Connect. Log in to your Apple Developer[1] account, and you'll see something like this:

---

1. https://developer.apple.com/account

On the left side (listed with the other Program Resources), click App Store Connect. Alternatively, you can log in to App Store Connect using its direct link.[2] In either case, you'll end up at the App Store Connect home page:

Before you can sell anything on the App Store, you must first accept the agreements,[3] specifically the *Paid Applications agreement*. You also need to enter the tax and banking information for the account holder. Once you have signed the agreements, you can add users and assign roles.

Adding a Sandbox Tester Account

To test in-app purchases, you need at least one user account and one sandbox tester account.[4] With sandbox tester accounts, you can test your in-app purchases without having to worry about live data and live payments.

Setting up users and sandbox tester accounts is not something this book covers; however, you can follow these steps as per Apple's documentation to add tester accounts:

1. Sign in to App Store Connect.
2. On the home page, click Users and Access.
3. Under Sandbox, click Testers.
4. Click "+" to set up your tester accounts.
5. Complete the tester information form and click Invite.
6. Sign out of your Apple ID on all testing devices and sign back in with your new sandbox tester account.

For more information about adding and editing users, please refer to Apple's online documentation.[5]

2.   https://appstoreconnect.apple.com/login
3.   https://help.apple.com/app-store-connect/#/deva001f4a14
4.   https://appstoreconnect.apple.com/access/testers
5.   https://help.apple.com/app-store-connect/#/devdbefef011

Now that you have the user accounts set up, you're ready to add a new app.

Adding a New App

From the App Store Connect home page, open the My Apps section. To add a new app, click the Add (+) button in the top-left corner and select New App, like so:

When the New App dialog appears, enter or select the following options:

- Platform: iOS
- Name: Gloop Drop
- Primary Language: English
- Bundle ID: {your bundle id}
- SKU: GLOOPDROP
- User Access: Full Access

Be sure to replace {your bundle id} with your Bundle ID. You may also need to change the Name and SKU values if you get an error about them already being in use. When you're done, you'll end up with something like this:

Click the Create button to create your new app. For more information about adding apps, please refer to Apple's online documentation.[6]

If everything works, you'll see the App Information page, which looks something like this:

You're ready to add some products.

Adding In-App Purchases

With the App Information page open, switch to the Features tab and you'll see the In-App Purchases page, which looks something like this:

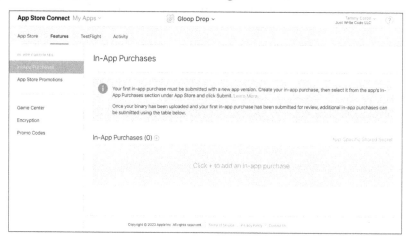

The In-App Purchases page is where you can set up your game's in-app purchases. For the gloopdrop project, you'll set up two in-app purchases: one that removes ads, and one that allows players to continue their game.

---

6. https://help.apple.com/app-store-connect/#/dev2cd126805

Click the Add (+) button to add a new in-app purchase and you will see the following:

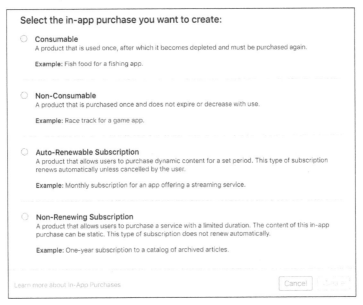

Here, you need to define the type of in-app purchase you're about to set up. You can choose from four types:

- Consumable: A product that is used once, after which it becomes depleted and the player must purchase it again.

- Non-Consumable: A product that is purchased once and does not expire or decrease with use.

- Auto-Renewable Subscription: A product that allows users to purchase dynamic content for a set period. This type of subscription renews automatically unless canceled by the user.

- Non-Renewing Subscription: A product that allows users to purchase a service with a limited duration. The content of this in-app purchase can be static. This type of subscription does not renew automatically.

Add a Non-Consumable

The first type you'll set up in this chapter is a *non-consumable* product. In other words, players buy it once and it's available—in theory—forever.

Select the Non-Consumable option and click the Create button. This action takes you to the Product page, as shown in the image on page 434.

At a minimum, you need to enter the Reference Name, Product ID, Price, and a localized Display Name and Description. However, before you can release a product on the App Store, you must also supply the rest of the metadata. You won't be supplying that data in this book, but know that it's something you'll need to think about when you're ready to create your own products. Apple has an excellent article[7] about promoting your in-app purchases and creating effective metadata.

For now, enter the following information for this new product:

- Reference Name: Remove Ads
- Product ID: {your bundle id}.removeads
- Price: USD 1.99
- Display Name: Remove Ads
- Description: Full version of the game with no ads

Don't forget to replace {your bundle id} with your Bundle ID, for example, net.justwritecode.gloopdrop, which gives you a Product ID of net.justwritecode.gloopdrop.removeads.

---

7. https://developer.apple.com/app-store/promoting-in-app-purchases

Examples aside, when you're ready to create your own products, here are some things to keep in mind:

- The Reference Name is for internal use only. This name shows up in App Store Connect and on your reports; it does not show up in the App Store.

- The Product ID must be a unique alphanumeric number, and it cannot be changed or reused—even after the product is removed.

- The Display Name and Description are what potential customers will see when viewing your product in the App Store. You can add additional localizations using the Add (+) button. However, with the gloopdrop project, you'll use only English (U.S.).

Naming Your In-App Purchases

When it comes to naming conventions and description text for your in-app purchases, you're limited in space, so choose wisely. Pick something players will recognize and easily understand what's being offered. Apple recommends avoiding generic names. Apple also recommends that you tie-in the name of your game in some way. For example, Forest Explorer offers an in-app purchase with the name Explorer Pack that unlocks premium maps and trail recommendations.

Add a Consumable

The next type of product you'll add is a *consumable* product that lets players continue their game when they miss a drop. Consumables are, well, consumed by the player. In other words, their quantity is reduced when used and not replaced until the player buys the product again.

Return to the Features page and click the Add (+) button to add another product. This time, when the Select the in-app purchase you want to create dialog appears, select the Consumable option and click the Create button.

For this new product, set up the following options:

- Reference Name: Continue Game (1x)
- Product ID: {your bundle id}.continue.1
- Price: USD 0.99
- Display Name: Continue Game (1x)
- Description: Continue your game up to one time

Once again, replace {your bundle id} with your Bundle ID.

The number 1 represents the quantity being purchased. This isn't something Apple forces you to do. Rather, it's more of a personal choice to help organize things. For example, you might want to sell a three-pack of continues for $1.99. In that case, you could set the ID to {your bundle id}.continue.3.

When you're done adding these two products, you'll end up with something like this:

At this point, you're ready to head back to Xcode and integrate in-app purchase support.

Add In-App Purchase Support to the Project

Similar to what you did in Chapter 18, Using Ads to Increase Revenue, on page 393, you'll use *helper* files to integrate in-app purchases. You'll also use a pre-built scene to speed up development.

Open Finder and drag the IAP folder from the resources folder into the Project Navigator; place it below the AdMobHelper.swift file, like so:

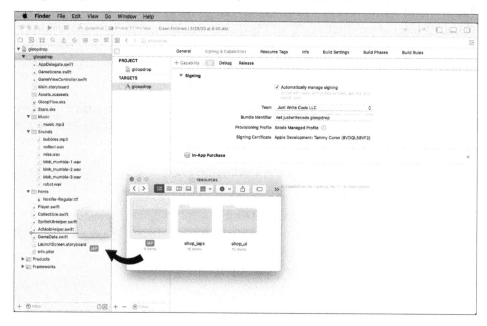

Don't forget to verify that the Copy items if needed and Add to targets options are both checked. Also verify that the option to Create groups is selected. Once confirmed, click the Finish button to add the contents of the folder to your project.

Back in Xcode, open the IAP group and have a look around. You'll see the following new files:

- ShopScene.sks
- ShopScene.swift
- StoreManager.swift
- StoreProducts.swift

You'll learn more about each of these files as you work through the rest of this chapter. The first stop on this tour, however, is the StoreProducts.swift file, which is the file you'll use to configure the products.

Configure Products in Xcode

With in-app purchases, nearly everything is tied to a product ID (or product identifier). As it turns out, there's no way to fetch product IDs from the App Store, so you'll need another way to load the product IDs into your Xcode project. For example, you could:

- Create a class or struct with static variables to hold the product IDs.
- Use a property list to include an array of product IDs in the app bundle.
- Use a remote server to host a JSON file containing the product IDs.

The first two options are typical implementations for scenarios where you have limited products or product updates. The third option is typically used when you have frequent updates and/or delivered content. For the gloopdrop project, you'll use a custom struct.

Open the StoreProducts.swift file. This file contains the StoreProducts struct and the StoreProducts.Product class—both of which are custom classes. It also includes a large comment block at the top of the file.

Take a few minutes to read the comment block; there's a lot of information in there, so take your time. When you're ready, look for the following block of code:

```
static let prefixID = "{your bundle id}" // include trailing dot

static let productIDsConsumables: Set<String> = [
  "\(prefixID){productid.qty}"
]
static let productIDsNonConsumables: Set<String> = [
  "\(prefixID){productid}"
]
```

Here, you need to update the value of the prefixID property to match your Bundle ID. You also need to add the product IDs you set up in Adding In-App Purchases, on page 432, minus their prefixes.

For example, after updating the code, you'll have something like this:

```
static let prefixID = "net.justwritecode.gloopdrop." // include trailing dot
static let productIDsConsumables: Set<String> = [
  "\(prefixID)continue.1"
]
static let productIDsNonConsumables: Set<String> = [
  "\(prefixID)removeads"
]
```

Notice there are two static properties: one to hold the consumable product IDs and one to hold the non-consumable product IDs. Because these two properties are sets, you can add additional product IDs when needed.

For example, if you were to add more than one consumable, like a Continue (1x) and a Continue (3x), you'd code it like this:

```
static let productIDsConsumables: Set<String> = [
  "\(prefixID)continue.1", "\(prefixID)continue.3"
]
```

Now that you have the product IDs set up in Xcode, the next step is to prepare the GameData class for storing purchases.

Modify the GameData Class to Store Purchases

When a player makes a purchase, you'll need some way to store that information. What better way than to use the GameData class you're already using to save the number of free continues? You added this class to the gloopdrop project in Save and Load the Number of Continues, on page 424.

In the Project Navigator, select the GameData.swift file. Below the freeContinues property, add a new variable, like so:

```
var products = [StoreProducts.Product]() {
  didSet {
    saveDataWithFileName("gamedata.json")
  }
}
```

This new property stores an array of StoreProducts.Product objects. These objects represent the player's purchases. Also, as you did with the freeContinues property, any time a change is made to this array, the gamedata.json data file is updated when the saveDataWithFileName(_:) method is called.

You also need to handle reloading the stored data. Locate and modify the loadDataWithFileName(_:) method and update it to match the following (the high-lighted code shows the updates):

```
func loadDataWithFileName(_ filename: String) {
  let fullPath = getDocumentsDirectory().appendingPathComponent(filename)
  do {
    let contents = try Data(contentsOf: fullPath)
    if let data = try
      NSKeyedUnarchiver.unarchiveTopLevelObjectWithData(contents) as? Data {
      let gd = try PropertyListDecoder().decode(GameData.self, from: data)

      // Restore data (properties)
      // propertyName = gd.propertyName
      freeContinues = gd.freeContinues
      products = gd.products

          // Print the list of products owned
      for p in products {
        print("GameData: \(String(describing: p.id)) | \(p.quantity)")
      }
    }
  } catch {
    print("Couldn't load Store Data file.")
  }
}
```

With this new code, you're populating the products property with the information from the data file. You're also printing the product information to the console so that you can verify things are working.

Now that you have a way to save and load the player's owned products, you can start modifying the rest of the code to use these products.

Modify the AdMob Helper to Disable Ads

When the player purchases the "Remove Ads" product, you need to stop the banner ads from running—and only the banner ads. You don't want to prevent rewarded ads from running because that's how players receive "free" continues (and you receive extra revenue).

To selectively hide banner ads, you need to update the adViewDidReceiveAd(_:) delegate method in the AdMob helper file. You added that helper file in Add the AdMob Helper File, on page 405.

Open the AdMobHelper.swift file and update the adViewDidReceiveAd(_:) delegate method to match this:

```
func adViewDidReceiveAd(_ bannerView: GADBannerView) {
  // print("adViewDidReceiveAd")
➤  // Check for "Remove Ads" purchase
➤  if GameData.shared.products.filter({ $0.id.contains("removeads")}).first
➤    != nil {
➤      print("Banner Ads Disabled")
➤      adBannerView.delegate = nil
➤      adBannerView.removeFromSuperview()
➤  } else {
      adBannerView = bannerView
      UIView.animate(withDuration: 0.5,
              animations: {[weak self] in self?.adBannerView.alpha = 1.0})

      // Auto-hide banner
      Timer.scheduledTimer(timeInterval: AdMobHelper.bannerAdDisplayTime,
                      target: self,
                      selector: #selector(hideBanner(_:)),
                      userInfo: bannerView, repeats: false)
➤  }
  }
```

With these changes, the code first checks to see if the player purchased the
"Remove Ads" product by checking the GameData.shared.products array for a match.
If a match is made, the code sets adBannerView.delegate = nil and removes the
adBannerView view from its superview. These two actions, effectively, hide the
banner ads.

Next up, it's time to modify the GameScene class to handle paid continues.

Modify the GameScene Class to Handle Paid Continues

Similar to how you added the numberOfFreeContinues property in Save and Load
the Number of Continues, on page 424, you need to add a property to track
the number of paid continues; one that uses a custom getter and setter.

Open the GameScene.swift file, and below the code that adds the numberOfFreeContinues property, add the following code:

```
var numberOfPaidContinues: Int {
  get {
    var qty: Int = 0
    for product in GameData.shared.products {
      if product.id.contains("continue") {
        qty += product.quantity
      }
    }
    return qty
  }
```

```
  set(newValue) {
    let product = GameData.shared.products.filter(
    {$0.id.contains("continue")}).first
    product?.quantity = newValue
    updateContinueButton()
  }
}
```

The getter and setter for the new numberOfPaidContinues property filters on the product ID using the string continue. The getter adds the quantity and returns the value. The setter grabs the first matching product and updates its quantity.

To present the player with an accurate total number of continues, you need to combine the number of free continues with the number of purchased continues. For that, you'll use another computed property. Add the following code below the code you just added:

```
var numberOfContinues: Int {
  get {
    return numberOfFreeContinues + numberOfPaidContinues
  }
}
```

With the new properties in place, you're ready to update the code that handles displaying and using continues.

Find the updateContinueButton() method—it should be near the bottom of the file—and modify it to match this:

```
func updateContinueButton() {
  if numberOfContinues > maxNumberOfContinues {
    let texture = SKTexture(imageNamed: "continueRemaining-max")
    continueGameButton.texture = texture
  } else {
    let texture = SKTexture(imageNamed:
      "continueRemaining-\(numberOfContinues)")
    continueGameButton.texture = texture
  }
}
```

While you're here, update the useContinue() method to pull from either the free continues or the paid continues, depending on which one has a continue available, like so:

```
func useContinue() {
  /* Verify the player has at least 1 continue.
   If so, reduce the continues by 1, first by checking the free
   continues. If no free continues exist, check the paid continues. */

  if numberOfContinues > 0 {
```

```
  // Check from where to pull
  if numberOfFreeContinues > 0 {
    numberOfFreeContinues -= 1
  } else if numberOfPaidContinues > 0 {
    numberOfPaidContinues -= 1
  }

  // Continue game
  isContinue = true
  spawnMultipleGloops()
 }
}
```

This new code first checks the quantity of the free continues. If none are available, it then pulls from the paid continues.

The next step is to prepare the shop UI.

Setting up the Shop Interface

In the Project Navigator, select the ShopScene.sks file and you'll see the following scene in the Scene Editor:

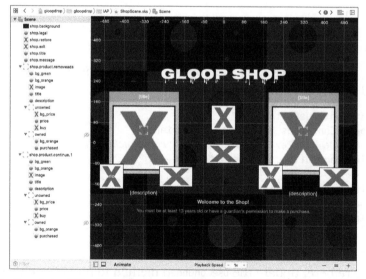

Whoa, that's a lot of Xs. If this were a treasure hunt, you'd be in for one heck of a haul—but it's not, so put away that shovel and get back to work.

The problem here is that you added the scene but didn't add the resources the scene uses.

Open the Assets.xcassets asset catalog and create two new sprite atlases. Name the first shop_ui and the second shop_iaps.

The shop_ui sprite atlas will hold the buy, exit, price, restore, and shop image sets:

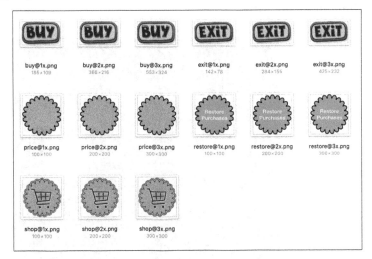

The shop_iaps sprite atlas will hold the continue-1, continue-3, continue, default, and removeads image sets:

Additional Image Resources

Note that the continue-3 and continue image resources aren't used in this chapter, but they're included in case you want to play around with some additional product options on your own.

After creating the new sprite atlases, copy the image files from the resources/shop_ui folder into the shop_ui sprite atlas, and copy the image files from the resources/shop_iaps folder into the shop_iaps sprite atlas. (Don't forget to delete the default Sprite image set from each new atlas.)

Back in Xcode, select the ShopScene.sks file in the Project Navigator and you'll see something more like this:

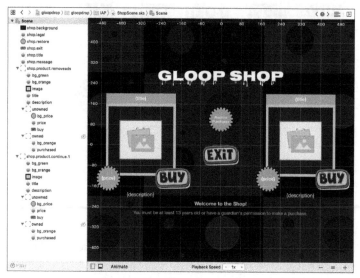

With the resources added to your project, and the shop scene looking less like a treasure map and more like an in-game shop, you're ready to configure the scene (and see what makes it tick).

Configure the Shop Scene

In the Project Navigator, select the ShopScene.swift file; this file is the brains behind the shop scene. Take a moment to look around and when you're ready to get into the thick of it, keep reading.

Viewing the Store Messages

Notice the static properties in the custom ShopMessages struct:

```
struct ShopMessages {
  static let welcome = "Welcome to the Shop!"
  static let success = "Thank you! Enjoy your purchase."
  static let restored = "Excellent! Your purchases have been restored."
  static let restoredComplete = "Restoration complete."
  static let makingPurchase = "Standby, attempting to make purchase."
  static let restoringPurchases = "Standby, attempting to restore purchases."
}
```

These are the messages players will see as they interact with the store. You're welcome to update these messages as you see fit.

This file also contains the ShopScene class. This custom class is what operates the shop scene behind the scenes (no pun intended). At the moment, though, it shows the following compile error:

```
override init(fileNamed fileName: String?) {
  super.init(fileNamed: fileName)

  self.name = "shopScene"
  self.zPosition = Layer.shop.rawValue                    ❶ Type 'Layer' has no member 'shop'
  self.alpha = 0.0
  self.setScale(1.0)
}
```

You probably already know why you're getting this error and how to fix it, but just in case, let's take care of that next.

Adding the New Layer Enum

Open the SpriteKitHelper.swift file, and in the Layer enum, add a new case for shop, like so:

```
enum Layer: CGFloat {
  case background
  case foreground
  case player
  case collectible
  case ui
➤ case shop
}
```

Save the file and return to the ShopScene.swift file. The error should now be resolved; if not, build the project (but don't run it), and the error will clear.

With the error gone, it's time to set up the shop.

Setting up the Shop

Working your way through the ShopScene.swift file, you'll see a beginInteraction() method and an endInteraction() method. These are the methods the GameScene calls when the player opens and closes the shop; they don't do anything fancy, but they are necessary to set up the scene:

```
func beginInteraction() {
  updateMessageText(with: ShopMessages.welcome) // reset message text
  updateUI() // reset UI

  let scale = SKAction.scale(to: 1.0, duration: 0.15)
  let fade = SKAction.fadeIn(withDuration: 0.15)
  let group = SKAction.group([fade, scale])
  run(group, completion: {})
}
```

```
func endInteraction() {
  let scale = SKAction.scale(to: 0.25, duration: 0.15)
  let fade = SKAction.fadeOut(withDuration: 0.15)
  let group = SKAction.group([fade, scale])
  run(group, completion: {})
}
```

Further down the file, you'll see the two methods that handle purchasing products and restoring purchases:

```
func purchaseProduct(node: SKNode) {
  let productIdentifier = node.userData?.value(forKey: "productId") as? String

  if let product = StoreManager.shared.availableProducts.first(where:
    { $0.productIdentifier == productIdentifier }) {
    updateMessageText(with: ShopMessages.makingPurchase)
    StoreManager.shared.buyProduct(product: product, qty: 1)
  }
}

func restorePurchases() {
  updateMessageText(with: ShopMessages.restoringPurchases)
  StoreManager.shared.restoreProducts()
}
```

You will also see the updateMessageText(with:) method, which updates the message text:

```
func updateMessageText(with message: String?) {
  if let shopMessage = childNode(withName: "//shop.message") as? SKLabelNode {
    shopMessage.text = message
  }
}
```

The next group of methods deals with notifications. You'll observe and use six notifications to handle the various in-app purchase delegate methods. You'll learn more about these delegate methods in Using the StoreKit Delegate Methods, on page 452.

Finally, you'll see a group of methods responsible for setting up and customizing the shop. There's a lot going on with these methods, but as you look through the code, you should start to see how it all works. Let's have a closer look.

The first notable method is setupShop(), which looks like this:

```
func setupShop() {
  for product in StoreManager.shared.availableProducts {
    setupProduct(product)
  }
}
```

With this method, you're looping through the StoreManager.shared.availableProducts array, and with each object, you're calling setupProduct(_:). Don't worry, you'll learn more about the StoreManager class in Interface with StoreKit Using the Store Manager, on page 451. For now, know that the StoreManager class is where most of the magic happens.

Next up is the setupProduct(_:) method. This method first grabs the product ID; it then uses that ID to set up the product information within the scene.

To get a better idea of how the setupProduct(_:) method works, look at the following image:

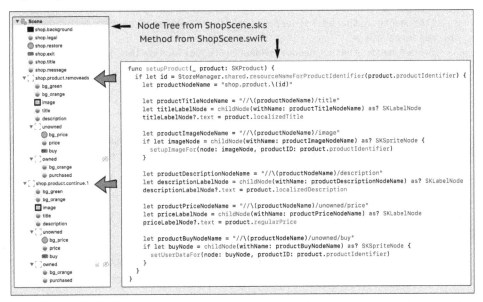

In this case, only two products are being sold, so the interface is rather simple. The two nodes, shop.product.removeads and shop.product.continue.1, are both part of the node tree.

Notice the call to the StoreManager.shared.resourceNameForProductIdentifier() method, which looks like this:

```
func resourceNameForProductIdentifier(_ productIdentifier: String)
  -> String? {
  let product = StoreProducts.Product(productID: productIdentifier)
  return product.id.replacingOccurrences(of: StoreProducts.prefixID, with: "")
}
```

This method returns the product ID after it removes the prefix. For example, net.justwritecode.gloopdrop.removeads is shortened to removeads, and net.justwritecode.gloopdrop.continue.1 is shortened to continue.1.

You then use the return string to build the node name:

```
let productNodeName = "shop.product.\(id)"
```

The result of which is shop.product.removeads and shop.product.continue.1.

With these two node names, you can build out each part of the product; this includes the title, image, description, price, and buy button.

Furthermore, to set the proper image, the setupProduct(_:) method makes a call to setupImageFor(node:productID:), which looks like this:

```
func setupImageFor(node: SKSpriteNode, productID: String) {
  let product =
      StoreManager.shared.resourceInformationForProductIdentifier(productID)
  let resourceName =
      StoreManager.shared.resourceNameForProductIdentifier(productID) ?? ""

  var imageName = resourceName.replacingOccurrences(of: ".", with: "-")

  let textureAtlas = SKTextureAtlas(named: "shop_iaps")
  if textureAtlas.textureNames.contains(imageName) == false {
    imageName =
          imageName.replacingOccurrences(of: "-\(product.quantity)", with: "")
    if textureAtlas.textureNames.contains(imageName) == false {
      node.texture = SKTexture(imageNamed: "none")
    }
  }

  node.texture = SKTexture(imageNamed: imageName)
}
```

There's also a call to another method, setUserDataFor(node:productID:), which sets up the node's userData, storing the value of product.id and product.quantity:

```
func setUserDataFor(node: SKNode, productID: String) {
  let product =
      StoreManager.shared.resourceInformationForProductIdentifier(productID)
  node.userData = NSMutableDictionary()
  node.userData?.setValue(product.id, forKey: "productId")
  node.userData?.setValue(product.quantity, forKey: "quantity")
}
```

The final method in this file is UpdateUI(). At the moment, it's empty (except for a TODO comment). You'll update this later in Buying Products and Restoring Purchases, on page 455.

Now that you have the shop set up and you're a little more familiar with the methods inside, you need to add the shop scene to the main game scene.

Add the Shop Scene to the Main Game Scene

What good would a shop be if the player couldn't access it?

Switch to the GameScene.swift file and add the following new properties (be sure to add them below the line that reads var isContinue: Bool = false):

```
// Reference Scene
let shopButton = SKSpriteNode(imageNamed: "shop")
var shopScene: ShopScene!
var shopIsOpen = false
```

You'll use these properties to show and hide the shop scene.

Jump to the end of the file, and inside the GameScene extension, below the useContinue() method, add the following code:

```
func setupShop() {
  // Set up Shop Button
  shopButton.name = "shop"
  shopButton.zPosition = Layer.shop.rawValue
  shopButton.position = CGPoint(x: frame.minX + 75, y: viewBottom() + 75)
  addChild(shopButton)

  // Set up Shop Scene and add it to the Game Scene
  shopScene = ShopScene(in: self)
  shopScene.zPosition = Layer.shop.rawValue
  shopScene.position = CGPoint(x: frame.midX, y: frame.midY)
  addChild(shopScene!)

  // Set up notification observers and Shop UI
  shopScene.setupObservers()
  shopScene.setupShop()
}
```

This method adds the shop scene as a reference node. You first learned about reference nodes in Use Reference Nodes in Your Scene, on page 181. It also calls the methods responsible for setting up the shop observers and products.

Next, in the didMove(to:) method (near the top of the file), below the setupContinues() method, add a call to the method you just created, like so:

```
setupShop()
```

Finally, jump to the touchDown(atPoint:) method and update the code from this:

```
func touchDown(atPoint pos: CGPoint) {
  let touchedNodes = nodes(at: pos)
  for touchedNode in touchedNodes {
    // print("touchedNode: \(String(describing: touchedNode.name))")
    if touchedNode.name == "player" && gameInProgress == true {
      movingPlayer = true
```

```
      } else if touchedNode == watchAdButton && gameInProgress == false {
        gameSceneDelegate?.showRewardVideo()
        return
      } else if touchedNode == continueGameButton && gameInProgress == false {
        useContinue()
        return
      } else if touchedNode == startGameButton && gameInProgress == false {
        spawnMultipleGloops()
        return
      }
    }
  }
}
```

to this (the highlighted code shows the changes):

```
func touchDown(atPoint pos: CGPoint) {
  let touchedNodes = nodes(at: pos)
  for touchedNode in touchedNodes {
    // print("touchedNode: \(String(describing: touchedNode.name))")
➤   if shopIsOpen == true {
➤     if touchedNode.name == "buy" {
➤       shopScene.purchaseProduct(node: touchedNode)
➤       return
➤     } else if touchedNode.name == "shop.restore" {
➤       shopScene.restorePurchases()
➤       return
➤     } else if touchedNode.name == "shop.exit" {
➤       shopScene.endInteraction()
➤       shopIsOpen = false
➤       return
➤     }
➤   } else if shopIsOpen == false {
➤     if touchedNode.name == "shop" && gameInProgress == false {
➤       shopScene.beginInteraction()
➤       shopIsOpen = true
➤       return
      } else if touchedNode.name == "player" && gameInProgress == true {
        movingPlayer = true
      } else if touchedNode == watchAdButton && gameInProgress == false {
        gameSceneDelegate?.showRewardVideo()
        return
      } else if touchedNode == continueGameButton && gameInProgress == false {
        useContinue()
        return
      } else if touchedNode == startGameButton && gameInProgress == false {
        spawnMultipleGloops()
        return
      }
    }
  }
}
```

The new code adds some additional checks: when the player taps on the Shop button in the bottom-left corner of the screen, the shop scene will open. Likewise, when the player taps the shop scene's Exit button, the shop will close. This new code also handles when the player taps the shop's Buy and Restore Purchases buttons.

Build and run the project to test opening and closing the shop. (You won't see any products yet, but don't worry, you'll take care of that next.)

Notice how the shop scene animates into and out of the game scene when you tap the Shop button and Exit button.

Now that you have the shop scene set up and added as a working reference node, you're ready to get into the nitty-gritty of *StoreKit*.

Wait, hold on a minute. StoreKit? What the heck is that?

Interface with StoreKit Using the Store Manager

In Add In-App Purchase Support to the Project, on page 436, you added a group of files. One of those files, StoreManager.swift, is responsible for interfacing with StoreKit.

StoreKit, or rather the StoreKit framework, is what handles all of the in-app purchases and interactions your game has with the App Store. This includes loading the product details, prompting the player for payment details, and validating receipts (something you won't do in this book).

When working with StoreKit and in-app purchases, you're mostly dealing with products, payments, requests, and transactions using classes like:

- SKProduct
- SKRequest
- SKPayment
- SKPaymentTransaction

These four classes (some of which you've already been using but may not have even realized) are just some of what's included with StoreKit—and what you can use to support in-app purchases within your games.

In fact, StoreKit offers more than just in-app purchase support. You can interact with Apple Music and also provide recommendations for third-party content and reviews for your games. But StoreKit is a big topic, and there's not much room left in this book to cover everything, so you'll need to keep your focus on using the helper files included with this book (while I'll explain just the important bits about StoreKit).

Using the StoreKit Delegate Methods

Open the StoreManager.swift file and have a look around. The first thing you'll see are some custom notifications.

With in-app purchases, and specifically these helper files, you'll track the following six actions:

- Successful purchases
- Purchasing failures
- Successful restorations
- Restoration failures
- Product requests

The ShopScene extension (ShopScene.swift) is observing these notifications. If you look at the ShopScene.setupObservers() method, you'll see that each notification calls a corresponding selector method:

- purchaseSuccess(_:)
- purchaseFailure(_:)
- restoredSuccess(_:)
- restoredComplete(_:)
- restoredFailure(_:)
- requestComplete(_:)

To give you an idea of what these methods do, here's a look at the purchaseSuccess(_:) method:

```
@objc func purchaseSuccess(_ notification: Notification) {
  updateMessageText(with: ShopMessages.success)
  updateUI()
}
```

And here's a look at the requestComplete(_:) method:

```
@objc func requestComplete(_ notification: Notification) {
  setupShop()
}
```

For the most part, these six methods do the same thing: they receive the notification object and act accordingly—whether it's setting up the shop or showing a message and updating the UI.

So, how do these notifications fit in? You're about to find out.

Loading Products and Reviewing Class Properties

Before getting too deep into the StoreKit delegate methods and custom notifications, have a look at the properties set up in the StoreManager class:

```
var availableProducts = [SKProduct]()
var invalidProductIdentifiers = [String]()

var purchasedTransactions = [SKPaymentTransaction]()
var restoredTransactions = [SKPaymentTransaction]()

private var productsRequest: SKProductsRequest?
```

You'll use these properties to interact with the store. Notice the productsRequest property. This property holds the main SKProductsRequest object.

The SKProductsRequest[8] object is what you'll use to grab a list of available products and their details from the App Store. These are the details stored in the SKProduct[9] object and what you're using in the ShopScene.setupProduct(_:) method to set up the shop and display the product details.

However, at the moment, your project has very little awareness of the ShopManager class or its objects, requests, and callbacks.

Open the AppDelegate.swift file, and inside the application(_:didFinishLaunchingWithOptions:) method, below the line that reads GameData.shared.loadDataWithFileName("gamedata.json"), add the following code:

```
// Attach an observer to the payment queue
SKPaymentQueue.default().add(StoreManager.shared)

// Fetch products
StoreManager.shared.fetchProducts()
```

---

8. https://developer.apple.com/documentation/storekit/skproductsrequest
9. https://developer.apple.com/documentation/storekit/skproduct

This code sets up a payment observer[10] and starts the request responsible for retrieving the product information from the App Store. Without a payment queue, your game would have no way to interact with the App Store for payment processing. And, without products, your players would have no way to purchase things.

Switch back to the StoreManager.swift file and look at the fetchProducts() method:

```swift
func fetchProducts() {
  productsRequest?.cancel()
  productsRequest = SKProductsRequest(productIdentifiers: productIdentifiers)
  productsRequest?.delegate = self
  productsRequest?.start()
}
```

This method creates a new SKProductsRequest object, passing in the product identifiers, and then starts the request.

Scroll through the rest of the StoreManager.swift file and look at the different delegate methods. (Yes, there are a lot, but each one includes an explanation above it.)

Stop for a moment and look at the productsRequest(_:didReceive:) method:

```swift
func productsRequest(_ request: SKProductsRequest,
                    didReceive response: SKProductsResponse) {
  print("productsRequest(_:didReceive)")

  // Populate the `availableProducts` array
  if !response.products.isEmpty {
    availableProducts = response.products
  }

  // Populate the `invalidProductIdentifiers` array
  if !response.invalidProductIdentifiers.isEmpty {
    invalidProductIdentifiers = response.invalidProductIdentifiers
  }

  // For testing and verifying
  for p in availableProducts {
    print(" - Product (available): \(p.productIdentifier) "
        + "\(p.localizedTitle) \(p.price.floatValue)")
  }

  for p in invalidProductIdentifiers {
    print(" - Product (invalid): \(p)")
  }

  // Send notification that the products request operation is complete
  NotificationCenter.default.post(name: .productsRequestComplete, object: nil)
}
```

---

10. https://developer.apple.com/documentation/storekit/skpaymentqueue

This method is just one of the delegate methods the shop uses. Notice how this codes reads the SKProductsResponse object and parses out the product information. It then posts a notification, which is observed by the ShopScene class, as you can see here:

```
NotificationCenter.default.addObserver(self,
                             selector: #selector(self.requestComplete),
                             name: .productsRequestComplete,
                             object: nil)
```

This particular observer calls the following method:

```
@objc func requestComplete(_ notification: Notification) {
  setupShop()
}
```

You saw this method earlier; it's the one that calls the method that sets up the shop scene.

You're ready to test. Build and run the project. Tap the Shop button and you'll see the Remove Ads and Continue (1x) products show up in the shop:

Now that you have products showing up in the shop, you're ready to hook up the code that handles purchases and restorations.

Buying Products and Restoring Purchases

When it comes to buying and restoring in-app purchases, it's important to know that players can restore only non-consumable products. Restoring consumable products is not (and should not be) supported. For example, players can't purchase a consumable product on device A, and then restore that consumable product to devices B and C. This is by design.

Two methods in the ShopScene class need updating to handle purchasing and restoration: purchaseSuccess(_:) and restoredSuccess(_:).

Open the ShopScene.swift file and add the following code in both the purchaseSuc-cess(_:) and restoredSuccess(_:) methods (be sure to place this code above the lines that read updateUI()):

```
if let productIdentifier = notification.object as? String {
  let product = StoreProducts.Product(productID: productIdentifier)

  if let gp = GameData.shared.products.first(where:
    { $0.id == productIdentifier }) {
    gp.quantity += 1
  } else {
    product.quantity = 1
    GameData.shared.products.append(product)
  }
}
```

This code verifies the product ID and then adds the product to the GameData.shared.products array, which indicates ownership of the product. Remember, when the products array changes (such as with an add or update), the game data is saved.

You also need to modify the shop's UI so that players know when a non-con-sumable product has been purchased. Locate the updateUI() method and update it to match this:

```
func updateUI() {
  gameScene?.updateContinueButton()

  for product in GameData.shared.products {
    if let id =
      StoreManager.shared.resourceNameForProductIdentifier(product.id) {
      let productNodeName = "shop.product.\(id)"
      if product.isConsumable == false {
        let ownedNodeName = "//\(productNodeName)/owned"
        let ownedNode = childNode(withName: ownedNodeName)
        ownedNode?.isHidden = false
        // print("   ownedNodeName: \(ownedNodeName)")

        let unownedNodeName = "//\(productNodeName)/unowned"
        let unownedNode = childNode(withName: unownedNodeName)
        unownedNode?.isHidden = true
        // print("   unownedNodeName: \(unownedNodeName)")
      }
    }
  }
}
```

This code checks the products' purchase status and shows or hides certain shop scene elements depending on the product's current state. However, because players can purchase non-consumable products only once and consumable products as many times as they want, the code behaves differently depending on what type of product it is. For example, once players purchase or restore the "Remove Ads" product, they'll see a badge showing them that they already own the product, like this:

Now that you have a way to purchase and restore products, it's time to test things out on a physical device, which is a necessary step for testing in-app purchases.

Why Can't I Access the Store?

 If you were eager and tried to buy a product while testing in the simulator, you likely saw the error message: Cannot connect to iTunes Store. The reason you see this error is because you must use a physical device to test in-app purchases.

Test In-App Purchases

The big moment is finally here: testing your in-app purchases. The thing about testing in-app purchases, though, is that you need to test on a physical device. You also need a sandbox account so that you can make purchases without getting charged "real" money.

Assuming you meet the requirements, build and run the project to your device. Open the shop and try to purchase a product. (You'll need to enter your sandbox tester credentials. See Adding a Sandbox Tester Account, on page 430 for more details.)

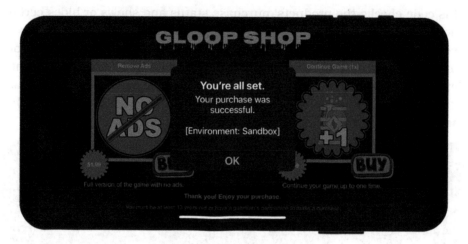

If everything goes well, you'll be able to purchase and restore products like nobody's business.

Next Steps

Congratulations, you made it through another long chapter. As you might have guessed, StoreKit and in-app purchase support are both huge topics, and this chapter only scratched the surface of what's possible. Not only did you get a brief introduction to StoreKit, you also learned how to use the pre-built helper files and shop scene to fetch products and make and restore purchases. But there's so much more you can do—not only with the shop scene, but also with what you can offer in your store. I encourage you to spend some time reviewing the files in the IAP group.

Index

Thank you!

How did you enjoy this book? Please let us know. Take a moment and email us at support@pragprog.com with your feedback. Tell us your story and you could win free ebooks. Please use the subject line "Book Feedback."

Ready for your next great Pragmatic Bookshelf book? Come on over to https://pragprog.com and use the coupon code BUYANOTHER2021 to save 30% on your next ebook.

Void where prohibited, restricted, or otherwise unwelcome. Do not use ebooks near water. If rash persists, see a doctor. Doesn't apply to *The Pragmatic Programmer* ebook because it's older than the Pragmatic Bookshelf itself. Side effects may include increased knowledge and skill, increased marketability, and deep satisfaction. Increase dosage regularly.

And thank you for your continued support,

The Pragmatic Bookshelf

SAVE 30%!
Use coupon code
BUYANOTHER2021

Distributed Services with Go

This is the book for Gophers who want to learn how to build distributed systems. You know the basics of Go and are eager to put your knowledge to work. Build distributed services that are highly available, resilient, and scalable. This book is just what you need to apply Go to real-world situations. Level up your engineering skills today.

Travis Jeffery
(258 pages) ISBN: 9781680507607. $45.95
https://pragprog.com/book/tjgo

Explore Software Defined Radio

Do you want to be able to receive satellite images using nothing but your computer, an old TV antenna, and a $20 USB stick? Now you can. At last, the technology exists to turn your computer into a super radio receiver, capable of tuning in to FM, shortwave, amateur "ham," and even satellite frequencies, around the world and above it. Listen to police, fire, and aircraft signals, both in the clear and encoded. And with the book's advanced antenna design, there's no limit to the signals you can receive.

Wolfram Donat
(78 pages) ISBN: 9781680507591. $19.95
https://pragprog.com/book/wdradio

Genetic Algorithms in Elixir

From finance to artificial intelligence, genetic algorithms are a powerful tool with a wide array of applications. But you don't need an exotic new language or framework to get started; you can learn about genetic algorithms in a language you're already familiar with. Join us for an in-depth look at the algorithms, techniques, and methods that go into writing a genetic algorithm. From introductory problems to real-world applications, you'll learn the underlying principles of problem solving using genetic algorithms.

Sean Moriarity
(242 pages) ISBN: 9781680507942. $39.95
https://pragprog.com/book/smgaelixir

Design and Build Great Web APIs

APIs are transforming the business world at an increasing pace. Gain the essential skills needed to quickly design, build, and deploy quality web APIs that are robust, reliable, and resilient. Go from initial design through prototyping and implementation to deployment of mission-critical APIs for your organization. Test, secure, and deploy your API with confidence and avoid the "release into production" panic. Tackle just about any API challenge with more than a dozen open-source utilities and common programming patterns you can apply right away.

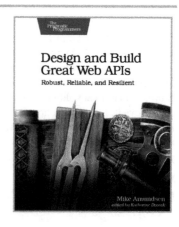

Mike Amundsen
(330 pages) ISBN: 9781680506808. $45.95
https://pragprog.com/book/maapis

Quantum Computing

You've heard that quantum computing is going to change the world. Now you can check it out for yourself. Learn how quantum computing works, and write programs that run on the IBM Q quantum computer, one of the world's first functioning quantum computers. Develop your intuition to apply quantum concepts for challenging computational tasks. Write programs to trigger quantum effects and speed up finding the right solution for your problem. Get your hands on the future of computing today.

Nihal Mehta, Ph.D.

(580 pages) ISBN: 9781680507201. $45.95

https://pragprog.com/book/nmquantum

A Common-Sense Guide to Data Structures and Algorithms, Second Edition

If you thought that data structures and algorithms were all just theory, you're missing out on what they can do for your code. Learn to use Big O Notation to make your code run faster by orders of magnitude. Choose from data structures such as hash tables, trees, and graphs to increase your code's efficiency exponentially. With simple language and clear diagrams, this book makes this complex topic accessible, no matter your background. This new edition features practice exercises in every chapter, and new chapters on topics such as dynamic programming and heaps and tries. Get the hands-on info you need to master data structures and algorithms for your day-to-day work.

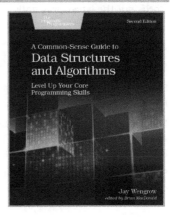

Jay Wengrow

(506 pages) ISBN: 9781680507225. $45.95

https://pragprog.com/book/jwdsal2

The Pragmatic Bookshelf

The Pragmatic Bookshelf features books written by professional developers for professional developers. The titles continue the well-known Pragmatic Programmer style and continue to garner awards and rave reviews. As development gets more and more difficult, the Pragmatic Programmers will be there with more titles and products to help you stay on top of your game.

Visit Us Online

This Book's Home Page
https://pragprog.com/book/tcswift
Source code from this book, errata, and other resources. Come give us feedback, too!

Keep Up to Date
https://pragprog.com
Join our announcement mailing list (low volume) or follow us on twitter @pragprog for new titles, sales, coupons, hot tips, and more.

New and Noteworthy
https://pragprog.com/news
Check out the latest pragmatic developments, new titles and other offerings.

Save on the ebook

Save on the ebook versions of this title. Owning the paper version of this book entitles you to purchase the electronic versions at a terrific discount.

PDFs are great for carrying around on your laptop—they are hyperlinked, have color, and are fully searchable. Most titles are also available for the iPhone and iPod touch, Amazon Kindle, and other popular e-book readers.

Send a copy of your receipt to support@pragprog.com and we'll provide you with a discount coupon.

Contact Us

Online Orders:	*https://pragprog.com/catalog*
Customer Service:	*support@pragprog.com*
International Rights:	*translations@pragprog.com*
Academic Use:	*academic@pragprog.com*
Write for Us:	*http://write-for-us.pragprog.com*
Or Call:	+1 800-699-7764

9 781680 507843